Selection of
Library Materials
in Applied and
Interdisciplinary
Fields

Selection of Library Materials in Applied and Interdisciplinary Fields

Beth J. Shapiro
John Whaley
Editors

Collection Management and Development Committee
Resources and Technical Services Division
American Library Association

AMERICAN LIBRARY ASSOCIATION · CHICAGO AND LONDON · 1987

Designed by Harvey Retzloff

Composed by Impressions, Inc. in
Sabon on a Penta-driven Autologic
APS-µ5 Phototypesetting system

Printed on 50-pound Glatfelter, a
pH-neutral stock, and bound in
B-grade Holliston linen cloth
by Edwards Brothers, Inc.

Library of Congress Cataloging-in-Publication Data

Selection of library materials in applied and
interdisciplinary fields.

    Sequel to: Selection of library materials in the
humanities, social sciences, and sciences.
    Bibliography: p.
    Includes index.
    1. Book selection.   2. Collection development
(Libraries)   3. Acquisitions (Libraries)   4. Libraries,
University and college—Collection development.
5. Inter-disciplinary approach in education.
6. Libraries, Technical college—Collection
development.   I. Shapiro, Beth J.   II. Whaley, John.
III. American Library Association. Collection
Management and Development Committee.
IV. Selection of library materials in the humanities,
social sciences, and sciences.
Z689.S353   1987   025.2'1   86-32101
ISBN 0-8389-0466-1

Printed in the United States of America.

Contents

v

Preface

Nearly five years have passed since the original editors of *Selection of Library Materials in the Humanities, Social Sciences, and Sciences* sat down to plan the project that resulted in its publication. At that time we realized that this would be a multivolume effort, and from its inception we intended to publish a total of three volumes. This is the second.

As in the first volume, we have attempted to offer advice and guidance to selectors who lack experience developing collections in an assigned field. The essays follow the general pattern of providing information on sources and strategies for identifying, evaluating, and acquiring materials in the field. Inevitably there will be some repetition due to the nature of the literature treated here. Our focus is on the interdisciplinary and applied fields, and they frequently draw upon other subjects for some of their material. Nonetheless, while each of the areas covered in this book owes something to other disciplines, each also has an identifiable literature, a core that sets it apart from the other fields. The writers of the essays have addressed this literature here.

Although our principal audience is intended to be the inexperienced selector, librarians with more knowledge of the disciplines also will find the book useful and interesting. The art of developing collections is constantly evolving, and many of the writers discuss the application of new technologies to the challenges of collection development.

Any success this book enjoys will be due to the efforts of a large group of people, generous with their time and willing to share their thoughts with colleagues. We thank all librarians dedicated to developing the best possible collections, the men and women who have contributed to the creation of a common body of knowledge widely and freely shared. Our essayists have drawn upon that knowledge, as well as their own experience, in making this contribution. This book provides another vehicle for further sharing the knowledge that shapes our profession.

Like its predecessor, this volume received the support and help of many colleagues on the Resources Section Executive Committee and the Collection Management and Development Committee. We are grateful for their assistance. We also wish to thank Michigan State University and Virginia Commonwealth University for providing vital administrative support for this project. The editors once again thank Bettina MacAyeal, our advocate and friend at ALA Publishing, for sustaining this effort and guiding it to fruition. Finally we thank the writers of these essays, for it is they who have made this book possible.

Introduction

The shopworn phrase "information explosion" has achieved a status close to that of a cliché in writings about libraries and collections, but it accurately conveys the situation confronted by librarians responsible for building and maintaining collections. The demand for information has fueled that explosion, and the appetite for materials seems insatiable. Publishers of every format have rushed to meet the needs of scholars and students in a bewildering variety of subjects, many of which have but recently emerged. Each year thousands of titles join the flood of materials that threaten to swamp our facilities. Much of the publication generated to feed our voracious consumers can be found in the applied and interdisciplinary fields discussed in this book.

These essays build upon those published in this volume's predecessor, *Selection of Library Materials in the Humanities, Social Sciences, and Sciences* (1985). General overviews of selection sources and strategies, buying out-of-print books, serials, and other specialized materials are well covered in that work and will not be repeated here. A third volume, in progress, will examine the problems and processes of building collections to support foreign-area study programs.

The eighteen essays in this volume focus on the work of identifying, evaluating, and acquiring materials in the applied and interdisciplinary fields. Collections in these areas are built by a broad spectrum of institutions that encompass public, academic, and special libraries. We have tried to discuss collection building in a way that addresses the general needs of all libraries acquiring materials in the applied and interdisciplinary fields. The intent is to provide practical advice for selectors having little knowledge of the subjects, either because of changes in assignments, or because they are new to the task of collection building in general. Experienced bibliographers also will find a useful refresher in these pages, while collection development administrators and library science students and faculty may discover value as well.

We have conceptualized this volume as two large groupings, applied or professional studies, which includes agriculture, business and management, criminal justice, education, engineering, health sciences, home economics, law, public administration, social work and urban planning, and interdisciplinary fields, comprising communications, environmental studies, geography and maps, race and ethnic studies, radical left and right, sports and recreation, and women's studies. In some cases the distinction we make between "applied" and "interdisciplinary" is admittedly arbitrary, since almost all of the subjects covered in this volume draw, to greater or lesser degree, upon a variety of disciplines. This volume is by no means a comprehensive treatment of all applied or interdisciplinary fields. Perhaps subsequent volumes will attempt to address those fields we were unable to include.

Selection of materials in the applied and interdisciplinary fields leads the bibliographer down a variety of paths perhaps not trod by collection developers in the more traditional subjects. While relying on the standard tools (*Publishers Weekly, Library Journal*, book reviews, flyers, etc.) for some current acquisitions, those librarians entrusted with building collections in the areas discussed in this book need to search more widely for appropriate titles. The literature of the disciplines is dynamic and reflects changes in the social and economic environment to a far greater extent than is usually encountered in the established and traditional fields. With some exceptions, current practice and experience shape the literature of the field. Consequently, it is important that the bibliographer stay abreast of events and influences in the regular work-a-day world, as well as be aware of the shifting interpretations of established disciplines that have an effect on the applied and interdisciplinary areas.

In describing their efforts and strategies in building collections, the authors of these essays frequently use terms such as "complex" and "unusual." In some cases the field itself is still being defined. For example, in women's studies, scholars are grappling with the problem of establishing its proper boundaries. As Rona Gregory notes in the essay on urban planning, "the inability to define planning in a neat and simple fashion is one of the salient characteristics of the field." Home economics is equally hard to define. As Neosha Mackey writes, "Nothing in Home Economics is as it appears." It is no wonder that the librarians charged with building the collections have difficulties identifying and acquiring the appropriate materials.

This literature is constantly changing and seems to be in a permanent state of flux. Engineering and communication arts and sciences are representative of this condition. Edwin Posey observes that "engineering is one of the most rapidly changing disciplines [and] the subject specialist is hard pressed to keep up with the burgeoning literature." Communications, "in common with fields applied by business and developed through sciences, . . . has changed radically in the last ten years because of rapidly changing and developing technologies." The torrent of literature on these subjects likewise has changed and the selector must keep abreast of these shifts to ensure that proper collections are built.

Materials for these fields are difficult to identify and locate; bibliographic control ranges from weak to nonexistent. Many of the authors treat this problem, but collecting the radical left and the radical right, as discussed by Janette Fiore, presents special challenges. Here the "publication" may be a skimpy pamphlet of severely limited distribution or merely a broadside. Items are produced in small quantities, and so the collector must be ever alert to their availability. While collecting the documents of political fringe groups represents perhaps the most striking example of acquiring fugitive materials, other areas present the same type of challenge. For example, publications needed for building collections in agriculture often fall outside of the mainstream of publishing. Selectors in women's studies also cast a wide net in gathering materials. In the case of collecting in sports and recreation, absence of bibliographic control is compounded by inadequate terminology provided by both the LC and Dewey schedules.

Even when the literature is well covered in standard sources, the selector in applied and interdisciplinary fields has additional challenges. Since these areas draw from a wide range of disciplines as well as generate their own literature, the selector must at the same time be both a generalist and a specialist. More than passing knowledge of publication in science, technology, and the social sciences is required, and while the arts and humanities generally are less well represented in the interdisciplinary and applied fields, subjects such as home economics, women's studies, ethnic studies, education, and communication arts draw heavily from them.

Builders of collections in the applied and professional studies such as agriculture, business and management, education, social work, and urban planning have additional collection decisions to make. Materials collected in these areas often are needed for performing some type of work or for training practitioners, in addition to academic research or analysis. Searching for the literature that deals with the practical as opposed to the theoretical aspects of the subject requires careful scrutiny of a variety of publications perhaps not as necessary for the research-oriented fields. Often that literature is found in the publications of associations and private organizations as well as in the hard to find documents issued by local, state, and federal governments. Selectors also must develop sensitivity to current events that presage the appearance of new trends in the field and its literature. As Neosha Mackey puts it, "one must be constantly on the alert when reading daily newspapers and news magazines [and] when watching television. . . ."

Selectors in these fields must cope with a variety of problems. They often have difficulty in defining the field. With the contributing disciplines identified, they must review that literature on a regular basis to find the pertinent titles. They must ferret out the fugitive and elusive materials produced within the field. Poor bibliographic control, in itself a reflection of the haphazard nature of publication, requires that the selector develop somewhat unconventional sources of information in order to ensure that titles are added to the collection in timely fashion.

The authors of these essays identify the tools needed and offer guidance to develop good collections. Building collections in the applied and interdisciplinary fields demands industry, intelligence, ingenuity, and imagination. It is up to each librarian to provide these ingredients.

AGRICULTURE

Arlene E. Luchsinger

The domestication of animals, the cultivation of soil, and the production and harvesting of crops have played a significant role in human history. Agriculture was synonymous with farming until the late nineteenth century. In 1862 federal support of agricultural education in the United States was established with the passage of the Land Grant College (Morrill) Act. This legislation resulted in the establishment of agricultural education institutions in each state as well as the creation of cooperative extension services and agricultural experiment stations.

After the Second World War, as agricultural programs expanded, the need for agricultural-related education and research heightened. Scientific approaches were applied to farming and agricultural research in order to increase the production of food. Today agriculture is big business and truly an interdisciplinary field. It includes plant pathology, animal science, horticulture, engineering, food science and technology, agricultural economics, marketing, commodities, and general business, as well as the pure sciences of chemistry and biology.

Library selectors in agriculture must be as knowledgeable about the literature of biology and chemistry as they are with that of agriculture. The reader of this chapter should become familiar with the essays on biology, chemistry, science, and government documents in *Selection of Library Materials in the Humanities, Social Sciences, and Sciences.* The *Quarterly Bulletin of the International Association of Agricultural Librarians and Documentalists* and *Agricultural Libraries Information Notes* should be added to the list of agricultural librarians' professional reading.

Guides to the Literature

While the guides to agricultural literature as such are few, bibliographers should become familiar with those that are available. Richard Blanchard

1

Blanchard, J. Richard, and Lois Farrell, eds. *Guide to Sources for Agricultural and Biological Research.* Berkeley: Univ. of California Pr., 1981.
Comprehensive sourcebook of agriculture-related literature published through 1980.
Annotated entries.
Extensive author, title, and subject indexes.
This book describes sources that will lead to primary resource materials pertaining to agriculture and related areas. The entries include abstracts and indexes, bibliographies, dictionaries, encyclopedias, handbooks, reviews, directories, conference proceedings, and literature guides. Nine broad subject chapters are divided into more specific topics.

---

and Lois Farrell's *Guide to Sources for Agricultural and Biological Research* is a comprehensive guide to bibliographic research sources in the production of food. It is arranged in nine broad subject sections. The first chapter of G. P. Lilley's *Information Sources in Agriculture and Food Science* provides an overview of agricultural literature, and bibliographers in agricultural libraries should acquaint themselves with it. Lilley also includes extensive lists of sources for specialized areas such as soils, agricultural engineering, field crops, and crop protection. *Keyguide to Information Sources in Agricultural Engineering,* by Bryan Morgan, provides a narrative survey of the literature of agricultural engineering as well as an annotated bibliography of sources of information.

Retrospective Selection

The *Dictionary Catalog of the National Agricultural Library, 1862-1965* and its supplement, the *National Agricultural Library Catalog,* are excellent sources when searching and verifying retrospective items. It is possible to locate materials in these catalogs by author, title, or subject. The subject portion of the *National Agricultural Library Catalog* is arranged by broad subject areas, such as nutrition, plant science, forestry, pesticides, soil science, and home economics.

"Pest Management Literature: Collection Development," an article by Syed Khan, is a more specialized but excellent annotated listing of books and serials within this subfield of agriculture. Frank Polach presents a short but extensively annotated bibliography of the sources needed in the reference collection of an agricultural library in "Current Survey of Reference Sources in Agriculture."

Another useful publication that provides information about bibliographies and directories is G. R. T. Levick's *Guide to Agricultural Information Sources in Asia and Oceania.* It is arranged by country and includes a subject and title index. *Agriculture in America, 1622–1860*, compiled by Andrea Tucker, is a bibliography of printed materials from the earliest period of printing in the United States to 1860 and should be of interest to those seeking complete bibliographic information for retrospective collecting.

The selection of retrospective materials is followed by locating the items to be purchased. Finding copies of out-of-print materials may be more difficult than the selection process. However, this part of a selector's job can be fun as well as a challenge. Peter Loewer, in his article, "Garden Book Dealers: A Catalog Review," discusses dealers who offer books in horticulture and agriculture. Other sources of out-of-print books are listed in *Smith's Guide to the Literature of the Life Sciences*.

Selection Sources for Current Publications

The selector has a variety of sources available to identify new and relevant agricultural publications. Scholarly papers and the results of research are most often published in journals and reflect current trends and ideas. Compilations of previous research, reference works, and treatments of a historical nature are published most often in book or monograph form.

Many of the places examined for notices of new publications are of a serial nature. It is helpful to keep a record of issues searched to save time. A convenient system is described in *Smith's Guide to the Literature of the Life Sciences*. A card recording volumes, issues, and years is kept for each journal title. As issues are examined the number is checked.

PERIODICALS

Special care is needed in selecting serials or periodicals for purchase, as subscriptions are a commitment to the expenditure of future funds. New serials may be advertised in existing journals. Also, notices of new periodicals are sent to libraries by the publishers, while some publishers will place libraries on their mailing lists for samples of all of their new journals. Most publishers are willing, upon request, to provide sample issues of periodicals for perusal. When examining a sample issue, the selector should note the content and its relevance to the existing collection and to the programs the library supports, the geographical scope, the editorial policies such as page charges, and whether or not the journal is refereed and where the journal is indexed. Note the members of the editorial committee or board.

The *Quarterly Bulletin of the International Association of Agricultural Librarians and Documentalists* has an occasional section called "New

---

Quarterly Bulletin of the International Association of Agricultural Librarians and Documentalists. v.1– . 1956– . London: International Assn. of Agricultural Librarians and Documentalists. Quarterly.
This journal provides a communications forum of an international scope for agricultural librarians. About once a year an extensive list of new agricultural serials is provided.

Periodicals" that includes bibliographic information for new agricultural periodicals. *Agricultural Libraries Information Notes* also has a listing of new serials. The *Monthly Catalog of United States Government Publications* has an annual serials supplement that is a compilation of federal serial publications. The classified lists in *Ulrich's International Periodical Directory* are also helpful in identifying agricultural periodicals.

MONOGRAPHS

Selecting monographs for an agriculture collection can be a real challenge. Book reviews traditionally have served as a source for the selection of new publications; and in addition to reviewing traditional library sources such as *Weekly Record* and *British National Bibliography*, selectors should review regularly those journals with book review sections. It must be noted, however, that there is often a time lag of a year or more between the publication of the book and the appearance of the review. The last section of *Biological and Agricultural Index* provides citations to book reviews, and the Commonwealth Agricultural Bureaux publications, such as *Animal Breeding Abstracts* and *Field Crop Abstracts*, have sections that abstract new books. *Booklist* includes reviews of materials related to agriculture, particularly horticulture.

Specialized subject journals publish reviews and may also include lists of materials they have received, but not reviewed. A few of the core agricultural periodicals in which reviews may be found are:

Agricultural and Forestry Meteorology
Agriculture, Ecosystems and Environment
Agronomy Journal
American Journal of Agricultural Economics
Association of Official Analytical Chemists Journal
Biological Agriculture and Horticulture

Canadian Journal of Agricultural Economics
Ceres: FAO Review on Agriculture and Development
Economic Botany
Energy in Agriculture
Grass and Forage Science
Journal of Animal Science
Journal of Soil and Water Conservation
Journal of Soil Science

Plant Pathology   Tropical Pest Management
Soil Science   World's Poultry Science Journal

The Monthly Checklist of State Publications is helpful in selecting items published by state agencies. State publications cor ain material of a regional nature and may be the only source for statistical information at the state level. About once a year Library Journal publishes a list of new scientific books, some of which are agriculture related. The U.S. Department of Agriculture and its specialized divisions issue publications on a variety of agricultural topics. The Monthly Catalog of United States Government Publications provides bibliographic access to these documents.

Trade publishers are eager to distribute their blurbs about new books and will add libraries to their mailing lists. Among those that publish books related to agriculture are AVI, Academic Press, Butterworths, CRC Press, Iowa State University Press, Wiley, Longmans, and Rodale.

Commercial vendors are helpful in providing information on the books they can supply. Harrassowitz, Nijhoff, and Blackwell North America are among those that will supply book selection forms. A profile can be written to include only those subjects that are of interest to a particular library.

Some libraries compile and distribute lists of current acquisitions. They are often willing to include other libraries on their mailing lists, especially if a reciprocal agreement can be worked out. The names and addresses of agricultural libraries may be found in Science and Technology Libraries.

Some of the most pertinent agricultural literature is published by professional societies and organizations such as the American Society of Agronomy, Crop Science Society of America, Soil Science Society of America, International Rice Research Institute, American Association of Cereal Chemists, and American Phytopathological Association. Addresses to these and other relevant organizations may be found in World Guide to Scientific Associations. It is possible to be placed on the mailing lists of organizations for their fliers or announcements of new and forthcoming materials. Associations' Publications in Print is an annual source of complete bibliographic information. In addition to a listing of publications by organization, there is a title and subject index.

FAO Documentation: Current Bibliography is a bimonthly list of documents produced or distributed by the Food and Agricultural Organization of the United Nations. It includes a subject index. The Commonwealth Agriculture Bureaux (CAB) prepares bibliographies with abstracts of literature relevant to specific agricultural topics such as dairy science, animal nutrition, plant breeding, and weeds. The cumulated index of these bibliographies may be obtained from CAB.

FAO Documentation: Current Bibliography. v.1– . 1967– . Rome: Food and
Agriculture Organization of the United Nations, Documentation Ctr.
Bimonthly.
Author, subject, and geographic indexes.
This publication includes selected documents and publications produced by or
on behalf of the Food and Agriculture Organization of the United Nations. The
Documentation Center in Rome can supply many of these documents on film.

Nonconventional Agricultural Literature

Abstracting or indexing services and other guides provide a link to the
commercially published literature. However, there is a substantial amount
of agricultural literature that is published in an unconventional form and
does not emanate from commercial publishers. This literature frequently
lacks bibliographic control and may be difficult to identify. Acquiring it
provides a challenge to bibliographers and acquisitions librarians.

This literature is frequently termed "gray" or "fugitive literature" and
may include reports, lectures, conference proceedings, in-house documents issued by industrial companies, booklets, pamphlets, and short press
runs of documents not intended for general distribution.

It is important to become familiar with the producers of these materials
in your state or region. They are generally willing to provide bibliographic
and ordering information. Some of these can be located by examining the
section for agricultural organizations in *Encyclopedia of Associations* or
by using the geographic index. In addition to addresses for the organization, the names and types of publications are identified. Some will place
libraries on their mailing lists or send complimentary copies of their publications. It is also necessary to scan the agricultural trade journals for
announcements and advertisements.

Conference proceedings are frequently issued by the organization sponsoring the meeting. If the publications are not well publicized they may
not be readily acquired. When a conference is announced, write to the
organization responsible for the meeting and ask that bibliographic and
ordering information be sent when the proceedings are published. Selectors may locate citations to previously published materials in *Index to
Scientific and Technical Proceedings, Index of Conference Proceedings
Received, Conference Papers Index*, and *Directory of Published Proceedings.*

The state agricultural experiment stations and the extension service of
universities generally issue publications in series, such as bulletins or research reports. However, these organizations also publish or sponsor other
materials less easy to identify. The addresses for these agricultural orga-

nizations may be located in the annual publication of the Professional Workers in State Agricultural Experiment Stations and Other Cooperating State Institutions' *Agriculture Handbook.*

Summary

The selector of agricultural literature must be aware of the subject matter and publishing trends in other areas of science and technology. Many of the sources needed by patrons will not be published by the commercial publishing houses. Agriculture librarians must be agressive in identifying, locating, and ordering relevant materials.

Selection Sources

Agricultural and Forestry Meteorology. v.31– . 1984– . Amsterdam: Elsevier. Monthly.
Agricultural Libraries Information Notes. v.1– . 1975– . Beltsville, Md.: National Agricultural Library. Monthly.
Agriculture, Ecosystems and Environment. v.9– . 1983– . Amsterdam: Elsevier. Monthly.
Agronomy Journal v.1– . 1907– . Madison, Wisc.: American Society of Agronomy. Bimonthly.
American Journal of Agricultural Economics. v.50– . 1968– . Ames, Iowa: American Agricultural Economics Assn. 5/year.
Animal Breeding Abstracts. v.1– . 1933– . Farnham Royal, Slough, U.K.: Commonwealth Agricultural Bureaux. Monthly.
Association of Official Analytical Chemists Journal. v.1– . 1915– . Arlington, Va.: Assn. of Official Analytical Chemists. Bimonthly.
Associations' Publications in Print. v.1– . 1981– . New York: Bowker. Annually.
Biological Agriculture and Horticulture. v.1– . 1982– . Berkhamsted, Herts, U.K.: A. B. Academic Publ. 4/year.
Biological and Agricultural Index. v.1– . 1916– . New York: Wilson. Monthly, except Aug.
Blanchard, J. Richard, and Lois Farrell, eds. *Guide to Sources for Agricultural and Biological Research.* Berkeley: Univ. of California Pr., 1981.
Booklist. v.1– . 1905– . Chicago: American Library Assn. 22/year.
British Library. Lending Division. *Index of Conference Proceedings Received.* no. 69– . 1974– . Boston Spa: British Lending Div. Annually.
British National Bibliography. v.1– . 1950– . London: Council of the British National Bibliography, British Museum. Weekly, with annual cumulations.
Canadian Journal of Agricultural Economics. v.1– . 1951– . Ottawa: Canadian Agricultural Economics and Farm Management Society. 3/year.
Ceres: FAO Review on Agriculture and Development. v.1– . 1968– . Rome: Food and Agriculture Organization of the United Nations. Bimonthly.
Commonwealth Agricultural Bureaux. *Annotated Bibliographies Price List.* Farnham Royal, Slough, U.K.: Commonwealth Agricultural Bureaux, 1983. (Supplements have been issued.)

Conference Papers Index. v.6– . 1978– . Bethesda, Md.: Cambridge Scientific Abstracts. Monthly.

Directory of Published Proceedings. Series SEMT—Science, Engineering, Medicine, and Technology. v.1– . 1965– . Harrison, N.Y.: Interdok. 10/year.

Economic Botany. v.1– . 1947– . Bronx, N.Y.: New York Botanical Garden. Quarterly.

Encyclopedia of Associations. v.1– . 1975– . Detroit: Gale. Annually.

Energy in Agriculture. v.1– . 1981– . Amsterdam: Elsevier. Quarterly.

FAO Documentation: Current Bibliography. v.1– . 1967– . Rome: Food and Agriculture Organization of the United Nations. Bimonthly.

Field Crop Abstracts. v.1– . 1948– . Farnham Royal, Slough, U.K.: Commonwealth Agricultural Bureaux. Monthly.

Grass and Forage Science. v.34– . 1979– . Oxford: Blackwell Scientific. Quarterly.

Index of Conference Proceedings Received. no. 69– . 1973– . Boston Spa, U.K.: British Library Lending Div. Monthly.

Index to Scientific and Technical Proceedings. v.1– . 1978– . Philadelphia: Institute for Scientific Information. Monthly.

Journal of Animal Science. v.1– . 1942– . Champaign, Ill.: American Society of Animal Science. Monthly.

Journal of Soil and Water Conservation. v.1– . 1946– . Ankeny, Iowa: Soil Conservation Society of America. Bimonthly.

Journal of Soil Science. v.1– . 1949– . Oxford: British Society of Soil Science. Quarterly.

Khan, Syed M. A. "Pest Management Literature: Collection Development." *Science & Technology Libraries* 4:57–87 (Winter 1983).

Levick, G. R. T., ed. *Guide to Agricultural Information Sources in Asia and Oceania.* The Hague: Federation Internationale de Documentation, 1980.

Library Journal. v.1– . 1876– . New York: Bowker. 20/year.

Lilley, G. P., ed. *Information Sources in Agriculture and Food Science.* London: Butterworths, 1981.

Loewer, Peter. "Garden Book Dealers: A Catalogue Review." *American Horticulturist* 64:11–13 (Feb. 1985).

McClung, Patricia A., ed. *Selection of Library Materials in the Humanities, Social Sciences, and Sciences.* Chicago: American Library Assn., 1985.

Monthly Catalog of United States Government Publications. no. 1– . 1895– . Washington, D.C.: U.S. Government Printing Office. Monthly.

Monthly Checklist of State Publications. v.1– . 1955– . Washington, D.C.: Library of Congress, Exchange and Gift Div. Monthly.

Morgan, Bryan. *Keyguide to Information Sources in Agricultural Engineering.* London: Mansell, 1985.

Plant Pathology. v.1– . 1952– . Oxford: Blackwell Scientific. Quarterly.

Polach, Frank. "Current Survey of Reference Sources in Agriculture." *Reference Services Review* 7:7–14 (July–Sept. 1979).

Professional Workers in State Agricultural Experiment Stations and Other Cooperating State Institutions. *Agriculture Handbook.* no. 305, rev. (1984).

Quarterly Bulletin of the International Association of Agricultural Librarians and Documentalists. v.1– . 1956– . London: International Assn. of Agricultural Librarians and Documentalists. Quarterly.

Science and Technology Libraries. v.1– . 1981– . New York: Haworth. Quarterly.

Smith, Roger C., W. Malcolm Reid, and Arlene E. Luchsinger. *Smith's Guide to the Literature of the Life Sciences.* 9th ed. Minneapolis: Burgess, 1980.

Soil Science. v.1– . 1916– . Baltimore: Williams & Wilkins. Monthly.

Subject Directory of Special Libraries and Information Centers. v.5. *Science and Technology Libraries.* Detroit: Gale, 1983.

Tropical Pest Management. v.26– . 1980– . London: Tropical Development and Research Institute. Quarterly.

Tucker, Andrea J., comp. *Agriculture in America, 1622–1860.* New York and London: Garland, 1984.

Ulrich's International Bibliography. v.1– . 1932– . New York: Bowker. Annually.

U.S. National Agricultural Library. *Dictionary Catalog of the National Agricultural Library, 1862–1965.* 73v. New York: Rowman & Littlefield, 1967–1970.

————. *National Agricultural Library Catalog.* 20v. Totowa, N.J.: Rowman & Littlefield, 1966–85.

Weekly Record. v.1– . 1974– . New York: Bowker. Weekly.

World Guide to Scientific Associations. 3rd ed. Munich: K. G. Saur, 1982.

World's Poultry Science Journal. v.1– . 1945– . Aylesbury, Bucks, U.K.: World's Poultry Science Assn. 3/year.

BUSINESS AND MANAGEMENT

Robert Bellanti
Tracey Miller

Collection development in business can take a variety of twists, primarily because business information needs often are very eclectic, ranging across a host of disciplines. For example, a user may need information on medical electronics as background for a market research study or to assess the sociopolitical climate in a particular country in order to make an investment decision. For situations like these it is almost impossible to rely solely on a business-focused collection development policy and expect that such wide-ranging needs can be fully met as a result of diligent collecting.

For collection development librarians working in the area of business, one of the first issues that must be addressed, therefore, is a clear explication of what subdisciplines to include. Obviously this will be dictated largely by the needs of the community served and available resources. Another consideration is the proximity of nearby collections that may have much to offer for those in need of business information. For example, government publications have valuable data of interest to business users. A small library may not want to extend its collecting efforts into this area if it is located near a depository library.

This chapter will focus on business collection development sources of major interest to librarians. The sources mentioned are useful for collection development work in areas traditionally considered to be within the core of business: accounting, finance, management, marketing, personnel, and the like. The wide array of sources useful for building specialized business collections, such as in banking or advertising, for the most part are not considered, although titles mentioned in this chapter are often good starting points for this purpose.

The authors would like to thank Corryn Crosby-Brown, Charlotte Georgi, Bob Rose, Milt Ternberg, Virginia Walter, and Eloisa G. Yeargain for their help in reviewing this chapter.

10

It should also be noted that the majority of the sources mentioned are useful for building a business collection that is comprised of items in print and microform. Despite the rapid pace of technological change and the increasing importance of computer databases and other innovations such as CD-ROM, items in print and microform will form the major part of business collections for some time to come. The primary focus of collection development in all but the most specialized libraries will continue to be in traditional formats, which is what this chapter emphasizes. The concluding section briefly discusses issues surrounding the acquisition and use of databases in business collection development work. This is an emerging area with major implications for business libraries. The impact of newer technologies has yet to be fully realized. It is clear they will grow in importance, making business collection development work more complex and challenging.

If this chapter contains any bias, it is its orientation towards collection development for business in academic libraries, reflecting the authors' background. However, collection development work in academic and public libraries is usually not too dissimilar; the titles and issues mentioned generally will be of interest to librarians working in both settings. Collection development work in corporate libraries varies more than in academic and public libraries, primarily because of the very specialized needs to which corporate librarians must respond. Therefore not everything mentioned in this chapter may be useful in the same degree to those working in the corporate sector.

Before discussing key collection development sources for business, it will be useful to review the nature of business information needs and the variety of formats that are encountered. Understanding the context in which business information is requested and used and the wide range of formats available provides a systematic framework for business collection development activities. This approach should also help librarians focus on key issues that collection development librarians face when working with business disciplines.

Business Information Needs

Business users' information needs frequently are analagous in many ways to user needs in the sciences. In both disciplines the emphasis is on current information and on the use of periodical literature and databases. Specific facts, particularly statistical data, are often required rather than broad expository treatments of a topic. Within both fields the tendency is towards ever greater specialization as well as a more interdisciplinary orientation.

Both fields are concerned with ethics; in business this concern includes the consequences of business decisions on other spheres of society.

This configuration of user needs and trends in the field provides a framework for a great deal of business collection development work. Because current information is in such great demand, serials form an important part of any business collection; considerable attention must be given to these publications. Also, because of their currency, databases play an ever-increasing role in business libraries. The issue of providing access to databases as part of a public service program is no longer the main question. Increasingly librarians must consider the acquisition of databases, or at least software, within the context of a business collection development policy.

Factual information is heavily requested in business libraries and much of it can be elusive to track down. Requests range the whole gamut of business endeavor—from the balance of trade payments in Brazil in a given year to the beta of a company's stock—and the collection development librarian must be alert for sources useful for this kind of information. Directories, statistical compendia, and government publications are all very useful in this regard and should be well represented in a business collection.

Works that provide a broad overview of a subject are not always as obviously in demand as those that provide the kinds of information described above. Often by the time a book is published, the information it contains is too dated to be of immediate interest for many users' purposes. However, such works are important because they provide the fundamentals on which business and management theory is based. The extended exposition afforded by a monograph or handbook is critical for users who need in-depth examination of a topic.

The recent upsurge of interest in business, as manifested by the popularity of books such as *Theory Z* and *In Search of Excellence* (which are solidly grounded in management theory, although written in a very accessible, nonacademic style), indicates that works providing an extended discussion of a topic do indeed have an important place in a business collection. Also, the interest in such works underscores the point that periodical literature and statistical compendia alone do not form a fully rounded business collection. Thus the challenge for the collection development librarian is to separate the wheat from the chaff, since much current business publishing output is not especially illuminating.

Works that provide a broad historical perspective are probably in least demand in an active business collection, but they should not be overlooked. A collection development librarian should ensure that at least representative samples of such works, particularly some of the classics of management theory (for example, Frederick Taylor's *Principles of Scientific Management* or Chester Barnard's *Functions of the Executive*) are available. Some of the fine histories of corporations (for example, Robert Sobel's *I.T.T.: The Management of Opportunity*) and the industries (for example, Anthony Sampson's *Empires of the Sky: The Politics, Contests and Cartels of World Airlines*) should similarly not be overlooked.

Time-series data constitute one type of historical information that will often be of interest. These statistical data, covering various economic or other quantitative variables, are normally collected and reported at given intervals, such as quarterly or annually. These data often are reported for long-term sequences in publications such as the U.S. Department of Commerce's *Business Statistics*, a biennial which presents annual data back to 1961 for approximately 1,900 series that are reported in the *Survey of Current Business*. Although much useful time-series data are available online (for example, PTS U.S. Statistics—U.S. Time series), the collection development librarian should be on the lookout for print sources like *Business Statistics* that help to meet users' needs.

Business Information Treatment

A few words should be said about the variety of treatments and forms that business information takes. One of the most vexing problems for any librarian attempting to build a serious business collection is the proliferation of popular, "how-to" books (for example, books that proclaim how one can get rich quickly by following the author's investment advice). These are commonly seen on the shelves of most bookstores and, while they may have their place, there is a limit to how many a library should collect. Many academic libraries will not want any material of this nature. Public libraries generally have user demands for books of this type and most likely will want to include this category in their collections. Unfortunately, titles can be misleading. Sometimes a book with a popular-sounding title turns out to treat a subject seriously. No easy solution to dealing with this problem exists short of being alert to authors and publishers for whom these works constitute their stock in trade.

Textbooks and workbooks are another common format encountered. While there is nothing inherently wrong with collecting texts and workbooks, many libraries choose not to, or collect these in a highly selective way. If this material is not wanted, the collection development librarian should be especially watchful because texts are not always identifiable by their titles and many trade publishers routinely include these in promotional literature and catalogs.

Loose-leaf services represent another common format for business information. With the exception of law, probably no other discipline matches business for the broad array of information that is available in loose-leaf treatment. The type of information varies widely, ranging from computers and information science, to company and stock data, to tax and accounting information, to international business. Generally expensive and always difficult to control, loose-leaf services form an integral part of any business collection and must be accommodated despite the difficulties they present.

Selection of Materials

BUSINESS INFORMATION FORMATS

Although format should not dictate a collection policy, it is useful to categorize those that typically are encountered when dealing with business information. Collection development librarians need to be aware of such formats, particularly those unique to business, to ensure that policies and procedures for processing and providing access to business materials have been formulated.

In this section, information formats are considered in a "generic" sense; for more detailed information on specific titles of collection development sources, consult the next section, "Bibliographic Sources for Selection."

STANDARD FORMATS

Monographs certainly are not unique to business. No dearth of monographs exist in this field and, as noted previously, often the problem is to identify the really useful publications from those written for the mass market. Works from major trade publishers generally are quite easy to identify; they comprise the core of what is collected in this format. Not to be overlooked, however, are nonserial publications issued by key associations (such as the American Management Associations or the Conference Board), the publishing output of university and research institutes, and dissertations.

It should be pointed out that collection development work in business is focused almost exclusively on works published in English (with the exception of serials). Even the largest business collections in academic or public libraries seldom require works published in other languages. Of course there will always be exceptions to this rule-of-thumb based on local needs, and collection development librarians should be alert to these exceptions. However, in business as in the sciences, English increasingly constitutes the universal language.

Serials form the heart of a business collection, and it is easy to be overwhelmed by the sheer output of titles relevant to business users' needs. They range from highly academic journals to practically oriented trade publications. Collection development librarians must have a clear understanding of their users' needs when considering serial titles because indiscriminate collecting in this format can quickly consume an acquisitions budget, thus resulting in a collection that is a hodgepodge of titles of marginal value.

In addition to journals, many other types of serial publications are of interest. These include newspapers, newsletters of all sorts (bank letters are an important subset in this category), directories, and regularly issued handbooks. Loose-leaf services, noted in the previous section, are another important serial type of great importance to any business collection. The latter are also among the most expensive items, so special care should be exercised when considering the addition of new loose-leaf services to a collection.

Microfilm and microfiche represent common formats in business collections. All kinds of publications are available in microformat—journals, newspapers, annual and 10K reports, state industrial directories, dissertations, periodical indexes, and the like. It is almost impossible to exclude microforms from an active business collection, and collection development librarians should not shy away from this format. Rather, the goal should be to ensure that the proper equipment and facilities are provided so that users can work comfortably with microforms.

Pamphlets and audiovisual materials are two formats with a relatively minor role in business collections. Although they can be immediately useful, often their long-term value is not that significant. Time, effort, and funds expended to acquire, provide access, and maintain these materials must be weighed against their potential usefulness to a library's user group. The usefulness of materials in these formats will be enhanced if access to them is provided through standard library holdings tools such as a card catalog. If separate files must be consulted to identify pamphlet or audiovisual items, they often remain out of the mainstream and underutilized.

FORMATS UNIQUE TO BUSINESS

A type of serial, although not often thought of as such, are annual reports to shareholders (ARS) and 10K and other reports that publicly held companies are required to file with the Securities and Exchange Commission (SEC). These reports are always in high demand. They provide much valuable information, particularly financial data, on individual companies. Annual reports and reports filed with the SEC are available in microfiche. Many libraries choose to maintain a hard-copy collection of annual reports instead of, or in addition to, collecting microfiche. However, unless the parameters of a hard-copy ARS collection are carefully defined, extensive collecting in this format can be very time-consuming. Hard-copy annual report collections consume a good deal of space as well. Since users' interest in older reports generally is quite low, maintaining a large hard-copy ARS collection is not recommended, except possibly in research-level collections. Even in research libraries it is often more effective to rely on the microfiche editions of the ARS for back sets and to select hard-copy editions carefully for retention.

Market research reports constitute another format unique to business collections. These highly specialized reports are researched and written by staff at professional consulting firms for fee-paying clients. They cover virtually any topic of interest to an individual client company—from an analysis of the wine market in California to the projected demand for German-made autos in New York. Because of the great amount of original data collecting that often goes into compiling these reports, and because they are frequently idiosyncratic to a client's needs, market research reports tend to be very expensive. The expense alone ($1,000 or more per report is not uncommon) is sufficient reason for most libraries to justify not collecting market research reports. Also, because they cover such a wide variety of topics, user demand for these reports can be unlimited. Collection development librarians should proceed with caution when dealing with these reports; once a user's need is satisfied by purchasing a market research report it may be difficult to turn down other requests. A collection development policy that clearly addresses this issue can be very helpful when dealing with this question.

Reports issued by securities and investment dealers are a third format unique to business. These reports generally provide an analysis of a company or an industry from the perspective of their investment potential (for example, *Time, Inc.* by Mary L. Kukowski, a company analysis of Time, Inc., issued by Kidder, Peabody & Co., August 1, 1984; *Industry Review* by Mark Biderman, a review of the banking industry, issued by Oppenheimer & Co., November 19, 1984). They are usually well researched and range anywhere from one to one hundred pages. Because they are written by people whose job is to monitor a company or an industry closely, their "insider" perspective can be very valuable. Securities and investment dealers reports are available in microfiche collections and online. Obtaining individual hard-copy reports can be quite difficult since bibliographic control for this material is elusive and the firms that issue the reports are not accustomed to dealing with library requests.

Bibliographic Selection Sources

CURRENT SELECTION SOURCES

Standard book trade publications, such as *Books in Print, Cumulative Book Index, American Book Publishing Record, Publishers Weekly*, and the *Weekly Record*, can be utilized to identify currently available materials in many subject areas, including business and economics. *Ulrich's International Periodicals Directory, Standard Periodical Directory* and *Standard Rate & Data Service: Business Publications Rates and Data*, are good sources to identify business serials. Harvard University's Baker Library maintains one of the most comprehensive academic business collections in the country, and their in-depth serials collection is listed in *Current Periodical Publications in Baker Library*, published annually.

Publishers' catalogs and announcements contain valuable information on new titles. Many of the major reputable trade publishers, such as John Wiley & Sons, McGraw-Hill, and Elsevier regularly publish lists of recent publications, with sections devoted to business. Wiley's *Librarians' Newsletter* appears bimonthly, while Elsevier's *New and Forthcoming Books and Journals* is published monthly. Adding one's name to one or more of these lists will insure that, in no time at all, the library should be receiving announcements and brochures from many other publishers.

Quite a few business libraries and departments publish bibliographies of recently acquired items. Sometimes these take the form of acquisitions lists, as in the case of Harvard's monthly *Recent Additions to the Baker Library*, or Stanford University's *Selected Additions to the J. Hugh Jackson Library*, published bimonthly. Others are more subject-oriented, such as the Brooklyn Public Library's *Service to Business and Industry*, and *Info*, published monthly by the Tulsa City-County Library. Frequently, as in the case of the last two items mentioned, there is no charge for these lists. However, a few current awareness titles do charge nominal sums for subscriptions. For example, *What's New in Advertising and Marketing*, published ten times a year by the Special Libraries Association, Advertising and Marketing Division, costs $15.00 per year. *Business Literature*, published five times a year by the Newark Public Library, costs $3.00 annually. Harvard's Baker Library also publishes an annual catalog of their reading room collection, entitled *Core Collection: An Author and Subject Guide*. The charge for this publication is approximately $15.00.

LIBRARY LITERATURE

Various sources from library literature can assist the librarian in business selection tasks. *American Reference Books Annual* provides annotated reviews of major business reference works. The first March issue of *Library Journal* contains an annotated list of "Business Books," preceded by an introductory essay commenting on the quality and quantity of the previous year's output. Forthcoming "Scientific, Technical, Medical and Business Books" is published in the first November issue of *Library Journal*. Regular monitoring of other library-related journals containing book

"Business Books: A Selection of Recommended Books." *Library Journal.* New York: Bowker. Annually.
An annual feature appearing in the March 1 issue, this list provides an overview of recommended business books published in the previous year. The introduction provides an informative and lively summary of key trends in business publishing. The list itself is organized by broad topical areas. Each entry is annotated and includes complete bibliographic information. Although the list is selective and one might take issue with the inclusion of particular titles, overall it is a good starting point for keeping current with the best business output. Because of its selectiveness, academic and larger public libraries will need to go well beyond the scope of this list.

reviews, such as *RSR: Reference Services Review, Serials Review*, and *College and Research Libraries* is a good way to identify additional titles.

SPECIFIC BUSINESS BIBLIOGRAPHIES

Selection sources that are specifically targeted for business include G. K. Hall's *Bibliographic Guide to Business and Economics*, which covers publications cataloged by the Research Libraries of the New York Public Library and the Library of Congress. R. R. Bowker has published *Business and Economics Books and Serials in Print* on an irregular basis for a number of years (as of this writing the most recent edition is 1981). Bowker has also produced a comprehensive, four-volume bibliography entitled *Business and Economics Books: 1876–1983.* It contains records of Library of Congress holdings, covering works published and distributed in the United States, including both in-print and out-of-print titles. Other useful sources include the *Wall Street Review of Books, Business Book Review*, and *Business Library Newsletter.*

Some standard business reference sources can also be tapped for collection development purposes. Lorna Daniell's *Business Information*

Bibliographic Guide to Business and Economics, v.1– . 1975– . Boston: Hall. Annually.
A listing of publications cataloged by the Library of Congress and the Research Libraries of the New York Public Library. Inclusion of titles is based on the LC classification HA through HJ. Volumes are arranged in a single alphabetical sequence, with access by main entry, added entries, title, series titles, and subject headings. Full bibliographic information is included with the main entry. Extremely valuable because of its comprehensiveness, although its usefulness for ongoing collection development work is lessened to some extent because of its annual frequency. Despite this it is an essential tool since there are few other sources with its scope.

Wall Street Review of Books. v.1– . 1973– . Bedford Hills, N.Y.: Redgrave. Quarterly.
Scholarly review journal.
About 20 critical reviews per issue.
6–12-month lag between book publication and review.
Author and title indexes in the final issue.
Featured are signed critical reviews for scholarly books in business and economics. Several books are frequently discussed in the same review, providing useful analyses of works on similar topics. Complete bibliographic information including price is given. An excellent source, although the time lag and the selective coverage lessen its usefulness for timely collection development work.

Daniells, Lorna M. *Business Information Sources.* Rev. ed. Berkeley: Univ. of California Pr., 1985.
The most comprehensive and respected compilation of key business sources by the leading United States business bibliographer. Arranged by broad topical areas, with subsections listing works in subdisciplines and by particular formats, such as handbooks, indexes, periodicals, etc. The book covers virtually hundreds of titles. Each entry is annotated and includes complete bibliographic information. The final chapter lists works recommended as a basic bookshelf for personal or business use or for a small public library. This book is indispensable for both business collection development and reference work.

Sources, revised edition, is an indispensable tool for selection as well as for reference purposes. *The Basic Business Library: Core Resources* is another helpful title that provides an overview of key sources. In addition, *The Directory of Directories, Encyclopedia of Associations, Encyclopedia of Business Information Sources, Directory of Industry Data Sources, Statistical Reference Index (SRI),* and *Where to Find Business Information* all contain listings of items of interest to business and economics.

BOOK REVIEWS FROM BUSINESS JOURNALS

In order to achieve collection depth in specific subject areas, the librarian may choose to examine business and economics journals that regularly feature book reviews. The drawback to this approach is time lag—some of these journals are notoriously slow in reviewing various titles. Listed below are representative journals useful to scan for book reviews:

Academy of Management Review. v.1– . 1976– . Mississippi State, Miss.: Academy of Management. Quarterly.
Accounting Review. v.1– . 1926– . Sarasota, Fla.: American Accounting Assn. Quarterly.
Administrative Science Quarterly. v.1– . 1956– . Ithaca, N.Y.: Graduate School of Business Admin., Cornell Univ. Quarterly.
American Economic Review. v.1– . 1911– . Nashville, Tenn.: American Economic Assn. Quarterly.

Business History. v.1- . 1958- . London: Frank Cass. 3/year.
Business History Review. v.1- . 1926- . Boston: Graduate School of Business Admin., Harvard Univ. Quarterly.
Business Horizons. v.1- . 1957- . Bloomington: Indiana Univ. Graduate School of Business. Bimonthly.
Harvard Business Review. v.1- . 1922- . Boston: Graduate School of Business Admin., Harvard Univ. Bimonthly.
Journal of Economic History. v.1- . 1941- . Iowa City: Economic History Assn. at the Univ. of Iowa. Quarterly.
Journal of Economic Literature. v.7- . 1969- . Nashville, Tenn.: American Economic Assn. Quarterly.
Journal of Finance. v.1- . 1946- . New York: American Finance Assn. 5/year.
Journal of International Business Studies. v.1- . 1970- . Columbia: Univ. of South Carolina and Academy of International Business. 3/year.
Journal of Marketing Research. v.1- . 1964- . Chicago: American Marketing Assn. Quarterly.
Management Review. v.1- . 1914- . New York: American Management Assn. Monthly.
Sloan Management Review. v.12- . 1970- . Cambridge, Mass.: Sloan Management Review Assn. at the Alfred P. Sloan School of Management, Massachusetts Institute of Technology. Quarterly.

Trade journals for specific industries can also be useful to locate reviews, especially if one is seeking to build an in-depth collection of industry-specific works. A few examples are *Advertising Age* (weekly, published by Crain Communications, Inc.), *California Real Estate Magazine* (monthly, published by the California Association of Realtors), and *Marketing News* (biweekly, published by the American Marketing Association).

CORPORATE REPORTS

A good financial reports collection often forms the cornerstone of a business library. Valuable information about publicly traded securities is contained in reports these companies are required to file with the Securities and Exchange Commission (SEC). Items reported in various documents may include descriptions of business, financial statements, corporate changes, legal proceedings, and compensation of top executives. Some of the more in-demand reports to collect are 10Ks, prospectuses, 8Ks, and Annual Reports to Shareholders. As of October 1, 1985, Bechtel Information Services of Gaithersburg, Maryland, is handling the more than 200,000 filings sent to the SEC. Bechtel will make these reports available to libraries and others interested in public companies. Disclosure, of Bethesda, Maryland, who handled this task before October 1, 1985, will continue to supply SEC reports to libraries. Micromoedia Limited of Toronto, Canada, offers a range of "insider" reports on Canadian companies registered with the Ontario Securities Commission.

Annual reports from foreign companies are also available from Disclosure, as well as from Bechtel.

Chadwyk-Healey Inc., with offices in Teaneck, New Jersey, has published a microfiche collection entitled *Annual Reports of the World's Central Banks*. The 1984 collection covers reports from 125 countries, and a retrospective collection is promised.

INVESTMENT ADVISORY SERVICES, NEWSLETTERS, BANK LETTERS, AND LOOSE-LEAF SERVICES

Investment advisory services, such as the *Value Line*, and newsletters that address a multitude of special topics, are high demand items in an active business collection. One of the best guides for identifying newsletters and advisory services is the *Directory of Business and Financial Services*, in which the authors list and describe more than 1,100 business and financial services worldwide. *Investment Newsletters* and the *Oxbridge Directory of Newsletters* are other sources to check for these materials.

Bank letters provide valuable statistical and narrative information. Utilizing publications such as *The Fed in Print* (free from the Research Library, Federal Reserve Bank of Philadelphia), one can find all the publications of the Federal Reserve's Research Department. *Banking Literature Index*, published by the American Bankers Association, also constitutes a good information source for banking serial titles.

Loose-leaf services also play a major role in any business collection because they provide the key element of currency. A few major publishers of such services include Standard and Poor's Corporation (S&P), Moody's Investor's Services, Prentice-Hall (P-H), Commerce Clearing House, the Bureau of National Affairs, Datapro Research Corporation, and Auerbach. Almost every business topic can be found in this popular format, ranging from profiles of publicly held companies (S&P and Moody's) to detailed tax information (CCH and P-H).

GOVERNMENT PUBLICATIONS

The acquisition of government publications poses a special challenge for the librarian. These publications contain statistics and reports crucial to the researcher, and timely acquisition is important.

Utilizing a subscription agent, such as Bernan Associates, can help eliminate much time-consuming legwork. Bernan acquires serial and nonserial government publications from the United States, Britain, Canada, Australia, Ireland, Hong Kong, and from organizations such as the United Nations, Organisation for Economic Co-operation and Development (OECD), World Bank, European Communities, International Labour Organisation (ILO), International Monetary Fund (IMF), and the Organization of American States (OAS), among others. Standing orders for many government serials can be placed with Bernan.

The U.S. Government Printing Office (GPO) also offers a "standing order service" for a number of their publications. Occasionally the GPO publishes announcements such as *U.S. Government Books Especially for Business Professionals.*

Other ways to monitor U.S. government publications include checking the *Monthly Catalog of United States Government Publications and New Books* (a bimonthly pamphlet of materials available from the Superintendent of Documents, arranged by broad subject areas) and by placing one's name on mailing lists of individual government agencies that publish items relevant to business, such as the Bureau of Labor Statistics and the Small Business Administration. The *Government Printing Office Sales Publications Reference File*, a microfiche catalog, lists currently available U.S. publications. This is a helpful source to determine if a government publication is still in print, its cost, and its stock number.

AGENCIES AND ASSOCIATIONS

Many specialized agencies and associations publish materials of particular interest to business. These include the World Bank, the OECD, American Management Associations, American Marketing Association, the Conference Board, and the American Institute of Certified Public Accountants (AICPA). The World Bank publishes an annual *Catalog of Publications,* available free upon request. The OECD publishes a *General Catalogue* in June of each year, updated by irregularly published supplements. In addition, they publish *OECD Recent Publications* monthly, available by writing the OECD Publications and Information Center. The Conference Board, a nonprofit, independent business research organization, publishes an annual *Cumulative Index,* which serves as a guide to their current publications. In addition, a publications price list and order form is available at no charge. The AICPA publishes a *Current List of AICPA Publications,* and a brochure describing their standing order plan. And last, for a broad overview of what is available in this area, *Associations Publications in Print* is an invaluable source.

MARKET RESEARCH REPORTS AND WORKING PAPERS

Market research reports present a dilemma for the collection development librarian. Since they are usually very costly and quite specific in subject coverage, most business collections do not include them, despite heavy user interest. However, sources such as *Findex* and the *Directory of U.S. and Canadian Marketing Surveys and Services* provide information helpful in identifying some of the reports available in the United States and Canada.

Working papers, usually described as unpublished drafts of possible journal articles, are produced by leading business schools in the United States and abroad, as well as by government agencies and companies. These papers can be very difficult to track down because they are viewed as "preliminary" works. A good, although selective, source for reviewing works in this category is Harvard University's *Working Papers in the Baker Library: A Quarterly Checklist*. Working papers are also included with research reports, pamphlets, and periodical articles, in the AUBER (Association for University and Business Economic Research) *Annual Bibliography*.

Two important collections of working papers, developed by the University of Warwick, Coventry, England, are available through Trans-Media/The Oceana Group in Dobbs Ferry, New York. *Economics Working Papers Bibliography* consists of a bibliography-index that lists about 3,000 economics working papers from over 400 institutions. A companion microfilm service reproduces the full text of nearly half of these papers. Trans-Media also publishes *Management and Accountancy Research Working Papers* annually as a printed index, with abstracts from the papers available on microfiche.

DISSERTATIONS AND MICROFORM

Dissertations in the fields of business and economics are indexed in *Dissertations Abstracts International*, and are available on demand in microform or paper format through University Microfilms International (UMI). UMI publishes many separate topical catalogs of available dissertations. They will, upon request, generate a specialized subject bibliography of dissertations in the area of business and economics. UMI Press has published several series of books based on dissertations. One of special interest is *Research for Business Decisions*, published irregularly since 1978.

Increasingly, many collections of interest to business are available only in microform. A few examples include *Statistical Reference Index (SRI), Cirr/Corporate & Industry Research Reports, Area Business Databank (ABD)*, and *Goldsmiths'-Kress Library of Economic Literature*. There is no one channel through which these publications are regularly reviewed. Therefore, libraries need to monitor carefully other sources mentioned in this chapter in order to keep up to date on new microform publishing endeavors.

One point to keep in mind with collections such as SRI is that they include some publications also easily obtainable in print format. For example, the *International Index of Statistics*, a companion collection to

SRI, includes OECD publications. It might be possible to rely on the microform collection for access to these publications and to forego acquiring the print copies. Whether or not this trade-off can be made will depend on factors such as the availability of funds, the amount of use the print copies receive, the availability and ease of use of microform reading equipment, user acceptance of microforms, and the like.

RETROSPECTIVE SOURCES

Several excellent retrospective sources, specifically directed towards business subjects, are available. One of the most comprehensive (and expensive) sets is Harvard University's *Author-Title Catalog of the Baker Library* and *Subject Catalog of the Baker Library*, published by G. K. Hall in 1971, both available with supplements published in 1974.

G. K. Hall's *Bibliographic Guide to Business and Economics*, mentioned earlier in this chapter, can also be utilized for retrospective selection purposes, as can Bowker's *Business and Economics Books: 1876–1983* and *Business and Economics Books and Serials in Print*.

Acquisitions Issues

Many business libraries, like their counterparts in other disciplines, utilize approval plans such as Blackwell North America's to facilitate timely acquisition of books. No one standing order plan can be recommended that focuses strictly on business books. As is the case with any other subject area, care must be exercised when creating the approval plan profile, in order to avoid receiving unwanted materials. Also, using an approval plan in business, as in any discipline, will not address all of a library's collection development needs. Collection development librarians should be on the alert for the many items and formats that an approval plan does not cover.

Some approval plans include foreign materials, most often from Great Britain, Canada, and Australia. When ordering items from other countries, utilizing a vendor in the specific geographic region of interest, such as Harrassowitz in West Germany or Blackwell's Ltd. in the United Kingdom, is recommended. *Who Distributes What and Where: An International Directory of Publishers, Imprints, Agents and Distributors* provides a useful list of vendors, arranged both alphabetically by company name and geographically by areas covered.

For serials, business librarians often choose to place orders with large subscription agents such as Faxon, rather than deal individually with each publisher.

A number of key business publishers, such as AMACOM and the AICPA, accept standing orders for their publications.

There are many reputable business book publishers. What follows is a partial list of some of the key business publishers:

Addison-Wesley	Institute of Internal Auditors
AMACOM Book Division	JAI Press
American Marketing Assn.	Jossey Bass
Auerbach Publishers Inc.	Knowledge Industry
Ballinger	Lexington
Basic	Longwood Publishing
Bowker	Matthew Bender
Brookings	Macmillan
Bureau of National Affairs	McGraw-Hill
Chicago Board of Trade	Moody's Investors Services
Commerce Clearing House Inc.	North Holland
Crain	Nichols
Datapro Research Corp.	Pergamon
Dow Jones-Irwin	Pitman
Dun and Bradstreet	Praeger
Free Press	Prentice-Hall
Gale Research	Reston
Garland (reprints)	Robert Morris Assoc.
Gower	Standard & Poor's Corp.
Graham Trotman Ltd.	Wadsworth
Greenwood	John Wiley & Sons
G. K. Hall	Wiley Interscience

Many university presses also offer excellent business titles, such as *Business Information Sources*, published by the University of California Press.

Occasionally, institutes, associations, and other organizations such as local chambers of commerce are willing to make their publications available at no cost to libraries. Since items published by these agencies can be difficult to obtain, it's always best to contact them directly.

When collecting retrospective material, it is helpful to establish contact with local out-of-print booksellers. It's a good idea to determine whether any local dealers specialize in business titles. Regular interaction with one or two booksellers will improve the chances of acquiring desired items.

Attendance at national library conferences, such as the Special Libraries Association, can be very beneficial. Many publishers and vendors mount displays in the exhibit halls. This presents an ideal opportunity to discuss current and future publishing output directly with them.

Databases

Databases play a central role in business libraries because of the wealth of information available and the timeliness they offer. Most often, online databases are available to library users as part of a public service/reference program. Their use as a collection development tool is frequently more limited, although they can be very helpful in this regard.

Databases can be extremely useful and time saving as a means of identifying titles when building a new collection, or in a new subject, or when adding depth to an existing collection. In such cases the cost of searching various online files is likely to be less than the personnel cost involved in manually searching print sources to identify titles of interest. The LC MARC and the REMARC databases, available through Dialog Information Services, are especially good for these purposes. Also helpful, if a library has access to them, are the bibliographic utilities such as OCLC and RLIN. These large files include many works relevant for business libraries.

Many titles mentioned in the previous section have online counterparts that can be especially useful for retrospective collection development work, including Books in Print, Dissertation Abstracts online, Encyclopedia of Associations, GPO Monthly Catalog, Find/SVP Reports and Studies Index (the online equivalent of *Findex: The Directory of Market Research Reports, Studies and Surveys*), and Ulrich's International Periodicals Directory, available through Dialog Information Service. Books in Print, Dissertation Abstracts online, GPO Monthly Catalog and Ulrich's International Periodicals Directory are also available through BRS.

The Wiley Catalog/Online, available through Dialog Information Services, is the online version of Wiley's *General Catalog*. It contains about 30,000 records and includes full citations, descriptions, and tables of contents for approximately 10,000 books, journals, software, databases, and other publications currently available from Wiley. It also includes about 20,000 records on forthcoming and out-of-print Wiley titles. Because of Wiley's large output of business and computer science books, this database may be of special interest to collection development librarians working in business. (Presumably other major publishers will mount online counterparts to their catalogs when it becomes cost effective for them to do so.)

While databases such as those mentioned above can expedite retrospective collection development activity, they also can be useful for on-going work. The cost involved may be more difficult to justify since it would be a regularly recurring expense as opposed to a one-time expenditure for retrospective work. However, databases certainly should be considered as an adjunct to the more traditional approaches used in business collection development.

ACQUISITION OF DATABASES

More and more, libraries will be confronted with the need to acquire databases or at least to provide access to them when there are no print or microform counterparts available. The issues surrounding this topic are complex and are not unique to business. Business collection development librarians need to be especially aware of developments in this area, since so many data files are of high interest to their user group.

Providing access to various files through online services vendors such as BRS or Dialog Information Services is not a new issue for libraries. Most libraries are well acquainted with their services and are set up to provide user access to needed files—usually for a fee.

More recently, many data files have become available that have no print counterparts or for which the printed publications represent but a fraction of the total data available. Data from the Bureau of the Census and the Bureau of Labor Statistics are examples in this category; they are of high interest to business libraries. Raw numeric data frequently comprise these files. Separate database management packages often must be utilized to extract the needed information from them in a format that meets a user's specific requirements. Thus, acquiring or providing access to these files is a much more complex issue than simply providing access to files available through online services vendors.

Although criteria for evaluating data files are similar to those for evaluating materials in other formats, several collection development issues unique to this form of information must be dealt with.[1] These include confidentiality (some files may include proprietary or restricted information); physical format (for example, magnetic tape, floppy disk, or disk pack format); online access (some files may only be available online); documentation and consulting (complex files may require staff to assist users with file manipulation); and special hardware and software issues.

Unfortunately, identifying data files that may be of interest as an acquisition for the library is not an easy task. Karin Wittenborg has comprehensively addressed issues related to acquiring data files in her chapter "Machine-Readable Data Files."[2] For business collections two sources are individual government agencies (such as the Bureau of the Census) and

1. Concepts discussed in this selection have been drawn from *Textual and Numeric Data Files*, a report from the LAUC ad hoc Committee on Textual and Numeric Databases (Librarians Assn. of the Univ. of California, Oct. 23, 1983).
2. Karin Wittenborg, "Machine-readable Data Files," in *Selection of Library Materials in the Humanities, Social Sciences, and Sciences*, ed. Patricia A. McClung (Chicago: American Library Assn., 1985), pp. 375–87.

the Inter-University Consortium for Political and Social Research (ICPSR) at the University of Michigan. The latter collects and disseminates machine-readable social science data and publishes an annual *Guide to Resources and Services*, a classified catalog of its holdings.

As Wittenborg points out, the federal government is a prolific producer of machine-readable data files but control of what is available is far from good. She notes that the *Directory of Federal Statistical Data Files*, published in 1981, is a major advance in providing control over the output from the federal government.[3]

Data files pose special challenges for collection development librarians. A great deal of coordination and integration with library staff and staff in nonlibrary departments may be required to insure that the acquisition and utilization of machine-readable data files fully supports the goals of the library and its parent institution. Because of the high value and importance of data files for business library users, business collection development librarians should be well acquainted with the issues and should plan actively for their inclusion in library holdings.

Selection Sources

ABD. v.1– . 1983– . Louisville, Ky.: Area Business Databank. Monthly.
American Book Publishing Record. v.1– . 1960– . New York: Bowker. Monthly.
American Reference Books Annual. v.1– . 1970– . Garden City, N.Y.: Literary Guild. Annually.
Association for University Business and Economic Research. *Annual Bibliography.* v.1– . 1977– . Morgantown: Bureau of Business Research, West Virginia Univ. Annually.
Associations Publications in Print. v.1– . 1981– . New York: Bowker. Annually.
Banking Literature Index. v.1– . 1982– . Washington, D.C.: American Bankers Assn. Monthly.
Books in Print. v.1– . 1948– . New York: Bowker. Annually.
Brownstone, David M. *Where to Find Business Information: A World Guide for Everyone Who Needs the Answers to Business Questions.* 2nd ed. New York: Wiley, 1982.
Business and Economics Books: 1876–1983. New York: Bowker, 1983.
Business and Economics Books and Serials in Print. New York: Bowker, 1981.
Business Book Review. v.1– . 1984– . Urbana, Ill.: Corporate Support Systems. Bimonthly.
Business Library Newsletter. v.1– . 1978– . Cambridge, Mass.: Business Library Newsletter. Monthly.
Business Literature. v.1– . 1983– . Newark, N.J.: Public Library of Newark, Business Library. 5/year.
CIRR/Corporate & Industry Research Reports. v.1– . 1982– . Eastchester, N.Y.: JA Micropublishing. Annually.

3. Ibid., p. 381.

College and Research Libraries. v.1- . 1939- . Chicago: American Library Assn. Bimonthly.
Conference Board. *Cumulative Index.* v.1- . 1971- . New York: Conference Board. Annually.
Core Collection: An Author and Subject Guide. v.1- . 1970/71- . Boston: Harvard Univ. Graduate School of Business Admin., Baker Library. Annually.
Cumulative Book Index. v.1- . 1928- . New York: Wilson. 11/year.
Current Periodical Publications in Baker Library. v.1- . 1971/72- . Boston: Harvard Univ. Graduate School of Management, Baker Library. Annually.
Daniells, Lorna M. *Business Information Sources.* Rev. ed. Berkeley: Univ. of California Pr., 1985.
Directory of Business and Financial Services. 8th ed. Ed. by Mary McNierney Grant and Riva Berleant-Schiller. New York: Special Libraries Assn., 1984.
The Directory of Directories. 2nd ed. Detroit: Gale, 1983.
Directory of Industry Data Sources: The United States of America and Canada. 2nd ed. Cambridge, Mass.: Ballinger, 1982.
Directory of U.S. and Canadian Marketing Surveys and Services. v.1- . 1976- . Fairfield, N.J.: H. Kline. Biennially, with two interim supplements.
Dissertations Abstracts International. v.1- . 1973- . Ann Arbor, Mich.: University Microfilms. Monthly.
Economics Working Papers Bibliography. v.1- . 1976- . Dobbs Ferry, N.Y.: Trans-Media. Annually.
Encyclopedia of Associations. v.1- . 1956- . Detroit: Gale. Biennially.
Fed in Print: Business and Banking Topics. v.1- . 1970/74- . Philadelphia: Federal Reserve Bank of Philadelphia. Semiannually.
Findex: The Directory of Market Research Reports, Studies and Surveys. v.1- . 1979- . New York: Find/SVP. Annually.
Goldsmiths'-Kress Library of Economic Literature. Microfilm ed. Woodbridge, Conn.: Research Publications, 1979.
Guide to Industry Special Issues. v.1- . 1984- . Cambridge, Mass.: Ballinger. Annually.
Harvard Univ. Graduate School of Business Admin. Baker Library. *Author-Title Catalog of the Baker Library.* Boston: Hall, 1971.
_____. _____. _____. *Recent Additions to the Baker Library.* v.1- . 1979- . Boston: Graduate School of Business Admin., Harvard Univ. Monthly.
_____. _____. _____. *Subject Catalog of the Baker Library.* Boston: Hall, 1971.
_____. _____. _____. *Working Papers in Baker Library: A Quarterly Checklist.* v.1- . 1969- . Boston: Graduate School of Business Admin., Harvard Univ. Quarterly.
Info. Tulsa, Okla.: Tulsa City-County Library. Business and Technology Dept. Monthly.
Inter-University Consortium for Political and Social Research. *Guide to Resources and Services.* Ann Arbor, Mich.: Inter-University Consortium for Political and Social Research. Annually.
Library Journal. v.1- . 1876- . New York: Bowker. Bimonthly.
Management and Accountancy Research Working Papers. v.1- . 1983/84- . Dobbs Ferry, N.Y.: Trans-Media. Annually.
Monthly Catalog of United States Government Publications. v.1- . 1895- . Washington, D.C.: Government Printing Office. Monthly.
New Books. v.1- . 1982- . Washington, D.C.: Government Printing Office. Bimonthly.

New York Public Library. Research Libraries. *Bibliographic Guide to Business and Economics.* v.1- . 1975- . Boston: Hall. Annually.
Oxbridge Directory of Newsletters. v.1- . 1979- . New York: Oxbridge. Annually.
Publishers Weekly. v.1- . 1872- . New York: Bowker. Weekly.
RSR: Reference Services Review. v.1- . 1973- . Ann Arbor, Mich.: Pierian. Quarterly.
Schlessinger, Bernard S., ed. *Basic Business Library: Core Resources.* Phoenix, Ariz.: Oryx, 1983.
Selected Additions to the J. Hugh Jackson Library. 195?- . Stanford, Calif.: Stanford Univ., J. Hugh Jackson Library. Bimonthly.
Serials Review. v.1- . 1979- . Ann Arbor, Mich.: Pierian. Quarterly.
Service to Business and Industry. v.1- . 1952- . Brooklyn, N.Y.: Brooklyn Public Library. Monthly.
Standard Periodical Directory. v.1- . 1932- . New York: Bowker. Annually.
Standard Rate & Data Service, Inc. *Business Publications Rates and Data.* v.1- . 1919- . Skokie, Ill.: The Service. Monthly.
Statistical Reference Index. v.1- . 1981- . Bethesda, Md.: Congressional Information Service. Monthly with quarterly and annual cumulations.
Ulrich's International Periodicals Directory. v.1- . 1932- . New York: Bowker. Annually.
U.S. Department of Commerce. Office of Federal Statistical Policy and Standards and the National Technical Information Service. *A Directory of Federal Statistical Data Files.* Washington, D.C.: Government Printing Office, 1981.
Wall Street Review of Books. v.1- . 1973- . Pleasantville, N.Y.: Redgrave. Quarterly.
Wasserman, Paul, Charlotte Georgi, and James Woy, eds. *Encyclopedia of Business Information Sources.* 5th ed. Detroit, Mich.: Gale, 1983.
Weekly Record. v.1- . 1974- . New York: Bowker. Weekly.
Weiner, Richard, ed. *Investment Newsletters.* New York: Public Relations Publishing, 1982.
What's New in Advertising and Marketing. v.1- . 1950- . New York: Advertising and Marketing Div., Special Libraries Assn. 10/year.
Who Distributes What and Where: An International Directory of Publishers, Imprints, Agents and Distributors. 3rd ed. New York: Bowker, 1983.

Addresses of Selected Library Publications

Business Literature. Newark Public Library, The Business Library, 34 Commerce St., Newark, NJ 07102.
Current Periodical Publications in Baker Library. Baker Library, Graduate School of Business Admin., Harvard Univ., Soldiers Field, Boston, MA 02163.
Fed in Print. Research Library, Federal Reserve Bank of Philadelphia, P.O. Box 66, Philadelphia, PA 19105.
Info. Business & Technology Dept., Tulsa City-County Library, 400 Civic Ctr., Tulsa, OK 74103.
Selected Additions to the J. Hugh Jackson Library. Jackson Library, Graduate School of Business, Stanford Univ., Stanford, CA 94305.
Service to Business and Industry. Brooklyn Public Library, Science and Industry Div., Central Library, Grand Army Plaza, Brooklyn, NY 11238.

What's New in Advertising and Marketing. Advertising and Marketing Div., Special Libraries Assn., Subscription and Circulation: Yvonne Gloede, Ally & Gragano, Information Center, 805 Third Ave., New York, NY 10022.

Addresses of Selected Associations and Organizations

American Bankers Assn., 1120 Connecticut Ave., N.W., Washington, DC 20036.
American Institute of Certified Public Accountants (AICPA), 1211 Avenue of the Americas, New York, NY 10036–8775.
American Management Assns., 135 W. 50th St., New York, NY 10020.
American Marketing Assn., 250 S. Wacker Dr., Chicago, IL 60606.
Conference Board, Publications Sales, 845 Third Ave., New York, NY 10022.
International Labour Organisation (ILO), 1750 New York Ave., N.W., Washington, DC 20006.
International Monetary Fund (IMF), 700 19th St., N.W., Washington, DC 20431.
Organisation for Economic Co-operation and Development (OECD), 1750 Pennsylvania Ave., N.W., Suite 1207, Washington, DC 20006–9990.
World Bank, 1818 H St., N.W., Washington, DC 20433.

COMMUNICATION ARTS AND SCIENCES

Nancy Allen

How many hours every week do we spend talking, reading, watching television, listening to the radio, going to films, admiring billboards, or reading our mail? During business hours and in our leisure time, we experience communication constantly, and in many different ways.

The literature of communication is just as diverse and extensive. It is composed of research, commentary, and theory; is connected to billion-dollar international industries; and interconnects with many other areas of study, such as sociology, psychology, economics, and the arts. This essay will attempt to introduce the librarian to the various fields of communication, emphasizing the mass media, but touching upon interpersonal communication.

As with all other interdisciplinary fields, a clear-cut categorization of the literature is impossible. In common with fields applied by business and developed through the sciences, communication literature has changed radically in the last ten years because of rapidly developing and changing technologies. However, the librarian new to selection in the mass media and communication must try to break this extensive topic into manageable parts. A look at "traditional" communication and media will provide a good start.

Person to person communication, which is neither transferred nor augmented by a medium or carrier such as a telephone or radio, is most basic to our lives. The literature of interpersonal communication is closely related to that of psychology, linguistics, sociology, and education, and has subdivisions such as nonverbal communication, organizational communication, and semiotics.

Literature on the press includes historical and trade studies of newspapers and magazines. Editorial journalism has a long history that includes cartooning and caricature, related to print advertising; in recent times this also includes photojournalism and other types of photography. Also related to editorial journalism are freedom of the press and other First Amendment issues.

Book publishing and book arts are closely related to print journalism and constitute a distinct area within communication, which ranges from the social history of book publishing to the paper pulp industry to the graphic and artistic elements of publication design.

Broadcasting traditionally has comprised radio and television. Broadcast content studies immediately link to radio and television advertising, and technical literature exists on station design, engineering, and broadcast production.

Film as a medium of communication might be fitted in next. This collaborative medium has a literature that is at once diverse and distinct. Film has been studied and written about as an industry, an educational tool, a political and persuasive weapon, a cultural problem, an art form, a branch of literature, a kind of language, and a way to spend leisure time.

Persuasive communication literature appears related to the mass media as well as to interpersonal communication. Public relations, propaganda, political communication, and advertising in all media—print, audio, and visual—are part of this group. The literature ranges from how-to books on advertising design to empirical investigations of the role of political marketing on voting behavior.

All media of mass communication have literature that is both critical and theoretical, and that is technical or oriented around production: broadcasting radio or television shows, typesetting and layout of papers, or the making of movies. The critical and theoretical works can be broken down into categories of history, theory, social effects, and individual effects. International and cross-cultural communication studies have been numerous, as have works on issues related to international communication, which fall into the category termed "new world information order."

Technical works are plentiful in the area that used to be called simply "broadcasting," and that is now more often and more inclusively called "telecommunications." The shift from the industrial society to the information society has been much explored, and this change can be seen dramatically in the literature of telecommunications. Hundreds of books and articles appear monthly on satellites, cable TV systems, teletext, videotex, the changing data and voice communication industry (telephone), multipoint distribution services (MDS), electronic messaging systems, teleconferencing, and on the impact of all these and other new media on the traditional media. Examples are visible everywhere. Newspaper production is often based on electronic text transmission, text processing, and satellite relay systems. The importance of satellite systems to modern television news is clear to any owner of a television set. Millions of people watch movies and programming originating in Atlanta or Chicago on cable TV,

---

Communication Booknotes: Recent Titles in Telecommunications, Information, and Media. v.1- . 1982- . Washington, D.C.: George Washington Univ. Ctr. for Telecommunications Studies. Monthly.
A reliable, inclusive, and well-informed source of annotated citations to current literature. It has international coverage and is the best single source of information on current media literature of all types, including trade publications, research literature, and hard-to-find publications such as working papers, conference reports, and documents.

---

and interactive television systems have existed in some British and European homes for a decade. Much is being written on these media phenomena, and it may be a challenge for a librarian with a social science or humanities background to select materials on these increasingly technical topics.

There are only a few selection sources for current material that cover all or most of these areas. Fortunately, those few are very useful and are annotated. The best is *Communication Booknotes: Recent Titles in Telecommunications, Information, and Media.* The editor, Christopher Sterling, has been doing this newsletter-format list, with its lengthy annotations and notes, for years. (Before 1982, it was called *Mass Media Booknotes.*) Sterling knows the field well and enters his views forcefully. The title is somewhat misleading, since he includes government publications, pamphlets, and serials, as well as books.

Long a standard research journal, *Journalism Quarterly* covers more than journalism. Much of each issue is taken up with bibliographic information on relatively current publications in most areas of communication. There are book reviews, an index, a list of important current articles in several major communication journals, and a section called "Other Books and Pamphlets," made of short annotations supplied by the University of Illinois at Urbana Champaign Communications Library. All are organized by topic.

Journalism Quarterly: Devoted to Research in Journalism and Mass Communication. v.1- . 1924- . College of Journalism, Univ. of South Carolina. Columbia, S.C.: Assn. for Education in Journalism and Mass Communication. Quarterly.
Journalism Quarterly is a wider-ranging publication than the title indicates. Each issue contains book reviews, a list of short annotations to current literature, and an index to journal articles published not only in *JQ* but in other mass media research journals as well. A large portion of every issue is useful to media librarians responsible for book selection.

Communication Abstracts. v.1– . 1978– . Beverly Hills, Calif.: Sage. Quarterly.
A very useful and commendably current index to the journal literature of media and information science, it also contains frequent entries on monographs and other longer works published separately. It is worth regular perusal by the communications selector.

Communication Abstracts is the most useful and inclusive research journal index and can be used to support collection development choices. It indexes monographs and research reports, as well as journal articles.

In addition to these quite comprehensive sources of current citations, new book lists are issued regularly by several major journalism or communication libraries, including the University of Illinois at Urbana-Champaign Communications Library, the Indiana University Journalism Library, the Ohio State University Journalism Library, the Library of the Canadian Radio-Television and Telecommunications Commission in Ottawa, and the Library of the International Telecommunication Union in Geneva, Switzerland. One may simply write to be placed on these mailing lists. Most book lists, if not all, are free of charge. They vary in usefulness, since not all libraries process new books with equal speed, and some of the library acquisition lists contain "new" titles that are actually one to two years old. The collecting policies of these libraries vary considerably, but this is desirable to the communication selector, who can see a wide range of citations in areas peripheral to communication by examining the accession lists. Not all library book lists are annotated, but a review of these lists can ensure that a selector has seen almost every publication of research or teaching interest, including some documents, since some of the U.S. government depository libraries include selected federal publications in their lists. Most of the lists are organized topically, which is very helpful for the selector.

Two current-contents type publications provide a review of current journal literature not limited to English. They are *Sommaire Mensuel des Livres et Revues,* which shows title pages of over 150 media-related serials; and *Teleclippings,* a monthly selection from the International Telecommunications Union of reprinted articles in many languages covering radio, television, telephone, information technology, and space communication.

Because many books on communication are of interest to the general public as well as to scholars, students, and communication practitioners, a close review of the large seasonal issues of *Publishers Weekly* will yield hundreds of advance and current title announcements. *Choice* and *Library Journal* regularly review media-related titles and reference volumes. This means that for librarians selecting communication material for public li-

---

Blum, Eleanor. *Basic Books in the Mass Media.* 2nd ed. Urbana: Univ. of Illinois Pr., 1980.

For years this has been the primary general bibliography for the field. The annotated guide to major works of the many fields of mass communication covers reference works, principal texts, and major research publications, as well as selected works of other kinds. The author was, for many years, the librarian of the Communications Library at the University of Illinois.

---

braries, a large number of key works, popular books, overviews, and basic texts are easily accessible. Most major publishers regularly include communication titles. Biographies, studies of the press, books about television and films, topics within the area of popular culture, and many very useful how-to books or laypersons' guides to the new media are available from Macmillan, Englewood Press, Little, Brown, Prentice-Hall, Simon and Schuster, New America Library, McGraw-Hill, Harper and Row, and others.

For retrospective selection, a good way to get a quick but accurate look at the traditional mass media literature is Eleanor Blum's 1980 annotated *Basic Books in the Mass Media.* It is selective, but describes most important works, including reference books, texts, and basic readings. It is an excellent source for retrospective collection development, and selections from the bibliography would comprise a strong central communication collection.

Surprisingly, there are not many bibliographies that cover all areas of communication. Neither is there a regular appearance of updated book-length bibliographies. A very useful title covering media effects research literature is Thomas Gordon and Mary Ellen Verna's *Mass Communication Effects and Processes: A Comprehensive Bibliography, 1950-1975.* A more recent title by Benjamin Shearer and Marilyn Huxford, *Communications and Society: A Bibliography on Communications Technologies and Their Social Impact,* has a somewhat misleading title, since it emphasizes the traditional media, but it covers a wide range of communications media and their social effects literatures.

Beyond these general sources for citations to current and retrospective communication literature, there are numerous bibliographies for each type of communication and for each medium. Research, technical, and popular literature listings are available for topics from advertising and public relations to space communication. A few of the principal bibliographies covering older literature on specific communication topics are listed with comments at the end of this essay.

Literature on new media, electronic communication, and telecommunication is very plentiful now and deserves special attention. New and

Horton, Forest Woody, Jr. *Understanding U.S. Information Policy: The Infostructure Handbook.* 4v. Washington, D.C.: Information Industry Assn., 1982.
While quickly losing value as a guide to current publications, this is still a valuable source of information on information. The information industries are covered here as well as policy production; and reference works, serials, newsletters, and other sources of information are listed for each of the new media technologies.

expensive newsletters are issued very frequently. Some of the many technical developments are reported in engineering and computer science literature. Policy issues and access issues are covered in information science literature. In a worthy effort to gain control of this boom in publishing, the *Basic Bibliography Series,* a helpful new series of short bibliographies (15-22 pages each) by Christopher Sterling, are being published by the George Washington University Center for Telecommunications Studies. A continuing bibliography limited to cable TV comes out every six months; it is called *BC TV.*

The government is an important determinant for the developing communication media. Regulation, or recently, deregulation, and the associated rulings, hearings, and discussions are traced in *Media Law Reporter. Public Affairs Information Service Bulletin* is a surprisingly useful literature source and index in communication. The FCC is obviously a source of information, but it is not the only source. United States and international policy issues are explained, and publishing and information sources are listed in two recent works: Jane Yurow's *Issues in International Telecommunication Policy: A Sourcebook,* and Forest Woody Horton's *Understanding U.S. Information Policy: The Infostructure Handbook.* The latter lists almost everything a librarian needs—selective bibliographies, journals, newsletters, organizations, conferences, etc.

Scholarly output in the many interdisciplinary fields of communication is widely distributed. A great many publishers produce occasional volumes on communication. Many studies come from British publishers. However, the communication bibliographer would certainly wish to see catalogs for this list of publishers, many of whom offer series: Longman (Longman Series in Public Communication), Praeger, Knowledge Industry Publication, Ablex (Studies in Communication, Communication and Information Science Series) Comedia—a London publisher of liberal media criticism, Wadsworth (Wadsworth series in Mass Communication), Plenum (Application of Communication Theory Series), and Sage, which has at least five relevant series. This is not by any means a comprehensive list of publishers' series for the field, but it includes some of the most active. A few university presses have published heavily about media, including the University of

Wisconsin, Indiana University, the University of California, and recently, the University of Illinois Press, which is distributing British Film Institute publications. Many other university presses are occasional publishers of media titles. This means that university press blanket order receipts should be monitored regularly for communication literature.

Two large working paper series continue to include works of interest to communication students and scholars: The Harvard University Center for Information Policy Research and the Columbia University Graduate School of Business Research Program in Telecommunications and Information Policy Research. The latter has been publishing book-length works in its working paper series. *A Directory of Communication Research Centers in U.S. Universities, 1984–1985*, by Barry Sapolsky, lists the publications of such centers.

Many of the organizations, societies, and institutes that publish regularly are most interested in practical aspects of communication but also publish surveys, studies, and criticism. Others regularly produce "best-of" awards or collections of prize winners. A list of a few of these would include: the American Society of Newspaper Editors, the American Association of Advertising Agencies, the Corporation for Public Broadcasting, the Speech Communication Association, the Media Institute (Washington, D.C), Action for Children's Television, the National Association of Broadcasters, the Television Information Office, the Associated Press Managing Editors, the International Telecommunications Union, the International Organization of Journalists, the Association for Education in Journalism, the Cable Television Information Center, the American Academy of Advertising, the Advertising Research Foundation, and the Broadcast Education Association. Many of these groups publish journals, news magazines, or reference works, but for the most part, although they publish regularly, no single group could be called a major publisher. However, on the whole societal and organizational publications form a sizable part of the literature.

Because of the great variations in types of publications and publishers and the large number of subject categories contributing to the literature of communication, approval plan profiles by subject or by publisher are difficult to create effectively. Of course, a well-designed approval profile will help, but in the best of circumstances it will bring only a portion of the most visible publications to the attention of the communication bibliographer. A variety of selection sources should supplement approval plans, including all those previously mentioned—library book lists, current specialized selection sources, older specialized bibliographies, mailing lists of publishers and organizations, listings of government and agency publications, and general selection sources.

So far, monographic publications of various kinds have been emphasized. However, serial literature is a vital source of information in these rapidly developing and changing fields. The selector has little to go on when faced with the confusingly large number of journals, newsletters, and magazines being published. A comprehensive and international listing of these would probably number at least 500 titles. Prices range from free to over a thousand dollars. Many indexing tools are available, but only a few cover any sizable percentage of the whole, and many libraries do not subscribe to most of these indexes; for example, as of 1984, only a handful of U.S. libraries subscribed to the excellent but slow *International Index to Television Periodicals*, now produced on microfiche.

Since indexing is a key factor in the selection decision, the bibliographer new to communications should examine coverage of several important tools. Already cited, *Communication Abstracts* has good coverage of many communication topics, emphasizes research, comes quickly, and has current coverage. *Journalism Abstracts* indexes theses and Ph.D. dissertations, but it arrives so slowly that one makes regular inquiries as to its continuing existence. *Business Periodicals Index*, a standard Wilson index, is strong in advertising literature and media business literature, and a small publication, *Topicator*, overlaps *Business Periodicals Index* coverage, listing articles in certain topical categories from about twenty advertising, marketing, and general communications periodicals. *Humanities Index* picks up some critical journal literature, as does *Social Sciences Index*. Also previously mentioned, *Journalism Quarterly* indexes articles in a handful of major communication journals. The *International Index to Film Periodicals* and *Film Literature Index* both cover film periodicals as well as selective indexing of television titles. The latter has better coverage of the range of American literature and is easier to use with one author and subject index. The former is published on microfiche and in annual hardbound volumes, emphasizing European literature, since indexing is contributed by members of the International Federation of Film Archives. A sister organization, the International Federation of Television Archives, produces the *International Index to Television Periodicals*, which does branch out into telecommunications somewhat. A new index called *Cable-Video Index* started in 1983 and emphasizes new technologies.

Most communication journals are not unduly expensive, but selectors will notice that some newsletters covering developments of new electronic media are very expensive. However, there is no better way of keeping informed of current issues, technical developments, and legal issues than such newsletters.

To aid in the selection of major communication periodicals, a selective and briefly annotated list of sixty titles is available in a chapter on mass media collections in *Media Librarianship,* edited by John Ellison. However, even this is dated. A recent essay that includes citations to periodical titles is Nancy Allen's "Sources of Information in the New Media" in *Crossroads*, the 1984 Library and Information Technology Association (LITA) Conference proceedings.

Experience shows that some material on communicating ends up in every library, even if no one is trying to create a communication collection. It is an interesting topic with broad appeal. As any college reference librarian knows, term papers on the effects of violence on television are all too common, and the staff of any public library must know how to find out who played Bat Masterson in the series. Librarians working with masters students in journalism are more likely to need information on why afternoon newspapers are failing, but the question could be asked of almost any reference librarian. The fact is that interpersonal and mass media communication is a topic that has changed the daily life of just about every person in the world. Librarians using selection sources cited here, and suggested methods of finding out what is being published and by whom, can better create collections to answer the many and varied communication questions being asked by trivia buffs and scholars alike.

Selected Bibliographies

JOURNALISM

McCoy, Ralph. *Freedom of the Press: An Annotated Bibliography.* Carbondale: Southern Illinois Univ. Pr., 1968.
_____. *Freedom of the Press: A Bibliocyclopedia: Ten Year Supplement (1967–77).* Carbondale: Southern Illinois Univ. Pr., 1979. (These two enormous works are very thorough. The first edition includes 8,000 citations and the supplement is about the same size.)
Nafziger, Ralph O. *International News and the Press.* New York: Arno, 1972. (Originally published in 1940.)
Price, Warren C. *The Literature of Journalism: An Annotated Bibliography.* Minneapolis: Univ. of Minnesota Pr., 1959. (Newspapers and magazines are covered in 3,147 entries.)
_____, and Pickett Calder. *An Annotated Journalism Bibliography, 1958–1968.* Minneapolis: Univ. of Minnesota Pr., 1970. (A supplement listing another 2,172 entries.)

BROADCASTING AND TELECOMMUNICATIONS

Atkin, Charles, John P. Murray, and Oguz B. Nayman. *Television and Social Behavior: An Annotated Bibliography of Research Focussing on Television's Impact on Children.* Rockville, Md.: U.S. Department of Health, Education and Welfare, 1971.
Chin, Felix. *Cable Television.* New York: IFI/Plenum, 1978. (Also contains a chronology, glossary, and other historical information.)

Comstock, George, et al. *Television and Human Behavior.* New York: Columbia Univ. Pr., 1978.

Lichty, Lawrence W. *World and International Broadcasting: A Bibliography.* Washington, D.C. Assn. for Professional Broadcasting Education, 1971.

McCavitt, William. *Radio and Television: A Selected, Annotated Bibliography.* Metuchen, N.J.: Scarecrow, 1978.

———. *Supplement, 1977–1981.* Metuchen, N.J.: Scarecrow, 1982.

Meyer, Manfred, and Ursula Nissen. *Effects and Functions of Television: Children and Adolescents: A Bibliography of Selected Research Literature 1970–1978.* Munich: K. G. Saur, 1979.

Smith, Myron J. *U.S. Television Network News: A Guide to Sources in English.* Jefferson, N.C.: McFarland, 1983.

Sterling, Christopher. *Electronic Media: A Guide to Trends in Broadcasting and Newer Technologies, 1920–1983.* New York: Praeger, 1984.

FILM

Armour, Robert, *Film: A Reference Guide.* Westport, Conn.: Greenwood, 1980. (Contains a selective list of periodicals.)

Austin, Bruce: *The Film Audience: An International Bibliography of Research.* Metuchen, N.J.: Scarecrow, 1983.

Ellis, Jack C., Charles Derry, and Sharon Kern. *The Film Book Bibliography, 1940–1975.* Metuchen, N.J.: Scarecrow, 1979. (Annotated and well indexed.)

Leonard, Harold, ed. *The Film Index.* New York: Arno, 1966. (Originally published in 1941, this is the major guide to early literature.)

Rehrauer, George. *Macmillan Film Bibliography.* 2v. New York: Macmillan, 1982. (This set of books contains many selections from Rehrauer's *Cinema Booklist* and supplements, plus new entries.)

PERSUASIVE COMMUNICATION

Bishop, Robert. *Public Relations, a Comprehensive Bibliography: Articles and Books on Public Relations, Communication Theory, Public Opinion, and Propaganda, 1964–1974.* Ann Arbor, Mich.: A. G. Leighton-James, 1974.

Cutlip, Scott. *A Public Relations Bibliography.* Madison: Univ. of Wisconsin Pr., 1965.

Lipstein, Benjamin, and William J. McGuire. *Evaluation Advertising: A Bibliography of the Communication Process.* New York: Advertising Research Foundation, 1978. (Covers most advertising research literature through the mid-70s.)

Pollay, Richard W. *Information Sources in Advertising History.* Westport, Conn.: Greenwood, 1979. (Contains annotations and bibliographic essays plus other information for researchers.)

Smith, Bruce Lannes, Harold D. Lasswell, and Ralph D. Casey. *Propaganda, Communication and Public Opinion: A Comprehensive Reference Guide.* Princeton: Princeton Univ. Pr., 1946. (Covers older books, periodicals, and articles.)

Selection Sources

Allen, Nancy, "Sources of Information in the New Media." In *Crossroads.* Chicago, Ill.: American Library Assn., 1985.

BC TV. v.1– . 1975– . San Francisco: Communications Library of the Commu-
nications Institute. Annually.
Blum, Eleanor. *Basic Books in the Mass Media.* 2nd ed. Urbana: Univ. of Illinois
Pr., 1980.
Business Periodicals Index. v.1– . 1958– . New York: Wilson. Quarterly.
Cable-Video Index. v.1– . 1983– . Muncie, Ind.: Cable-Video Index. Monthly.
Communication Abstracts. v.1– . 1978– . Beverly Hills, Calif.: Sage. Quarterly.
*Communication Booknotes: Recent Titles in Telecommunications, Information,
and Media.* Ed. by Christopher Sterling. v.1– . 1982– . Washington, D.C.: George
Washington Univ. Ctr. for Telecommunications Studies. Monthly. (Supersedes
Mass Media Booknotes. Philadelphia: Temple Univ. Dept. of Radio, TV, Film.)
Ellison, John, ed. *Media Librarianship.* New York: Neal-Schuman, 1986.
Film Literature Index. v.1– . 1973– . Albany, New York: Filmdex. Quarterly.
Gordon, Thomas F., and Mary Ellen Verna. *Mass Communication Effects and
Processes: A Comprehensive Bibliography, 1950–1975.* Beverly Hills, Calif.: Sage,
1978.
Horton, Forest Woody, Jr. *Understanding U.S. Information Policy: The Info-
structure Handbook.* 4v. Washington, D.C.: Information Industry Assn., 1982.
Humanities Index. v.1– . 1974– . New York: Wilson. Quarterly.
International Index to Film Periodicals. v.1– . 1972– . New York: St. Martin's
Pr. Annual printed cumulation; monthly for microfiche.
International Index to Television Periodicals. v.1– . 1980– . London: International
Federation of Film Archives (FIAF). Annual printed cumulation; monthly for
microfiche.
Journalism Abstracts. v.1– . 1963– . Minneapolis: Assn. for Education in Jour-
nalism. Annually.
*Journalism Quarterly: Devoted to Research in Journalism and Mass Communi-
cation.* v.1– . 1924– . Coll. of Journalism, Univ. of South Carolina, Columbia:
Assn. for Education in Journalism and Mass Communication. Quarterly.
Library Journal. v.1– . 1876– . New York: Bowker. Monthly.
Media Law Reporter. v.1– . 1977– . Washington, D.C.: Bureau of National Affairs.
Weekly.
Public Affairs Information Service Bulletin. 1915– . New York: Public Affairs
Information Service, Inc. Semimonthly.
Publishers Weekly. v.1– . 1872– . New York: Bowker. Weekly.
Sapolsky, Barry S. *A Directory of Communication Research Centers in U.S. Uni-
versities, 1984–1985.* Tallahassee: Florida State Univ., 1984.
Shearer, Benjamin, and Marilyn Huxford, comps. *Communications and Society:
A Bibliography on Communications Technology and Their Social Impact.*
Westport, Conn.: Greenwood, 1983.
Social Sciences Index. v.1– . 1974– . New York: Wilson. Quarterly.
Sommaire Mensuel des Livres et Revues. 1980– . Bry sur Marne: Documentation
sur L'Audiovisuel, Institut National de L'Audiovisuel. Monthly.
Sterling, Christopher. *Basic Bibliography Series.* v.1– . 1983– . Washington, D.C.:
George Washington Univ. Ctr. for Telecommunications Studies. Irregularly.
Teleclippings. Geneva: International Telecommunications Union. Bimonthly.
*Topicator: A Classified Article Guide to the Advertising/Communications/Mar-
keting Periodicals Press.* v.1– . 1965– . Golden, Colo.: Topicator. Bimonthly.
Yurow, Jane H. *Issues in International Telecommunication Policy: A Sourcebook.*
Washington, D.C.: George Washington Univ. Ctr. for Telecommunications Stud-
ies, 1983.

CRIMINAL JUSTICE

Eileen Rowland

In the broadest sense, the study of criminal justice is concerned with the causes and manifestations of criminal behavior and with both the formal and the informal societal responses to that behavior. Academic criminal justice offerings run the gamut from narrowly constructed associate degree programs geared toward professional careers in law enforcement and corrections to doctoral programs that investigate social, economic, and biological roots of criminality.

The literature of criminal justice is drawn from sociology when the focus is on the social pathology of crime and delinquency, from law when dealing with law enforcement and issues of constitutional interpretation, from public administration when concerned with managing institutions such as police agencies and prisons, from psychology when studying deviant behavior, and from the sciences when dealing with investigative methodologies. Graduates of criminal justice programs pursue careers in fields such as police administration, criminal investigation, and parole work, and also as social theorists and academicians.

What more could a book selector in so cross-disciplinary a field want than a clearinghouse of the national and international literature in the discipline—one that offers such services as monthly accessions lists, regularly updated bibliographies, readily accessible and extensively annotated online and microfiche catalogs of its collection, and a microfiche publication program for virtually all of its traditionally hard to obtain noncopyright holdings? A selector might ask for perfect convergence between the collection profile of the clearinghouse and the home institution. Failing that, the hope might be for so great a divergence of profile or so poor a level of performance that one could safely, albeit sadly, ignore the inevitable steady stream of seductive fliers and brochures.

The really good news for a criminal justice selector is that there is such a clearinghouse. More mixed is the news that while it is unlikely that even

43

a small academic library will find the clearinghouse an adequate one-source collection-building tool, it is much too valuable to ignore. The effect of all this news is that the criminal justice book selector has to keep a constant eye over his or her shoulder, not only to avoid duplicating the efforts of colleagues in the numerous related and tangential disciplines, but also to anticipate and monitor the behavior of the clearinghouse. The base line of the selector's responsibility is to keep in touch with institutional priorities, of course, and to participate in and/or respond to programmatic shifts and developments. This essay will suggest the short cuts and end runs made possible by the clearinghouse's existence, while reserving more or less traditional collection establishment, maintenance, and enrichment techniques for filling in gaps.

The National Criminal Justice Reference Service (NCJRS) was established by the National Institute of Justice (NIJ) in the early 1970s to meet the technical information needs of criminal justice professionals. Currently its sponsors include additional agencies such as the National Institute for Juvenile Justice and Delinquency Prevention and the Bureau of Justice Statistics. Despite involvement of a descending hierarchy that begins with the Department of Justice and runs through the National Institute of Justice to the NCJRS, clearinghouse services are provided by a private vendor holding an NIJ contract. This arrangement does not affect the service mandate of NCJRS, but it does help to explain the marketing hype that characterizes much of the clearinghouse's promotional materials and a drive to expand and improve services that seems to occur as contract renewal time approaches. It should be noted, however, that the arrangement appears to be working quite well.

With a primary target audience of practitioner/professionals who operate in the highly charged arena of criminal justice planning and administration, it is entirely appropriate that urgency and action-oriented pragmatism should inform collection building efforts at NCJRS. That this is an inappropriate stance for most academic or research libraries is a given; an academic selector needs an in-depth overview of the field that goes beyond the world of practitioner/professionals.

A discovery to be made in this search for an overview is that there is not at present, and indeed there may never be, consensus on whether criminal justice is a discipline with its own distinctive theory and literature or an interdisciplinary field dependent on a variety of methodologies and knowledge bases. Indeed, if there were definitional clarity, a collection-building policy might be simpler to arrive at, but executing that policy would probably not be nearly so much fun. "Fun" may not be a sufficiently formal descriptor, but I would argue for its applicability to a field that examines the cases of both Socrates and Son of Sam, administration of justice in both the Garden of Eden and Watergate, and conditions of imprisonment on both Rikers and Devil's Island.

It would be an impoverished criminal justice orientation that did not acknowledge the religious, philosophical, historical, sociological, and psychological roots of the pressing contemporary problems that gave rise to the establishment of NCJRS. It is the good fortune of the selector that the field has achieved sufficient status and maturity to have seen the recent publication of a disciplinary encyclopedia that is fully up to the task of supplying the desired breadth and depth.

The *Encyclopedia of Crime and Justice* is an excellent introduction to scholarly concerns under the criminal justice umbrella, in all of their historical, analytical, and philosophical complexity. In addition to intellectual stimulation, the set can also serve as a first step for retrospective selection efforts. The generally excellent bibliographies that follow major articles are an invaluable and relatively painless route to identification of seminal and significant works. It is also the selector's good fortune to have access to a sense of how the field and its literature are interpreted for those who aspire to the status of practitioner or scholar.

Robert O'Block, a professor of political science and criminal justice, wrote *Criminal Justice Research Sources* to ease the frustration his students were experiencing in the course of their research assignments. The handbook combines guidance in the research process with a comprehensive listing of research sources. The list of sources is substantial and interesting; whether or not one considers it comprehensive depends on how one defines the field. O'Block's definition seems to encompass a level of enrichment a bit beyond the NCJRS orientation but somewhat short of what the *Encyclopedia of Crime and Justice* would suggest. As a selection tool, the lists of sources are of limited use since there are few annotations; what annotations there are, are descriptive rather than evaluative. Nevertheless, a criminal justice selector might want to return and scan the lists as a kind of double-check after collection-building efforts are well advanced.

Criminal Justice Research in Libraries: Techniques and Strategies was written by two criminal justice reference librarians: Marilyn Lutzker of the John Jay College of Criminal Justice and Eleanor Ferrall of Arizona State University. Since it has a broader and deeper approach to the field than O'Block's guide, and takes a somewhat more sophisticated approach to the research process by focusing on issues such as the formal and informal communications networks that operate in the criminal justice system and on the structure of information in the discipline, it adds a valuable dimension to the sought-for overview. There is also a fundamentally different approach to source lists: there is an annotation for every title, and selective—rather than comprehensive—coverage is the goal. What we have, therefore, from a selector's point of view, is the possibility that less might well be more. That indeed is the case.

Establishing and Maintaining the Collection

REFERENCE MATERIAL

Judicious use of Lutzker and Ferrall's book will yield a sound criminal justice reference collection for a program of any dimension. A large research library may find that, except for rather narrowly defined abstracts, indexes, directories, and statistical compendiums, it already has a collection that offers strong support for the new program. Conversely, the smaller library with more limited resources may well find that it must strengthen reference holdings in unanticipated areas such as management and toxicology. The burden for the smaller library may appear doubly difficult where the program is both career-oriented and focused on a particular aspect of the system, such as law enforcement. Even here, the reference collection's attention to the judiciary, corrections, and social services should be as fulsome as possible. To do otherwise would be a denial of the one point on which there seems to be little disagreement, that there is indeed a "system" of some sort.

New criminal justice-specific reference materials are picked up and highlighted in a timely fashion in the NCJRS bimonthly current awareness bulletin, *NIJ Reports*. For the selection of new reference materials in related disciplines, one must fall back on traditional methods of browsing

---

NIJ Reports. v.1– 1983– . Rockville, Md.: National Institute of Justice/ NCJRS. Bimonthly.
Research and information service announcements and reports.
About 30 abstracts per issue.
Regular column by Director of National Institute of Justice.
Several research-in-progress reports per issue.
Calendar of events.
Principal source of information on federal government's criminal justice information services. The columns and reports in each issue make this an excellent tool for keeping abreast of national priorities, while the "Calender of Events" broadens the picture to include regional and academic concerns. About half of the material in each issue is directly related to the National Criminal Justice Reference Service (NCJRS): announcements of information products and services; changes in existing services; abstracts of significant additions to their collection and database. Abstracts are descriptive rather than evaluative and include both ordering information and the accession number that can be used to borrow material from the agency. For sponsored research, the sponsoring agency and contract number are included.

a wide range of announcements and reviews or of examining the actual volumes where approval plans are in place.

THE GENERAL BOOK COLLECTION: RETROSPECTIVE

Every library with a commitment to a criminal justice program should consider using the *Document Retrieval Index (DRI)*, NCJRS's catalog, for the purpose of retrospective collecting. *DRI* not only identifies a good portion of the criminal justice trade and nontrade monograph, document, and report literature published since 1970, but also indicates the name and address of the source. If you can afford the time and effort, consider using the *Library Catalogue of the Radzinowicz Library* and the *Catalog of the Police Library of the Los Angeles Public Library*, which you will probably have selected as items for the reference collection, as retrospective selection tools for materials that predate the NCJRS library.

Approximately ten percent of the *DRI* entries are for monographs, proceedings, and dissertations that are in the NCJRS collection but which must be purchased through conventional sources. Collection policy will determine how much attention to pay to dissertations. Textbooks are included in the *DRI* entries and many libraries have fairly firm exclusionary policies in this area. Even where the ban is less than absolute, proliferation of new criminal justice programs and attendant proliferation of new textbooks in the late 60s and early 70s create a problem. While much was published of little enduring value, others helped to define and shape the academic field. As a rule of thumb in this matter, one might consider bypassing the generally pedestrian Prentice-Hall textbook series and being extremely wary of the prolific output of Charles C. Thomas and Sage. Caution and wariness can best be exercised by physical examination of the books in question or by limiting purchase to reviewed or frequently cited titles.

Where comprehensiveness is not an issue, and a library is committed to substantive collecting in only a very specific portion of the criminal justice system, one might sidestep the *DRI* and select retrospectively from appropriate hard-copy NCJRS subject bibliographies. An alternative route to a starter collection of significant older titles is purchase of complete or partial sets of criminal justice reprint series. *Books in Series in the United States* lists the titles in such series as the "Patterson Smith Reprint Series in Criminology, Law Enforcement and Social Problems" (213 titles) and the AMS Press's "Foundations of Criminal Justice" (49 titles). Many of the volumes in these two series will disappear or wear out from overuse; others will be shelf sitters. Cross-checking individual titles against the book catalogs referred to above and the bibliographies in the *Encyclopedia of Crime and Justice* will help to eliminate some of the less significant material in cases where dollar savings are more important than saving time.

Document Retrieval Index (DRI) v.1– . 1972– . Washington D.C.: National
Criminal Justice Reference Service. Basic set 1972–78.
Annual updates; 5-year cumulations.
Microfiche catalog of the NCJRS collection.
Includes subject, title and personal name indexes and thesaurus of indexing
terms.
Basic collection approximately 40,000 titles; about 10,000 titles added per
year.
Covers print and nonprint formats, dissertations, periodical articles.
The best currently available compilation of English language criminal justice
information resources including such elusive material as unpublished research
reports. Unfortunately, the values inherent in breadth of coverage are partially
offset by a cumbersome access mechanism. The principal file, which includes
brief annotations and full bibliographic, ordering, and sponsorship data, is arranged by accession number. All entries in the subject, title, and personal name
indexes, the only user-oriented access points, refer back to the primary file. A
lesser problem is that the inclusion of periodical articles adds an unwelcome
bulk to the catalog when used as an acquisitions tool. *NIJ Reports*, although
selective, is a useful hard-copy update between cumulations; the NCJRS database, available through DIALOG, provides comprehensive current access.

If I were facing retrospective general book selection for a new criminal
justice collection at this time, I would opt for postponing efforts to add
that portion of the scholarly literature not covered by the NCJRS outlook
or not of such obvious significance that one or more reprint publishers
had anticipated the need. Rather than scanning a decade of assorted bibliographies and reviews in scholarly journals and *Choice*, I would wait for
the publication of the third edition of *Books for College Libraries* in 1988
and hope that it would prove an adequate one-source alternative.

THE GENERAL BOOK COLLECTION: CURRENT

For comprehensive collections, a full subscription to NCJRS monthly
accessions lists should prove a substantial aid for identifying current mainstream criminal justice publications. For those less comprehensive collections, one might subscribe to one or more of the monthly accessions list
parts: courts, law enforcement, corrections, crime prevention, or juvenile
justice.

How a criminal justice collection builder goes about the task of selecting
current scholarly materials to add the breadth and depth that distinguish
the institution's collection from that of the clearinghouse will be a function
of the library's general practices. Where a general approval plan is in place
some alteration in the profile may be desirable. If you tend to rely on the
daily mail for current awareness you should place yourself on the mailing
lists of trade and university presses and of the associations, agencies, and

think tanks listed in the O'Block book. I would take it as an act of faith that any press or agency you have missed will find you in short order.

Using reviews for current selection is as satisfying and as frustrating in criminal justice as in any other field. Pay careful attention to prominent reviews in the *New York Times* or your local Sunday newspaper supplements. A provocative new look at any part of the criminal justice system will evoke interest well beyond the program's normal constituency. Since reviews in the scholarly journals generally lag far behind publication dates and represent only a small portion of relevant material, they are inadequate as selection tools. Nevertheless, scholarly review-scanning keeps one abreast of intellectual trends in the field; similarly, some wallowing in the daily mail maintains a link with publishing trends and directions. Both are essential for the creation and nurturing of the monomania that defines a subject specialist. Also useful is the practice of tuning into future trends by attending disciplinary conferences. The key scholarly associations in this case are the Academy of Criminal Justice Sciences (which has a Library Committee) and the American Society of Criminology. Since neither association publishes conference proceedings, a selector might want to scan conference programs as an additional way of tuning in.

REPORTS AND DOCUMENTS

As mentioned earlier, NCJRS has a publication program of its own. Virtually all of the noncopyright material that may have been initially available in hard copy from a variety of sources will be available later on fiche from NCJRS. A small portion of this material, such as significant reports of national commissions, predates the establishment of the clearinghouse.

There are various options offered by NCJRS for purchasing fiche publications. For the not-insubstantial price of about $10,000, one can buy the entire basic set covering 1972–80 and the annual updates from 1981–84; for an additional $1,290/year, one will receive approximately 1,200 documents annually. Through 1984, this comes to some 25,000 titles, about twenty-five percent of the listings in the *DRI*. Alternatively, one can purchase various NCJRS SLIM (Selective Libraries in Microfiche) packages devoted to a particular subject such as POLICE or TERRORISM. Then again, there is nothing barring title-by-title selection.

Wherever possible, I would urge purchase of the full collection. The chief reason is the richness of the materials; a secondary reason is the ease with which students and researchers will be able to move from *DRI* or online database searches to the materials themselves. If your library is a Government Printing Office depository or has a significant government document collection, you will be getting some duplicate material if you purchase the entire NCJRS collection, but you will save a good deal of your time and that of your users. Avoiding duplication of material is complicated by the difficulty of determining, without a title-by-title check, exactly what it is that the clearinghouse will or will not have available on microfiche. While it is safe to assume that the fiche program will include all of the documents of the several sponsoring agencies and a portion of the GPO output in the field, it is impossible to predict which publications of various agencies will be noncopyright and available on fiche and which will have to be ordered directly.

What I do know is that a library that attempts to collect a sampling of municipal criminal justice agency reports by subscribing to the fiche program of the *Index to Current Urban Documents* will be getting some unique items and some duplicates of titles available through the NCJRS program. Whether to subscribe to one or to both will depend on available resources and the depth of coverage a library aspires to. The same will be true where a library seeks to cover criminal justice issues in Congressional Hearings by subscribing to selective Senate or House Committee materials through the Congressional Information Service (CIS). NCJRS coverage will be broader since it regularly picks up the stray justice-related materials from sources not likely to be included in partial subscriptions.

When building both a retrospective and a current document and report collection, one must bear in mind that before there was an NCJRS there was an NCCD, the National Council on Crime and Delinquency. The council, founded in 1909, published and marketed (through the Microfilming Corporation of America) a significant portion of its noncopyright document and report holdings in the 1970s. The basic collection and annual updates through 1984 in the *Crime and Juvenile Delinquency* set numbers some 3,000 fiche documents. Unfortunately only about eight percent of these date from the first half of the century, so that its complementarity to the NCJRS collection is less than one would hope for, given the wide gap in their founding dates. Since there is no option for title-by-title purchase in this case, a library again must decide how comprehensive it wants to be and/or how much duplication it is willing to pay for in the interest of saving time and energy.

A notable aspect of the NCCD collection is that access is through both a printed index and sets of catalog cards. Where reference staff does not gravitate to an online database such as NCJRS and/or is not socialized to directing users to access tools beyond the card catalog, this feature might make a difference.

THE PERIODICAL COLLECTION

Not long after NCJRS first saw the light of day (1975), the *Criminal Justice Periodical Index* (*CJPI*) made its first appearance. Criminal justice students

Criminal Justice Periodical Index. v.1- . 1975- . Ann Arbor, Mich.:
University Microfilms International. 3/year with annual cumulations.
Standard format periodical index with separate alpha listings for authors
and subjects.
Particularly useful for maintaining a basic criminal justice periodical collection,
since editors are responsive to librarian and practitioner recommendations for
expanding coverage. About 100 indexed titles span the full range of scholarly,
association and agency journals and newsletters. Subject headings BOOK REVIEWS,
PERIODICAL REVIEWS, and REPORTS also make this a valuable tool for overall
selection purposes. Entries under the various review headings are conveniently
arranged by author of the material under review rather than by review's author.
Also available online through DIALOG.

and librarians probably would have difficulty deciding which was the more
significant event for the field. The one hundred-plus indexed journals are
representative of the major currents in the discipline. *CJPI* is generally a
first stop for students and researchers. If your library can possibly afford
it, subscribe to the entire list, including those pariah periodicals categorized
as "newsletters." Career-minded upper level students will be grateful for
the "positions available" notices in many of the newsletters; everyone will
be grateful for the fact that they can proceed without frustration from a
manual or computer search (through DIALOG) of *CJPI* directly to the
materials themselves. Short of purchasing the entire list, be guided by such
factors as sponsorship, affiliation, and frequency of citation in the *DRI*.

If you can afford to go beyond the *CJPI* list, the older and more scholarly
criminal justice abstracting services such as *Criminal Justice Abstracts,
Police Science Abstracts,* and *Criminology and Penology Abstracts* have
a more international outlook and are a good source for identifying the
major foreign language journals in the field. *Forensic Science Abstracts,*
which was spun off *Excerpta Medica* in 1975, is a good source if your
institution prepares students for careers in the scientific aspects of criminal
investigation.

For the richness contributed by related disciplines, the selector probably
has little choice other than to let the criminal justice student thrive or
suffer in accord with the quality and currency of the institution's general
collections.

LAW: A SPECIAL CASE

One more "given" in our subject is that every criminal justice student will
have to become familiar with basic legal research—familiar in a "hands
on" rather than a "reading about" sense. If you are fortunate enough to
be affiliated with a large university that has its own law school, you may

be spared the need to decide how much time, money, and shelf space you are ready to allocate to legal resources. Even with a law library there is still the potentially explosive task of negotiating access for relatively naive undergraduates. In the absence of a captive law school, or in the presence of one that restricts access, it is conceivable that a tactful administrator might work out limited access at a local bar association or government agency.

Failing the options mentioned above, the selector should accept the fact that creating a law collection in support of a criminal justice program will be at best only marginally successful. Lutzker and Ferrall's volume is a good source for identifying the basic legal encyclopedias and dictionaries. *LEX: A Bibliography of Legal Resources for the Layman,* a publication of the New York Metropolitan Reference and Research Library Agency (METRO), which addresses law needs in nonlaw libraries, is a useful second step. You might even acquire basic treatises in criminal evidence and criminal procedure without getting into too much trouble. For a more detailed discussion of selecting law materials for a general collection, you should refer to the essay on law in this volume.

A minimal collection will contain copies of local and regional penal codes; a more comprehensive collection will be rich in statutory, regulatory, and case law. Whatever the collecting level, one must keep in mind that the purchase of each law set, volume, or service commits funds in perpetuity for the loose-leaf pages, pocket parts, or new volumes that will provide the critical currency the subject demands.

The criminal justice selector will not want to enter this whirlpool without some self-study to cover terminology and structure of the law. Thus armed, the vital next step is earnest consultation with the criminal justice teaching faculty. There are numerous brief introductions to the law that can help in the preparation for the faculty get-together. The one I am most familiar with and can recommend without reservation is a fifty-nine page pamphlet prepared by Antony Simpson, *Basic Legal Research.* Despite the fact that it is designed for use in the John Jay College Library, the guide is parochial only for call number and location information. The collection it describes is comprehensive for federal and New York State case, regulatory, and statute law and something less than that for everything else. By substituting one's own state for New York, the collection will serve a fairly rich undergraduate and graduate criminal justice program.

One more word of warning is in order before meeting with the faculty. Stay alert to the possibility that while you are thinking curriculum, some of the people you are talking to may be thinking private law practice. This is simply in the nature of the criminal justice faculty. Dealing with it may require no more than natural wit and charm. In extremis, you may have to call on a higher authority. Good luck.

No less problematic than the above is selection of law reviews. In creating a reference collection, a range of abstracts or indexes to legal literature will have been acquired. As a nonlaw library, however, it is unlikely that many of the indexed law reviews will have been added to the collection. Short of taking a sabbatical, the only advice I would offer is to appeal to the faculty to confine their recommendations to the most important reviews, boost interlibrary loan and plead poverty. It may be helpful to point out to the faculty that even large universities without law libraries infrequently subscribe to all nine leading law reviews recommended by the American Bar Association.[1]

When I suggested early in this essay that building a criminal justice collection was fun, I was not referring to legal materials; that can best be described as "challenging."

Collection Enrichment

Even the newest criminal justice collection will soon find itself stretching beyond basic reference, serial, monograph, document and report boundaries. Indeed, I would be inclined to worry where faculty engagement with the discipline is such that they do not press for broader and deeper coverage. Several possible directions for enrichment are suggested below.

DISSERTATIONS

Standing orders, by subject and/or by granting institutions, can be arranged with University Microfilms International. Since dissertation bibliographies tend to be both extensive and narrowly focused, they are invaluable resources for the serious student or faculty researcher in a program of any dimension. Be careful to make your subject description quite specific. Crime- and justice-related dissertation topics regularly crop up in virtually every discipline and you may find yourself with bigger bills (and a bigger cataloging backlog) than you anticipated.

COMPUTER READABLE DATA FILES

If or when data sets are called for in your collection, the *Criminal Justice Data Directory* is a prime selection tool. The directory, available online as a SPIRES subfile on the University of Michigan's computing system (MTS) and in hard copy, is a product of the Criminal Justice Archive and Information Network (CJAIN). The directory describes files in the CJAIN collection and in a number of other fully identified sources as well.

1. S. W. Beal, *Legal Reference Collections for Non-Law Libraries: A Survey of Holdings in the Academic Community* (Ann Arbor, Mich.: Pierian, 1973), p. 29.

The Criminal Justice Data Directory. 1982– . Ann Arbor Mich.: Inter-University Consortium for Political and Social Research. Continuously updated online.
Directory of publicly available computer-readable criminal justice datasets. Online version available as SPIRES subfile.
Access by principal investigator or keyword.
434 datasets through 1982.
Until comprehensive control of criminal justice datasets is achieved, the combination of the print and online versions of this directory with the personal networks of like-minded researchers is apt to be the best possible substitute. Dataset entries include title, principal investigator, keyword, source, and a description of the file's informing purpose and content. An appendix expands the source information for the benefit of those seeking the files themselves or further information on research methodology and file design. In addition, scattered throughout the introductory material, there are the names of organizations and individuals available to guide potential acquirers and/or users through the often confusing dataset universe.

PRIMARY SOURCES

With the wonders of micropublishing, it is feasible to encourage the use of archival collections by undergraduate as well as graduate students. *Guide to Microforms in Print—Subject* and *Microform Review* are sources for identifying a variety of exciting criminal justice-related collections. Some are as specific as the proceedings of the American Correctional Association; others represent social agencies whose activities had significant impact on the reform of the criminal justice system.

In addition to purchasing published packages of primary source material, the selector should consider searching out fresh materials such as the annual reports of local agencies or prisoner publications in the regional correctional institutions. Local materials add a collection dimension that can be especially stimulating for students. It can also foster constructive and mutually supportive relationships between the college and the agencies involved.

POPULAR LITERATURE

Somewhere on every campus, there are popular culture buffs and among them there will be at least one whose interest is crime or justice related. Feeding such an interest is wonderful for the particular faculty member, enriching for students since curriculum will surely follow available resources, and (to bring this essay full circle) "fun" for the selector. It matters little whether the road leads to police procedural mysteries, female detectives, true crime pulps, prison biographies or crime-fighter comic books. Help will come from unexpected sources, kindred spirits will find one another, and some portion of the selector's pleasure will have been passed along.

Selection Sources

Books in Series in the United States. v.1- . 1980- . New York: Bowker. Biennial.

Choice. v.1- . 1964- . Middletown, Conn.: Association of College and Research Libraries. 11/year.

Criminal Justice Abstracts. v.9- . 1977- . Monsey, N.Y.: Willow Tree. Quarterly. (Formerly *Abstracts on Crime and Delinquency, Crime and Delinquency Literature.*)

The Criminal Justice Data Directory. Ann Arbor, Mich.: Inter-University Consortium for Political and Social Research, 1982.

Criminal Justice Periodical Index. v.1- . 1975- . Ann Arbor, Mich.: University Microfilms International. 3/year.

Criminology and Penology Abstracts. v. 20- . 1980- . Amsterdam: Kugler. Bimonthly. (Formerly *Excerpta Criminologica, Abstracts on Criminology and Penology.*)

Document Retrieval Index. v.1- . 1972- . Rockville, Md.: National Criminal Justice Reference Service. Quarterly.

Encyclopedia of Crime and Justice. 4v. New York: Free Pr., 1983.

Forensic Science Abstracts. v.1- . 1975- . Amsterdam: Elsevier. Monthly.

Guide to Microforms in Print. Subject. v.1- . 1978- . Westport, Conn.: Microform Review. Annually.

Index to Current Urban Documents. v.1- . 1972- . Westport, Conn.: Greenwood. Quarterly.

LEX: A Bibliography of Legal Resources for the Layman. New York: METRO, 1980.

Los Angeles. Public Library. Municipal Reference Library. *Catalog of the Police Library of the Los Angeles Public Library.* 2v. Boston: Hall, 1972.

Lutzker, Marilyn, and Eleanor Ferrall. *Criminal Justice Research in Libraries: Techniques and Strategies.* Westport, Conn.: Greenwood, 1986.

Microform Review. v.1- . 1972- . Westport, Conn.: Greenwood. Quarterly.

Monthly Accessions List Series. v.1- . 1985- . Rockville, Md.: National Institute of Justice/NCJRS. Monthly.

NIJ Reports. v.1- . 1983- . Rockville, Md.: National Institute of Justice/NCJRS. Bimonthly. (Formerly *SNI.*)

O'Block, Robert L. *Criminal Justice Research Sources.* 2nd ed. Cincinnati: Anderson, 1986.

Police Science Abstracts. v.1- . 1973- . Amsterdam: Kugler. Bimonthly. (Formerly *Abstracts on Police Science.*)

Simpson, Antony Eric. *Basic Legal Research.* 2nd ed. New York: John Jay College of Criminal Justice Library, 1982.

University of Cambridge. Radzinowicz Library. *The Library Catalogue of the Radzinowicz Library.* 6v. Boston: Hall, 1979.

EDUCATION

Charles B. Thurston

The word "education" itself has taken on a muddled definition, according to [Cleanth] Brooks.

"Education comes from a Latin root meaning 'to draw out,' " he said. "The idea is to lead students out of their limited worlds, out of provincial thoughts and prejudice, out of the self, and into the broader culture."[1]

You've all heard that old commencement speech, haven't you (I hope none of you have *given* it), about "education" coming from *e-ducere*, to lead out, so that teaching is just drawing out all those good, true, beautiful, and valid ideas humming around inside the head of every schoolchild? The sad fact is that *educate* is derived not from *ducere* but from a causative form of *edo*, the verb for "to eat," and hence "education" means something far more like "to stuff in."[2]

Everything we "stuff in" our collections may be considered educational, but Brooks's interpretation of the meaning of *e-ducere* is a worthy goal.

The academic discipline of education is fluid and subject to debate regarding its scope, but a fairly standard model incorporates fourteen major subdisciplines: (1) higher education; (2) bilingual and bicultural education; (3) multicultural education; (4) special education; (5) adult, community, and continuing education; (6) vocational and technical education; (7) comparative and international education; (8) early childhood education; (9) health and physical education; (10) history and philosophy of education; (11) educational psychology; (12) educational sociology; (13) curriculum and instruction; and (14) educational administration. James R. Kennedy provides a more detailed outline in *Library Research Guide to Education: Illustrated Search Strategy and Sources*.

1. Sheppard Ranbom, "Humanities Laureate Cites Illiteracy As a Threat to American Democracy," *Education Week* 4:6 (May 15, 1985).
2. Mary C. Preus, "St. Augustine on Teaching," *Luther* 20:7 (Aug. 1984).

Theoretical and practical problems rest in the inclusive meaning of *edo.*
Each of the fourteen categories can be divided ad infinitum. For instance,
the National Clearinghouse for Bilingual Education defines twelve major
subject areas within its acquisitions scope for the Bilingual Education
Bibliographic Abstracts (BEBA) database.[3]

Then there are the fuzzy areas of the curriculum that deal with the
education of special populations, such as the deaf or the incarcerated;
various teaching methods, such as distance education or total physical
response; and different settings where formal education occurs, including
laboratory schools and home instruction.

It is a daunting task to grasp the subtle distinctions between seemingly
similar fields, such as bicultural and multicultural education, and yet relate
their similarities to the broader category of the education of racial and
linguistic minorities. But the tensions between broad and narrow concep-
tions of what it means to educate, and to be an educated person, are
resolved by embracing both the particular and the general.

Background Reading

The bibliographer unfamiliar with the social and historical foundations
of American education will profit from reading Henry J. Perkinson's *The
Imperfect Panacea: American Faith in Education, 1865–1976.* Chapters
such as "Racial Inequality and the Schools," "Economic Opportunity and
the Schools," and "The Government and the Schools," describe vexing
problems and attempted remedies. Historians use David Tyack's *The One
Best System: A History of American Urban Education* as a framework
for interpreting the push toward centralization of many functions of American government. Diane Ravitch's *The Troubled Crusade: American Education, 1945–1980* is an excellent critique of contemporary trends.

It is difficult to keep up with the literature of the education reform
movements sweeping across the states. *Education Week* reported:

> According to the Education Commission of the States, 275 state-level task
> forces on education were created in the year following the April 1983 pub-
> lication of [*A Nation at Risk*], the report of the National Commission on
> Excellence in Education.[4]

It is helpful to read the commission reports pertaining to one's own
state as well as major trade books such as *High School: A Report on
Secondary Education in America* by Ernest Boyer and *The Good High
School: Portraits of Character and Culture* by Sara Lawrence Lightfoot.

3. National Clearinghouse for Bilingual Education, *Guide to NCBE Priority/Scope Areas*
(Rosslyn, Va.: National Clearinghouse for Bilingual Education, 1982), p. i.
4. "Quizmaster," *Education Week* 4:4 (June 5, 1985).

Finally, three books in *A Study of High Schools,* the series of reports cosponsored by the National Association of Secondary School Principals and the National Association of Independent Schools, are worthy of attention: (1) *Horace's Compromise: The Dilemma of the American High School,* by Theodore Sizer; (2) *The Shopping Mall High School: Winners and Losers in the Educational Marketplace,* by Arthur Powell, Eleanor Farrar, and David K. Cohen; and (3) *The Last Little Citadel: American High Schools since 1940* by Robert Hampel.

The current focuses of scholarship are teacher education and elementary education.

GUIDES TO THE LITERATURE

The benchmark is the second edition of *A Guide to Sources of Educational Information,* by Marda Woodbury. It is an annotated bibliography of some 700 print and nonprint sources, each succinctly described.

Richard Durnin's *American Education: A Guide to Information Sources* contains a valuable "Bibliographical Essay" and an annotated bibliography arranged by 107 subject areas.

These and other general surveys should be consulted to develop a feel for the structure of the discipline. Few bibliographers are as ambitious as Woodbury or Durnin, preferring to cover in comprehensive fashion discrete areas, such as the politics of education, international education, or the education of specific minority groups. Specialized bibliographies are very useful when developing particular aspects of the collection.

Current Sources of Information

There are fine distinctions between the journals and monographs an education reference librarian should read and those an education bibliographer ought to skim, but both should read the following six newspapers and journals.

WEEKLY

The Chronicle of Higher Education, as the newspaper of record for faculty and administrators at American colleges and universities, is very useful to the bibliographer. The *Chronicle* tracks trends in scholarship, instruction, and legislation at every educational level, although its main focus is the university.

The *Chronicle* has several regular features that should be checked. "New Books on Higher Education," a descriptive rather than evaluative bibliography, lists reference and trade books, university press monographs, and publications of academic and professional organizations. Listings appear near publication dates. Another feature, "New Scholarly Books," typically lists three to five titles in the Education category. Other categories such as sociology, psychology, and public policy occasionally list interdisciplinary books of interest to the education bibliographer.

The *Chronicle* frequently prints the entire texts of reports such as the National Commission for Excellence in Teacher Education's *A Call for Change in Teacher Education*. It usually provides ordering information for studies mentioned in articles; occasionally specialized bibliographies accompany feature articles.

The primary audience of *Education Week*, published forty-two times a year, is elementary and secondary school administrators who must keep abreast of court decisions, statutes, and regulations. The newspaper's format is similar to that of the *Chronicle* and it has several parallel features. One of these is "New in Print," listing books, directories, and ephemeral publications. "Research and Reports" summarizes findings of studies and provides ordering information. In many instances, the reports are free. The "States" section is required reading for legislative and economic news.

Education Week occasionally runs multipart series such as "Schooling in Japan: The Paradox in the Pattern," which appeared in three consecutive issues in 1985. The eighty-six-page article concluded with a fifty-eight-item bibliography.

Important bureaucratic developments, such as the Office of Educational Research and Improvement's (OERI, formerly the National Institute of Education) proposed network of research and development centers, are thoroughly reported. The centers have tremendous import for collection development:

> According to N.I.E., almost 60 percent of its $51.2-million annual budget is earmarked for the support of the centers—which sponsor research in areas such as teaching, reading, and educational policymaking—and a system of regional laboratories that sponsor research on the particular needs of the geographic areas that they serve.[5]

These centers will undoubtedly publish reports of value to almost every collection.

Even the advertisements in the *Chronicle* and *Education Week* can provide valuable information. For example, in the March 20, 1985, issue of *Education Week* Mary Hatwood Futrell, president of the National Education Association, discussed Japan's "Fundamental Law of Education," calling it "the philosophical bedrock of Japan's education system," as well as the practice of *juken senso*, or "examination war," in a pro-

5. Tom Mirga, "New Study Panel Gets Cautious Nod from Researchers," *Education Week* 4:13 (Apr. 10, 1985).

motional essay.[6] Such material provides deep background, but one never knows when it will prove useful.

The third essential publication is *Resources in Education (RIE)*, "a monthly abstract journal announcing recent report literature related to the field of education, permitting the early identification and acquisition of reports of interest to the educational community."[7] Familiarity with *RIE* is assumed here, but an excellent overview is provided in the microfiche document *Development and Current Status of the Educational Resources Information Center (ERIC): A Model Bibliographic Control System Covering the Literature of Education in the United States,* by Charles Hoover and Ted Brandhorst.

Some 3,500 libraries and organizations subscribe to *RIE*, and 735 maintain ERIC microfiche collections.[8] *RIE* is available as a U.S. Government Printing Office depository item or from ORI, Inc., in which case it is distributed by Baker and Taylor and Blackwell North America.

The sixteen ERIC clearinghouses solicit conference papers before their presentation dates, which facilitates quick entry into the education pipeline. For instance, the National Endowment for the Humanities report *To Reclaim a Legacy: A Report on the Humanities in Higher Education* was released in November of 1984 and announced in the January, 1985, issue of *RIE*. Not every ERIC document is indexed with such alacrity, but *RIE* is also an excellent retrospective bibliography.

A good place to begin one's monthly scanning of *RIE* is the "Clearinghouse Number/ED Number Cross-Reference Index," located at the back of each issue. The / / symbol following an ED number indicates that the document is not available on microfiche. These documents should be checked against the public catalog. Even libraries with ERIC microfiche collections will find it useful to duplicate in hard copy some microfiche publications.

Two hours a month devoted to scanning the "Document Resumés" section and noting the title and publisher of each ERIC document pays handsome dividends. Within two years, one begins to have a feel for the major yearbooks, directories, conference proceedings, and sources of statistics.

Each clearinghouse publishes information bulletins and short digests on specific topics of current interest. They list recently accessioned ERIC documents as well as publications available only from the clearinghouses.

American Education (ED1.10:) is published ten times a year by the U.S. Department of Education. It is a general interest journal covering all levels of education. Two useful sections are "Recent Publications," a bibliog-

6. Mary Hatwood Futrell, "A Lesson from Japan," *Education Week* 4:6 (Mar. 20, 1985).
7. Educational Resources Information Center, *Resources in Education* 21:iii (Mar. 1986).
8. Pamela W. McLaughlin, Coordinator of User Services, ERIC Clearinghouse on Information Resources, letter to author, Apr. 10, 1985.

raphy of approximately thirty books, directories, and audiovisual materials, and "Statistic of the Month," worth noting for the source of the statistic, rather than the statistic itself.

QUARTERLY

Another essential journal for bibliographers is the *Harvard Educational Review (HER)*. It frequently has special issues such as "Symposium on the Year of the Reports: Responses from the Educational Community," or "Education and the Threat of Nuclear War." Excellent bibliographies are appended to first-rate articles. There is tremendous competition to publish in *HER*; manuscripts go through a lengthy review process. Consequently, the articles' references are often better for retrospective collection development than for currency of information. The "Essay Reviews" section consists of lengthy book reviews and essays that discuss the themes of the books in broader contexts.

TRIANNUALLY

Last on the required reading list is *Education Libraries*, published by the Education Division of the Special Libraries Association. Individual and institutional subscriptions are available through the editor, Hope Tillman, Rider College Library, 2083 Lawrenceville Road, Lawrenceville, New Jersey 08648.

Education Libraries is a gold mine of information. Bibliographically-oriented articles such as "Software Reviews: A Guided Tour," and "Latchkey Children: A Bibliography," offer outstanding sources to consider purchasing. Regular columns include "New and Forthcoming at Reference," "Education/Psychology Journals," and "Education/Psychology Tests." Each issue is thematically oriented.

Finally, the bibliographer will find it useful to read the newsletter or bulletin published by one's state education agency. Two parochial examples demonstrate why this type of publication is important. The Texas Education Agency, in its monthly *Report*, recently announced the publication of guidelines on the duties of school board members. Another issue of the *Report* discussed a rule requiring school districts to collect and publish data. These publications would probably come in under state library depository plan profiles, but advance information enables the bibliographer to stay a step ahead of the process.

The bibliographer new to education should budget twelve to fifteen hours a month for reading the six publications discussed above. A year of such reading will develop a feeling for those that are most important and those that are optional. Nobody can keep up with the literature of education writ large, but these sources provide a general overview.

Retrospective Sources

In this discussion, "retrospective" applies to reviews of books published within the past two years.

BOOK REVIEWS IN JOURNALS

The journals below carry timely reviews. Each journal in one's collection should be examined for regular review columns and publication dates of

Adolescence: An International Quarterly Devoted to the Physiological, Psychological, Psychiatric, Sociological, and Educational Aspects of the Second Decade of Human Life
American Educational Research Journal
American Journal of Education
Athletic Journal
Australian Journal of Reading
Childhood Education
Comparative Education: An International Journal of Comparative Studies
Comparative Education Review
Contemporary Education Review
Contemporary Psychology: A Journal of Reviews
Curriculum Review
ELT Journal
Educational Forum
Educational Leadership
Educational Record: The Magazine of Higher Education
Harvard Educational Review
International Review of Education
Journal of Child Language
Journal of Higher Education
Journal of Learning Disabilities
Journal of Reading Behavior
Modern Language Journal
NASSP Bulletin
Peabody Journal of Education
Phi Delta Kappan
Psychology in the Schools
Reading Teacher
Roeper Review
Scholastic Coach
School Science and Mathematics
Social Education
T.H.E. Journal
Teachers College Record
Times Educational Supplement
Times Higher Education Supplement
Vocational Education Journal
Young Children

the books reviewed. It is also helpful to note journals such as *Educational Studies: A Journal in the Foundations of Education* or *History of Education Quarterly* which review somewhat less recent books, since many will not have found their way into either current or retrospective bibliographies.

Book reviews are not the sine qua non of collection development, but three abstracts of the education literature are noteworthy for their reviews.

Child Development Abstracts and Bibliography, a triannual publication of the Society for Research in Child Development, features "Book Notices," lengthy reviews (300 to 1,200 words) of scholarly and professional books. Each issue reviews twenty to forty books. An occasional "Books Received" section is useful for identifying ephemeral titles.

Language Teaching: The International Abstracting Journal for Language Teachers and Applied Linguists is relevant to the study and teaching of phonetics, reading, testing, and other topics of interest to teachers of reading and foreign languages. The "New Books" section provides brief, uncritical annotations of books published within the past year. Another regular feature, "Books Received," is less comprehensive than the similar column in *Child Development Abstracts and Bibliography* but serves the same purpose. In addition, an unannotated "Bibliographies" section lists specialized bibliographies appearing in recent issues of journals.

Approximately 250 books, yearbooks, and reference books are described, rather than reviewed, in *Resources in Education* each year. Monthly, semiannual, and annual issues of *RIE* include a "Publication Type Index," thirty-six numerical categories that list ERIC documents according to their form or organization (reports, reference materials, dissertations/theses, and the like) rather than by subject. The 010 category designates books, most of which are not available as ERIC microfiche documents.

Teachers College of Columbia University has long been an outstanding teacher training and research institution. Its library has benefited from philanthropic gifts since 1880. G. K. Hall's *Dictionary Catalog of the Teachers College Library*, a thirty-six volume set, is the primary bibliography in education. The "Introduction" notes its scope:

> The [Teachers College Library] collections include basic reference resources dealing with approximately two hundred distinct educational systems in the world. More than eighteen hundred periodicals, in many languages, are received. The publications dealing with American elementary and secondary

education are exceptionally comprehensive. These include original documents, historical and contemporary textbooks, early catalogs and histories of academies and schools, courses of study, administrative reports of school systems, and surveys.[9]

Supplements comprising seventeen volumes were published in 1971, 1973, and 1977. Additional annual supplements, entitled *Bibliographic Guide to Education*, have been published since 1978. They list material on Teachers College Library OCLC tapes, with additional entries cataloged by the Research Libraries of the New York Public Library for selected publications in education. The library collection should also include the annual bibliographies.

The "Publication Type Index" of *RIE* is a second valuable bibliographic tool. Its eighteen major categories and eighteen subcategories give it a serviceable classification scheme lacking in a dictionary catalog arrangement.

Joseph Drazan's compilation, *An Annotated Bibliography of ERIC Bibliographies, 1966–1980*, lists 3,200 bibliographies arranged under some 600 subjects.

To update Drazan or to search for a specific topic not covered in his work, an online ERIC search works well. Combining the descriptors "Bibliographies," "Annotated Bibliographies," or "Literature Reviews" with the subject is an effective search strategy.

Publishers of Bibliographies. Social sciences bibliographers will be familiar with many publishers of education bibliographies. Oryx Press titles such as *Higher Education Literature: An Annotated Bibliography* ($55.00) by Jane Write and Collins Burnett, strain the acquisitions budget, but generally are of high quality. Garland Publishing's *School Prayer and Other Religious Issues in American Public Education: An Annotated Bibliography* ($20.00) by Albert Menendez, is competently done, while its *Bilingual Education: A Sourcebook* by Alba Ambert and Sarah Melendez falls within the "overpriced but essential" category at $50.00. Greenwood Press also has good bibliographies such as Mark Beach's *A Subject Bibliography of the History of American Education*. Its retail price of $35.00 is typical for Greenwood. Of more importance, all of these bibliographies make significant contributions.

Highly specialized, dearly priced bibliographies such as Garland's *American Education 1622–1680* ($71.00), consisting of "those works printed prior to 1861 in the collections of the American Philosophical Society, the Historical Society of Pennsylvania, and the Library Company of Phil-

9. Columbia University, *Dictionary Catalog of the Teachers College Library* (Boston: Hall, 1970), 1, p. iii.

adelphia which related to American education," are indispensable for scholars but optional purchases for the smaller library.[10]

Bibliographers. The preeminent bibliographer of American educational history is Lawrence Cremin, Frederick A. P. Barnard Professor of Education, Teachers College of Columbia University. Cremin is not, per se, a bibliographer, but his three-volume study promises to be the authoritative work for years to come. *American Education: The Colonial Experience, 1607–1783* and *American Education: The National Experience, 1783–1876* contain lucid "Bibliographical Essays" of monumental scholarship. The projected third volume, *American Education: The Metropolitan Experience, 1876–1976*, will undoubtedly also prove a boon to bibliographers. It would seem to the reader of Cremin's essays that he consulted every source in the *Dictionary Catalog.*

Francesco Cordasco is perhaps the most prolific education bibliographer. His works, published by Gale, Arno Press, and AMS Press, encompass bilingual and bicultural education, vocational education, immigrant education, urban education, and school desegregation.

Philip G. Altbach is well known as a scholar, editor of *Comparative Education Review*, and as a bibliographer of comparative, international, and higher education. His bibliographies include *A Select Bibliography on Students, Politics, and Higher Education* (revised edition published by Harvard University, Center for International Affairs in 1970) and (with others) *Research on Foreign Students and International Study: An Overview and Bibliography.*

PRICES OF MONOGRAPHS

Education is not an inordinately expensive discipline, nor are an overwhelming number of books published each year.

1985 preliminary *Weekly Record* figures indicate that the average per-volume price of a hardcover education title was $27.66 for the 506 volumes analyzed.[11] The education category ranked thirteenth in average per-volume price of hardcover books, and nineteenth in total hardcover and trade paperback volumes published, of the twenty-three categories tracked.[12]

The *Chronicle of Higher Education* often reports hardcover and paperback prices of the same title in its "New Books" column. Noting significant price differences between editions can mean savings of hundreds of dollars each fiscal year. For example, Cambridge University Press pub-

10. Cornelia S. King, comp., *American Education, 1622–1860* (New York and London: Garland, 1984), p. ix.
11. Chandler B. Grannis, "Title Output and Average Prices: 1985 Preliminary Figures," *Publishers Weekly* 229:40 (Mar. 14, 1986).
12. Ibid, p. 40.

lished *Functional Syntax and English Grammar* at $59.50 in hardcover and $19.95 in paperback.

Periodicals

New periodicals in educational computing, bilingual and multicultural education, educational policy, and interdisciplinary areas such as written communication and child development appear monthly. Although one will want to obtain review copies, it is helpful to consult directories of more established journals.

There are at least eight general directories of education journals, and many specialized guides to periodicals in educational administration, art education, educational psychology, higher education, instructional technology, science education, and special education.[13]

Journal selection information is also found in directories marketed to education faculty members seeking journals in which to publish. Two good directories are *Cabell's Directory of Publishing Opportunities in Education* and *Journal Instructions to Authors: A Compilation of Manuscript Guidelines from Education Periodicals.* The latter

> includes the current instructions to authors/notes to contributors from more than 475 journals in the field of education that publish material in the English language. All of the editors/publishers of the journals indexed in *Current Index to Journals in Education* and *Education Index* were requested to submit their current guidelines.[14]

Education Index and *Current Index to Journals in Education* (CIJE) are excellent starting points for periodical collection building. A comparison of the number of publications covered in their January, 1983, issues found that *Education Index* covered 312 titles, all cover-to-cover, while *CIJE* covered 733 publications, 140 cover-to-cover.[15]

Libraries with smaller education budgets and those whose institutions offer only baccalaureate degrees in education would do well to concentrate on the core coverage of journals and yearbooks in *Education Index.*

On the other hand, *CIJE*, with its international coverage and inclusion of obscure but important publications, is a more appropriate selection source for larger collections. In addition, its "Journal Contents Index," a table of contents index, is useful for obtaining a clearer view of a particular journal's coverage than afforded by a single sample issue. Several issues

13. Tara Fulton, "Writing for Professional Publication," *Education Libraries* 10:18–24 (Winter 1985).
14. Barbara A. Parker, ed., *Journal Instructions to Authors: A Compilation of Manuscript Guidelines from Education Periodicals* (Annapolis: PSI, 1985), p. i.
15. Pamela W. McLaughlin, letter to author, Apr. 10, 1985.

of a journal's tables of contents are frequently listed in the same issue of the "Journal Contents Index."

Online searches of ERIC provide good sources of information on which journals tend to be retrieved on frequently searched broad topics. ERIC searches on reading, for instance, often retrieve citations from *Reading Research Quarterly, Journal of Reading Behavior,* and *Australian Journal of Reading.*

Other important publications are journals, bulletins, and newsletters published by associations of teacher educators, teachers, school administrators, and school boards in one's own state. They are inexpensive sources of information on topics such as pending legislation, teacher competency testing, and legal responsibilities of teachers and administrators. The publications often mention reports and studies that can be purchased from colleges of education and school districts. *State Education Journal Index,* covering eighty publications, is the only index that specifically tracks such literature.

PRICES OF PERIODICALS

In 1984 the average price of education periodicals published in the United States was $34.01, ranking twelfth among twenty-four subject areas.[16] A scanning of the February, 1986, issue of *Education Index* shows that many journals fall within the price range of $15.00 to $50.00 a year.

As in any discipline, there is no direct correlation between cost and quality, nor are the more expensive journals necessarily better suited to one's collection. It is possible that *Bilingual Review,* at $20.00 a year, will see more use than *Journal of Multilingual and Multicultural Development,* at $76.00 a year. Focusing on appropriateness, rather than price, works best. Indeed, some of the most valuable periodicals may be free.

PUBLISHERS OF MONOGRAPHS AND PERIODICALS

Many of the premier social sciences publishers such as Jossey-Bass, Macmillan, and Taylor and Francis also publish important scholarly and professional trade books and journals in education. Each of the fourteen areas of educational studies enumerated at the outset of the chapter is worthy of its own listing of publishers; bilingual and multicultural education have been given special attention because of their recent emergence as scholarly fields.

The standard techniques of reviewing publishers' fliers and requesting catalogs are important, since there are hundreds of reputable trade, association press, and small press publishers in education. The "Book Pub-

16. Dennis E. Smith, "Prices of U.S. and Foreign Published Materials," in *Bowker Annual of Library & Book Trade Information,* 30th ed. (New York: Bowker, 1985), p. 472.

lishers—Classified by Subject Matter" index in the 1986 edition of *Literary Market Place* lists 199 education publishers.

Standing Orders for Monographs and Periodicals

Standing orders for monographic serials such as yearbooks, annual reviews of the literature, and directories account for a substantial portion of the education budget. A good rule of thumb is to allocate approximately forty to forty-five percent of the budget for serials.

Many educational organizations offering standing orders are listed in chapter 5 of the *Encyclopedia of Associations.* A useful although laborious technique is to read the descriptions of associations whose publications are likely to be relevant to one's collection development guidelines. Contact the groups for additional information.

Important education serials bear the imprints of commercial publishers and scholarly and professional societies. A discussion of standing orders offered by three organizations in the latter categories follows; they are noted because their publications are pertinent to most education collections.

The National Education Association (NEA) offers several standing order plans; fulfillment is through the association or jobbers. The latter may not offer all the incidental publications available directly from the association.

NEA's comprehensive plan includes every title (except periodicals) published by the NEA Professional Library, which is composed of "materials created expressly to help teachers maintain and extend their expertise in working directly with students. These materials address classroom concerns of all members of the profession, all grade levels, and all content areas."[17] The library includes print and audiovisual materials.

Plan B is less comprehensive; it includes only printed matter. But it includes at least seventeen series as well as some monographs that are not parts of series. The price is approximately $115.00 a year. Plan B is adequate for most libraries.

Another organization whose publications should be purchased is Phi Delta Kappa (PDK), a professional education fraternity. PDK fastbacks are succinct (thirty to fifty pages) pamphlets on timely topics such as the "Philosophy for Children" movement, merit pay, and tuition tax credits. The fastbacks report research findings in a style of writing accessible to the informed layperson. There are 240 fastbacks; 164 are in print, and 8 are published twice a year. An annual list is available from PDK.

17. National Education Assn., *Catalog 1984–85* (Washington, D.C.: National Education Assn., n.d.), p. 2.

TRADE

Academic Press
Addison-Wesley
Allen & Unwin
Allyn & Bacon
Aspen Systems Corporation
Bergin & Garvey
Boynton/Cook
Charles C. Thomas
Croom Helm
Falmer Press
Free Press
Greenwood Press
Grune & Stratton
Harcourt Brace Jovanovich
Human Kinetics Press
John Wiley & Sons
Jossey-Bass

Lawrence Erlbaum Associates
Little, Brown
Longman
Macmillan
McGraw-Hill
NFER-Nelson
Oryx Press
Paul H. Brookes
Pergamon
Peterson's Guides
Prentice-Hall
Routledge & Kegan Paul
Sage
Schenkman
St. Martin's Press
Taylor & Francis

UNIVERSITY

Cambridge University
Harvard University Press
Southern Illinois University Press

Teachers College Press
University of Chicago Press
Yale University Press

BILINGUAL/MULTICULTURAL

Alemany Press
Bilingual Review/Press
Center for Applied Linguistics (dist.
   by Harcourt Brace Jovanovich)
Chicano Studies Resource Center

John Benjamins North America
Multilingual Matters
Newbury House
Relampago Press

SCHOLARLY AND PROFESSIONAL ASSOCIATIONS

American Alliance for Health, Physical Education, Recreation and Dance
American Association of Colleges for Teacher Education
American Council on Education
American Educational Research Association
American Educational Studies Association
Association for Supervision and Curriculum Development
Council for Advancement and Support of Education
Council for Exceptional Children
International Reading Association
John Dewey Society
National Association for Bilingual Education
National Association of Elementary School Principals
National Association of Secondary School Principals
National Council for the Social Studies
National Council of Teachers of English
National Council of Teachers of Mathematics
National Education Association
Phi Delta Kappa
Society for Research in Child Development
Society of Professors of Education
Teachers of English to Speakers of Other Languages

Libraries may be able to obtain free fastbacks through the establishment of a Reavis Reading Area (RRA), a community service activity of local PDK chapters and the PDK Educational Foundation.

> Each chapter is allowed to establish five RRA's in its service area. The chapter contacts local institutions (schools, libraries, etc.) to see if they would like to house the RRA collection. If they agree to do so, they are sent the initial kit of publications and continue to receive new publications as they are released.[18]

If an RRA is composed of several institutions, the local chapter determines which library would maintain the collection.

John Dewey is regarded by many philosophers of education as the preeminent theorist of the twentieth century. Dewey's corpus and commentaries are bedrocks of any education collection. The Center for Dewey Studies at Southern Illinois University (SIU) at Carbondale contains the Dewey archives, and SIU Press has published most of Dewey's works. Consult the SIU "Series Index" in the *Publishers' Trade List Annual* for additional information.

Finally, every academic library, and many public and school libraries, should have a complete ERIC microfiche collection. The monthly price varies according to the number of microfiche received in each shipment, but a year's worth of microfiche costs approximately $1,700.00.

An additional incentive to receive ERIC microfiche on standing order is *RIE*'s reduction in price, beginning February 1, 1985, from $95.00 to $51.00 ($70.00 foreign) for a year's subscription.[19]

State Documents

To speak of an American educational system is misleading, since education is not a power specifically delegated to the federal government by the Tenth Amendment to the U.S. Constitution. Education is largely a state function.

The education or state documents collection should contain every publication of one's state education agency. The agency is responsible for implementing statutes enacted by the state legislature. It also issues rules or regulations, advisory opinions, and orders. School administrators, teachers, and local school board officials look to the education agencies for standards and guidelines in administrative and curricular areas. This is the primary reason for acquiring state education agency materials.

A second reason to acquire state documents is for information on timely topics such as testing students' academic achievement. For example, as

18. Derek L. Burleson, editor, Special Publications, Phi Delta Kappa Educational Foundation, letter to author, Apr. 10, 1985.
19. "Subscription to RIE Now Costs Less," *ERIC Information* n.p. (Spring 1985).

more states begin to require that high school seniors pass competency tests before graduating, there has been a concomitant interest in testing students at several grade levels in elementary and secondary schools to insure that they are performing according to prescribed standards. The Texas Assessment of Basic Skills (TABS) is an annual test of academic achievement in reading, writing, and mathematics, administered to students in six grade levels. The Texas Education Agency publishes documents pertaining to TABS score interpretation, sample test items, instructional guidelines, and regional and statewide results. These types of documents are useful to educational researchers, policymakers, teachers, administrators, and parents.

State documents are also valuable primary sources of information on historical surveys of the curriculum, statutes long since deleted from the education codes, statistical data, and principles and standards regarding school accreditation. Such publications often escape national and trade bibliographies.

Depository collections are traps for the unwary; the tendency not to review newly received depository items, on the assumption that one can always retrieve them later, should be avoided.

Textbooks

Elementary and secondary school textbooks are a major, on-going expense for academic libraries supporting teacher education programs.

There are no nationally uniform standards or procedures for purchasing textbooks, so it is impossible to describe how each state's libraries go about the task. The following model holds true for many states.

Each year, state textbook selection committees review several categories of textbooks (language arts, vocational education, and music, for example) that will be adopted for classroom use for the next several years. The committees listen to publishers and citizen interest groups discuss the merits and demerits of particular books under consideration. They then issue lists of textbooks that are either mandated for use in public schools or from which local school districts can make their own choices.

The college or university director of teacher certification is familiar with state teacher education policies and procedures, and is interested in seeing that the library textbook collection meets accrediting agencies' requirements. He or she will also know the schedule of accreditation teams' visits to the campus, including the library. Furthermore, the director of teacher certification can inform the bibliographer what textbooks are not needed, or those categories where one need only demonstrate that the library is making a good faith effort to purchase some of the state-adopted books in a particular field. Not every textbook need be purchased, as a rule; there is little point to buying cosmetology textbooks if one's institution does not offer courses in cosmetology.

EDITIONS

The lists of state-adopted textbooks sometimes offer little bibliographic information. *Subject Guide to Children's Books in Print* and *El-Hi Textbooks and Serials in Print* are useful for verification.

Elementary level student's and teacher's editions of textbooks are frequently identical, although the latter sometimes also has answers to exercises and suggestions for additional activities. Student teachers need to work with the teacher's editions.

Secondary textbooks should be purchased in student's editions. The teacher's guides, which substitute for teacher's editions, are often little more than worksheets. In addition, purchasing student's editions eliminates theft or mutilation of answer keys.

ACQUISITIONS

Textbooks should be purchased from state textbook depositories, which generally have an adequate supply. Major jobbers do not stock elementary and secondary textbooks. Publishers will ship textbooks in a timely manner, but their mailing addresses are frequently separate from their main mailing addresses. *Literary Market Place* and *Publishers, Distributors, and Wholesalers of the United States* are good sources for these addresses.

The state education agency may provide advance information on categories being considered for adoption to superintendents, school boards, and purchasing agents, who need to set their budgets far in advance. The bibliographer should obtain this preliminary announcement. It can be difficult to track down, but well worth the effort when it comes to setting the coming year's acquisitions budget.

PRICES

Textbook expenditures are a black hole in the education budget. No matter how much money one sets aside for them, it seems there is never enough. Some years are particularly expensive (such as when mathematics, language arts, and natural sciences texts are adopted), and other years less costly; spelling and music books are relatively inexpensive. Average costs are difficult to derive; prices range from $2.00 for preprimers to $28.00 for biology textbooks.

Curriculum Materials

Other quagmires in the acquisitions budget are curriculum guides, kindergarten systems, activities kits, and audiovisual materials. No library can afford to purchase in all subjects and at every grade level. Education faculty, whose research and teaching interests can be tapped by the bibliographer, will assist in winnowing the choices.

Curriculum guides are scope and sequence outlines of what is to be taught and in what order. State education agencies may specify that a minimum number of curriculum guides be in the library collection. Write to school districts listed in *Patterson's American Education* for information on locally produced curriculum guides. Anticipate spending several dollars for each; few school districts still supply free copies. Another source to consider is *Kraus Curriculum Development Library*, a microfiche collection of 3,423 guides developed by school districts, state education agencies, and curriculum development contractors throughout North America. Approximately 300 guides are added each year. See Kraus International Publication's catalog in *The Publishers' Trade List Annual*.

Kindergarten systems substitute for textbooks and offer a variety of items. The Scott, Foresman Kindergarten System approximates systems published by Houghton Mifflin, DLM, Scholastic, Addison-Wesley, and others.

> The Scott, Foresman Kindergarten System provides a complete set of teaching materials to help you [the teacher] guide each child's intellectual, social, and physical development. Included are [a] Teacher's Manual, with information, management aids, scope and sequence charts, vocabulary lists, and blackline masters, Teacher's Editions for individual content areas, two Big Books (poster-size teaching charts for reading and math), and two audio cassettes.[20]

Libraries supporting teacher education programs in bilingual education should also purchase Spanish and English as a Second Language kindergarten systems.

One caveat: shelf space is a crucial consideration. The Scott, Foresman kit measures 21″ × 25″ × 3″.

Other types of curriculum materials include manipulatives, educational games, science and social studies kits, and the like. Many faculty members who teach early childhood education and elementary education methods courses keep publishers' catalogs. Ask them to prioritize specific requests. It is also useful, from political and fiscal standpoints, to rotate major subject areas of purchasing. One fiscal year, social studies may be emphasized; the next year, science may come in for the major share of the

20. Scott, Foresman, *The Scott, Foresman Kindergarten System Teacher's Manual* (Glenview, Ill.: Scott, Foresman, 1982), p. 3.

budget. This technique also ensures that unintended imbalances in the collection do not occur.

The time spent searching for a jobber is hard to justify if one does not have access to a major school supplier such as Heffernan School Supply in San Antonio, Teaching Resources in Hingham, Massachusetts, or Educational Teaching Aids in Chicago. Such suppliers function in the same manner as library jobbers in other fields. A ten percent discount from the retail price is fairly standard. Many curriculum materials are inexpensive ($2.00 to $10.00), so it may not be worth the monies saved to order through a major vendor in order to obtain a state discount.

It is useful to examine the materials budgets of the 170 institutions listed in the second edition of *Directory of Curriculum Materials Centers*, published by the Association of College and Research Libraries in 1985. It also lists centers' holdings of textbooks, curriculum guides, realia, and special collections.

Another useful ACRL publication is their 1984 *Curriculum Materials Center Collection Development Policy*. It covers the scope of the collection, sources of reviews, selection criteria, and weeding.

Software

Any inclinations to build an extensive software collection should be tempered by the realities of how schools and teacher education programs select microcomputer software. Many states and major school systems require computer literacy instruction, but,

> one major obstacle [to exploiting the computer's potential] is a shortage of teachers who understand both their regular subjects and fast-changing technology. Training programs are spreading, but most of them focus on the basics of handling and maintaining computers, printers and floppy disks. They don't necessarily equip a teacher to sort through new products and find the programs that might work best for a particular class.
>
> As a result, schools generally aren't savvy purchasers of computer materials. They frequently buy primitive software, for example, and wind up with little more than a print workbook flashed on a video screen.[21]

State education agencies realize that a good deal of money has been wasted on inappropriate software, and they are bringing some quality control to the purchasing process:

> California, Florida, and Texas have taken pioneering action in educational computing by expanding their statewide textbook adoption programs to include or consider microcomputer software in adoption decisions.

21. "Schools Keep Buying Computers, but Pupils May Not Benefit Much," *Wall Street Journal* 17:1 (Apr. 1985).

But state officials hasten to add that software usually figures in adoptions only if it's part of a program that centers on text materials—and they don't see a change in this policy in the near future.[22]

BACKGROUND READING

Many "how-to" books on educational computing are hastily assembled, inaccurate, and obsolete even before publication. Rather than reading books on specific programming languages or their applications to specific areas of the curriculum, the bibliographer would do well to gain an overview of how students, teachers, administrators, and librarians are using microcomputers at all educational levels.

Several perspectives are offered in Oryx Press's *Educational Microcomputing Annual*. Volume 1 (1985) consists of journal article reprints in chapters such as "Microcomputers in Education: Where Are We Now?" and "Integrating Micros into the Curriculum." Annotated bibliographies are appended to each chapter.

Another excellent source is *Computers in Schools* (McGraw-Hill, 1985). The textbook is clearly written and assumes that the reader has little knowledge of computers. Chapter 7, "Evaluating Instructional Software," is particularly useful.

A third useful book is *School Administrator's Guide to Computers in Education*, published in 1986 as part of the Addison-Wesley Series on Computers in Education. The book's intended audience allows the bibliographer to approach the field from the perspective of the end-users.

DIRECTORIES

Collection development starts with building a good reference collection of educational software directories. Many directories simply list available software, but several contain evaluations and recommendations. A discussion of two outstanding directories in both categories follows, but there are many other good ones.

Moore Data Management Services publishes *Softwhere*, a two-volume semiannual directory (*Education Administration Softwhere* and *Education Courseware Softwhere*). What distinguishes *Softwhere* from other directories is the amount of detailed information supplied by the vendors. A brief abstract of each package identifies applications and special features; other information includes compatible hardware, source language, operating system, memory required, suggested retail price, availability of training manuals, and number of copies sold.

22. "Software Creeps into State Textbook Adoptions," *SchoolTechNews* 3:1 (Jan./Feb. 1986).

Every bibliographer should be familiar with *Only the Best: The Discriminating Software Guide for Preschool–Grade 12*. The publisher, Education News Service, culled through reviews published by twenty-two evaluation services, including the New York City School District, the Texas Microcomputer Courseware Evaluation Network, and *Classroom Computer Learning*. The 1986 edition consists of "meta-reviews" of 281 programs judged "most highly rated" or nearly so.

REVIEWS IN PERIODICALS

Software reviews are found in dozens of periodicals, including *Childhood Education, Classroom Computer Learning* ("CCL Picks"), *Collegiate Microcomputer, Compute!, Educational Technology* ("Ed Tech Product Reviews"), *Journal of Reading, Journal of School Psychology* ("Software Review Section"), *School Microcomputing Bulletin, School Science and Mathematics, Science and Children, Science Teacher* ("Reviews"), *Social Education,* and *Teaching Learning Computing*. Other journals containing reviews are listed in *Educational Microcomputing Annual*.

As with book reviews, the goal is not to read every review but rather to identify several journals that consistently provide critical reviews of software relevant to one's collection guidelines and regularly scan them.

Conclusion

There is a strong temptation to devote extra attention to several of the fourteen fields mentioned at the beginning of the chapter. That would be unfair, for each is worthy of its own treatment.

It is a daunting task to obtain a bibliographic overview of education, and an understanding of its jargon ("time on task," "visual literacy," and "superlearning" come to mind), but the challenge is rewarding to the bibliographer who stuffs himself or herself full of knowledge in the pursuit of wisdom.

Selection Sources

Ambert, Alba N., and Sarah E. Melendez. *Bilingual Education: A Sourcebook.* Garland Reference Library of Social Science, v.197. New York: Garland, 1985.
Altbach, Philip G., David H. Kelly, and Y. G-M. Lulat. *Research on Foreign Students and International Study: An Overview and Bibliography.* Praeger Special Studies Series in Comparative Education. New York: Praeger, 1985.
Beach, Mark, comp. *A Subject Bibliography of the History of American Higher Education.* Westport, Conn.: Greenwood, 1984.

Bibliographic Guide to Education. v.1- . 1978- . Boston: Hall. Annually.
Cabell, David W. E., ed. *Cabell's Directory of Publishing Opportunities in Education.* Beaumont, Tex.: Cabell, 1984.
Columbia University. *Dictionary Catalog of the Teacher's College Library.* 36v. Boston: Hall, 1970.
_____. _____. *First Supplement.* 5v. Boston: Hall, 1971.
_____. _____. *Second Supplement.* 2v. Boston: Hall, 1973.
_____. _____. *Third Supplement.* 10v. Boston: Hall, 1977.
Durnin, Richard G. *American Education: A Guide to Information Sources.* American Studies Information Guide Series, v.14. Detroit: Gale, 1982.
El-Hi Textbooks and Serials in Print. v.1- . 1985- . New York: Bowker. Annually.
Mattas, Linda L. *Only the Best: The Discriminating Software Guide for Preschool-Grade 12: A Special Report from the Editors of SchoolTechNews.* v.1- . 1985- . Carmichael, Calif.: Education News Service. Annually.
Menendez, Albert J. *School Prayer and Other Religious Issues in American Public Education: An Annotated Bibliography.* Garland Reference Library of Social Science, v.291. New York: Garland, 1985.
Moore Data Management Services. *Softwhere: Education Administration.* 2v. 1985- . Minneapolis: Moore Data Management Services. Semiannually.
_____. *Softwhere: Education Courseware.* 1985- . Minneapolis: Moore Data Management. Semiannually.
Parker, Barbara A., ed. *Journal Instructions to Authors: A Compilation of Manuscript Guidelines from Education Periodicals.* Annapolis: PSI, 1985.
Subject Guide to Children's Books in Print. 1970- . New York: Bowker. Annually.
White, Jane N., and Collins W. Burnett, eds. *Higher Education Literature: An Annotated Bibliography.* Phoenix, Ariz.: Oryx, 1981.
Woodbury, Marda. *A Guide to Sources of Educational Information.* 2nd ed. Arlington, Va.: Information Resources Pr., 1982.

JOURNALS

American Education. v.1- . 1964- . U.S. Department of Education, Washington, DC 20202. 10/year.
Child Development Abstracts and Bibliography. v.1- . 1927- . Pennsylvania State Univ., 442 B.V. Moore Bldg., University Park, PA 16802. 3/year.
Current Index to Journals in Education. v.1- . 1969- . Oryx, 2214 North Central at Encanto, Phoenix, AZ 85004. Monthly.
Education Index. v.1- . 1929- . H. W. Wilson, 950 University Ave., Bronx, NY 10452. Monthly.
Education Libraries. v.1- . 1976- . Special Libraries Assn., Education Div., Rider College Library, 2083 Lawrenceville Road, Lawrenceville, NJ 08648. Triannually.
Educational Studies: A Journal in the Foundations of Education. v.1- . 1970- . American Educational Studies Assn., Box 655, Georgia State Univ., University Plaza, Atlanta, GA 30303. Quarterly.
Harvard Educational Review. v.7- . 1937- . Longfellow Hall, 13 Appian Way, Cambridge, MA 02138-3752. Quarterly. (Supersedes *Harvard Teachers Record.*)
History of Education Quarterly. v.1- . 1961- . History of Education Society, School of Education, Indiana Univ., Bloomington, IN 47405. Quarterly.
Language Teaching: The International Abstracting Journal for Language Teachers and Applied Linguists. v.15- . 1982- . Cambridge Univ. Pr., 32 East 57th St.,

New York, NY 10022. Quarterly. (Supersedes *Language Teaching & Linguistics: Abstracts.* v.8- . 1975- .)

Resources in Education. v.10- . 1975- . U.S. Department of Education, Office of Educational Research and Improvement, Educational Resources Information Center, Washington, DC 20208. Monthly with semiannual and annual cumulations. (Supersedes *Research in Education.* v.1- . 1966- . U.S. Department of Health, Education and Welfare, Washington, DC 20202.)

State Education Journal Index. v.1- . 1963- . P.O. Box 244, Westminster, CO 80030-0244. Semiannually.

NEWSPAPERS

Chronicle of Higher Education. v.1- . 1966- . 1255 23rd St., N.W., Washington, DC 20037. Weekly.

Education Week. v.1- . 1981- . Editorial Projects in Education, 1255 23rd St., N.W., Suite 755, Washington, DC 20037. 42/year.

ENGINEERING

Edwin D. Posey

The field of engineering is characterized by a richness and diversity of subject emphases. Historically, the term is applied to human efforts to alter the physical environment. From Archimedes' lever, the Egyptian pyramids, and the irrigation systems of the ancients to modern genetic engineering, the record has been a mostly successful chronicle of harnessing the forces of nature to meet human needs.

The literature of engineering, as distinct from that of the natural sciences, assumed a recognizable form about the time of the Industrial Revolution. Early contributions were mainly concerned with what is now civil engineering—that is, the construction of dams, roads, and buildings, as well as surveying. Mechanical engineering was also represented somewhat earlier in the fields of military weapons and fortifications, as well as that of horological devices.

Modern engineering may be classified into broad areas; with, however, a considerable overlap not only within the arbitrary classifications, but also with bordering areas in the overall scheme of knowledge. The basic genera, fairly well established near the end of the nineteenth century, is: civil, mechanical, electrical, and chemical. A number of other subdisciplines have been created, several of which have assumed almost equal importance with the "parent" disciplines: notably aeronautical, materials, mining, bioengineering, nuclear, industrial, environmental, and others. These classifications reflect the organization of most academic institutions involved in the education of engineers.

The literature of engineering, however, does not divide itself into such convenient classification schemes. For instance, the mechanical engineer concerned with the physical properties of bone will immediately become involved with the literature of both medicine and engineering. Environmental engineers will need to draw upon the literature of chemical engineering, civil engineering, biology, and other disciplines. One rather an-

79

cient device to attempt to differentiate between "engineering" and "science" is the test of theory versus application. This is unworkable on the face of it, since most meaningful applications in engineering are based upon sound theoretical considerations.

The practice of engineering encompasses many different pursuits, and a consideration of the literature of engineering must take into account the differing needs of practitioners, depending upon their professional situation—the academic engineering professor, the "project" engineer in industry, the design/research and development engineer, and engineers in governmental research establishments, to name a few. The informational needs of the various groups, however, can be considered under two major headings; research and application.

Despite these caveats and inconveniences, there is a large body of information concerned directly with engineering, and it is this corpus that the present chapter addresses. The preprint problem in physics, the classification systems of biology, and the nomenclature difficulties in mathematics will be left to the respective practitioners of those arts, although the outcome of their efforts will impinge, in at least some instances, upon the engineer.

Engineering literature appears in numerous formats—traditional monographs and journals, handbooks, data compilations, technical drawings, patents, codes and specifications, maps, etc. Physically, in addition to the traditional ink-on-paper medium, the information is also packaged in microforms, magnetic tapes, computer readable disks, and video disks.

Engineering software, although a vital element in modern engineering practice, is excluded from consideration in this chapter. While there is no doubt as to its being "engineering information," the topic is covered in the books, journals, and other categories that are considered, at least in a bibliographical sense. For instance, many engineering journals have regular columns announcing and reviewing new software within their purview. There is little doubt, however, that computerized methods are revolutionizing the entire field of engineering and will undoubtedly affect its bibliographic apparatus.

This chapter is written from the standpoint of an academic engineering librarian, but it is hoped that the information herein will also interest fellow engineering librarians in all of the various types of engineering libraries.

General Considerations

The field of engineering poses unique problems in collection development. As engineering is one of the most rapidly changing disciplines, the subject specialist is hard pressed to keep up with the burgeoning literature.

A major complicating factor is the rate at which engineering monographs become "out-of-print"; publishers try to gauge immediate demand and, since demand is always increasing, the net result is that if material is not acquired promptly it is likely to be unavailable.

For academic librarians, the institutional setting is of paramount importance in relation to collection development activities. Procedures for an engineering collection embedded in a large central library will quite likely be different from those practiced in a decentralized facility. Practitioners can attest to the difficulty of drawing the line between, say, chemical engineering and chemistry, to give but one example. Close cooperation between the subject specialist/bibliographers is extremely important, as is a good knowledge of the research and teaching activities of the engineering faculty. These problems, of course, are usually not present in the corporate or special library setting.

GUIDES TO THE LITERATURE

A good introduction and source of general background information on the literature of engineering, as well as the idiosyncrasies of several subdisciplines, is provided by K. W. Mildren's *Use of Engineering Literature.* This book's thirty-five essays are written by British engineers and librarians and, although published in 1976, much of its contents is still quite useful. The essays introduce and describe the scope, reference sources, abstracting and indexing services, established engineering journals, and some standard texts for twenty various fields of engineering.

Another very useful guide is Ellis Mount's *University Science and Engineering Libraries;* the chapter on library collections is especially helpful, and the book includes a detailed treatment of scientific and engineering literature.

Krishna Subramanyam's *Scientific and Technical Information Resources* is yet another superior bibliographic tool and provides a wealth of references.

BUDGETARY CONSIDERATIONS

The inflationary spiral has been particularly devastating to the entire field of scientific/technical literature, and has wreaked havoc on many engineering collections. "Collection development" as a meaningful goal has had to be put aside; instead, many libraries have been forced into a posture

---

Mount, Ellis. *University Science and Engineering Libraries.* 2nd ed. Westport, Conn.: Greenwood, 1985.
Covers all aspects of sci/tech libraries, including the acquisition of materials.

of responding to demand as best as is possible instead of systematically building a collection.

Ideally, the engineering library or collection should have just one book fund. Where funds are divided by departments (mechanical, chemical, etc.) or, worse yet, controlled by these departments, collection development as a meaningful activity for the librarian becomes an absurdity. Faculty and staff have a strong tendency to select materials of immediate interest, with little or no regard for the other responsibilities of the library, such as support of undergraduate programs, and even less consideration of inevitable changes in research and teaching programs.

The prudent engineering selector will find it necessary to divide funds between approval plan/firm order purchasing, and faculty/staff requests. Further, it is essential to try to pace expenditures to coincide with the fiscal year, given the stochastic nature of publishing and inevitable short-falls due to unusually expensive items, as well as general inflation.

Selection by Types of Materials

MONOGRAPHS

Engineering patrons, generally speaking, contribute much less to the se-lection process than do those from other disciplines. Therefore, it is nec-essary for the engineering librarian to diligently seek out appropriate items to add to the book collection. Major publishers in the field (see the list under "Approval Plan," below) should be contacted for catalogs and an-nouncements. The *American Book Publishing Record* should be consulted monthly under engineering categories—as a suggestive checklist for a gen-eral academic library, the following Dewey numbers should be scanned: 0-100; 307-308.99; 333-333.99; 338.43-338.499; 363-363.799; 380.5-381.55; 385-388.5; 500-550; 600-629; 651-652.99; 655 (all); 660-673; and 686 (all). This list will, of course, vary from library to library, de-pending upon the subject emphases at the institution. *Weekly Record* covers the same books more promptly, but is more difficult to use. *Tech-nical Book Review Index* and *New Technical Books* should also be ex-amined monthly. *Books in Print* is yet another essential tool, as is *Forth-coming Books*. Bowker also publishes *Scientific and Technical Books and Serials in Print*, which may be a better choice than *Books in Print*, al-though it is nearly as expensive as is the more complete latter item.

A word of caution is in order, however, as to ordering "forthcoming" books either from the publication of the same name or from publishers' announcements. Publishing schedules tend to be honored more in the breach than in the accomplished fact, and it is quite possible to encumber substantial amounts of book funds for long periods of time should the

Scientific and Technical Books and Serials in Print. v.1– . 1978– . New
York: Bowker. Annually.
Over 100,000 sci/tech books listed in the 1985 volume, indexed by subject,
author, and title with full ordering information. 19,500 sci/tech serials are also
treated.

publisher fail to deliver as promised. The acquisitions department should
be geared to spot unusual delays, and then give the engineering librarian
the opportunity to cancel the order if necessary.

Some engineering librarians have found the Library of Congress' *CDS
Alert Service* (proof slips) with cataloging in publication (CIP) data a useful
mechanism for selection before a book's publication date. This service is
available on cards for selected classifications, e.g., all of the Ts. More
information is available on this service from the Cataloging Distribution
Service's brochure of LC's Customer Service Section.

Reviews, summaries, and notifications of new books are often published
in the official journals of various engineering societies. The choice and
timeliness of these announcements vary considerably from journal to journal. Two journals that provide coverage of the major books in their fields
are *Civil Engineering* (ASCE) and *Mechanical Engineering* (ASME). *Civil
Engineering* devotes several pages in each of its monthly issues to describing the contents of about twenty books. Coverage includes materials
in the areas of engineering management, structural, geotechnical, construction, environmental, sanitary, energy, water, and transportation engineering. Adequate bibliographical information is provided, and the books
are treated within a few months of their publication. The books covered
are about evenly divided between commercial and society, institute or
association-sponsored material. Some English-language foreign books are
included, but the primary focus is on American imprints.

Mechanical Engineering includes signed reviews, uncritical abstracts,
and bibliographic citations to books recently added to the Engineering
Societies Library in New York City. A separate column lists American
Society of Mechanical Engineers (ASME) publications. The books treated,
the number of which varies from a few to over fifty an issue, come almost
entirely from commercial publishers (with the exception of ASME, of
course!). Timeliness varies from a few months to as much as two years
after the publication date.

JOURNALS

Journals typically consume seventy to eighty percent of the materials budget for most engineering libraries. Further, their inflation rate (as much as
twice the overall national average for all periodicals) threatens to crowd

out other materials entirely. This trend has caused more emphasis to be placed on deacquisition of journals in the immediate past—both to try to contain them within inelastic budgets as well as to free some money for new journals, which continue to spawn at a rapid pace.

For these reasons, it would probably be fatuous to point out ways to find out about "new" journals; most librarians would rather not hear about them, but do anyway. Seriously, the journal literature is the heart of the research collection, and must be considered. Faculty input is usually adequate, since they receive blurbs on most journals that might remotely interest them. The catalogs and announcements of major journal publishers should be monitored. The latest edition of *Ulrich's International Periodicals Directory* can be checked by broad subject categories. The companion publication, *Irregular Serials and Annuals*, complements the coverage for the items mentioned in its title. *PIE; Publications Indexed for Engineering* lists over 2,000 journal titles, many of which are essential for engineering libraries with multidisciplinary responsibilities. The quarterly supplements to this publication are useful for identifying new journals.

It should be emphasized that a new journal is always a gamble—some die aborning, others wither after the initial store of articles is exhausted, and still others are too specialized for most audiences. Generally speaking, those published by reputable commercial publishers and major professional societies are most likely to endure, and to be of lasting value.

A number of the commercial publishers listed in the section on approval plans also publish journals—Academic, Wiley, Pergamon, and others. The European commercial publishers, such as Noordhoff and Elsevier, generally produce the most expensive journals—they seem to be trying to redress the balance of trade for their countries!

Professional societies are also a prolific source of journals—IEEE, for instance, publishes about fifty titles.

SOCIETY PUBLICATIONS

Society publications are an essential component of academic engineering library collections. Most engineering faculty are members of at least one major society relating to their professional interests. Depending upon the curricula at the institution, it will be necessary to acquire as many of these as the budget permits.

A selective listing of major societies includes:

AIAA (American Institute of Aeronautics and Astronautics)
AIChE (American Institute of Chemical Engineers)
AIIE (American Institute of Industrial Engineers)
AIME (American Institute of Mining Engineers)

ANS (American Nuclear Society)
ASM (American Society for Metals)
ASTM (American Society for Testing and Materials)
ASCE (American Society of Civil Engineers)
ASHRAE (American Society of Heating, Refrigeration and Air
  Conditioning Engineers)
ASME (American Society of Mechanical Engineers)
IEEE (Institute of Electrical and Electronics Engineers)
SAE (Society of Automotive Engineers)
SME (Society of Manufacturing Engineers)
SPE (Society of Plastics Engineers)

In addition, there are literally dozens of smaller, more specialized organizations. Most publish voluminously, and their publications are useful to many academic engineering libraries.

The best arrangement, if the library can afford it and if the society offers the service, is to establish standing orders with those societies most important to the research efforts of the institution. This is possible with IEEE, ASME, ASTM, and ASCE (the latter quite recently, and greeted with loud hurrahs). Standing orders can be quite expensive, and selective acquisition may be a viable alternative, whereby only those publications of direct interest to the patrons will be acquired.

Associations' Publications in Print is a useful tool for retrospective acquisition; however, current announcements from the societies are necessary for timely acquisition of new items. This is especially true since many society publications become out-of-print quite rapidly.

The above-mentioned tools for locating monographs are also useful for society publications, particularly those of the major societies. For the more specialized societies, it is frequently necessary to request their publication lists and catalogs.

TECHNICAL REPORTS

Technical reports have been roundly cursed in numerous library publications and justly so from this writer's standpoint. Bibliographical control, for the most part, is very poor; acquisition procedures difficult; and quality is erratic, to say the least. Nevertheless, they have become firmly embedded in the informational fabric, and they must be dealt with by engineering librarians (poetic justice, since engineers are responsible for the bulk of them).

Acquisition activites should be tailored to the research programs of the particular institution. Faculty or professional staff advice is essential. If access is available to similar report series, it is frequently possible to arrange for exchange with sister institutions. Often, however, these arrangements

---

Government Reports Announcements and Index. v.1- . 1961- . Washington, D.C.: National Technical Information Service. Bimonthly with annual cumulative indexes.
About 70,000 reports are treated each year. Individual issues arranged in 22 subject categories, further divided into 178 more specific subjects. Minutely indexed by keywords, personal and corporate authors, contract/grant numbers, and NTIS/report numbers. An essential tool for accessing the voluminous government-sponsored technical report literature.

---

must be established between corresponding academic departments rather than the libraries. The trend lately has been for academic institutions to *sell* technical reports, imposing further burdens upon already overextended budgets. This is especially true in "hot" research areas, such as artificial intelligence, robotics, and CAD/CAM.

The types of technical reports most easily acquired (U.S. Department of Energy, National Aeronautics and Space Administration, etc.), are also those under best bibliographical control through published abstracts and indexes. If the institution is a government depository, the DOE problem is solved. Likewise, if NASA research is carried out locally, this veritable flood can also be tapped. The National Technical Information Service, on the other hand, is a prime producer of reports generated by government-funded research, and their products must be purchased (particularly galling to engineering librarian taxpayers who have to buy something already paid for). For a comprehensive output in microfiche of NTIS reports covering only the major areas of engineering, their fee is $5,000 or so per year. Many engineering libraries have perforce opted to acquire these selectively, or on demand, due both to the expense and the overall low rate of use.

Major selection tools include *Government Reports Announcements and Index*, NASA's *Scientific and Technical Aerospace Reports* (STAR) and *International Aerospace Abstracts* (IAA), and *Energy Research Abstracts*.

STANDARDS, SPECIFICATIONS, AND CODES

Standards, both industrial and governmental, are frequently needed by patrons of engineering libraries. They are more likely to be of importance in a library associated with strong programs in manufacturing technology. The American National Standards Institute standards are probably of most general interest, since they incorporate the standards issued by a number of professional societies and cover a wide range of professional activities. These are available on subscription, and are listed in their annual *ANSI Catalog*.

Other important standards publications include those of the American Society for Testing and Materials (now in some fifty volumes per year!), the triennial American Society of Mechanical Engineers *Boiler and Pressure Vessel Code*, the *National Electrical Code*, the National Electrical Manufacturers Association standards, the Building Officials and Code Administrators of America (BOCA) building codes, the International Conference of Building Officials (ICBO) *Uniform Building Code*, etc.

In addition to the above abbreviated list, data con munications interface standards promulgated by the Electronics Industries Association (EIA), the Consultative Committee for International Telegraph and Telephone (CCITT) of the International Telecommunications Union, and the International Organization for Standardization (ISO) are important tools for many technical libraries. The International Electrical Commission, composed of over 200 committees from 42 countries, provides international standardization in the electrical and electronic fields. The U.S. National Bureau of Standards is yet another valuable source of information on engineering standards.

While all of the above standards and codes may be obtained from the issuing agencies, several commercial enterprises offer good service on individual standards: NSA National Standards Association, Information Handling Services, and others. Information Handling Services also publishes a very useful index—*Index and Directory of U.S. Industry Standards*.

The *World Guide to Scientific Associations and Learned Societies* is an excellent source for the addresses of the above organizations, as well as of the engineering associations listed under "Society Publications."

GOVERNMENT PUBLICATIONS

While DOE, NASA, and NTIS technical reports (covered in the preceding section) may be considered as government documents, there are a great many other governmental publications of interest to engineering clienteles. Examples include the U.S. Office of Surface Mining reports, U.S. Environmental Protection Agency material, U.S. Department of Transportation research reports, and many other agency publications. The *Monthly Catalog of United States Government Publications* covers many of these.

CONFERENCE PROCEEDINGS

Symposia, meetings, conferences and their various aliases are almost as difficult to deal with as are technical reports. However, their importance to engineering patrons is difficult to overstate—the papers in these publications frequently do not make their way into the journal literature and, in many cases, are more timely than the versions that are formally published later. Those sponsored and published by major professional societies are generally the least complicated to identify and obtain, while the ones published in the third floor offices of some professor in Uruguay and such

Directory of Published Proceedings: Science, Engineering, Medicine and Technology. v.1– . 1965– . Harrison, New York: InterDok. Monthly with various cumulations.
Basic arrangement is by the date of the conference. Exhaustive indexing by editor, location, subject/sponsor. The subject/sponsor index provides a useful tool for timely acquisition of newly published conference proceedings on topics of interest.

---

places drive both acquisitions and engineering librarians up the wall. One complication, as with monographs, is that press runs are likely to be quite small; frequently only enough copies are produced to distribute to conference participants. Inevitably, however, these papers *will* be heavily cited, at least to the extent where they will be requested at the library. Most librarians could easily expend their entire book budget on conference proceedings, but this would not be a prudent course. A conscientious effort should be made to identify meetings of particular importance to the faculty and professional staff, and to then acquire proceedings if possible. The clientele can frequently provide valuable pointers as to which items should be acquired—indeed, at one institution in particular, the engineering librarian monitors the travel requests of faculty for this information!

Directory of Published Proceedings: Science, Engineering, Medicine and Technology is a particularly valuable tool for the identification of available items, since it provides broad subject access and identifies publishers and prices.

Approval plans, through form notifications, can also be of great assistance.

MANUFACTURERS' DATA

Catalogs and product specifications are yet another component of a well-equipped engineering library. In a recent paper by William LeBold and Carl Frey on the utilization of engineers, the use of catalogs and manufacturers' literature ranked third highest among sources of information, topped only by "informal contact with coworkers" and "personal store of information."

The emphasis on the manufacturers' data collection should depend on the professional activities of engineering patrons. Typically, engineers involved in the design process, especially those working in electrical and mechanical engineering, have a greater requirement for this type of information. The collection should be tailored with specific groups of users in mind, since it is difficult to maintain and keep up-to-date, and requires a substantial amount of staff effort.

While much of this information is distributed freely to the manufacturing community, academic librarians usually find it more difficult to acquire since the materials are expensive to produce, and the vendors are apt to view libraries as poor sales prospects. Regular attention is required if the catalog collection is not to become obsolete. This usually involves form letters to be sent regularly to assure continuity, filling out reader service cards from various periodicals, and dealing with salespeople. Some vendor catalogs must be purchased. User requests are the most reliable guide as to the types of catalogs to collect.

Much of the needed information can also be obtained through several commercial services. *Thomas' Register* and the Sweets services are convenient and relatively inexpensive sources. In the field of electronics, a number of useful tools are available to either supplant or shore up the catalog collection—for example, the D.A.T.A. series on semiconductors and devices, and the *IC Master* are noteworthy efforts along these lines. The 1985 D.A.T.A. *Microprocessor Integrated Circuits*, for instance, provides complete technical information on some 8,000 devices made by more than fifty manufacturers. The information is arranged by "functional equivalence," "cross index," "technical sections," schematics, etc. This, along with twenty-five other volumes in the series, provides very good coverage of this important field. For about $1,600 per year, one can be assured of having the latest technical information from literally hundreds of manufacturers, and the saving in staff time, added to the patron benefits, makes this a worthwhile investment for any library associated with research in electronics.

Yet another commercial service dedicated to product information is that provided by Information Handling Services. For a fee, online access can be obtained to the *Industrial Product Catalog Data File*, or, alternatively, this material may be subscribed to in microform. Over 75,000 vendor catalogs are included in the collection. The file is frequently updated, and is organized into broad categories—Gas Appliance Data Bank, Medical Equipment, Devices, etc. Another similar service is provided by Information Marketing International, who offer over 25,000 catalogs on cartridge reels with a printed index. IMI's service, although less comprehensive, is viewed by some librarians as being better in certain areas, e.g., military specifications, and as having better indexing. These services are not inexpensive, but may be cost effective if there is a heavy demand for product specifications in the library.

PATENTS

The above remarks pertaining to manufacturers' literature apply also to patents. Strong manufacturing programs and associated research are almost necessary requisites to justify large patent collections in engineering libraries. However, it is still important to be able to respond to occasional requests for patents. Coupons may be obtained from the U.S. Patent Office for this purpose. For engineering libraries situated near large public or academic libraries maintaining patent depositories, it may be more feasible to utilize their services. This is especially true since the Patent Office files are machine searchable at most depository libraries utilizing their online system.

Implementation of Procedures

APPROVAL PLAN

The approval plan approach can be of great benefit to the academic engineering librarian. Properly planned, executed, and monitored, it can relieve the librarian of the necessity for identifying and acquiring routine items of interest, enabling the pursuit of the more esoteric and difficult materials. A typical plan would include all of the major areas covered by subject discipline (aeronautical engineering, etc.), and provide form notification of new items of peripheral interest. For example, "mechanical engineering" might be covered completely, with form notification only for "magnetohydrodynamics." Limits should be established, such as language, maximum cost, country of origin, etc.

Faculty or professional staff involvement in screening the books produced by the approval plan is highly recommended. Typically, the books shipped in a certain period are listed, and the list distributed to interested faculty and staff. The books are then displayed, with a recommendation form attached to each, and the faculty/staff reviewers are encouraged to examine the books and give their opinions as to the suitability of each item for acquisition. Besides providing essential guidance for the librarian, this active involvement of the library patrons in collection development is a very good public relations device.

The approval plan just described is subject oriented; it is also possible to devise a plan restricted to certain publishers. Of the several thousand publishers of technical books in this country, a relatively small number produce the bulk of high quality engineering monographs. The following group would appear on most engineering librarians' "must" list:

Academic Press	Oxford University Press
Addison Wesley	Pergamon
Marcel Dekker	Plenum Press
Elsevier/North Holland	Prentice-Hall
Macmillan	Springer Verlag
McGraw-Hill	Van Nostrand Reinhold
MIT Press	John Wiley

This publisher approach should be distinguished from the "standing order" programs offered by many publishers—the essential difference between an approval plan or blanket order program and a standing order plan is, of course, that in the first instance unwanted materials may be returned, while standing order plans assume all books sent will be kept by the library. Publisher plans may not be practical for engineering libraries that are a component of a library system with an overall approval program.

One of the disadvantages of approval plans is the subject classification process of the vendors. Key books, particularly those in peripheral areas, stand a good chance of being classified in nonengineering categories—for instance, "cybernetics" and "artificial intelligence" may be classified under "philosophy" or "science." For this reason, the input from the approval program must be constantly compared with announcement and review media to be sure that the proper books are obtained.

Approval plans must be used with caution, and supplemented by numerous other acquisition tools such as publishers' catalogs, *American Book Publishing Record*, LC proof slips, and book reviewing media. Again, faculty or staff input is very important; they are likely to receive blurbs on items in their fields. If it can be arranged, it is also quite useful to review interlibrary loan requests regularly, as they are reliable indicators of deficiencies in the collection, as well as pointers to new research directions in the institution.

Several vendors offer approval plans suitable for engineering collections. Baker & Taylor and Blackwell North America both provide good coverage of the field. Harrassowitz is recommended for European literature, and is particularly strong in conference proceedings. Scholarly Books has a new plan that is publisher oriented; however, it is too early to evaluate their program. For a more complete discussion of approval plans see *Approval Plans and Academic Libraries* by McCullough, Posey, and Pickett.

GIFTS

Gifts can be a valuable resource for the academic engineering collection, and should be actively solicited. Faculty members typically buy and otherwise acquire materials of interest in their specialties, and are prime sources. An example is conference proceedings—frequently, these are either given to attendees or are paid for by registration fees. Furthermore, they may not even be "published" officially, and are thus available only through gifts. The utility of gifts, with resulting tax benefits to the donors, can be made known to the faculty either on an individual basis or through appropriate library committees. Where institutions have an overall gift policy, of course, this must be followed. Even older materials have value—in the replacement of worn or missing copies, for instance, as well as providing needed duplicates to support heavy use.

OUT-OF-PRINT MATERIALS

It has been remarked several times that engineering books go out-of-print rapidly, and are thus unavailable through normal channels. Interlibrary loans, while occasionally effective although always slow, are not really a long-term solution to permanent collection deficiencies. It is essential for the acquisitions department of the institution to learn how to secure out-of-print materials, and it may become the job of the engineering librarian to assume the role of teacher in the process.

There are a number of retail book dealers who either specialize in out-of-print technical books or can provide a search service to locate them. PAB (Princeton Antiques Books) covers all scholarly fields. An example of a specialized dealer is John Roby, who maintains a large stock of out-of-print books and journals on all aspects of aeronautics and aviation. *AB Bookman's Weekly* publishes a yearbook with a subject index to specialized booksellers. Another listing of out-of-print dealers is that of Ruth Robinson's *Buy Books Where—Sell Books Where*.

RECORDS

Engineering libraries usually either have, or can get, computer facilities. In addition to the established advantages of online catalogs and circulation systems, it is relatively easy to devise a system that will aid the harried engineering selector in his or her job. First, a "search" file should be initiated to keep track of items being considered for acquisition. Next, a file of books actually on order should be formed. Finally, a file containing books already received is needed. These three files should cover a time period of perhaps a year, to allow for the various stochastic new book information inputs, ranging from premature publisher blurbs (as are most!) to delayed reviews. Little keyboarding is required after the initial entry, as most items can be moved successively from file to file as the order process progresses.

A major benefit of such a system is that the librarian can search all of the files, usually with one command, and find out if a book is in the acquisitions system and, if so, at what stage. With the plethora of inputs (approval plans, blurbs, patron requests, selection tools, etc.), such a system is necessary to preserve one's sanity, not to mention the reduction of the possibility of duplication. Another advantage is that delays can be spotted, and remedial action taken. By scanning order versus received dates, the efficiency of the acquisition process can be monitored. The system also facilitates the preparation of new book lists and, if properly augmented, can even keep track of the budget.

ONLINE SERVICES

As one of the newer phenomena, the implications of online searching for the acquisitions process should be briefly examined. In the long run, it will prove to be an extremely important tool, and is already making its mark. Many of the aforementioned problems regarding conference proceedings, patents, technical reports, journals, etc., can be at least ameliorated by judicious use of online services. When an item can be identified in a database, it is a simple matter in most cases to request a copy of the full text online, and have it in the patron's hands within a few days. The economics are obvious—why spend perhaps $500 to acquire the Eurasian Conference of Semiobioticalurgictal Endymosis when all the patron wants is the paper by Zygmund, and a copy can be obtained online for $10? Interlibrary loan is yet another route, should time permit.

There are at least 2,000 commercially available databases, and the number grows apace, covering many areas of technology. The *Directory of Online Databases* is updated quarterly, and is one of several publications keeping track of this burgeoning field. The major vendors with good coverage of engineering databases include:

BRS (Bibliographical Retrieval Services) .
Dialog Information Services
SDC Information Services

The acquisition implications for engineering libraries of online searching are only beginning to be recognized; the results of patron searches can and do place severe demands on collections, and provide valuable inputs as to research directions, as well as to areas where collection enhancement is needed.

COLLECTION DEVELOPMENT

This rubric, like networking, has become a buzz word in librarianship— indeed, a new level in the bureaucratic hierarchy has become well established—CDOs, or Collection Development Officers. Collection development statements are written, usually after extensive and expensive staff effort including committee meetings and other more or less well regulated activities. The present chapter, as well as the larger publication of which it is a part is, indeed, devoted to "collection development," or at least the mechanics of the process.

The basic problem with formal collection development policies for engineering collections is that they are usually out of date before they are written, unless they confine themselves to generalities that are unlikely to be helpful in practical situations; for instance, "we will only collect materials written in the English language." The field is moving so fast that only the foolhardy would attempt to forecast what type of materials will be bought even as early as next year!

Several processes have been suggested for monitoring the efficiency of the collection in doing what it is supposed to do—reviewing interlibrary loan requests, scrutinizing the results of online database searches, etc. These, plus active involvement with the faculty and professional staff who understand the research emphases at the host institution, are the most valid resources for structuring the development of the collection.

Selection Sources

AB Bookman's Weekly Yearbook. AB Bookman's Weekly, P.O. Box AB, Clifton, NJ 07015. Annually.

American Book Publishing Record. v.1- . 1960- . New York: Bowker. Monthly; annual cumulations available.

Associations' Publications in Print. v.1- . 1981- . New York: Bowker. Annually.

Baker & Taylor Companies, Professional and Technical Center, 6 Kirby Ave., Somerville, NJ 08876.

Blackwell North America, Inc., 1001 Fries Mill Rd., Blackwood, NJ 08012.

Books in Print. v.1- . 1948- . New York: Bowker. Annually.

BRS (Bibliographic Retrieval Services), div. of Information Technology Group, Thyssen Bornemisza Inc., 1200 Rt. 7, Latham, NY 12110.

Catalog of American National Standards. v.1- . 1985- . New York: National Standards Institute. Annually.

Civil Engineering ASCE: Environmental Design/Engineered Construction. 1930- . New York: American Society of Civil Engineers. Monthly.

D.A.T.A., Inc., P.O. Box 26875, San Diego, CA 92126.

Dialog Information Services, Inc., 3460 Hillview Ave., Palo Alto, CA 94304.

Directory of Online Databases. v.1- . 1979- . Santa Monica, Calif.: Cuadra Associates. Annually.

Directory of Published Proceedings: Science, Engineering, Medicine and Technology. v.1- . 1965- . Harrison, N.Y.: Interdok. Monthly with various cumulations.

Energy Research Abstracts. v.1- . 1977- . Oak Ridge, Tenn.: Technical Information Center, U.S. Dept. of Energy. Semimonthly; cumulative indexes available.

Forthcoming Books. v.1- . 1966- . New York: Bowker. Bimonthly. (Subject guide also available.)

Government Reports Announcements and Index. v.1- . 1961- . Springfield, Va.: National Technical Information Service. Semimonthly; cumulative indexes available.

Otto Harrassowitz, POB 2929, D-6200, Wiesbaden, W. Germany.

IC Master. v.1- . 1977- . Garden City, N.Y.: United Technical Publications. Annually.

Index-Directory of U.S. Industry Standards. Englewood, Colo.: Information Handling Services, 1985.

Information Handling Services, 15 Inverness Way East, Englewood, CO 80150.

Information Marketing International, Oak Park, MI 48237.

International Aerospace Abstracts. v.1- . 1961- . Washington, D.C.: National Aeronautics and Space Administration. Semimonthly; cumulative indexes available.

International Electrotechnical Commission, 3 rue de Varembe, 1211 Geneva 20, Switzerland.

Irregular Serials & Annuals; An International Directory. v.1- . 1967- . New York: Bowker. Irregularly. 10th ed., 1985.

LeBold, William K., and Carl Frey. "Major Findings & Methodology of 1985 Research Project on Utilization of Engineers." Boston Univ., IEEE Careers Conference, Oct. 1985. (Not yet published.)

Library of Congress. Cataloging Distribution Service. Customer Service Section. Washington, DC 20540.

McCullough, Kathleen, Edwin D. Posey, and Doyle Pickett. *Approval Plans and Academic Libraries.* Phoenix, Ariz.: Oryx, 1977.

Mechanical Engineering. 1906– . New York: American Society of Mechanical Engineers. Monthly.

Microprocessor Integrated Circuits. Ed. 1– . 1981– . San Diego: D.A.T.A. Semiannually.

Mildren, K. W., ed. *Use of Engineering Literature.* London: Butterworths, 1976.

Monthly Catalog of United States Government Publications. v.1– . 1895– . Washington, D.C.: U.S. Government Publications Office. Monthly.

Mount, Ellis, *University Science and Engineering Libraries.* 2nd ed. Westport, Conn.: Greenwood, 1985.

New Technical Books. v.1– . 1915– . New York: New York Public Library. Monthly.

NSA National Standards Assn., Inc., 5161 River Rd., Bethesda, MD 20816.

PAB (Princeton Antiques Bookshop), 2915–17 Atlantic Ave., Atlantic City, NJ 08401–6395.

PIE: Publications Indexed for Engineering. v.1– . 1971– . New York: Engineering Information. Annually.

Robinson, Ruth, and Daryush Farudi. *Buy Books Where—Sell Books Where; A Directory of Out-of-Print Booksellers and Their Author-Subject Specialties.* 4th ed. Morgantown, W.Va.: Ruth E. Robinson Books, 1984.

John Roby, Bookseller, 3703-K Nassau Dr., San Diego, CA 92115.

Scholarly Book Center, 3816 Hawthorn Ct., Waukegan, IL 60085.

Scientific and Technical Aerospace Reports. v.1– . 1961– . Washington, D.C.: National Aeronautics and Space Administration. Semimonthly; cumulative indexes available.

Scientific and Technical Books and Serials in Print. v.1– . 1978– . New York: Bowker. Annually.

SDC Information Services, System Development Corp., 2500 Colorado Ave., Santa Monica, CA 90406.

Subramanyam, Krishna. *Scientific and Technical Information Resources.* New York: Marcel Dekker, 1981.

Sweet's General Building Catalog File. v.1– . 1906– . New York: McGraw-Hill. Annually.

Technical Book Review Index. v.1– . 1935– . Pittsburgh: JAAD. Monthly, except July–Aug.

Thomas' Register of American Manufacturers and Thomas' Register Catalog File. v.1– . 1905– . New York: Thomas. Annually.

Ulrich's International Periodicals Directory. v.1– . 1943– . New York: Bowker. Annually with quarterly supplements.

Weekly Record. v.1– . 1975– . New York: Bowker. Weekly.

World Guide to Scientific Associations and Learned Societies. New York: Saur, 1982.

ENVIRONMENTAL STUDIES

Bill Robnett

The impact of human activity on the environment is not unique to contemporary society. However, earlier societies had a much more direct
dependence on the natural environment without that intervening buffer
of technology that seems to isolate us today.[1] Therefore, creating imbalances in ecosystems was potentially more disastrous for our forebearers
than for twentieth-century inhabitants. Technology has seemingly allowed
us a degree of control that, upon closer examination, may be much more
apparent than real. The study of humankind's attempts to live in balance
with, or more frequently, purposeful or incidental exploitation and manipulation of its environment has generated an extensive wealth of literature.

In the New World, agriculture, population increases, urban expansion,
and westward migration, and later the almost exponential growth of industry and manufacturing, began processes whose environmental consequences are strongly felt in the latter twentieth century. American environmentalism evolved from science and its methodology, growth of the
conservation movement, and challenges to Darwinian science in society's
manipulation of the natural environment. Audubon, Muir, Roosevelt, and
Olmstead, among many others, were key figures in the development of
the American environmental conscience.[2] Environmental activism has not
been confined to the latter nineteenth and early twentieth centuries. Very
few people have not heard of Rachael Carson and *Silent Spring*, Friends
of the Earth, the Nature Conservancy, and the Sierra Club. Neither has
environmental abuse, such as deforestation or desertification due to poor
agrarian practices, been confined to earlier times. Love Canal, Times Beach,

1. J. Donald Hughes, *Ecology in Ancient Civilizations* (Albuquerque: Univ. of New Mexico
Pr., 1975), pp. 3–4.
2. Donald Worster, *American Environmentalism: The Formative Period, 1860–1915* (New
York: Wiley, 1973), pp. 1 ff.

dioxin, strip-mining, acid rain, and the Superfund are issues of contemporary environmental abuse.

Federal and state governments have also been responsive to environmental concerns well before the passage of the National Environmental Policy Act in 1969 and the establishment of the Environmental Protection Agency (EPA) the following year. A list of major laws and ordinances from 1626 through 1974 is found in David and Barbara Harrah's *Conservation/Ecology: Resources for Environmental Education.* And the recognition that petroleum is not an infinite resource has prompted the federally supported search for alternative energy sources—and the often extreme environmental impact of extracting, then processing and refining such resources. Governments are in the forefront of energy/environment research.

The disparate nature of information sources resulting from our attempts to understand the ecosystem requires the selector in environmental studies to monitor scientific, technical, social, historical, political, economic, and legal publishing. Environmental studies also has generated its own literature with the development of research in environmental engineering, environmental toxicology, environmental history, environmental policy, environmental geology, etc.; but the lines between the pure and the applied disciplines and environmental studies are not clearly drawn. The selector not only should be alert to sources of selection with the terms "environment" or "conservation" prominently printed on the title page, but also should utilize sources associated with other disciplines such as biology, chemistry, agriculture, and history.

Because of the large role played by the federal government in environmental research and development, selectors need to be aware of major legislation and administrative regulations and their historical and current versions, as found in the *U.S. Code* and the *Code of Federal Regulations.* A very great percentage of publications in environmental studies is based upon these laws.

Guides to and Reviews of the Literature

An excellent guide to the literature of environmental studies is Kenneth Hammond's *Sourcebook on the Environment: A Guide to the Literature.* That the copyright was held by the Association of American Geographers until the end of 1984 (when it became part of the public domain) reiterates the very interdisciplinary nature of environmental studies. Contributors to the *Sourcebook* discuss environmental philosophies, perspectives, and trends; present case studies in major areas such as water quality, mining, urbanization, and agriculture; and describe major elements of the envi-

---

Environment Index/Environment Abstracts. v.1– . 1971– . New York: Environment Information Center. Annually. (*Environment Abstracts* monthly with annual cumulation.)

Subject and author index to books, conferences, films, government reports, and periodical articles about the environment.

Periodical articles, reports, and proceedings abstracted in *Environment Abstracts.*

Review section highlights major environmental issues of the year.

Entries for articles, reports, etc., published up to three years earlier.

Periodicals list included in annual index. Publications are abstracted rather than critically reviewed, and abstracts of periodical articles predominate. Both technical and more popular periodicals are covered. Full-text documents can be purchased from EIC, but many are available through NTIS. Directory of state, federal, and nongovernment organizations in each annual index. Index entries and abstracts are in subject-classified arrangement.

---

ronment. Another, perhaps more timely source is published annually in *Environment Index.* The *Index* includes overviews of national and international environment-related developments and environmental literature to keep the selector abreast of information upon which to base collection development decisions.

For selectors unfamiliar with the relevant literature of pure and applied sciences, Robert Malinowsky and Jeanne Richardson's *Science and Engineering Literature: A Guide to Reference Sources* and Dolores Owen's *Abstracts and Indexes in Science and Technology: A Descriptive Guide* may be useful in defining sources for these areas. For clarification of terms and concepts to the new selector, Sybil Parker's *McGraw-Hill Encyclopedia of Environmental Science and Engineering* and J. R. Pfafflin and E. N. Jiegler's *Encyclopedia of Environmental Science and Engineering* are useful. The former title also provides introductory material to environmental protection, urban planning, environmental analysis, and other areas, and the brief bibliographies at the end of the entries may be used as selection sources.

Research scientists, educators, and selectors in environmental studies face similar situations in keeping abreast of publishing in the field. One type of publication that is helpful is the literature review, which attempts to touch upon major developments in a research area and is generally broader in scope than the published article on a specific, more focused research topic. To the selector these present two choices: selection of the literature review serials for the environmental studies collection and then use of the reviews as checklists for the collection, as these literature reviews usually include extensive lists of references with which the collection can be compared. Although the references are mainly citations of journal articles, also referenced are conference proceedings, technical reports and notes, and occasional monographs.

In the interdisciplinary area of environmental studies, the following may be important to the collection: *Advances in Environmental Science and Engineering, Advances in Environmental Science and Technology, Annual Review of Public Health,* and CRC *Critical Reviews in Environmental Control.* The *Index to Scientific Reviews* can help the selector locate reviews on specific topics in review serials or in other serials that occasionally publish the longer review articles.

Current Selection

MONOGRAPHS, CONFERENCE PROCEEDINGS, AND REPORTS

Because of their broad scope, general selection tools such as *Choice, British Book News, Booklist/Reference Books Bulletin,* and *RQ* occasionally will review environmental studies publications. Environmental science reviews are more frequent in the science/technology-oriented *Science Books & Films, New Technical Books, Technical Book Reviews Index, Scientific American, Quarterly Review of Biology,* and *Nature.* The latter two titles tend to include reviews of titles more ecological than technical in emphasis.

The association journals, *Air Pollution Control Association Journal* and *Water Pollution Control Federation Journal,* publish reviews. The former also includes microcomputer software reviews and a bibliography of articles by subject, which may be used as a literature checklist for the collection. The journal *Environment* reviews a variety of publications, including new titles on environmental policy analysis. The reviews in the quarterly issues of *Urban Ecology* are in-depth. *Water, Air and Soil Pollution* and *Water Research* both include frequent reviews, while *Environmental Review* publishes reviews of titles with a historical emphasis.

Environment. v.1– . 1958– . Washington, D.C.: Heldref Publications. Monthly.
Current environmental issues periodical with monthly book review section. 1–2 year lag time between publication and review.
Monographs reviewed are professional and scholarly rather than popular. Selection of materials for review reflects emphasis of published articles—that is, future trends, environmental policy, economic aspects, government regulation, and social/historical issues, rather than technical publications. Complete bibliographic information and price are given for each title reviewed.

The *Journal of Economic Literature* has a review section on Natural Resources.

Although journal articles are predominant in abstracts and indexes in science and technology, these reference tools are also sources for selection of monographs, documents, and proceedings. *Ecological Abstracts, Pollution Abstracts, Environment Abstracts, Selected Water Resources Abstracts, WRC Information,* and *Biological Abstracts/RRM* all publish descriptive abstracts of these types of publications. In those abstracting services with a subject-classified arrangement, entries for journal articles published about specific topics can be used as a checklist to evaluate periodical holdings in the collection and to add titles where lacunae exist. Since conference proceedings are a challenge to you, the selector, who must determine the timeliness, relevance, and potential use of these usually costly publications, *Environment Index* is a useful guide. This annual has a list of important conferences during the preceding year with contact names, associations, etc. Selecting from this list can create a core collection of published proceedings, when these become available.

Bibliographies are a good selection source, and the selector in environmental studies may consider very useful the *CPL Bibliography* series from the Council of Planning Librarians, many of which cover environmental topics. The individual bibliographies include entries for monographs, reports, and journal articles, and many are annotated. The Rand Corporation produces bibliographies of its publications, entitled *A Bibliography of Selected Rand Publications*, followed by the subject. When there is no standing order for Rand reports, papers, notes, or memoranda, the subject bibliographies are selection tools for these publications. Rand will also send to selectors its monthly *Rand Checklist* of newly published documents in specific subject areas. Because the U.S. government contracts with the Rand Corporation for many of its projects, there may be some duplication when there is a U.S. depository documents collection within the library system. Subject bibliographies are also published by the federal government and will be discussed in the government publications section of this essay. Other examples of published bibliographies to be used as selection sources are Brian Clark's *Environmental Impact Assessment*, and Seymour Gold's *Man and the Environment Information Guide Series*, published by Gale Research.

Major trade publishers in environmental studies include Pergamon, Plenum, Elsevier, John Wiley, Springer-Verlag New York, Academic Press, and Bureau of National Affairs. All these publishers or their affiliates maintain mailing lists for their numerous brochures and flyers on forthcoming publications, both monographic and serial. Mailing addresses are in *Books in Print, Ulrich's,* or any of several other publishers' directories.

A selector will infrequently encounter a collection with no environment-related periodicals, particularly if science or engineering literature constitutes a major part of the collection. The interdisciplinary nature of the subject area is such that periodical holdings in life science, agriculture, or engineering periodicals generally include titles relevant to environmental studies. When adding new titles, index coverage should be considered, and lists of periodicals indexed in reference serials should be reviewed. The *Sourcebook on the Environment* appendix includes a selected list of periodicals, and *Conservation / Ecology: Resources for Environmental Education* has a relevant periodicals checklist. *Ulrich's* will need to be consulted to determine if these titles are current or have undergone name changes, since both guides are somewhat dated.

Publishers of journals will send review issues when requested. When Elsevier announces a new journal title in its monthly *New and Forthcoming Books and Journals*, there is usually a tear-out request card preaddressed to its Journal Information Center. Reviews of periodical titles are infrequent in published review sources, although the new journals issue of *Nature* may include titles that are environment-oriented.

Government Publications

One of the most active participants in and also publishers of environmental studies is the United States government. Its Environmental Protection Agency publishes numerous technical reports, which fortunately are provided a degree of bibliographic control by the *EPA Publications Bibliography* and its cumulations, useful as selection sources for EPA reports. The National Technical Information Service (NTIS), under the Department of Commerce, distributes EPA publications.

NTIS also publishes *Government Reports, Announcements and Index* (GRAI), which groups technical reports of the federal government into twenty-two subject areas. Although no section is devoted exclusively to the environment, NTIS abstract newsletters on numerous subjects, such as Environmental Pollution and Control, are available. These newsletters can be used as both selection sources and bibliographies for government publications. NTIS also compiles and publishes specialized subject bibliographies of reports, etc., that can be similarly used. These bibliographies are also identified in GRAI.

The U.S. Superintendent of Documents Government Printing Office's *Monthly Catalog* is another major bibliographic source of reports and publications for government agencies and departments. Environmental

---

EPA Publications Bibliography. v.1- . 1970- . Washington, D.C.: Library
Systems Branch, U.S. Environmental Protection Agency. Quarterly.
Abstracts of EPA technical reports available from NTIS.
6–18-month lag between publication and appearance in bibliography.
Report entries are arranged by NTIS number with keyword, sponsoring EPA
office, corporate and personal authors, and title indexes. Selection tool for collections requiring current information about applied technology in environmental protection and monitoring.

---

reports produced by the Army Corps of Engineers, Fish and Wildlife
Service, National Institute of Environmental Health Sciences, Office of
Technology Assessment, Council on Environmental Quality, etc., can be
identified for selection. GPO also compiles its own subject bibliographies
(class number GP3.22/2:), many of which are on environmental studies
topics and can be used as report selection tools. Similarly *LC Tracer Bullets*
are distributed by the GPO. Many of these bibliographic guides cover
environmental topics.

The U.S. Geological Survey is involved in monitoring water resources
and groundwater pollution, and its *Publications of the Geological Survey*
is another selection tool for reports, monographs, etc. The *Bibliography
and Index of Geology* includes some government publications and may
also be helpful when selecting in a subject area such as water pollution
and environmental geology.

ENVIRONMENTAL IMPACT STATEMENTS

The *Monthly Catalog* lists numerous government agencies involved in the
environmental impact assessment process. Most of these agencies issue
both draft and final environmental impact statements (EIS), which are
sources of information on proposed environmental modifications and their
potential effects upon water, soil, air, noise, as well as the cultural, social,
and archaeological aspects of the environment. Cambridge Scientific Abstracts publishes a useful selection tool entitled *EIS: Digests of Environmental Impact Statements.* This tool abstracts EIS, provides EPA numbers,
and has an agency/organization index for EIS developed under one body,
e.g., Department of the Army. The digest reports EIS often before they
appear in the *Monthly Catalog* or the *EPA Publications Bibliography.* If
a smaller core collection of representative EIS is preferred, *Environment
Index* lists major EIS submitted to EPA during the year and can be used
as a selection tool. Another resource for EIS is Northwestern University
Transportation Library, which owns nearly all EISs issued since 1969 and
will loan through regular interlibrary channels or through telephone or

---

EIS: Digests of Environmental Impact Statements. v.1– . 1977– . Bethesda, Md.: Cambridge Scientific Abstracts. Monthly with annual cumulations. Synopses of current draft and final environmental impact statements. 50–60 statements per issue in topical arrangement. Multiple indexes, including agency and subject. Selection source of environmental impact statements for research or specialized collections. Descriptions include purpose, positive and negative impacts, legal mandates, and prior references to draft statements.

---

written requests. The noncopyrighted materials can be reproduced, but requesting the reasonably priced EIS on microfiche from Cambridge Scientific Abstracts is probably more cost-effective.

Bibliographic control for government documents is a challenge to the environmental studies selector. *Guide to U.S. Government Publications* is very helpful in identifying sources, name changes, cessations, etc., that plague government documents.

Since U.S. government publications are in the public domain, there are publishers, such as Noyes Publications, that will republish government report data under a new title at a substantially increased cost, especially when compared with the microfiche format. The selector in environmental studies should be aware of this practice.

FOREIGN AND INTERNATIONAL GOVERNMENT PUBLICATIONS

United Nations (U.N.) publications are an excellent source of information on the environment, especially in the Third World. The U.N. Environment Program and the U.N. Educational, Social, and Cultural Organization are two agencies actively involved in studies of the environment.

Many countries have environment programs supported by government agencies. For example, in Great Britain, Her Majesty's Stationery Office distributes materials for the Department of the Environment. Government printing offices generally publish catalogs for document selection in environmental studies and other subject areas.

Although dated by the time of publication (and further complicated by determining which agency will actually provide documents), the Library of Congress publishes accessions lists for various regions of the world, such as Southeast Asia. These are another source for documents (and trade publications). Occasionally the Library of Congress will also prepare environmental assessment studies of other countries for government agencies, such as the Agency for International Development. GRAI will include some of these publications since NTIS often distributes them.

Organization Publications

Research, government, conservation, and protection organizations for the environment are numerous, and many of these groups publish as part of their educational, scholarly, or lobbying efforts. *Environment Index*, *Conservation Directory* (National Wildlife Federation), *World Environmental Directory* (Gough), *Environment U.S.A.* (Onyx Group), *Directory of Governmental Air Pollution Agencies*, and the journal *Water and Pollution Control* (for Canadian governmental agency information) are helpful in identifying these governmental, educational, and private organizations. *Associations' Publications in Print* and *Sources of Serials* list many of these groups' publications suitable for environmental studies collections. Many conservation and environmental protection groups publish but do not have the monetary resources to distribute brochures and flyers in large numbers like trade publishers. Directories, therefore, are essential for locating organizations to obtain publication information. These do become dated; e.g., *World Environmental Directory* (Gough) and *Environment U.S.A.* (Onyx Group); but much of the information is still useful.

Reference Publications

Eugene Sheehy's *Guide to Reference Books*, the Selected Reference Books feature in *College & Research Libraries*, *American Reference Books Annual*, *RQ*, and *Booklist/Reference Books Bulletin* are sources of existing and new reference publications in environmental science, as well as in related fields such as biology, chemistry, history, engineering, and economics. Dolores Owen's *Abstracts and Indexes in Science and Technology: A Descriptive Guide* describes the major abstracting and indexing services in the field of energy and environment. These include several titles published by the U.S. government, such as *Energy Research Abstracts*, *Selected Water Resources Abstracts*, and *Pesticides Abstracts*.

Retrospective Collection Development

The *Environmental History Series* provides an outstanding series of monographs, most with very extensive bibliographies, for sources in retrospective collection development. Loren Owing's *Environmental Values, 1860–1972: A Guide to Information Sources*, one volume of Seymour Gold's *Man and the Environment* series from Gale Research, is a bibliography emphasizing the historical development of awareness and concern for nature. Reviews of published works and also the references of the journal articles in *Environmental Review* may serve as a source of titles for retrospective collecting. In an environmental studies collection emphasizing technology and engineering, retrospective collecting is often limited to journal backruns, fill-ins, or earlier published technical reports, such as those from EPA.

Vendors are very helpful in retrospective collection development. For example, Blackwell North America can generate complete bibliographic records for titles published back to 1970 on subjects chosen from their detailed subject descriptor list. B. H. Blackwell, Ltd., is able to do the same back to 1979 for British books.

Conclusion

Organized and methodical collection development in environmental studies requires monitoring a wide and varied range of selection tools. The sources and strategies in this essay are meant to introduce or reacquaint librarians involved to one extent or another in that process. The selector will usually need to establish priorities for selection, since librarians in many institutions are not full-time bibliographers or select in several subject areas. Library policies and procedures may help dictate the priorities; e.g., some libraries are complete depositories. Also, financial constraints may allow little, if any, retrospective purchasing.

With experience you will develop your own methods and approaches to the subject area and will need to become familiar with new selection tools. The process evolves continually.

Selection Sources

Air Pollution Control Association Journal. v.1- . 1951- . Pittsburgh: The Assn. Monthly.
American Reference Books Annual. v.1- . 1970- . Littleton, Colo.: Libraries Unlimited. Monthly.
Associations' Publications in Print. v.1- . 1981- . New York: Bowker. Annually.
Bibliography and Index of Geology. v.1- . 1973- . McLean, Va.: Documents Index. Monthly. (Supersedes *Bibliography and Index of Geology Exclusive of North America.* 1933- .)
Biological Abstracts/RRM. v.1- . 1980- . Philadelphia: Biosciences Information Services. Semimonthly. (Supersedes *Bioresearch Index.* 1967- .)
Booklist/Reference Books Bulletin. v.1- . 1980- . Chicago: American Library Assn. 22/year.
Books in Print. v.1- . 1947- . New York: Bowker. Annually.
British Book News. v.1- . 1940- . London: British Council. Monthly.

Choice. v.1- . 1964- . Middletown, Conn.: Assn. of College and Research Libraries. Monthly.

Clark, Brian D., Ronald Bisset, and Peter Wathern. *Environmental Impact Assessment: A Bibliography with Abstracts.* London: Mansell, 1980.

College & Research Libraries. v.1- . 1939- . Chicago: American Library Assn. Bimonthly.

CPL Bibliography [series]. v.1- . 1979- . Monticello, Ill.: Council of Planning Librarians. (Supersedes *Exchange Bibliography* [series]. 1958- .)

Directory of Governmental Air Pollution Agencies. v.1- . 1955- . Pittsburgh: Air Pollution Control Assn. Annually.

Ecological Abstracts. v.1- . 1974- . Norwich, U.K.: Geo Abstracts. Bimonthly.

EIS: Digests of Environmental Impact Statements. v.1- . 1977- . Bethesda, Md.: Cambridge Scientific Abstracts. Monthly.

Environment. v.1- . 1958- . Washington, D.C.: Heldref. Monthly.

Environment Abstracts. v.1- . 1971- . New York: Environment Information Ctr. Monthly.

Environment Index v.1- . 1971- . New York: Environment Information Ctr. Annually.

Environmental History Series. v.1- . 1980- . College Station: Texas A&M Univ. Pr.

Environmental Review. v.1- . 1976- . Pittsburgh: American Society for Environmental History. Quarterly.

EPA Publications Bibliography Quarterly Abstracts Bulletin. v.1- . 1977- . Washington, D.C.: Library Systems Br. USEPA. Quarterly.

Gold, Seymour M., ed. *Man and the Environment Information Guide Series.* v.1- . 1975- . Detroit: Gale. Irregularly.

Gough, Beverly E., ed. *World Environmental Directory.* 4th ed. Silver Spring, Md.: Business Publishers, 1980.

Government Reports, Announcements and Index. v.1- . 1975- . Springfield, Va.: National Technical Information Service. Biweekly. (Supersedes *Government Reports Index* and *Government Reports Announcements* and other earlier publications.)

Guide to U.S. Government Publications. v.1- . 1973- . McLean Va.: Documents Index. Annually. (Supersedes Andriot, John L., ed. *Guide to United States Government Serials and Periodicals.* 1959- .)

Hammond, Kenneth A., George Macinko, and Wilma B. Fairchild, eds. *Sourcebook on the Environment: A Guide to the Literature.* Chicago: Univ. of Chicago Pr., 1978.

Harrah, David F., and Barbara K. Harrah. *Conservation/Ecology: Resources for Environmental Education.* Metuchen, N.J.: Scarecrow, 1975.

Index to Scientific Reviews. v.1- . 1974- . Philadelphia: Institute for Scientific Information. Semiannual.

Journal of Economic Literature. v.1- . 1963- . Nashville, Tenn.: American Economic Assn. Quarterly.

LC Tracer Bullets. 1972(?)- . Washington, D.C.: Library of Congress. Irregularly.

Library of Congress. Library of Congress Office, Djakarta. *Accessions Lists. Southeast Asia.* v.1- . 1975- .

Malinowsky, H. Robert, and Jeanne M. Richardson. *Science and Engineering Literature: A Guide to Reference Sources.* 3rd ed. Littleton, Colo.: Libraries Unlimited, 1980.

Monthly Catalog of United States Government Publications. v.1- . 1895- . Washington, D.C.: U.S. Superintendent of Documents. Monthly.

National Wildlife Federation. *Conservation Directory*. v.1- . 1956- . Washington, D.C.: The Federation. Annually.

Nature. 1869- . London: Macmillan.

New Technical Books: A Selective List with Descriptive Annotations. v.1- . 1915- . New York: New York Public Library.

Onyx Group, Inc., comp. and ed. *Environment U.S.A.: A Guide to Agencies, People, and Resources*. New York: Bowker, 1974.

Owen, Dolores B. *Abstracts and Indexes in Science and Technology: A Descriptive Guide*. 2nd ed. Metuchen, N.J.: Scarecrow, 1985.

Owings, Loren C. *Environmental Values, 1860-1972: A Guide to Information Sources*. Man and the Environment Information Guide Series. Detroit: Gale, 1976.

Parker, Sybil P., ed. *McGraw-Hill Encyclopedia of Environmental Science*. 2nd ed. New York: McGraw-Hill, 1980.

Pfafflin, J. R., and E. N. Jiegler. *Encyclopedia of Environmental Science and Engineering*. 2nd ed. New York: Gordon & Breach Science Pub., 1983.

Pollution Abstracts. v.1- . 1970- . Bethesda, Md.: Cambridge Scientific Abstracts. Bimonthly.

Publications of the Geological Survey. 1879/1961- . Alexandria, Va.: American Geological Inst.

Quarterly Review of Biology. v.1- . 1926- . Stony Brook, N.Y.: State Univ. Quarterly.

Rand Corporation. *A Bibliography of Selected Rand Publications*. v.1- . 1974- . Santa Monica, Calif.: Rand Corp. Irregularly.

_____. *Rand Checklist*. v.1- . 1979(?)- . Santa Monica, Calif.: Rand Corp. Monthly.

RQ. v.1- . 1960- . Chicago: American Library Assn. Quarterly.

Science Books and Films. v.1- . 1976- . Washington, D.C.: American Assn. for the Advancement of Science. 5/year.

Scientific American. 1845- . New York: Scientific American. Monthly.

Selected Water Resources Abstracts. v.1- . 1968- . Washington, D.C.: Water Resources Scientific Information Ctr., U.S. Dept. of the Interior. Monthly.

Sheehy, Eugene P., comp. *Guide to Reference Books*. 10th ed. Chicago: American Library Assn. 1986.

Sources of Serials. v.1- . 1977- . New York: Bowker. Irregularly.

Technical Book Review Index. v.1- . 1935- . Pittsburgh: JAAD Publishing Co. Monthly.

Ulrich's International Periodicals Directory. v.1- . 1932- . New York: Bowker. Annually.

Urban Ecology. v.1- . 1975- . Amsterdam: Elsevier. Quarterly.

Water, Air and Soil Pollution. v.1- . 1971- . Dordrecht, Netherlands: Reidel. 20/year.

Water and Pollution Control. v.1- . 1893- . Don Mills, Ont.: Southam Communications. 6/year. (Supersedes *Canadian Municipal Utilities*.)

Water Pollution Control Federation Journal. v.1- . 1928- . Washington, D.C.: The Federation. Monthly.

Water Research. v.1- . 1967- . Elmsford, N.Y.: Pergamon. Monthly.

WRC Information. Stevenage, U.K.: Water Research Ctr., 1974. (Supersedes *Water Pollution Abstracts* and *Water Research Assn. Library List*.)

GEOGRAPHY AND MAPS

Judith L. Rieke

Geography and maps are assumed to be inextricably linked and are often uttered in the same breath. And, indeed, there is an innate relationship between the two. Maps are the tools of geographers and constitute the end product of one of the divisions of geography—cartography. Geographers often utilize maps liberally to illustrate and express their ideas and findings.

As a result, some overlap is found in their literature, but since maps are a special and unique format, some materials are specific to them. Maps are also more difficult to obtain than standard geographical materials, whose acquisition process closely resembles that of printed materials for other academic disciplines. Due to these factors, a specific discussion on the literature and acquisition of maps follows the more general one on geographic materials.

Geography cannot be categorized as either a social or a physical science. It is truly interdisciplinary, in that it integrates knowledge and information from many areas. Geographers are comfortable using the language of the sociologist as well as that of the geologist.

Geography is concerned with providing an accurate, orderly, and rational description and interpretation of the various characteristics of the earth's surface. Geographers also study human ideas, feelings, and attitudes toward particular environments and places. Throughout this century the discipline has evolved from its strong heritage in earth science to a growing emphasis on human-land relationships, with much contemporary research

The author wishes to thank members of the Publications Committee of the Map and Geography Round Table of the American Library Association for their assistance. Phil Hoehn, Map Library, University of California, Berkeley, and Arlyn Sherwood, Illinois State Library, Springfield, Illinois, were particularly helpful. In addition, the author wants to thank Stan Hodge, Department of Library Service, Ball State University, Muncie, Indiana, for his comments.

108

centering on spatial relationships. Geography is involved in the locational significance of phenomenon.

It is very important to understand the interdisciplinary nature of the discipline when developing a geography collection. Often geographers need materials from several other fields that appear out of "scope" in terms of geography's general conception. There is no way to second guess what geographic researchers will need from other areas, so this discussion addresses only the acquisition of materials identified as "geographical" in the literature. When peripheral materials are needed, the librarian must rely on the researcher to identify specific materials and to accept such requests as legitimate.

Before acquiring materials in a discipline as diverse as geography, it is essential that the desired "level" of the collection be established. Considerable thought needs to be expended on who will use the geographical materials and for what purpose. Obviously, a library in a large university granting academic degrees in geography will need different, more specialized, and a larger number of materials from a library serving the general public.

Bibliography of Geography

After a clear idea of the needs of the collection's users is established, the next step is to ascertain whether or not the collection contains the "standard" geographical materials. This is most effectively accomplished by using guides to the geographical literature, or in cases where only basic sources are needed, guides to the general literature containing geographical sections. A good introduction to the literature is the chapter on geography by Chauncy D. Harris in the third edition of *Sources of Information in the Social Sciences,* edited by William H. Webb. The chapter is very comprehensive with bibliographic information on the most important works in geography. The approach is scholarly and topics covered include the history of geography, economic geography, physical geography, and regional geography.

After an introduction to the discipline, any standard guide lists sources needed by nearly all collections. For instance, the tenth edition of *Guide to Reference Books,* compiled by Eugene P. Sheehy, has much geographical information organized into four sections: general works, gazetteers, geographical names and terms, and atlases. Each section lists individual titles with bibliographic data and brief annotations. In addition to other standard guides, most basic reference texts also have a geographical section such as the one in *Fundamental Reference Sources* by Frances Neel Cheney and Wiley J. Williams (2d ed., 1980).

Cheney's book gives very thorough coverage to geographical information and discusses the subject in general before describing the various sources available. The arrangement begins with bibliographies, then covers literature guides, library catalogs, selection aids, government publications, maps and atlases, serial publications, dissertations, and place names. The extensive section on maps and atlases provides excellent suggestions for evaluating atlases.

It is interesting and beneficial to compare these and similar sources. Many of the same titles appear in each work, attesting to their necessity in a geography collection. They are not intended as "buying guides," but the basic information is presented so that only current price and availability are needed to make purchases.

SPECIALIZED BIBLIOGRAPHIES

For more extensive collections, specialized guides to the geographical literature need to be consulted. While there is not a large number from which to choose, the ones that exist are helpful in identifying retrospective works in a particular division of geography or about a particular region of the world. Thus, even if research interests of faculty members vary, these guides will enable the librarian to decide if the library's collection is sufficient to support their activities.

One of the easiest to use and most helpful of the guides is *Bibliography of Geography: Part I. Introduction to General Aids*, by Chauncy D. Harris. It has recently been reprinted and is available in paperback from the Department of Geography at the University of Chicago; it updates *Aids to Geographical Research: Bibliographies, Periodicals, Atlases, Gazetteers and Other Reference Books* by John Kirtland Wright and Elizabeth T. Platt. The first edition of this book was published in 1923, with the second edition appearing in 1947 as number twenty-two in the American Geographical Society Research Series.

Together, the 1976 Harris work and the 1947 Wright study cover most of the general aids published in the field of geography. Entries are annotated and sometimes evaluated. Wright and Platt's book begins with a section on "general aids" such as general bibliographies, serials and pe-

---

Harris, Chauncy D. *Bibliography of Geography: Part I. Introduction to General Aids*. Research Paper no.179. Chicago: Univ. of Chicago, Dept. of Geography, 1976.
Very comprehensive coverage of available sources. It is necessary to examine this work when evaluating a geographical collection. Order from Dept. of Geography, Univ. of Chicago, 5828 University Ave., Chicago, IL 60637.

riodicals, gazetteers, maps, and atlases. A section on "topical aids" for the divisions of geography, such as physical and human, follows; finally, the section Regional Aids discusses sources for different geographic regions of the world. Harris's book is exclusively devoted to the general aids because other volumes designed to provide a more comprehensive coverage of the works pertaining to the divisions and regions of the field are planned. Part II, published in 1984, is entitled *Bibliography of Geography: Part II. Regional. Vol.1. The United States of America.* Four other volumes are planned to cover the Soviet Union; the Americas (excluding the United States); Europe (excluding the Soviet Union); and Africa, Asia, Australia, and the Pacific.

A Guide to Information Sources in the Geographical Sciences by Stephen Goddard gives an overview of the retrospective literature as well as defining ways to keep a collection current. The book is organized in three parts: the systematic approach, which approximates subdivisions in geography such as geomorphology, historical, agricultural, and industrial geography; the regional approach, featuring Africa, South Asia, the United States, and the Soviet Union; and the tools of the geographer, such as maps, atlases, gazetteers, aerial photographs, archival materials, statistical methods, and the computer. Each section was written by a prominent geographer and is quite comprehensive. Both monographic and serial materials are covered; the extensive section on the United States is subdivided regionally.

However, Goddard's book presents problems for the user. Lack of an index prevents easy verification of titles. The reader must determine which section to browse through to find a title. It ignores Latin America in regional considerations. The citations are complete, but require current publishing information such as whether an item is still in print and its current price. Another problem is its style, which embeds the sources in the brief narrative. Selecting a particular source can be very tiresome.

Another guide, *The Literature of Geography* by J. Gordon Brewer, serves as an introductory guide, identifying the most useful, significant, and authoritative sources in geography. The 1978 book is very tightly organized and begins with a general discussion of the literature of geography that contains a section on the organization of geographical literature in libraries. This is somewhat weighted with a British bias, but is nonetheless very helpful. First, the main body of the work concentrates on general geography (bibliographies, reference works, periodicals, monographs, textbooks, and collections). This is followed by sections on maps, statistics, government publications, history of geography, geographical techniques, and methods. Finally are found the different divisions of geography: physical, human, and regional. A detailed index makes this a

Harris, Chauncy D. *A Geographical Bibliography for American Libraries.*
Washington, D.C.: Assn. of American Geographers, 1985.
Very current source designed specifically for libraries.
Covers literature from 1970 to the present.
Very extensive and thorough coverage.
The expressly stated purpose is to "assist libraries in the United States, Canada,
and other countries to identify, select, and secure publications of value in geography." Entries are arranged by major categories: general aids and sources;
history, theory and methodology of geography; the fields of physical geography;
the fields of human geography; applied geography; regional geography; and publications suitable for school libraries. It focuses on publications from 1970 to
1984. The index is thorough and contains authors, editors, and compilers, short
titles, and major subjects.

very usable source. Here again, citations need to be verified for current
information, but overall it is well organized and easy to use.

C. B. Muriel Lock's 1976 *Geography and Cartography: A Reference
Handbook* has a dictionary format containing an alphabetic listing of
names and terms from the geographical bibliographic world. The index
is extensive and, although somewhat dated, is still useful to verify standard
titles. This must be supplemented with current publishing information
before items can be purchased.

Examples of more specialized bibliographies include those published by
the Gale Research Company of Detroit as part of the *Geography and
Travel Information Guide Series.* In the series are *Remote Sensing of Earth
Resources,* edited by M. Leonard Bryan; *Historical Geography of the
United States; Travel in Asia,* edited by Neal Edgar and Wendy Ma; *Travel
in Canada,* edited by Nora T. Corley; *Travel in Oceania, Australia and
New Zealand,* edited by Robert E. Burton; and *Travel in the United States,*
edited by Joyce Post and Jeremiah B. Post. Those devoted to travel are
oriented toward recreation.

A few selection guides, intended primarily for librarians, target certain
works as essential for a collection. *A Geographical Bibliography for American Libraries,* edited by Chauncy D. Harris and published in 1985 by the
Association of American Geographers as a joint project with the National
Geographical Society, is the most current.

This work has two predecessors, *A Basic Geographical Library: A Selected and Annotated Book List for American Colleges* edited by Martha
Church, Robert E. Huke, and Wilbur Zelinsky in 1966 and *A Geographical
Bibliography for American College Libraries,* edited by Gordon Lewthwaite, Edward T. Price, Jr., and Harold A. Winters in 1970. The former
was publication number two of the Association of American Geographers
and was updated by the latter, which was published as Association of
American Geographers publication number nine.

These works were also expressly intended for librarians attempting to provide adequate coverage of the geographical literature for undergraduates. Their arrangement is similar to the 1985 work, but are not quite as extensive. There are major sections on general works and aids, geographical methods (including cartography, statistical methods), thematic geography (history, human, political, physical), and regional geography. The two earlier works have author (but no title) indexes so they can not be easily used for information about a specific title. Entries have complete bibliographic information including price, which must be checked for accuracy. There are brief annotations with some evaluations included.

CURRENT SELECTION SOURCES

Once standard works and other retrospective materials are identified through the guides and bibliographies, it is mandatory to monitor new publications in the field to keep the collection current. This is accomplished primarily through constant and routine examination of the current literature. The sources used depend on the level of the collection. To maintain a basic collection on a timely basis, the general library literature, such as *Library Journal, Choice,* and *Booklist,* as well as such general geographical or scientific journals as *Journal of Geography, Scientific American,* and *Science,* need to be consulted routinely for reviews.

More comprehensive collections require a more rigorous perusal of the geographic literature. The sources available can be categorized into three types: current bibliographies, periodicals in the field containing reviews, and publishers' catalogs. There are two major bibliographies currently being published in the English language, *Geo Abstracts* and *Current Geographical Publications.* The only other bibliography to match them in size is *Referativnyi Zhurnal: Geografiia,* published in the Soviet Union. *Geo Abstracts* is published by Geo Abstracts, Ltd. at the University of East Anglia (Norwich NR4 7TJ, England). It was previously known as *Geographical Abstracts* from 1972 to 1973 and before that as *Geomorphological Abstracts* from 1966 to 1971. There are seven separate series, each with six numbers a year. They are Landforms and the Quaternary, Climatology and Hydrology, Economic Geography, Social and Historical Geography, Sedimentology, Regional and Community Planning and Remote Sensing, and Cartography. The abstracts make it a very valuable source. Not only are periodical articles and monographs indexed and abstracted, but they are also accessible online through the GEOREF database.

Current Geographical Publications: Additions to the Research Catalogue of the American Geographical Society Collection of the University of Wisconsin–Milwaukee Library was previously published in New York when the collection was located there, but since March of 1978 it has been published in Milwaukee. It contains references to books, periodical articles, pamphlets, government documents, maps, and atlases that are located in the American Geographical Society (AGS) Collection. Arrangement utilizes the AGS classification scheme in four sections: topical, regional, maps, and selected books. Entries are just title entries with no annotations or abstracts. There are also a few selected reviews in each issue and annual cumulative indexes.

There are several geographic periodicals that publish lengthy and informative reviews of recently published materials. The titles listed at the end of this chapter represent only a sample of the English-language journals being published. It takes time to decide which journals are most helpful in the selection process. The research interests of faculty members must be taken into consideration when deciding which one to read. The most comprehensive list of geographical periodicals, the 1980 *International List of Geographical Serials* compiled by Chauncy D. Harris and Jerome D. Fellmann, as a University of Chicago Department of Geography research paper, contains 3,445 titles. A less formidable list is the *Annotated World List of Selected Current Geographical Serials*, another University of Chicago Department of Geography research paper by Chauncy Harris. It is a list of 443 current titles selected after a study to determine those titles most frequently cited in geographical indexes and bibliographies. In both lists, complete bibliographic information is given, including the publisher's name and address.

Collecting catalogs from publishers who emphasize geographical works is another way of "keeping current." Once on their mailing list, blurbs of any new publications occurring between catalog publications will be noted. After reading reviews and becoming familiar with the collection, the selector will quickly recognize those publishers specializing in different areas of the field. While there will always be unusual cases of material being published by an unknown or uncharacteristic publisher, most of the publishing will be predictable. At the end of this chapter is a partial list of the commercial publishers actively publishing works in geography. Not listed individually, but very prominent in the geographical publishing scene, are the university presses of this country and Great Britain; it is important to closely monitor their publishing activities.

Other additional sources of geographical information are the publications of the professional geographic organizations; a partial list of names and addresses is also found at the end of the chapter. These sources should be contacted directly for placement on their mailing lists.

Atlases

Atlases are a major source of geographical information of interest to all types of libraries, and their literature needs to be singled out and emphasized. Most general and specific geographical sources contain sections on atlases. In addition, some sources are dedicated solely to atlases. Well known, but out of date, S. Padraig Walsh's *General World Atlases in Print, 1972-1973: A Comparative Analysis*. It does have evaluations and a good introduction on evaluating an atlas. Another well known carto-bibliography is Kenneth L. Winch's 1976 *International Maps and Atlases in Print*. This focuses on bibliographic data, with a brief contents note. The geographic arrangement is helpful because it provides a picture of the atlases (or maps) available for a particular locale. Because it does not have a regular schedule for revision and updating, it cannot be relied upon in the same way as *Books in Print*. Materials listed are for sale at Stanford's International Map Centre (12/14 Long Acre, London WC2E 9LP) or GeoCenter Internationales LandKartenhaus (Honigwiesenstrasse 25, Postfach 80 08 30, D-7000 Stuttgart 80, Federal Republic of Germany). Many items might be for sale directly from publishers for a lower price, but dealing directly with foreign publishers is often expensive in terms of time and effort.

The recently published *Kister's Atlas Buying Guide: General English-Language World Atlases Available in North America*, by Kenneth F. Kister, accomplishes its purpose. It is limited to English-language material but has a valuable section on "Finding the Best World Atlases," as well as helpful appendixes such as a map and atlas bibliography, out-of-print map and atlas dealers, and atlas publishers and distributors.

Keeping current on newly published atlases is done in the same manner as other geographic materials; they are listed in many of the same sources previously discussed.

Acquisitions

Once needed materials are identified, the actual acquisition process is similar to that of other printed literature. Major publishers respond to orders placed through jobbers or agents. Many participate in approval plans and standing order arrangements. Favored publishers need to be approached on an individual basis to determine which method works most effectively.

When acquiring geographical materials, develop a profile of areas desired, establish the "levels of collection intensity," and formulate selection strategies. In this way the number of items needed will be more manageable and their magnitude will not be overwhelming. The collection will develop in a specified direction designed to best meet user needs.

Maps

Before purchasing maps for a library, it is important to determine who will be using them and for what purpose. Deciding what geographic areas will be collected is especially crucial. The levels of the map collection can be established through a collection development policy. There are excellent articles in the literature about this process in terms of maps and they should be consulted.[1] No policy is written in stone and any policy may need to be expanded or condensed on occasion. But at the outset, it will provide the necessary guidelines.

After levels are established, identification and acquisition of maps can proceed. Many of the geographical sources already discussed include maps and can be used to identify both retrospective and current ones. The problem found when using older guides is that often only small numbers of a map are produced; thus they are generally not available as long as standard print materials. This renders retrospective guides and bibliographies less useful for acquisition of maps than other geographic materials.

In order to obtain maps in a timely fashion at the level desired, use the same types of current sources as for geographic materials: current bibliographies, periodicals, and publisher's catalogs. Both of the current bibliographies mentioned. *Geo Abstracts* and *Current Geographical Publications*, contain new maps, as do most of the geographic periodicals listed at the end of the chapter. The most important of the periodical publications are those of major map librarians' associations. These list and review new maps as well as atlases and other geographic materials. Using them saves time and eliminates some of the need for searching other sources. In addition to containing valuable acquisitions information, they also have other tips that are invaluable to map keepers. The major ones are *Base Line*, the *Bulletin* of the Special Libraries Association, the *Newsletter* of the Association of Canadian Map Libraries, and the *Information Bulletin* of the Western Association of Map Libraries. Complete bibliographic information is given at the end of this chapter.

To a beginner, the selection of maps from a perusal of the current literature can appear overwhelming. If there is little familiarity with the

1. Charles Seavey, "Map Collection Development Planning: Mapkeeper and Library Administrator Working Together Can Tailor a Rational Acquisitions Policy," Western Assn. of Map Librarians, *Information Bulletin* 15:268–79 (June 1984); Alberta G. Koerner, "Acquisition Philosophy and Cataloging Priorities for University Map Libraries," *Special Libraries* 63:511–16 (Nov. 1972); Mary Larsgaard, *Map Librarianship: An Introduction* (Littleton, Colo.: Libraries Unlimited, Inc., 1978), pp. 40–42.

collection, it is often easier to get catalogs from publishers, check them against holdings, order maps needed. There are a large number of map publishers in existence, so it is important to determine which publishers produce the needed types of maps. At the end of this chapter is a selective list of publishers and the types of maps they publish. Nancy Kandoian compiled a very complete list of commercial publishers arranged by subject in *Base Line*. Another useful subject list appears in Appendix F of *Mapping Your Business* by Barbara Shupe and Colette O'Connell.

By far the largest publishers of maps are federal, state, local, and foreign governments. They publish not only topographic maps but also several types of thematic maps. Morris Thompson's 1981 *Maps for America* does an excellent job of explaining the types of maps published by the federal government, with emphasis on the topographic map. It also has an appendix with the addresses of various governmental agencies. Those addresses are often subject to change, but can be updated by consulting a federal directory.

The easiest way to obtain government mapping is through a depository agreement. State and local governments may establish agreements, but each agency needs to be contacted individually to solidify them. In terms of the federal government, the majority of depository agreements are with either the Government Printing Office (GPO), which handles maps produced by the United States Geological Survey (USGS) and the Defense Mapping Agency (DMA), or the National Ocean Service (NOS). Usually if a library is a depository for government documents, maps published by GPO can be selected also. Some examples of those maps are the national forest and census maps. Consult the government documents librarian to ascertain exactly which maps can be received or write to GPO directly.

USGS distributes maps for the GPO. Shipping lists are included with shipments so there is better control over items being received. To keep current on everything the survey is publishing, the monthly *New Publications of the U.S. Geological Survey* needs to be read. It is free upon request from the survey and is cumulated yearly under the title *Publications of the Geological Survey*. Beginning in 1879, it serves as a good record of mapping done in this country by USGS. Access is by subject, author, and geographic location. However, the cumulations contain only thematic maps, not topographic maps.

To get an overview of government mapping for a particular area, obtain an index map of the locale in question. Index maps are usually free and can be requested from the governmental agency responsible for producing them. They show an outline of the geographic area with the map quadrangles marked off and identified so the specific maps needed are easily selected. For instance, if it is necessary to know what USGS topographic maps are available for a state, write to the survey and request the state

Field, Lance. *Map Users Sourcebook*. New York: Oceana Publications, 1982. Brings together in one book the many sources of obtaining maps. Also provides some narrative and explanation that is very helpful to the novice.

index map. The index maps also list dealers in each state from whom the maps can be purchased. Purchasing directly from USGS is also possible. Maps for areas east of the Mississippi can be purchased from the Branch of Distribution, USGS, 1200 S. Eads St., Arlington, VA 22202; for areas west of the Mississippi, purchase from the Branch of Distribution, USGS Box 25286, Denver Federal Center, Denver, CO 80225.

In addition, state agencies dealing with conservation or geology often have USGS maps for sale. There are, in addition, nine regional Public Inquiries Offices of the U. S. Geological Survey that sell maps and can also offer a great deal of assistance with any map-related questions. Contact the National Cartographic Information Center (NCIC) for the address and telephone number of the nearest office. NCIC is part of the U. S. Geological Survey and is located at 507 National Center, Reston, VA 22092 (703) 860-6045. It was established to give assistance to cartographic users and has affiliate offices in nearly every state. Addresses, telephone numbers, and the names of contact persons for the state affiliates are available upon request from the NCIC in Reston. Since there is some variability in services of state affiliates, it is necessary to find out the details directly from them.

For further assistance through the government mapping maze there are some excellent publications available. The July-August, 1983, issue of *Government Publications Review* is devoted entirely to government mapping. Topics include international mapping, federal mapping, state and local map publishing, maps of western nations and mapping in developing countries. *Map User's Source Book* by Lance Field gives many addresses for purchasing maps produced by the public sector. The book contains an alphabetic list by state that usually includes the tourist bureaus, highway department, state geological survey, or department of conservation. At the federal level the different offices and products are described and detailed lists of addresses are given. Particularly helpful is the list of offices of the Bureau of Land Management, U.S. National Forest Service, U.S. National Park Service, and U.S. National Wildlife Refuges. It is often difficult to determine what mapping exists for those areas; thus, having a direct address and telephone number enables one to ferret out the information more quickly. The Shupe and O'Connell book *Mapping Your Business* explains in clear and concise terms the different government agencies and their products. There is an extensive, annotated list of federal and state government map sources in Appendixes C and D.

Shupe, Barbara, and Colette O'Connell. *Mapping Your Business.* New York: Special Libraries Assn., 1983.
Although written expressly for the business community, this compact volume provides background information about maps that any novice mapkeeper can use. A section on computerized cartography is particularly helpful. There are extensive appendixes with sources of maps.

Maps of local areas are usually the most in demand, and it is only logical that a collection should have strong holdings of maps of the immediate surroundings. If there is more than one map collection in an area, an effort to contact the other responsible librarians to find out about their collections should be made. Usually a cooperative collection policy can be established, so that collections will complement one another and duplication can be kept to a minimum except for very heavily used items. Obtaining local mapping is difficult because local governmental mapping usually is not organized under one agency. Maps will be scattered throughout several city and county offices, such as the tax assessor's, planning, and zoning offices. A directory of city offices and some telephone calls often leads to several sources. Even though they are generally not in the map-selling business, if paper is provided they may be willing to make copies for a nominal fee. Although it takes more time and effort to acquire local maps, it will be well worth the effort.

Mapping done by other countries' governments can be equally mystifying. The U.S. Geological Survey Circular number 934, *Worldwide Directory of National Earthscience and Related International Agencies*, lists the national earth science agencies of 160 countries in the world as well as eighty-seven international organizations. Most of those listed are the map producers for their countries. This list is updated every few years. Another source for some of these addresses is the annual August issue of *Geotimes* (see the list of journals at the end of the chapter). It lists international mapping agencies as well as state geological agencies. Countries may be contacted directly requesting index maps and price lists for the areas of interest. It is cheaper to buy maps directly from map-producing agencies in English-speaking countries, such as Canada and Great Britain, but beyond that there are often problems in dealing with foreign governments in terms of currency exchange, communications, and prepayments.

A more expensive, though sometimes easier, method of attaining foreign mapping is through a map dealer. Two were previously mentioned in conjunction with Kenneth Winch's *International Maps and Atlases in Print*—Stanford's in England and GeoCenter in Germany. Geo Center also has a separate catalog available in two sections for purchase. The first part, *Band 1. Touristische Veröffentlichungen*, is more tourist oriented

Allison, Brent. "Map Acquisition: An Annotated Bibliography." Western
Assn. of Map Libraries, *Information Bulletin* 15:16–25 (Nov. 1983).
Brings together all the various articles written about map acquisitions. The an-
notations help point out which are "must" reading.

and has maps, plans, guides, atlases and globes. It is produced annually
in a bound volume. The second part, *Band 2. International. Amtliche
Geographisch-Thematische Karten und Atlanten* (official geographic-the-
matic maps and atlases), is in two loose-leaf volumes with updates several
times each year. There are index sheets for each country showing the
status of publication and availability of maps in key topographic and
thematic series. It is supplemented by *Geo-Kartenbrief*, published four to
six times each year, listing major new publications. If using a dealer, orders
are placed, maps and invoices are received, and invoices are paid just as
with other library materials. This is much more pleasant than hassling with
a foreign government over the receipt of a map that was prepaid months
ago. There are other small companies and also some individuals who sell
maps of various countries. Their names and addresses appear frequently
in the map librarian publications previously mentioned.

Many libraries maintain collections of city street maps. While it is possible to solicit free maps, many cities are now charging for them. Use the
U.S. Chamber of Commerce Directory for addresses of cities whose maps
are needed, but if solicitation does not yield satisfactory results, the maps
of major cities can be purchased from a commercial map publisher (See
the list at the end of this chapter).

Commercial publishers also produce a variety of other maps as noted
in the annotations at the end of the chapter. Ordering from a commercial
publisher is similar to purchasing other library materials. The order information needs to be as specific as possible; always note whether or not
prepayment is required. Commercial publishers usually invoice, whereas
government agencies often require prepayment if items are purchased.

The vagaries of map acquisitions have long been lamented by librarians,
and this brief overview serves only as an introduction. A recent annotated
bibliography "Map Acquisition" was compiled by Brent Allison. This book
should be thoroughly examined by anyone involved in cartographic acquisitions. Two other helpful items are the lengthy *Map Sources Directory*
by Janet Alin, and "Sources of U.S. Maps and Map Information" by Mary
Galneder.[2] Seeking out maps is truly an endeavor that requires energy and
ingenuity but is very rewarding to the persistent.

2. Mary Galneder, "Sources of U.S. Maps and Map Information," *American Cartographer*
suppl. to v.11:73–77 (Summer 1984).

Selection Sources

Alin, Janet. *Map Sources Directory.* 2nd rev. ed. Downsview, Ont.: York Univ., Scott Library, Map Library, 1982. Periodic updates; loose-leaf.

Bibliographic Guide to Maps and Atlases. v.1- . 1979- . Boston: Hall. Annually.

Brewer, J. Gordon. *The Literature of Geography.* 2nd ed. London: Clive Bingley, 1978.

Cheney, Frances Neel and Wiley J. Williams. *Fundamental Reference Sources.* 2nd ed. Chicago: American Library Assn., 1980.

Church, Martha, Robert E. Huke, and Wilbur Zelinsky. *A Basic Geographical Library; A Selected and Annotated Book List for American Colleges.* Publication no. 2. Washington, D.C.: Assn. of American Geographers, 1966.

Field, Lance. *Map User's Source Book.* London and New York: Oceana, 1982.

Goddard, Stephen. *A Guide to Information Sources in the Geographical Sciences.* Totowa, N.J.: Barnes & Noble, 1983.

Harris, Chauncy D. *Annotated World List of Selected Current Geographical Serials.* Research paper no.194. 4th ed. Chicago: Univ. of Chicago. Dept. of Geography, 1980.

_____. *Bibliography of Geography: Part I. Introduction to General Aids.* Research paper no.179. Chicago: Univ. of Chicago. Dept. of Geography, 1976.

_____. *Bibliography of Geography: Part II. Regional. Vol. 1. The United States of America.* Research paper no.206. Chicago: Univ. of Chicago. Dept. of Geography, 1984.

_____. *A Geographical Bibliography for American Libraries.* Washington, D.C.: Assn. of American Geographers, 1985.

_____, and Jerome D. Fellmann. *International List of Geographical Serials.* Research paper no.194. 3rd ed. Chicago: Univ. of Chicago, Dept. of Geography, 1980.

Kandoian, Nancy. *Base Line* 4(1983).

Kister, Kenneth F. *Kister's Atlas Buying Guide: General English-Language World Atlases Available in North America.* Phoenix, Ariz.: Oryx, 1984.

Larsgaard, Mary, ed. "Map Librarianship and Map Collections." *Library Trends* 29 (Winter 1981).

Lewthwaite, Gordon, Edward T. Price, Jr., and Harold A. Winters. *A Geographical Bibliography for American College Libraries.* Publication no.9. Washington, D.C.: Assn. of American Geographers, 1970.

Lock, C. B. Muriel. *Geography and Cartography: A Reference Handbook.* 3rd rev. ed. London: Clive Bingley, 1976.

Nichols, Harold. *Map Librarianship.* 2nd ed. London: Clive Bingley, 1982.

Seavey, Charles, ed. *Government Publications Review* 10 (July–Aug. 1983).

Sheehy, Eugene. *Guide to Reference Books.* 10th ed. Chicago: American Library Assn., 1986.

Shupe, Barbara, and Colette O'Connell. *Mapping Your Business.* New York: Special Libraries Assn., 1983.

Thompson, Morris. *Maps for America.* 2nd ed. Washington, D.C.: Government Printing Office, 1981.

Walsh, S. Padraig. *General World Atlases in Print, 1972-1973: A Comparative Analysis.* 4th ed. New York: Bowker, 1973.

Webb, William H., ed. *Sources of Information in the Social Sciences.* 3rd ed. Chicago: American Library Assn., 1986.

Winch, Kenneth L., ed. *International Maps and Atlases in Print*. 2nd ed. New York: Bowker, 1976.
Wright, John Kirtland, and Elizabeth T. Platt. *Aids to Geographical Research: Bibliographies, Periodicals, Atlases, Gazetteers and Other Reference Books*. 2nd ed. (1947). Repr.: Westport, Conn.: Greenwood, 1971.

Journals

American Cartographer. v.1- . 1974- . Washington, D.C.: American Congress on Surveying and Mapping. Semiannually. (Has reviews of atlases and "Cartographic News.")
Association of American Geographers. *Annals*. v.1- . 1911- . Washington, D.C.: The Assn. Quarterly. (Has lengthy book reviews and advertisements.)
Association of Canadian Map Libraries. *Newsletter*. v.1- . 1969- . Ottawa, Ont.: The Assn. Irregularly. (Lists and reviews all types of cartographic materials.)
Base Line. no.1- . 1980- . Chicago: American Library Assn., Map and Geography Round Table. Bimonthly. (Very current information and lists of maps, atlases, books, publishers.)
Cartographic Journal. v.1- . 1964- . London: British Cartographic Soc. Semiannually. (Lists new maps received by the Map Library at the Royal Geographic Society since the discontinuance of its *New Geographical Literature and Maps*. Also lists recent maps and atlases received in the Bodleian Library and has book reviews. Has a British perspective.)
Economic Geography. v.1- . 1925- . Worcester, Mass.: Clark Univ. Quarterly. (Has book reviews.)
Geographical Journal. v.1- . 1893- . London: Royal Geographical Soc. Quarterly. (Has reviews of books, maps, and atlases.)
Geographical Magazine. v.1- . 1935- . London: IPC Magazines. Monthly. (British counterpart to *National Geographic*. Some book reviews; tends to be oriented toward travel and recreation.)
Geographical Review. v.1- . 1916- . New York: American Geographical Soc. Quarterly. (Has critical book reviews.)
Geotimes. v.1- . 1956- . Falls Church, Va.: American Geological Institute. Monthly. (Has book reviews and lists of new maps, but emphasis is geological.)
Journal of Geography. v.1- . 1902- . Chicago: National Council for Geographic Education. Monthly, except July and August. (Designed for geographic educators; has book reviews.)
Professional Geographer. v.1- . 1949- . Washington, D.C.: Assn. of American Geographers. Bimonthly. (Has many book reviews and also advertisements from geographical publishers.)
Special Libraries Assn. Geography and Map Div. *Bulletin*. v.1- . 1947- . New York: The Assn. Quarterly. (Has book reviews as well as lists of new books, maps, and atlases.)
Western Assn. of Map Libraries. *Information Bulletin*. v.1- . 1969- . Santa Cruz, Calif.: The Assn. 3/year. (Book reviews as well as lists of new maps and other cartographic information.)

Publishers

Academic Press, 111 Fifth Ave. New York, NY 10003.
Allen & Unwin Inc., 9 Winchester Ter., Winchester, MA 01890.

Blackwell Scientific Publishers, 52 Beacon St., Boston, MA 02108.
Elsevier Science Publishing Co., Inc., 52 Vanderbilt Ave., New York, NY 10017.
W. H. Freeman & Co., 41 Madison Ave., 37th Fl., New York, NY 10010.
Harper & Row Pubs., Inc., 10 E. 53rd St., New York, NY 10022.
Methuen, Inc., 733 Third Ave., New York, NY 10017.
Pergamon Press, Inc., Maxwell House, Fairview Park, Elmsford, NY 10523.
St. Martin's Press, Inc., 175 Fifth Ave., New York, NY 10010.
Springer-Verlag New York, Inc., 175 Fifth Ave., New York, NY 10010.
John Wiley & Sons, 605 Third Ave., New York, NY 10158.
University presses, especially Oxford Univ. Pr., 200 Madison Ave., New York, NY
10016 and Cambridge Univ. Pr., 32 E. 57th St., New York, NY 10022.

Professional Societies

American Cartographic Assn. (ACA). c/o American Congress on Surveying and
Mapping, 210 Little Falls St., Falls Church, VA 22046. (703) 241-2446.
American Geographical Society (AGS). 156 Fifth Ave., Suite 600, New York, NY
10010. (212) 242-0214.
American Society of Cartographers (ASC). P.O. Box 1493, Louisville, KY 40202.
Assn. of American Geographers (AAG). 1710 16th St. N.W., Washington, DC
20009. (202) 234-1450.
Commonwealth Geographical Bureau (CCB). J. T. Parry, Dir., Geography Dept.,
McGill Univ., 805 Sherbrook St. West, Montreal, PQ H3A 2K6 Canada.
International Cartographic Assn. (ICA). c/o Don Pearce, Secy. Treas., 24 Strickland
Rd., Mt. Pleasant, Perth 6153, Australia.
International Geographical Union (IGU). Univ. of Chicago, 5828 University Ave.,
Chicago, IL 60637.
International Map Dealers Assn. (IMDA). c/o MAPSCO, Inc., 1644 Irving Blvd.,
Dallas, TX 75207.
National Geographic Society (NGS). 17th and M St., N.W., Washington, DC
20036. (202) 857-7000.
North American Cartographic Information Society (NACIS). c/o Ronald M. Bol-
ton, 8060 13th St., Rm. 1112, Silver Spring, MD 20910.
Pan American Institute of Geography and History (PAIGH). Ing Leopold Rodri-
guez, Ex-Arzobispado 29, Col Observatorio, 11860 Mexico 18 DF.
Socially and Ecologically Responsible Geographers (SERGE). Dept. of Geography,
Mail Location 131, Univ. of Cincinnati, Cincinnati, OH 45221. (513) 475-3421.
Society of Women Geographers (SWG). 1619 New Hampshire Ave., Washington,
DC 20009. (202) 265-2669.

Selected Map Publishers

American Map Co., Inc., 46-35 54th Rd., Maspeth, NY 11378. (Specializes in
educational maps, especially small outline maps.)
Champion Maps, P.O. Box 5545, Charlotte, NC 28225. (Good source of road and
street maps for American cities.)
George F. Cram Co., Inc., 301 S. La Salle St., P.O. Box 426, Indianapolis, IN
46206. (Specializes in educational maps, especially large wall maps.)

Facts on File, Inc., 460 Park Ave. South, New York, NY 10016. (Outline maps in a loose-leaf binder, handy for copying. Called *Maps on File.*)

Gousha/Check-Chart, 2001 The Alameda, P.O. Box 6227, San Jose, CA 95150. (Another reliable source of city and state maps.)

Hammond, Inc., 515 Valley St., Maplewood, NJ 07040. (Many types of maps, predominantly political. Good source for state and city street maps.)

National Geographic Society, 17th and M Streets, N.W., Washington, DC 20036. (Maps familiar to all readers of the *National Geographic Magazine.*)

Rand McNally & Co., P.O. Box 7600, Chicago, IL 60680. (Well-known publishers of highway and street maps.)

Ryder Geosystems, 445 Union, Suite 304, Denver, CO 80228. (Deals largely with cartographic products related to space imagery; emphasis on geology.)

Sanborn Map Co., Inc., 629 Fifth Ave., Pelham, NY 10803. (Produces maps for city and other governmental agencies. Very detailed city maps; older ones are invaluable for historical purposes.)

HEALTH SCIENCES

Beth M. Paskoff

Librarians in hospital and medical school libraries collect health science materials to support the research, education, and clinical practices of those health professionals who use such libraries. When other librarians in general academic or public libraries collect health sciences materials, they may do so for similar reasons. They may be supporting research or education programs whose staff needs access to medical information, or they may have a sufficient number of users who want to read sources of information available to physicians. Other health science collections are based not on the professional books and journals, but rather are developed for those readers who seek easier materials that are health, rather than disease, oriented. Such collections have come to be referred to as consumer health information libraries, and the librarians responsible for selecting these health sciences materials will use different sources to identify appropriate purchases.

The librarian collecting professional medical books and journals will find the publishing emphasis similar to that in most of the science and technology disciplines. Primary sources, especially journal articles, are the most frequently used means of remaining current with the new developments in medicine. Monographic publications, with the exception of a core collection of texts, are less frequently used, but can still be important sources of synthesized information. The texts, used both in medical education and by practicing physicians, are references used on a daily basis in medical libraries and could serve as a basic book collection in most upper level academic libraries.

One of the areas most strongly affected by the rise in consumerism has been the health care industry. The explosion of interest in diets, jogging, and electronic blood pressure monitors is reflected in libraries by the increased demand for consumer health information. Librarians collecting to meet this demand will be looking not for the classic text in internal

125

medicine, but rather for material written for the lay reader. There is an abundance of such information published in books, popular magazines, and pamphlets, much more than any one library will want to collect. Many of these publications promote fads or unconventional medical practices, or duplicate information already available in the collection. The accuracy of the information also varies, and librarians will need to rely on reviews and bibliographies to wisely select from the wide range of available quality and quantity.

Guides to the Literature

Several excellent guides to the health sciences literature are available. Volume 2 of the Medical Library Association's *Handbook of Medical Library Practice*, edited by Louise Darling, includes chapters on collection development and acquisition of health sciences library materials. Although intended primarily for medical librarians, there is much in this fine overview that will be of use to any librarian responsible for selecting health sciences materials. *Introduction to Reference Sources in the Health Sciences*, by Fred Roper and Jo Anne Boorkman, is a more detailed look at specific bibliographic and informational sources. Librarians interested in guides to information for the lay reader will find Alan Rees and Jodith Janes's *The Consumer Health Information Source Book* and Rees's *Developing Consumer Health Information Services* to be excellent sources for those developing or evaluating such collections. Occasionally, general library publications include reviews of medical information sources, such as the entire April, 1985, issue of *Illinois Libraries*, which was devoted to health information resources.

In addition, a number of more general publications can be used to identify standard health sciences works. *Guide to Reference Books* by Eugene Sheehy and *Walford's Guide to Reference Materials* can be sources

---

Rees, Alan M., and Jodith Janes. *The Consumer Health Information Source Book*. 2nd ed. New York: Bowker, 1984.
Bibliographies of consumer health information.
Very current in 1984; now slightly out of date.
Includes annotated bibliographies of selection guides, health magazines, health information clearinghouses and hotlines, as well as more specific topics including human sexuality, pregnancy and childbirth, mental health, substance abuse, and cancer. Within these categories there are separate listings of books and pamphlets. Appendixes of publishers and pamphlet suppliers, author, title and subject indexes follow. Also includes a section on medical consumerism and the need for libraries to provide reliable health information to the public.

Brandon, Alfred N., and Dorothy R. Hill. "Selected List of Books and Journals for the Small Medical Library." *Bulletin of the Medical Library Association* 73:176–205 (Apr. 1985).
Core collection.
Approximately 550 books, 135 journals.
Very current; announces forthcoming new editions.
Since 1965, "The Brandon List" has been a standard guide for development of medical collections. The core list is categorized by subject, and can be used either as a selection aid or as a guide for evaluating existing collections. Very small collections may purchase only the asterisked titles, representing thirty to forty percent of the total list. The list is updated every two years, and is published in the April issue of the *Bulletin of the Medical Library Association* in odd-numbered years.

to identify common reference works. The third edition of *Science and Engineering Literature: A Guide to Reference Sources*, by H. Robert Malinowsky and Jeanne Richardson, has a chapter on the biomedical sciences that includes references to other guides to the literature as well as standard reference sources.

Selectors in the health sciences are fortunate to have a number of core lists available for evaluating existing collections or for selecting new acquisitions. The best known of these is Alfred Brandon and Dorothy Hill's "Selected List of Books and Journals for the Small Medical Library," a standard work that identifies core collections for smaller medical libraries, such as those in hospitals. Larger, more general libraries with small health sciences collections will also find this list to be a sound selection of clinical books and journals. Now in its eleventh revised version, the list of more than 500 titles is updated every two years in the *Bulletin of the Medical Library Association* and has become a benchmark for evaluating current health sciences collections. Monthly updates to the "Brandon List" are published in *A Majors Report*, a newsletter published by Majors Scientific Books. Some approval plan vendors can also supply books designated as on the "Brandon List."

The entries in the "Brandon List" are grouped by subject and include price information to help in budgeting. Although $45,200 would be required to subscribe to all of the journals and purchase all of the books on the 1985 list, a shorter list of asterisked titles is available for much less. Rees also provides a very short core list in *The Consumer Health Information Source Book* consisting of one index, four journals, and thirteen books that can be purchased for less than $800.

Other core lists are available in specialized fields, such as "Selected List of Nursing Books and Journals" and "Selected List of Books and Journals in Allied Health Sciences," both by Brandon, or "Sports Medicine" by

Pat McCandless. Extensive bibliographies, such as that by Susan Salisbury on occupational health, T. Austin on socioeconomic resources, or A. Kowitz on dentistry, can also be used by collection development librarians. As part of a project funded by the New York State Library, the Onondaga County Public Library Health Information Clearinghouse Project developed a core collection of consumer health publications for public libraries, described by Christine Bain in *Health Information for the Public Library*. Regardless of the list selected, it is important not to rely exclusively on these core lists because they may not be current or specific enough to meet the needs of each library, but they can be a good starting place for many health science collections.

PUBLISHERS

Major trade publishers in the health sciences include Aspen Systems Corporation, Churchill Livingston, Grune & Stratton, Lange Medical Publications, Lippincott, Mosby, Saunders, and Williams & Wilkins. Scholarly and professional societies sponsor the publication of many of the journals in the health sciences, and may publish monographs as well. Among the most significant are the American Dental Association, the American Hospital Association, the American Medical Association, the American Nurses Association, the American Psychiatric Association, and the National League for Nursing. Material for the lay reader is readily available from the publication offices of the American Cancer Society, the American Diabetes Association, the American Heart Association, the National Kidney Foundation, and other voluntary health organizations. An extensive list, with addresses, is available in the *Consumer Health Information Source Book* by Alan Rees and Jodith Janes. Most societies will provide publication catalogs when requested, and large associations may keep libraries on their mailing lists to receive regular updates. With others, it will be necessary to write annually in order to receive a current list. Pharmaceutical companies and large insurance companies may also publish appropriate consumer health information. The United States government is a major (and often overlooked) publisher of health sciences information, including a large quantity of free or inexpensive consumer health information. The World Health Organization, an allied agency of the United Nations, is also a significant publisher of international information.

BOOK SELECTION

Naturally, no single source can be relied upon exclusively in health sciences materials. Reviews of general and popular books and audiovisual materials can be found in *Library Journal, Choice, Science Books and Films* and other standard collection development review tools. Medical journals that

---

JAMA: Journal of the American Medical Association. v.1- . 1848- . Chicago: American Medical Assn. Weekly.
Clinical medical journal.
5–10 signed reviews per issue.
Average lag time 6–8 months.
One of the most important U.S. medical journals, *JAMA* publishes five to ten signed book reviews each week. In addition, several pages of "books received" are listed, arranged by subject. The books reviewed are primarily of interest to clinical practitioners or libraries supporting medical research.

---

publish book reviews include *JAMA: Journal of the American Medical Association*, which publishes five to ten signed reviews each week and lists many other books received, grouping them by subject. The *New England Journal of Medicine* also publishes a weekly list of books received as well as signed reviews of books of particular interest as space permits. The lengthy reviews in the *British Medical Journal* are among the best available, with as many as fifteen published in a single week. Lists of additional new titles are also included. *Lancet*, the other major British medical weekly, also publishes two to four signed reviews in each issue. The *Mayo Clinic Proceedings,* sent free monthly to medical libraries, also publishes signed reviews of books on a variety of health sciences topics, including books of interest to patients. Most of the reviews in these publications are quite timely and can be considered good sources for very current information.

Specialty journals, such as *Annals of Internal Medicine*, which reviews books, audiovisual programs, and computer software, *Clinical Chemistry*, or *Bulletin of the History of Medicine*, also regularly publish reviews. Nursing books, a good source of relatively easy to understand information for the general reader, are reviewed monthly in the *American Journal of Nursing* and *Nursing Outlook*. The *American Dietetic Association Journal* publishes signed reviews each month, as well as announcements of publications received, pamphlets, government publications, computer software, films, and other media. Abstracts of recent articles in other periodicals are also published. *Contemporary Psychology: A Journal of Reviews* publishes more than fifty lengthy, signed reviews of books, films, etc., each month, as well as a list of additional books received. One section, "Previews," publishes brief, timely reviews of undergraduate texts.

Health science book reviews are indexed in *Technical Book Review Index, Cumulative Index to Nursing and Allied Health Literature,* and indexes to specific periodicals such as *JAMA: Journal of the American Medical Association.* Ann Van Camp and Lynn Smith have advocated using online databases to identify reviews of medical books in a more timely and cost-effective manner, rather than browsing through current journals.

Additional sources for selection of current health science books that do not involve waiting for reviews to be published include publishers' announcements; the weekly *National Library of Medicine Current Catalog Proof Sheets* and the quarterly *National Library of Medicine Current Catalog*, that contain the catalog records for English-language materials cataloged at the National Library of Medicine; and *Current Contents/ Clinical Practice* or *Current Contents/Life Sciences*.

Health sciences materials may be received as part of general science approval plans or, in a collection devoted primarily to medicine, a separate health sciences plan may be established. In either case, it will be important to develop the approval plan profile carefully to eliminate unwanted materials either by subject or level of treatment. Ballen Booksellers International and Majors Scientific Books are two of the companies known to specialize in health sciences approval plans and are especially familiar with the literature.

Consumer Health Information, by Kelly Jennings, includes a good section on evaluation and selection of health materials that lists a dozen criteria to be used when considering the purchase of consumer health information. Leslie Dalton and Ellen Gartenfeld have suggested eight selection criteria, including accuracy, currency, and audience level, to be used in evaluating consumer health information. Alan Rees includes a book evaluation form in *Developing Consumer Health Information Services*. Such a form can be used by librarians to measure whether a potential purchase meets established criteria for the collection. Popular books, for example, should generally be added only if they are accurate presentations of subjects not already available in the library.

SERIALS SELECTION

Medicine has always been one of the most expensive subject areas for a library to collect, ranked second only to chemistry and physics in costs of subscriptions, according to Norman Brown and Jan Philips. When coupled with the esoteric subjects of many clinical titles, librarians are wise to consider new health science subscriptions carefully. When considering a possible new title, criteria for evaluation can include subject content, intended audience, publisher, editorial board, inclusion in printed or online indexes, and cost. Certainly, the most important criteria will be use, either already indicated by interlibrary loan records, or anticipated use based on faculty requests or knowledge of existing research programs.

The lists of titles included in *Abridged Index Medicus*, the medical lists in *Science Citation Index*, and the titles in the previously mentioned core lists can be used to evaluate or initiate subscriptions. In order to identify new periodicals, librarians can consult publishers' lists, scan the lists of new titles received at the National Library of Medicine as they are published in *NLM News*, or use standard library tools such as *New Serial Titles*. Reviews of new medical journals are difficult to find, but *Nature* publishes reviews of new journals every October, and *Choice* and *Library Journal* occasionally include reviews of medical journals.

Even with careful selection, many libraries may find that they cannot afford subscriptions to the expensive health sciences journals. If the use of interlibrary loan is necessary to meet the needs of patrons, there is a well-established network of medical libraries to provide this service. Regional medical libraries, listed in *Index Medicus*, are able to fill most health sciences loan requests. If the regional library cannot fill the request, the library will refer it to the National Library of Medicine. As with any loan network, the borrower will have to allow several weeks to receive a photocopy of the requested material from the regional library; even more time is needed for requests that have been sent on to the National Library of Medicine. If time is a consideration, libraries may avail themselves of fee-for-service document delivery sources, such as Information-on-Demand or The Information Store, and pay for the faster service these companies provide.

Much discretion must be exercised in the selection of consumer health magazines. A recent report by the American Council on Science and Health evaluated the reliability of nutrition information published in popular magazines. Half of the magazines that provided extensive nutrition coverage were found to be unreliable or at best inconsistent in their accuracy. As much as eighty percent of the information in some magazines was found to be incorrect. Reviews of this sort, or the recommendations in Rees's *Consumer Health Information Source Book*, can provide reliable advice in the selection of health related magazines, newsletters, and consumer publications.

GOVERNMENT PUBLICATIONS

As noted in the section on publishers, United States government documents are an excellent source of health science information. While many of the standard indexes do not provide thorough coverage of government publications, identification of such publications is especially easy through *MEDOC: Index to U.S. Government Documents in the Medical and Health Sciences*. Prepared by the Eccles Health Science Library at the University of Utah, the index is published quarterly, with an annual cumulation. It is also available online through Bibliographic Retrieval Services. Both depository and nondepository items are indexed by title, subject, series and

Superintendent of Documents number. More than eighty percent of the libraries in Valerie Florance's study of documents in medical libraries use *MEDOC* for collection development, as well as for reference assistance.

Bibliographies such as *Health Information Resources in the Federal Government* or the more than twenty consumer health bibliographies available from the Government Printing Office are excellent introductions to the wide variety of publications available from the U.S. government. The National Library of Medicine (NLM), one of the National Institutes of Health, is also a significant source of health science information, including such significant publications as *Index Medicus* and *Bibliography of the History of Medicine*. *National Library of Medicine Literature Searches* and the *Specialized Bibliography Series* are current bibliographies on topics of wide interest available at no charge directly from NLM. A list of the *Literature Searches* and bibliographies is included in the front pages of each issue of *Index Medicus*. The National Health Information Clearinghouse in Washington, D.C., provides referrals to a wide variety of health information. There are many other federal clearinghouses of health information as well, such as those at the various National Institutes of Health that publish very reliable pamphlets designed for lay readers. These may form an integral part of consumer health collections. The Consumer Product Safety Commission also provides a clearinghouse and is the source of publications on health problems associated with consumer products. The extensive collections available at regional depository libraries may be convenient places for librarians to look at samples of government publications before making selections for acquisitions in their own libraries.

TECHNICAL REPORTS

The National Technical Information Service (NTIS) distributes the reports resulting from federally sponsored research. The index to the vast array of publications available from NTIS is *Government Reports Announcements and Index* (*GRA&I*), issued twice a month and available online, as well. Standing orders through the NTIS Selected Research in Microfiche (SRIM) service may be placed in such health sciences subject areas as toxicology, pharmacology, clinical medicine, or industrial (occupational) medicine.

AUDIOVISUALS

Libraries that collect audiovisuals may wish to add health sciences materials to their collections. Some medical societies produce films and video and audio cassettes for use by health care professionals. Audiovisuals designed for the instruction of nursing students may be more readily understood by a lay audience. As consumer health awareness has become more popular, audiovisuals in many formats have been produced for the public.

The National Library of Medicine publishes the quarterly *National Library of Medicine Audiovisual Catalog* (available online as AVLINE), which contains abstracts and recommendations by physicians and librarians about a wide variety of health sciences audiovisual materials for both medical professionals and the public. Other major bibliographies are available from the National Institute of Mental Health, which publishes *Selected Audiovisuals on Mental Health,* and the National Information Center for Educational Media, which produces the *Index to Health and Safety Education.* Other reviews are included in some medical and nursing journals.

PAMPHLETS

Libraries that choose to offer a wide variety of current health information for consumers will need to acquire a large number of pamphlets. These are readily available, often at no charge, from voluntary health organizations such as the American Cancer Society; insurance companies, including Blue Cross and Kaiser-Permanente; and pharmaceutical companies, such as E. R. Squibb and Merck, Sharp, and Dohme. As one might expect, the United States government is also a prolific publisher of pamphlets for the lay reader, and lists of free and inexpensive items may be obtained from the Consumer Information Center and the National Health Information Clearinghouse, as well as from the individual National Institutes of Health or the Centers for Disease Control. If collecting and organizing pamphlets is considered to be too time consuming for a library, packaged collections of health sciences pamphlets, such as *CHIS: The Consumer Health Information Service,* are available. This microfiche collection includes the full text of 1,350 publications of more than 150 organizations, as well as a subject index. If this microfiche file is locally

---

National Health Information Clearinghouse. P.O. Box 1133, Washington, DC 20013. Telephone (800)336–4796; in Virginia only call collect (703)522–2590.

Bibliographies, referral service.

Very current information on health publications.

The National Health Information Clearinghouse (NHIC) has been funded by the Public Health Service, the Office of Disease Prevention and Health Promotion, and the Department of Health and Human Services since 1979, to provide public access to health information. There is an in-house database of health related organizations and the staff has prepared "Healthfinders" on current topics such as herpes, exercise, and health fairs. A toll free number is available for information or to request publications.

available, smaller libraries could use *CHIS* as a convenient selection aid when considering the acquisition of new pamphlets.

RETROSPECTIVE SELECTION

When there is scholarly interest in the history of medicine, historical lists such as Leslie Morton's *A Medical Bibliography* or Lee Ash's *Serial Publications Containing Medical Classics* can be used to identify valuable works worth adding to or retaining in the collection. The John Blake and Charles Roos *Medical Reference Works, 1679–1966* and Pieter Smit's *History of The Life Sciences* are also thorough retrospective guides to historical sources. Current bibliographies include *Bibliography of the History of Medicine, Current Work in the History of Medicine,* and the *ISIS Cumulative Bibliography,* which is based on the bibliographies included in the history of science journal, *ISIS.*

Classic sources that have been reprinted due to high demand may be identified in *Guide to Reprints.* On-demand publishing reprints are available from University Microfilm. Out-of-print dealers and antiquarian book dealers who specialize in the health sciences may be identified in such sources as the *American Book Trade Directory* or *Bookdealers in North America.* Serials backfiles may be available from the publisher, or from back-issue dealers such as those listed in William Katz and Peter Gellatly's *Guide to Magazine and Serial Agents.* Librarians may find individual issues or complete runs of journals from the Universal Serials and Book Exchange (USBE) or from the serials exchange lists published quarterly by the Medical Library Association. Some regional or local exchanges of medical journals also exist and may be identified through local medical school libraries or a regional medical library.

If there is no marked interest in the history of medicine, retrospective selection may have little value in a general health science collection. Journal articles are readily available through interlibrary loan, and clinical materials should always be the most current published. Because of the rapid obsolescence of health science information, librarians should resist the temptation to add older editions that may be available as gifts. The inaccurate information contained in such materials adds little or nothing to the utility of the collection, detracts from its value, and does a disservice to the user.

Summary

Although the selection of health sciences materials in a nonmedical library may at first seem difficult, the variety of guides to the literature, core lists, book reviews, and the assistance available through reliable publishers of both medical and consumer health information can ease the task considerably. Librarians should not hesitate to enrich their collections by adding health sciences information.the combination of common sense, professional training, and the available bibliographic guides will enable even those new to selection to proceed with confidence.

Selection Sources

Abridged Index Medicus. v.1– . 1970– . Bethesda, Md.: National Library of Medicine. Monthly.

American Book Trade Directory. 31st ed. New York: Bowker, 1985.

American Dietetic Association Journal. v.1– . 1925– . Chicago: American Dietetic Assn. Monthly.

American Journal of Nursing. v.1– . 1900– . New York: American Journal of Nursing Co. Monthly.

Annals of Internal Medicine. v.1– . 1922– . Philadelphia: American College of Physicians. Monthly.

Ash, Lee. *Serial Publications Containing Medical Classics; An Index to Citations in Garrison/Morton (3rd ed., 1970).* 2nd ed. Bethany, Conn.: Antiquarian, 1979.

Austin, T. "Socioeconomic Resources in Medicine: Review of the Literature." *Bulletin of the Medical Library Association* 72:287-94 (July 1984).

Bain, Christine A., ed. *Health Information for the Public Library: A Report on Two Pilot Projects.* Albany: Univ. of the State of New York, 1984.

Bibliography of the History of Medicine. v.1– . 1964– . Bethesda, Md.: National Library of Medicine. Annually.

Blake, John B., and Charles Roos, eds. *Medical Reference Works, 1679-1964: A Selected Bibliography.* Chicago: Medical Library Assn., 1967.

Bookdealers in North America; A Directory of Dealers in Secondhand and Antiquarian Books in Canada and the United States of America. 9th ed. London: Sheppard, 1983.

Brandon, Alfred N., and Dorothy R. Hill. "Selected List of Books and Journals for the Small Medical Library." *Bulletin of the Medical Library Association* 73:176-205. (Apr. 1985).

———. "Selected List of Books and Journals in Allied Health Sciences." *Bulletin of the Medical Library Association* 72:373-91(Oct. 1984).

———. "Selected List of Nursing Books and Journals." *Nursing Outlook* 32:92-101(Mar./Apr. 1984).

British Medical Journal. v.1– . 1832– . London: British Medical Assn. Weekly.

Brown, Norman B., and Jan Philips. "Price Indexes from 1983; U.S. Periodicals and Serial Services." *Library Journal* 108:1659-62 (Sept. 1983).

Bulletin of the History of Medicine. v.1– . 1933– . Baltimore, Md.: Johns Hopkins Univ. Pr. Quarterly.

CHIS: The Consumer Health Information Service. Ann Arbor, Mich.: Univ. Microfilms, 1983.

Choice. v.1– . 1964– . Middletown, Conn.: Assn. of College and Research Libraries. Monthly.

Clinical Chemistry. v.1– . 1955– . Winston-Salem, N.C.: Assn. for Clinical Chemistry. Monthly.

Consumer Information Center, Pueblo, Co. 81009.

Consumer Product Safety Commission, Washington, DC 20207.

Contemporary Psychology; A Journal of Reviews. v.1– . 1956– . Washington, D.C.: American Psychological Assn. Monthly.

Cumulative Index to Nursing and Allied Health Literature. v.1– . 1961– . Glendale, Calif.: Glendale Adventist Medical Center. Bimonthly and annually.

Current Contents/Clinical Practice. v.1– . 1973– . Philadelphia: Institute for Scientific Information. Weekly.

Current Contents/Life Sciences. v.1– . 1958– . Philadelphia: Institute for Scientific Information. Weekly.

Current Work in the History of Medicine. v.1– . 1954– . London: Wellcome Institute for the History of Medicine. Quarterly.

Dalton, Leslie, and Ellen Gartenfeld. "Evaluating Printed Health Information for Consumers." *Bulletin of the Medical Library Association* 69:322–24 (July 1981).

Darling, Louise, ed. *Handbook of Medical Library Practice.* 2v. 4th ed. Chicago: Medical Library Assn., 1983.

Florance, Valerie. "Government Documents in Medical Libraries." *Government Publications Review* 12:457–61 (Sept.–Oct. 1985).

Government Reports Announcements and Index. v.1– . 1974– . Springfield, Va.: National Technical Information Service. Biweekly.

Guide to Reprints. Kent, Conn.: Guide to Reprints, Inc., 1967– .

Hatfield, Denise. "New ACSH Survey Rates Magazine Nutrition Accuracy." *ACSH News and Views* 5:1, 8–10 (1984).

"Health Information Resources." *Illinois Libraries* 67:333–428 (Apr. 1985).

Health Information Resources in the Federal Government. Washington, D.C.: National Health Information Clearinghouse, 1984.

Index Medicus. v.1– . 1960– . Bethesda, Md.: National Library of Medicine. Monthly.

Index to Health and Safety Education. 4th ed. Los Angeles: National Information Center for Educational Media, Univ. of California, 1980.

Information on Demand, Inc., Box 9550, Berkeley, CA 94709.

Information Store, Inc., 140 Second St., San Francisco, CA 94105.

ISIS: Cumulative Index, 1953–1982. Philadelphia: History of Science Society, 1985.

ISIS: International Review Devoted to the History of Medicine. v.1– . 1912– . Philadelphia: History of Science Society. 5/year.

JAMA: Journal of the American Medical Association. v.1– . 1848– . Chicago: American Medical Assn. Weekly.

Jennings, Kelly. *Consumer Health Information: The Public Librarian's Role.* Tulsa: Tulsa City-County Library, 1983.

Katz, William, and Peter Gellatly. *Guide to Magazine and Serial Agents.* New York: Bowker, 1975.

Kowitz, A. *Basic Dental Reference Works.* 5th ed. Chicago: American Dental Assn., 1983.

Lancet. v.1– . 1823– . London: Lancet. Weekly.

Library Journal. v.1– . 1876– . New York: Bowker. 22/year.

McCandless, Pat. "Sports Medicine." *Illinois Libraries* 67:385–89 (Apr. 1985).

A Majors Report. v.1– . 1979– . Dallas: Majors Scientific Books.

Malinowsky, H. Robert, and Jeanne M. Richardson. *Science and Engineering Literature: A Guide to Reference Sources.* 3rd ed. Littleton, Colo.: Libraries Unlimited, 1980.

Mayo Clinic Proceedings. v.1– . 1926– . Rochester, Minn.: Mayo Clinic. Monthly.

Medical Library Assn. *Bulletin.* v.1- . 1911- . Chicago: Medical Library Assn. Quarterly.

MEDOC: Index to U.S. Government Documents in the Medical and Health Sciences. Salt Lake City: Univ. of Utah, 1979.

Morton, Leslie T. *A Medical Bibliography (Garrison and Morton): An Annotated Checklist of Texts Illustrating the History of Medicine.* 3rd ed. Philadelphia: Lippincott, 1970.

National Health Information Clearinghouse, P.O. Box 1133, Washington, DC 20013.

National Library of Medicine Audiovisuals Catalog. v.1- . 1978- . Bethesda, Md.: National Library of Medicine. Quarterly.

National Library of Medicine Current Catalog. v.1- . 1966- . Bethesda, Md.: National Library of Medicine. Quarterly.

National Library of Medicine Current Catalog Proof Sheets. v.1- . 1966- . Bethesda, Md.: National Library of Medicine. Weekly.

National Library of Medicine Literature Searches. Bethesda, Md.: National Library of Medicine. Irregularly.

National Library of Medicine News. v.1- . 1945- . Bethesda, Md.: National Library of Medicine. Monthly.

Nature. v.1- . 1869- . London: Mcmillan Journals.

New England Journal of Medicine. v.1- . 1812- . Boston: Massachusetts Medical Society. Weekly.

New Serial Titles. v.1- . 1953- . New York: Bowker. Monthly.

Nursing Outlook. v.1- . 1953- . New York: American Journal of Nursing Co. Bimonthly.

Rees, Alan M., ed. *Developing Consumer Health Information Services.* New York: Bowker, 1982.

————, and Jodith Janes. *The Consumer Health Information Source Book.* 2nd ed. New York: Bowker, 1984.

Roper, Fred W., and Jo Anne Boorkman. *Introduction to Reference Sources in the Health Sciences.* 2nd ed. Chicago: Medical Library Assn., 1984.

Salisbury, Susan. *Getting the Facts: How to Organize a Labor Health Library; An Occupational Health Bibliography.* Berkeley: Regents of the Univ. of California, 1981.

Science Books & Films. v.1- . 1965- . Washington, D.C.: American Assn. for the Advancement of Science. 5/year.

Science Citation Index. v.1- . 1961- . Philadelphia: Institute for Scientific Information. 6/year.

Selected Audiovisuals on Mental Health. Rockville, Md.: National Institute of Mental Health, 1975.

Sheehy, Eugene, comp. *Guide to Reference Books.* 10th ed. Chicago: American Library Assn., 1986.

Smit, Pieter. *History of the Life Sciences: An Annotated Bibliography.* New York: Hafner, 1974.

Specialized Bibliography Series. 1980- . Bethesda, Md.: National Library of Medicine.

Technical Book Review Index. v.1- . 1935- . Pittsburgh: AAD Publishing. Monthly.

Van Camp, Ann J., and Lynn R. Smith. "Use of BRS PRE-MED Database for Collection Development." *Bulletin of the Medical Library Association* 70:414–16(Oct. 1982).

Walford, Albert John. *Walford's Guide to Reference Material.* 4th ed. London: Library Assn., 1982.

HOME ECONOMICS

Neosha A. Mackey

What is home economics, or human ecology, as it is known in some cases? The *Dictionary of Education* defines home economics as

> A discipline that draws from the biological, physical and social sciences and the humanities the content needed to help people solve problems of food, clothing, shelter, and relationships and that deals with the development of understandings, skills, and attitudes essential to the improvement of the ways of living of individuals, families, and community groups.[1]

In 1902, a committee of the Fourth Lake Placid Conference developed the following definition, adopted at that time. "Home economics . . . is the study of the laws, conditions, principles and ideals concerned with man's immediate physical environment and his nature as a social being, and specifically the relation between those two factors."[2] Both of these definitions represent home economics today. In most colleges and universities, one will find the five traditional areas of home economics: home economics education, home management and housing, family relations and human development, human nutrition and food management, and textiles and clothing. The emphasis in each area and the level of study will vary. Home economics most certainly draws from the physical, biological, and social sciences and the arts and humanities, so a selector must be a generalist and a specialist at the same time. To effectively build a collection, one needs to know and understand the strategies in other professional and interdisciplinary fields.

In general, home economics is a difficult field in which to select because of its diversity. A comprehensive collection in home economics can legitimately contain something in every LC or Dewey class. It is unreason-

1. Carter V. Good, ed., *Dictionary of Education*, 3rd ed. (New York: McGraw-Hill, 1973), p. 284.
2. Marjorie East, *Home Economics: Past, Present and Future* (Boston: Allyn and Bacon, 1980), p. 11.

Journal of Home Economics. v.1– . 1901– . Washington, D.C.: American
Home Economics Assn. Quarterly.
Reviews only a few (1–3) books per issue. Has more value as an indicator of
current areas of interest in the field. "Research in Brief" provides abstracts of
articles in the *Home Economics Research Journal.* Each issue is on a particular
theme and the bibliographies for the articles provide useful sources.

able, though, to expect a selector or bibliographer to have such comprehensive knowledge. One way to cover the field in general is to read regularly
the *Journal of Home Economics* and the *Home Economics Research
Journal,* both of which are published by the American Home Economics
Association. The *Journal of Home Economics* has book reviews and descriptions of research and other types of professional material in each
issue. The *Home Economics Research Journal,* as one would expect, reports on research being done. It also, in recent years, has provided a list
of theses and dissertations completed in home economics. If no other
sources are utilized in collection development, these two are required. By
reading them, one can keep up with trends, research, publications, association offerings, and names of leaders in the field.

A common means of acquiring current imprint material is to use approval plans. The selector cannot examine only the "Ts" or "640s"; many
titles appropriate for home economics would thus be missed. For example,
The Language of Clothes by Alison Lurie appeared with the Ps, and books
on play and children are often found in the "Gs." It is necessary to examine
all the books that come on approval plans.

Home Economics Education

Home Economics Education is the field that imparts knowledge on the
teaching of home economics in grade schools, secondary schools, vocational settings, colleges, and universities. It may fall either within an academic area called home economics or under education. Research in the
field appears in the professional journals, association publications, and
proceedings of meetings.

The Teacher Education Section of the American Home Economics
Association and the Home Economics Education Association, an affiliate
of the National Education Association, are important for the field. Publications of the Teacher Education Section are announced in the *Journal
of Home Economics.*

Other journals of value are *Forecast for Home Economics, Vocational
Education Journal, Tips and Topics,* and *What's New in Home Eco-*

Tips and Topics. v.1- . 196-- . Lubbock: Texas Tech Univ., College of
Home Economics, Home Economics Instructional Materials Ctr. Quarterly.
"Designed for in-service and pre-service education of persons involved in any
phase of home economics education" is the way this publicaton describes itself.
Only eight pages long, each issue is devoted to a specific subject with contents
designated as "Topics" or "Tips." The "Resources" section makes up the last
page and lists a variety of books and articles on the subject at hand. There are
no reviews provided but from checking numerous issues it appears that the items
have been carefully selected for their relevance. Since teachers (and prospective
teachers) at all levels use this publication, the titles in "Resources" may be more
frequently requested.

nomics. The *Forecast* provides current information on what is taught in
elementary and secondary schools. There are reviews of special types of
material such as software and bibliographies for some of the feature articles. If curriculum materials are to be purchased this is a good source
of titles. The *Vocational Education Journal* covers all aspects of vocational education and provides coverage of the American Vocational Association. In addition to articles on all aspects of vocational education,
there are book reviews of both curricular and professional materials. *Tips
and Topics* has a theme for each issue and provides information on trends,
issues, curricula, and research in home economics, emphasizing classroom
applications. Each issue has a "Resources" list of articles and books on
the issue theme. *What's New in Home Economics* reports on research
being done at universities and on trends and developments in all areas of
home economics. "Teaching Material" is a column that reviews books,
audiovisuals, pamphlets, and other types of material, some of which is
free or inexpensive. If you are selecting material for a vertical file, this list
can be useful. For the more general education resources, consult the education essay in this volume.

It is especially difficult to identify publishers of home economics education material at the academic level, though Jossey-Bass does publish a
number of titles of interest. If secondary level materials are needed as

What's New in Home Economics. v.1- . 1936- . Philadelphia: North
American Publishing Co. 8/year.
The value of this publication is its section on "Teaching Materials." All types
of materials are reviewed with the exception, for the most part, of standard
books. Films, documents, extension material, association publications, teaching
kits, and periodicals are reviewed. It will occasionally have a special list of
materials aimed at adolescents. Provides costs and complete addresses for acquiring items.

ACCI Newsletter. v.1– . 1953– . Columbia, Mo.: American Council on
Consumer Interests. Monthly, Sept.–May.
Has reviews of books, documents, pamphlets, and articles with ordering information. Because consumer publications are not easily identifiable in approval
plans or by call number categories, these reviews often uncover titles that would
be overlooked. Reviews free and inexpensive material that would be good for
vertical files. Consumer education materials, including teacher's guides, textbooks, and media, are reviewed and—in the case of films—rental information
is provided.

---

resources, publishers such as South-Western Publishing, Webster Division
of McGraw-Hill, and Goodheart-Wilcox can be contacted for catalogs
and other promotional materials.

Research related to teaching often appears in the form of ERIC documents. The selector is fortunate if the library is a depository of ERIC
items. Otherwise, the ERIC index needs to be monitored for publications.
The journal *American Education* lists new government documents of
special interest in education. The National Center for Research in Vocational Education publishes *Centergram*, which describes research activities and publications of importance to the field.

Home Management and Housing

Home management and housing, sometimes called consumer economics,
family economics, or family resource management, is a difficult area in
which to select materials. It may or may not include interior design and
home planning (floor plans, sizes, purchasing) or consumer advocacy.
Equipment, including ergonomics, family economics, and government involvement may be other areas of emphasis.

Much research is disseminated at professional meetings. The American
Association of Housing Educators, the American Council of Consumer
Interests (ACCI), and the Association for Consumer Research are three of
the associations that have publications of particular interest. The *ACCI
Newsletter, Ergonomics, Journal of Marketing Research*, and *Monthly
Labor Review* are serials that should be read on a regular basis. The *ACCI
Newsletter* reports not only on ACCI but also on other associations and
on federal and state consumer laws and actions. A lengthy list of resources
(books, pamphlets, audiovisuals, articles) is reviewed and a brief listing of
completed theses and dissertations is provided.

Ergonomics, an international journal focusing on human factors in
equipment design and task analysis, reports research, has book reviews,

and prints association news. Research on consumerism, customer relations, and consumer surveys is reported in the *Journal of Marketing Research*. Very good reviews of books are provided. This is a quarterly publication, so reviews may be dated, but since these titles probably have not surfaced in other home economics sources, they are good to scan nevertheless. *Monthly Labor Review*, in addition to articles and statistics of use in consumer economics, also contains book reviews and a list of new Bureau of Labor Statistics publications.

In the area of consumerism and consumer economics, *Consumer Reports*, *Consumers' Research Magazine*, and *Changing Times* are essential. Each of these reports on consumer issues, evaluates appliances and goods, and lists resources available either from that publisher or others. Many of the trade associations publish useful booklets, as do manufacturers, so being on such mailing lists can be of help. Some relevant trade associations include the Association of Home Appliance Manufacturers, the Gas Appliance Manufacturer's Association, and the National Housewares Manufacturer's Association. If you attend the annual meetings of the American Home Economics Association, check the exhibitors or review relevant sections of the *Encyclopedia of Associations*.

Home management and housing can be closely allied with business, engineering, art, architecture, and sociology. Business is the basis of much that is studied in consumer economics and personal finance, while housing and equipment topics relate to industrial engineering and architecture. The literature of art and sociology are excellent sources for information on interior design and the sociological aspects of housing.

Family Relations and Human Development

The study of family relations and human development is all encompassing. In many institutions, the emphasis is on young children from infancy through preschool. Family groupings of all kinds may be studied. In recent years, parenting and aging also have been important research areas. When family relations are covered separately from education, psychology, social work, and sociology, it is necessary to carefully define the coverage and consider such aspects as counseling, abnormal behavior, and early childhood education and how they relate to family relations and human development. The essays on education and social work in this volume should be reviewed, as should the essays on psychology and sociology in the *Selection of Library Materials in the Humanities, Social Sciences, and Sciences*.

Some journals to check regularly for book reviews and review articles are *Family Relations, Childhood Education, Child Care Information Ex-*

Young Children. v.1- . 1945- . Washington, D.C.: National Assn. for the Education of Young Children. Bimonthly.
Reviews children's books and records, books for adults, and lists new books. Reviews 6–10 children's books and records in each issue, and provides suggested age level for books. "Book Reviews" are for adult books. Each of the 4–6 reviews is signed. Books for teachers, child care providers, and parents are covered. The list of "New Books" is also very valuable; approximately 42 new titles are listed. The list provides an excellent way to keep up with the field of child care and early childhood education. All reviews and the book list give complete bibliographical information.

---

change, *Young Children,* and *Journal of Marriage and the Family. Family Relations* has good reviews, as does *Journal of Marriage and the Family,* although both are quarterly and may be somewhat dated. Checking these reviews against your approval plan is a good way to see if appropriate items are forthcoming. *Childhood Education* has reviews of books for children and adults, highly selective reviews of magazine articles, and a review of audiovisuals, including records and computer software. If you must purchase books for children, this is an important source. *Child Care Information Exchange* is essential if your library supports a preschool or nursery school program. It lists professional materials available from the exchange and discusses the "hot" topics in child care. Book reviews and a list of new books, both covering all aspects of child development and education, are given in *Young Children.*

Research appears in major journals and books; *Journal of Marriage and the Family* is one of the most important. All aspects of marriage and the family are discussed. The international perspective is provided in a separate section devoted to marriage and family in other countries. *Child Development,* a journal of the Society for Research in Child Development, reports on research covering all phases of child development. There are no book reviews, but some of the extensive bibliographies may be useful. The society also publishes a series, *Monographs of the Society for Research in Child Development.* These publications report in greater depth on child development. They can be purchased either on a subscription basis or individually, depending on your needs.

Sage Family Studies Abstracts and *Child Development Abstracts and Bibliography* provide abstracts of books and articles by subject. These can be useful when there is a need to build up a certain subject area. Sage publishes many books, journals, and abstracts of interest in this area. The National Association for the Education of Young Children is also a major publisher in this field.

One difficulty for the selector in this area is that so much popular material is published. One must be constantly alert to popular press books

Journal of the American Dietetic Association. v.1– . 1925– . Chicago:
American Dietetic Assn. Monthly.
Has abstracts of articles in many nutrition, medical, and management journals.
Signed, lengthy reviews of books including annual volumes of series and pro-
ceedings are provided. Gives abstracts of special types of material such as doc-
uments, association publications, teaching materials, and product information.
Has list of "Recent Books Received." Reviews cookbooks for special needs or
types of foods. Complete bibliographical information is provided.

of the kind reviewed in *Library Journal* or *Publishers Weekly*. Many of
these publications will be wanted in public libraries. If an academic collection serves a large lay population or has a strong program in parenting,
some of the better self-help and parenting books will be needed.

Human Nutrition and Food Management

Nothing in home economics is as it appears; here again, the problem is
one of definition. Dietetics and nutrition are standards in this department
and may be the only subjects covered; but institutional food service, food
science, and restaurant and/or hospitality management issues also may be
included. The focus of your institution will make a tremendous difference
in what is collected.

The *Journal of the American Dietetic Association* is essential for maintaining currency in the field and for its many reviews of books, audiovisual
items, and articles. Research in the various areas will appear in journals
and annual reviews. Three such annual review series are *Advances in Food
Research, Annual Review of Nutrition*, and *World Review of Nutrition
and Dietetics*. The contents of these are usually indexed in *Nutrition
Abstracts and Reviews. Journal of Food Science, Nutrition Reviews,
American Journal of Clinical Nutrition, School Food Service Research
Review, British Journal of Nutrition*, and *Journal of Agriculture and Food
Chemistry* are periodicals in which one will find current research reported.

In restaurant and hospitality management the *Cornell Hotel & Restaurant Administration Quarterly (Cornell Quarterly)* is the primary journal.
The *Cornell Quarterly* has a book review section that can be dated, but
often the professional books for the hotel and restaurant fields will surface
here and no place else. It also publishes an annual bibliography of articles
and books, manuals and other materials good to check for coverage.
Restaurants & Institutions and *Restaurant Business* are trade publications
that have occasional reviews of books and advertise a great deal of product
literature.

Publishers range from the American Association of Cereal Chemists to Prentice-Hall, with AVI Publications a particularly important source to check in food science. Publications of the American Dietetic Association are difficult to acquire and are frequently available only as photocopies, which may be unsuitable for binding.

The federal government is a necessary source of material, as the U. S. Department of Agriculture (USDA) is a major supplier of information. Most of the books, serials, or pamphlets that are of interest are listed in *New Books*, which should be carefully examined every two months. Also *U.S. Government Books*, published by the Government Printing Office, is a good source. The necessity of having certain parts of the Code of Federal Regulations will depend on what is taught. Oryx Press publishes a variety of guides to the National Agriculture Library that can be useful in locating documents. One recent publication of interest is Robyn Frank's *Directory of Food & Nutrition Information Services & Resources*.

Often covered in this area, at least from the collection development point of view, are cookbooks! Each library should have specific policies on the selection of cookbooks. Some cookbook series, such as the *Time-Life International Series*, are useful in many ways (language and culture courses, anthropology). Others such as the American Heart Association or American Diabetic Association cookbooks are essential reference tools. The *Journal of the American Dietetic Association* does review the more research-based cookbooks and ones for special diets. If cookbooks are part of your collecting responsibility, *Library Journal* and *Publisher's Weekly* will provide reviews. Cookbooks are important in public libraries and these two journals will help greatly with selection.

An abstracting source of particular interest is *Nutrition Abstracts and Reviews, Series A, Human and Experimental*. It has abstracts of articles, books, and conference proceedings and in general is a useful resource. For a straight index, the *General Science Index* provides good coverage for nutrition. Because of the interdisciplinary nature of nutrition and food service, in this volume the essays on agriculture, business, sports and recreation, and the government publications essay in *The Selection of Library Materials in the Humanities, Social Sciences, and Sciences* would provide useful information.

Textiles and Clothing

The primary areas of interest in textiles and clothing are textile science, fashion merchandising, clothing construction, and costume history. Research is reported in conference proceedings and journals. The Association of College Professors of Textiles and Clothing (ACPTC) publishes pro-

> *Textile Booklist.* v.1- . 1985- . Arcata, Calif.: Kaaren Buffington and Kay Hofweber. Quarterly. (Continues the same title previously published by R.L. Shep.)
>
> Reviews 30–50 books on all aspects of textiles and clothing including textile technology and history, costume and fashion, design, clothing construction, handwork, basketry, dolls, quilting and spinning, and fabric art. Reviews are succinct and straightforward. There is a list of exhibits with descriptions that provides a way to get exhibit catalogs if these are useful. The new book list in each issue allows one to keep up with the large number of publications in this area. A guest editorial is featured in each issue. Complete bibliographical information and publishers' addresses are given.

ceedings of its meetings. The *Textile Research Journal* is a primary source for research in textile science. Published by ACPTC, *Clothing and Textiles Research Journal* is a recent journal that reports research on all aspects of textiles and clothing. *Dress* and *Costume* are sources for historical studies of costume.

A good review source, *Textile Booklist* offers reviews of books on the whole spectrum of textiles and clothing. Textile science titles are reviewed in such journals as *Textile Chemist and Colorist, Textile World,* and *Textile Horizons* (British). There is, at the more advanced level, much overlap with chemistry and a decision will sometimes need to be made as to which selector should be responsible for collecting in the hard science aspects of textiles.

Fashion merchandising is not an area with a great deal of published materials. There are a few basic works that must be acquired, such as Elaine Stone's *Fashion Merchandising* and Sidney Packard's two books, *Fashion Buying and Merchandising* and *Consumer Behavior and Fashion Marketing.* Style books from Cho to Wallach will be needed, depending on the emphasis. Usually style books are reviewed by *Library Journal* and *Publishers Weekly. Textile Booklist* also covers these popular books with critical reviews. As a quarterly publication, there is a time lag with *Textile Booklist,* but the reviews of the popular titles are worth waiting for. Many of these books are very light in coverage and substance, so be careful—check several reviews. Public libraries may have a big demand for personal beauty and style books and the reviews from the above sources will prove useful. Since much of fashion merchandising is the application of business principles to the fashion industry, a familiarity with the business collection, its indexes and abstracts also is necessary.

Clothing construction may or may not be emphasized, perhaps with an arts or craft direction. A careful definition of teaching and research is needed here. Again, *Textile Booklist* is a good source. Fairchild Publications publishes a number of basic works in construction, textiles, and fashion merchandising. There are some very good construction books available primarily through fabric stores; these are listed in publications such as *Sew News*. Depending on your library's emphasis, such a periodical may be important for collection development.

The general study of clothing and dress covering psychological, sociological, and historic aspects is, of course, very broad. Reviews in *Dress* and *Costume* are useful, though dated. A good publishing firm for books on costume is Batsford in England. There does not appear to be an equivalent firm in the United States that consistently publishes high quality costume books. For out-of-print items, R.L. Shep is a dealer in Washington state who carries materials on all aspects of costume, dress, textiles, and interiors.

Home Economics Extension

If you are at a land grant institution, extension services will be a part of home economics in each of the five areas above. The *Journal of Extension* reports on research and programs and has some reviews of books. Most of the work of the extension faculty is reported through extension publications and government reports. These are not easy to track down. If you are lucky, your library will have been subscribing to a number of extension bulletins for many years. If not, determine, with your faculty, which university publications are most important for the different areas of emphasis and begin collecting those. Cornell, Ohio State, Iowa State, Oklahoma State, and the University of California are a few to consider.

Home Economics as an Agent of Change

Home economics is a dynamic profession and its literature is changing as it changes. In the past few years, areas such as entrepreneurship, computers and the family, aging, and variant life styles have received new attention in home economics. Since home economics concerns itself with human activity and life, it naturally must interact with all other areas of scholarly pursuit. To keep abreast of these changing interests, I have found membership in the American Home Economics Association (AHEA) to be useful. In the College and University section, there is a Librarians Committee that sponsors programs and poster sessions and has meetings at the Annual Conference of AHEA. In addition, one must be constantly on the alert when reading daily newspapers and news magazines, when watching television, or participating in community affairs, for it is in these areas that the emerging issues for home economics first appear. What is being reported, reviewed, and analyzed? What is the impact on home economics? Collection development in home economics can be at once challenging, mind-expanding, and fun!

Selection Sources

ACCI Newsletter. v.1– . 1953– . Columbia, Mo.: American Council on Consumer Interests. 9/year.

Advances in Food Research. v.1– . 1948– . Orlando, Fla.: Academic. Irregularly.

American Assn. of Housing Educators. c/o Joyce Gregg, Dept. of Family Economics, Justin Hall, Kansas State Univ., Manhattan, KS 66506.

American Council on Consumer Interests. 240 Stanley Hall, Univ. of Missouri, Columbia, MO 65211.

American Education. v.1– . 1965– . Washington, D.C.: U.S. Dept. of Education. Monthly. Jan./Feb. and Aug./Sept. nos. combined.

American Journal of Clinical Nutrition. v.1– . 1952– . Bethesda, Md.: American Society for Clinical Nutrition. Monthly.

Annual Review of Nutrition. v.1– . 1981– . Palo Alto, Calif.: Annual Reviews, Inc. Annually.

Assn. for Consumer Research. c/o Keith Hunt, Graduate School of Management, 632 TNRB, Brigham Young Univ., Provo, UT 84602.

AVI Publications Company, Inc., 250 Post Rd. E., P.O. Box 831, Westport, CT 06881.

British Journal of Nutrition. v.1– . 1949– . Cambridge, N.Y.: Cambridge Univ. Pr. 2 vols./year.

Centergram. v.1– . 1965– . Columbus, Ohio: National Center for Research in Vocational Education.

Changing Times. v.1– . 1947– . Washington, D.C.: Kiplinger Washington Editors. Monthly.

Child Care Information Exchange. v.1– . 1978– . Redmond, Wash.: Exchange Pr. Bimonthly.

Child Development. v.1– . 1930– . Chicago: Univ. of Chicago Pr. Bimonthly.

Child Development Abstracts and Bibliography. v.1– . 1927– . Chicago: Univ. of Chicago Pr. 3/year.

Childhood Education; A journal for Teachers, Teachers-in-Training, Students, Parents, Church-school Workers, Librarians, Pediatricians and Other Child Caregivers. v.1– . 1924– . Wheaton, Md.: Assn. for Childhood Education International. 5/year.

Cho, Emily. *Looking Terrific: How to Express Yourself through the Language of Clothing.* New York: Putnam, 1978.

————. *Looking, Working, Living Terrific 24 Hours a Day.* New York: Putnam, 1982.

Clothing and Textiles Research Journal. v.1– . 1982– . Reston, Va.: Assn. of College Professors of Textiles and Clothing. Semiannually.

Consumer Reports. v.1– . 1936– . Mount Vernon, N.Y.: Consumers Union of United States. Monthly.

Consumers' Research Magazine. v.1– . 1927– . Washington, D.C.: Consumers' Research, Inc. Monthly.

Cornell Hotel and Restaurant Administration Quarterly. v.1- . 1960- . Ithaca, N.Y.: Cornell Univ., School of Hotel Admin. Quarterly.

Costume. no. 1/2- . 1967/68- . London: Costume Society. Annually.

Dress. v.1- . 1975- . New York: Costume Society of America. Annually.

East, Marjorie. *Home Economics: Past, Present and Future.* Boston: Allyn and Bacon, 1980.

Encyclopedia of Associations. 3v. Detroit: Gale 1986.

Ergonomics. v.1- . 1957- . Hants, U.K. Taylor & Francis. Monthly.

Family Relations; Journal of Applied Family & Child Studies. v.1- . 1952- . St. Paul, Minn.: National Council on Family Relations. Quarterly.

Forecast for Home Economics. v.1- . 1952- . New York: Scholastic. Monthly.

Frank, Robyn C. *Directory of Food & Nutrition Information Services & Resources.* Phoenix, Ariz.: Oryx, 1984.

General Science Index. v.1- . 1978/79- . New York: Wilson. Monthly except June and Dec.

Good, Carter V., ed. *Dictionary of Education.* 3rd ed. New York: McGraw-Hill, 1973.

Home Economics Research Journal. v.1- . 1972- . Washington, D.C.: American Home Economics Assn. Quarterly.

Journal of Agricultural and Food Chemistry. v.1- . 1953- . Easton, Pa.: American Chemical Society, Books and Journals Div. Bimonthly.

Journal of Extension. v.1- . 1963- . Madison, Wisc.: Extension Journal, Inc. Quarterly.

Journal of Food Science. v.1- . 1936- . Chicago: Institute of Food Technologists. Bimonthly.

Journal of Home Economics. v.1- . 1901- . Washington, D.C.: American Home Economics Assn. Quarterly.

Journal of Marketing Research. v.1- . 1964- . Chicago: American Marketing Assn. Quarterly.

Journal of Marriage and the Family. v.1- . 1939- . Minneapolis: National Council on Family Relations. Quarterly.

Journal of the American Dietetic Association. v.1- . 1925- . Chicago: American Dietetic Assn. Monthly.

Lurie, Alison. *The Language of Clothes.* New York: Random House, 1981.

Monographs of the Society for Research in Child Development. v.1- . 1935- . Chicago: Univ. of Chicago Pr.

Monthly Labor Review. v.1- . 1915- . Washington, D.C.: U.S. Dept. of Labor, Bureau of Labor Statistics. Monthly.

New Books. v.1- . 1982- . Washington, D.C.: U.S. Government Printing Office.

Nutrition Abstracts and Reviews. Series A: Human and Experimental. v.47- . 1977- . Farnham Royal, U.K.: Commonwealth Agricultural Bureaux. Monthly.

Nutrition Reviews. v.1- . 1942- . Pittsburgh, Pa.: Nutrition Foundation. Monthly. Oryx Press. 2214 N. Central Ave. Phoenix, AZ 85004–1483.

Packard, Sidney. *Consumer Behavior and Fashion Marketing.* Dubuque, Iowa: W.C. Brown, 1979.

_____. *Fashion Buying and Merchandising.* New York: Fairchild, 1983.

Restaurant Business. v.1- . 1902- . New York: Bill Communications. 18/year.

Restaurants and Institutions. v.88- . 1981- . Chicago: Cahners. Fortnightly.

Sage Family Studies Abstracts. v.1- . 1979- . Beverly Hills, Calif.: Sage. Quarterly.

School Food Service Research Review. v.1- . 1977- . Denver, Colo.: American School Food Service Assn. Semiannually.

Selection of Library Materials in the Humanities, Social Sciences, and Sciences. Chicago: American Library Assn., 1985.

Sew News. v.1- . 1983- . Peoria, Ill.: PJS Publishing. Monthly.

Shep, R. L., P.O. Box C-20, Lopey Island, WA 98261.

Stone, Elaine. *Fashion Merchandising: An Introduction.* 4th ed. New York: Gregg Div. McGraw-Hill, 1985.

Textile Booklist. Arcata, Calif.: Karen Buffington and Kay Sennott-Hofweber, 1985- . (Continues same title published by R. L. Shep.)

Textile Chemist and Colorist. v.1- . 1969- . Research Triangle Park, N.C.: American Assn. of Textile Chemists and Colorists. Monthly.

Textile Horizons. v.1- . 1981- . Manchester, U.K.: Textile Institute. Monthly.

Textile Research Journal. v.1- . 1931- . Princeton, N.J.: Textile Research Institute. Monthly.

Textile World. v.1- . 1888- . Atlanta: McGraw-Hill. Monthly.

Tips and Topics in Home Economics. v.1- . 1960- . Lubbock: Texas Tech Univ. College of Home Economics. Home Economics Instructional Materials Ctr. Quarterly.

U.S. Government Books. v.1- . 1982- . Washington, D.C.: U.S. Government Printing Office. Quarterly.

Vocational Education Journal. v.1- . 1926- . Alexandria, Va.: American Vocational Assn. Monthly except Nov./Dec., Jan./Feb. combined.

Wallach, Janet. *Working Wardrobe: Affordable Clothes That Work For You!* Washington, D.C.: Acropolis Books, 1981.

What's New in Home Economics. v.1- . 1936- . Philadelphia: North American Publishing. Bimonthly.

World Review of Nutrition and Dietetics. v.1- . 1959- . Basel, N.Y.: Karger. Annually.

Young Children. v.1- . 1945- . Washington, D.C.: National Assn. for the Education of Young Children. 6/year.

LAW

Carl A. Yirka

All law book collections are alike to the extent that they collect a portion of the tremendous body of primary legal sources. However, as libraries seek to serve a specific clientele, their collections will vary. As in any library, the scope of a law collection is bound by the needs of its users. Law collections differ to the degree that their primary users are practicing lawyers, law school students and faculty, or the general public.

The primary goal of this chapter is to discuss academic law book collections. Only secondarily will it provide some insight into the collection patterns of public and practitioner's law libraries. The goal of the academic library's law book collection development is to collect primary sources of law, finding aids, and secondary legal materials of a general nature.

While all lawyers' work is not litigation, a brief overview of how the adversary model of American law works will suggest how lawyers think and thus how legal literature is used. In the American legal system disputes are resolved through adjudication. Plaintiff and defendant (in a civil case) or prosecutor and defendant (in a criminal case) meet before a court. Each presents his or her case, citing pertinent facts and applicable law. The judge decides which law is applicable; the jury applies the law to the facts and determines liability (guilt or innocence in a criminal case). The losing party has the opportunity to appeal. The facts are not generally reviewed on appeal— the appellate court limits its inquiry to the question of whether the law was properly applied. The role of lawyers in this process is to explain the facts and elucidate relevant law.

It is fair to view the lawyer's job as the collection and analysis of fact information and legal information. Fact research, while an important part of the work of the practicing bar, plays a very small role in law book collection development. The practicing attorney must not only ascertain

The author gratefully acknowledges the assistance of Fred Shapiro and Mary Ellen Benz-Voelkl, both of New York Law School Library.

what facts took place in a dispute, but also must put them in their context, necessitating research into science, history, medicine, or other fields according to the nature of the matter in dispute. Law collections are unable to collect across the entire panorama of possible areas of litigation. Of course, some libraries will try to collect in one or another area of fact research. Some libraries may support special programs in a substantive area that may necessitate the collection of materials in, say, psychiatry for a mental health law collection or cable television and satellite technology for a communications law collection. In general, however, that a case might turn on a given set of facts is not a question of legal research.

Legal analysis revolves around the attempt to discover a rule that resolves a case. Legal disputes are not decided in the abstract. Earlier cases are searched to find a rule resolving the dispute. These earlier cases are called precedents. It is argued by analogy that because a current dispute is similar to a previous dispute, justice requires that the later case be decided on the same principle as the earlier case. The opposing side argues that that precedent can be distinguished—that the earlier case is insufficiently similar to the later case, indeed it is so different that the rule of the earlier case should not be followed. Furthermore, not all precedents, not all earlier statements of the rule, are equally authoritative. It is important whether the rule derives from a statute or from a judicial opinion. It is also important who stated the rule. Lower courts are free to interpret an ambiguous legal rule—be it in a statute or judicial opinion—in different ways. However, if a higher court, such as the United States Supreme Court, has interpreted the rule one way, its voice is authoritative and lower courts must follow.

Authority differs depending upon where a case is argued. The legal rules of one jurisdiction may or may not be relevant in arguing a case in another jurisdiction. American law is not merely the law of one jurisdiction, but one federal jurisdiction and fifty state jurisdictions. The rules of law in New York may or may not be the same as the rules of law in California. The rules developed by the United States Congress and United States courts are only supreme as they apply to federal issues.

Libraries attempt to collect authoritative and precedential statements of legal rules. These statements are found in the primary sources of law: state and federal statutes, decisions of state and federal appellate courts and state and federal administrative regulations. Libraries also collect secondary sources, such as treatises and law reviews, which although not authoritative, are persuasive and serve as finding aids for the primary sources.

This chapter will discuss the various types of legal literature from a collection development point of view. It is not a goal of this chapter to rival the standard legal bibliographies. The reader of these pages must of necessity refer to Cohen, Cohen and Berring, Hicks, Jacobstein and Mersky, and Price and Bitner for a more complete discussion of law books and their uses.

Primary Sources

The primary sources of American law include federal and state statutes, case reports, and administrative materials. Statutes are legislation; that is, the laws passed by legislatures. Reports are the decisions of the courts, primarily appellate courts. Administrative materials are the rules, regulations, rulings, and opinions of administrative agencies. As might be expected, these most important legal materials are the least problematic from a selection point of view: because they are primary materials, they should be purchased.

Primary sources are often published in both official and nonofficial formats. Official publications are those whose printing is authorized by statute. Unfortunately, authorization to publish is not authorization to publish well. Official publications, whether published by federal or state government, suffer from the same general characteristics. They are slow to publish and have few editorial enhancements. The official federal publications are all government documents that many libraries receive as part of their government depository program. These publications include the *United States Code, United States Reports,* the *Code of Federal Regulations*, and the *Federal Register*. Unofficial publication of these primary sources is undertaken by private publishers. The unofficial publications are generally more convenient to use, with better indexes, finding aids, and cross-references. Of course these features are the reason that unofficial publications are very expensive.

STATUTES

Federal statutes are first officially published individually as "slip laws," which are then compiled into chronological volumes called *Statutes at Large* and later codified, that is, recompiled by subject, as the *United States Code*. In their unofficial form, federal statutes are published chronologically as the *United States Code Congressional and Administrative News* and are codified as the *United States Code Annotated* by West Publishing Company and as the *United States Code Service* by Lawyers Co-operative Publishing Company. There is no question that the federal statutory codes should be purchased. Most law libraries only have one copy of the official code, but buy more than one copy of the West or Lawyers Co-op editions of the code. The unofficial codes provide substantial cross-references and interpretive annotations. These annotations consist of notes on court cases that have interpreted the statute, and references to law review articles discussing the statute. The West and Lawyers Co-op editions are, of course, executed by different editors, so the annotations to the statutes may differ. Most researchers who wish to ensure a complete search will check both annotations. Cross-references from sections of various codes will differ. The West version will cite to West publications while the Lawyers Co-op one will cite to their own publications.

While purchase of these codes is not at issue, retention of superseded volumes is. Generally researchers will want to know what the state of the law is today. In some instances, however, it is necessary to know what the state of the law was at a previous time, before the statute was amended to its present form. Reference to *Statutes at Large*, which contains the statutes as originally passed rather than as codified, is an incomplete answer at best. In order to facilitate this kind of research, some libraries save superseded volumes and pocket parts of the codes. Retention of superseded volumes becomes a tremendous storage and bibliographic control problem. While all law libraries ponder the retention question and generally resolve it by retaining only bound superseded volumes, or only superseded materials for their own state, other academic libraries should refrain from any attempt to collect superseded volumes and pocket parts. The *United States Code* is now available on microfiche. This may well settle the retention issue for federal statutes.

One of the important issues that arises in statutory research is determining the meaning of an ambiguous statute. Statutes, it must be remembered, are the products of legislative compromise. They are often unclear either because they were purposely drafted with some ambiguity or because they are being applied to unforeseen situations. For this reason, an attempt is sometimes made to determine what the drafters of the document intended. In order to establish this, the researcher will compile a legislative history, gathering together all the documents that went into the passage of a given statute. To this end, law libraries collect, usually as part of their government depository program, substantial numbers of the House and Senate hearings and reports. Collection of these legislative history materials, while important, consumes considerable shelf space. The Government Printing Office now publishes many of these materials in microfiche, thus making storage substantially easier. Partial legislative history material is published in the *United States Code Congressional and Administrative News*.

The difficulties of research in state statutes are compounded by the ever-present fact that the United States is a federal system. Each of the fifty separate state jurisdictions and the District of Columbia publishes its own code. On the state level, once again, there is an official-unofficial distinc-

A Uniform System of Citation. 14th ed. Cambridge, Mass.: Harvard Law Review Assn, 1986.
The "Blue Book," prepared by the law reviews of Columbia, Harvard, the University of Pennsylvania, and Yale Law Schools, is the citation manual for law. The importance of citation to legal authorities also makes it a crucial selection tool. The "Tables" of primary sources for United States law (federal and state), foreign law (common law and other jurisdictions) and international legal materials are excellent guides for the purchase of primary sources. The "Blue Book" is not written for selectors, however—only title information is provided—so selectors should refer to other sources, such as the standard legal bibliographies, for more complete purchase information.

tion. While most states still publish official session laws (the chronological publication of the statutes) very few states publish an official code. Most states now authorize commercial publication of their codes. Some law libraries no longer purchase state session laws in hard copy, since they are now available on microfiche from William S. Hein and Company. Academic libraries need not collect state session laws. For a number of states, more than one edition of the statutory code is published. Academic law libraries generally purchase the edition of the code required for citation purposes by the *Uniform System of Citation.*

Most law libraries do, however, collect all editions of the codes published for their home state. While academic libraries may want to collect the state statutes of their own state, there is generally no need for them to collect the state statutes of any other state. We have seen that retention of superseded volumes is an issue on the federal level; it is an even greater problem on the state level. The physical format of the state codes ranges from loose-leaf pages to bound volumes with pocket part and supplemental volume updates. Except for their home state, few law libraries have tried to retain these superseded volumes, pocket parts or loose-leaf pages. Libraries soon find themselves inundated if they attempt to do this for all fifty state jurisdictions. Academic libraries should refer users to law libraries for superseded state statutes.

CASE REPORTS

The most important federal case laws are the opinions of the United States Supreme Court. They are published both officially and unofficially. The official form is the *United States Reports.* West Publishing Company publishes the *Supreme Court Reporter* and Lawyers Co-op publishes *The Lawyers' Edition of the United States Supreme Court Reports.* For the lower federal courts—the Courts of Appeals and the District Courts—only unofficial publications exist: respectively, the *Federal Reporter* and the

Federal Supplement, both published by West. There is no question that all academic law libraries should collect all the federal case reporters in all their various formats. The *United States Reports* come as part of the government depository program. Once again, the editorial material in the West and Lawyers Co-op publications may differ, most notably in that the *Lawyers' Edition* publishes excerpts from the briefs filed in court. One collection development issue that does arise is that early volumes of the federal reporters, particularly of the *United States Reports*, have deteriorated even in their early reprint forms. The issue confronting libraries is whether to replace these earlier volumes or rely on online databases such as LEXIS or WESTLAW for coverage of the early federal reports. Hard-copy reprint editions are available, and libraries that do not have the luxury of access to LEXIS or WESTLAW will want to keep complete hard-copy runs.

On the state level, the multiple jurisdiction issue arises again. Each state has its own court system that publishes its own reports. Larger states sometimes have more complicated court systems (including specialized trial courts and more than one level of appellate courts), and therefore publish a larger array of reports. A number of states (twenty-six to date) have dropped their official publication of the state reports, deferring to West's publication of the state reports as part of the National Reporter System (NRS).

The National Reporter System, begun in 1879, is by far the largest system of unofficial reports, covering the appellate courts of all the states. Comprehensive law collections still purchase state reports in all of their formats, both official and unofficial. Libraries with limited budgets or with limited shelf space no longer collect the state reports for those states where West is now the official publisher because these materials are available in the National Reporter System. Libraries with limited shelf space have withdrawn volumes of the official reports after the date in which they begin to appear as parallel citations in the National Reporter System. Some libraries no longer retain in hard copy the pre-National Reporter System official state reports. These pre-NRS state reports are available on microfiche. It should be noted that the online legal databases, LEXIS and WESTLAW, also contain coverage of state reports. To date this coverage is not complete, but both LEXIS and WESTLAW seem committed to completing their retrospective coverage of the state reports. Law libraries generally have hard-copy editions of the state reports because at the time libraries purchased these materials, they were only available in hard copy. Libraries that do not already have hard-copy editions should certainly consider whether their needs can be fulfilled by LEXIS or WESTLAW.

While self-contained indexing exists for the state and federal statutory codes, this is not true for case law. Indexing for case law exists in the form of digests, most of which are published by West Publishing Company. The American Digest System provides a classification scheme (the "key number system") for all American case law. The hard-copy collection of the American Digest System runs to hundreds of volumes. The information contained in this set is also available in a variety of smaller sets broken down by jurisdiction. Rather than purchasing the comprehensive digest for all state and federal case law, one can purchase digests covering a single state, a single region, federal courts only, or in some cases a single court such as the United States Supreme Court. Along with providing subject access to the case reports, the digests contain tables of case names so the researcher who only knows the name of the case can, by checking the table of cases volumes, find the citations for that case.

Law libraries handle the duplication of information question in a variety of different ways. Some libraries buy all of the West digests. Others try to limit the duplication by buying the regional digests but not the individual state digests. Still other libraries might simply purchase the American Digest System in order to have one comprehensive digest. As we have seen above, the question of jurisdiction is very important in doing legal research. It is inadequate merely to suggest what the law in the United States is. The law in the United States is the law in fifty states and the federal jurisdictions. Once a library has determined which jurisdictions are of particular interest to their patrons, it is then worthwhile to purchase digests for those jurisdictions.

ADMINISTRATIVE LAW

Federal administrative regulations are published first chronologically as part of the *Federal Register* and then codified by subject in the *Code of Federal Regulations* (CFR). Both of these are official publications available from the Government Printing Office. Both began publication in the late 1930s and have grown tremendously over the years. To date a bound collection of the *Federal Register* would run to hundreds of volumes. Many libraries obtain the *Federal Register* on microfiche and discard the hard copy. As with the statutory codes, the issue arises of whether to retain superseded volumes of the *Code of Federal Regulations*. A complete set of the *CFR* is available on microfiche. Most academic libraries will find their basic needs fulfilled by the current set of the *CFR* and a current subscription to the *Federal Register*.

Issues of interpretation arise as to the meaning of administrative language. Interpretation of administrative regulations by the administrative agencies has necessitated an array of administrative agency opinions and reports. Most law libraries collect these administrative reports as part of their government depository program.

The state administrative registers and administrative codes are relatively new publications, most of which began publication within the past ten or fifteen years. Before that time, individual rules or regulations were available from the pertinent state administrative agency. Publication in this area is quite diffuse, with some states publishing only a chronological register and no administrative code, other states publishing only administrative codes, and still other states lacking chronological or codified publication. Only the largest academic law libraries attempt to collect all the administrative codes and registers for all states. Most law collections purchase registers and codes for their own states, if available, and also for neighboring states or "important" states such as California and New York. Academic libraries will generally attempt to collect state administrative materials only if they are depositories of state documents.

Secondary Sources

While secondary sources lack the authority of primary sources, they are nonetheless important legal research tools. Aside from the obvious use of secondary materials as guides to the primary sources, another important use exists. The first step of legal research generally requires the researcher's determining whether the issue is a federal or local question, and whether it is an issue governed by statutory or case law. While the answers to these questions may be obvious to the seasoned practitioner, narrowing the scope of the legal issue in these ways is essential for all legal researchers. Such narrowing can best be accomplished through research in the secondary sources. In particular, since indexes to the primary sources are keyed to either case law or statute law, and the researcher may not intuitively know whether the issue is common law or statutory law, it is desirable to begin research in those sources that do not distinguish between case law questions and statutory questions. The most important secondary legal sources are law reviews and legal treatises.

LAW REVIEWS

Law reviews are the periodical literature of law. It is a unique feature of legal professional literature that such an important source may be edited by students rather than faculty or experts in the field. Each law school publishes at least one review. Many schools publish more than one, some devoted to specific topics such as international law, criminal law, human rights, etc. Law review issues typically follow a standard format: lead articles written by established scholars are followed by student notes and comments on recent cases and statutes. The paucity of book reviews has been much lamented, but recent steps have been taken to remedy this situation. *Michigan Law Review*, for example, publishes an annual issue devoted to book reviews, and the *Maryland Journal of International Law* has recently begun to do the same for international law titles.

For the collection development librarian the important questions are which law reviews should be subscribed to and how many copies should be purchased. The first question is easier to answer than the second. Law reviews are the cheapest form of legal publishing; annual subscriptions generally cost no more than twenty-five or thirty dollars. Most law libraries resolve this issue by purchasing all the American law school law reviews. One obvious method of limiting purchases is to buy only those titles indexed in the standard indexes: the *Index to Legal Periodicals (ILP)* or the *Current Law Index (CLI)*. The *ILP* indexes over 400 titles and the *CLI* indexes almost 700. A common method for determining the number of copies of law reviews to purchase is to subscribe to multiple copies of those law reviews that are most frequently cited. Olavi Maru's article, "Measuring the Impact of Legal Periodicals," contains a citation study of law reviews, and law libraries have commonly used this list to determine which reviews should be purchased in multiple copies. Other law collections could also utilize the Maru ranking as a guide to choosing law reviews.

A complete collection of even the indexed law reviews would take up substantial shelf space. Recently more and more law reviews have become available on microfiche. Both LEXIS and WESTLAW feature online collections of law reviews. The LEXIS database covers complete runs of several dozen law reviews, as does WESTLAW, but WESTLAW also includes selected articles from a broader array of journals.

While law libraries generally do not collect compilations of reprints of important law review articles, these titles may be ideally suited for nonlaw library collections. One example of such a compilation is the recently published Garland Publishing series *United States Constitutional and Legal History*, edited by Kermit L. Hall and containing 450 articles in twenty-one volumes.

MONOGRAPHS AND LEGAL TREATISES

Roughly three-fourths of the book budget in law libraries is committed to serial purchases. The remaining quarter of the book budget is devoted to monographic purchases, which account for the bulk of new book selection. As is true for all collection development, the first goal of law book selection is to determine what subjects to collect. In academic collections this policy is based on curricular offerings, faculty interests, historical strengths of the collection and other factors. Traditionally the law has been viewed as self-classifying. Law books could be purchased and libraries arranged along the traditional schema of classes taught to law students: contracts, torts, procedure, constitutional law, evidence, etc. Today these topics are often too broad to provide much assistance to the selector. While in the past limited numbers of titles were published, those that did exist attempted to be comprehensive. Large multivolume treatises covering an entire subfield of law were the standard. Indeed these large treatises were so important that their authors became synonymous with the field they covered: Williston on contracts, Wigmore on evidence, Appleman on insurance. So few and so comprehensive were these treatises that it is only within the last thirty years that general agreement came to exist on the need for a classification scheme for law collections: the Library of Congress schedule for American law (KF) was only published in 1967. In more recent times the multivolume treatise era has come to a close. Now more and more is published about less and less. Rather than producing comprehensive treatises covering an entire subfield of law, legal authors treat narrower and narrower slices of the legal panorama, often covering the law in only one jurisdiction or discussing only one aspect of a subfield. Where fifty years ago treatises were published on torts, today monographs are published on drunk driving law in New York or damages in civil rights cases. This trend complicates the work of book selection.

Libraries for the practicing lawyer collect "practice books." These are "how-to" books for practicing attorneys. Law school libraries and other libraries with legal collections prefer to collect scholarly works. In the area of law, scholarly publications are generally written by law school faculty, rather than the practicing bar. Often the selector will not have sufficiently complete information about the author to determine whether he or she is a practitioner or a legal scholar. Law school faculty can be identified by use of the *Directory of Law Teachers*. Alumni publications of law schools are useful for identifying the publishing law faculty. Some seemingly nonlaw titles published by law faculty will be of interest in law book collections because they are written from the point of view of legal scholars. For example, a monograph on tax law might not be of interest in a legal collection if the author were an accountant, but might be of interest to a legal collection if the author were a legal scholar.

At one time selectors relied on the acquisitions lists of the largest academic law libraries as selection tools. Today few academic law libraries distribute their acquisitions lists. However, the *National Legal Bibliography*, edited by Peter Ward, serves the same purpose. The *National Legal Bibliography* furnishes combined new cataloging of materials from twenty-five large, primarily academic law libraries.

A few sources of preselected information on titles for academic libraries are available. One is the "green slips," officially known as the *Advance*

National Legal Bibliography. v.1– . 1984– . Ed. by Peter Ward. Buffalo, N.Y.: William S. Hein. Monthly with annual compilation.

Part I is a monthly list of all post-1982 books, serials, theses, and dissertations cataloged by twenty-five major law libraries within the preceding thirty to ninety days. Titles appear on only one monthly list. Entries appear by subject within the relevant jurisdiction (United States, International, Foreign and Regional, Religious Systems and Early Systems). New subscriptions are listed separately, alphabetized by title.

Part II lists post-1982 state, federal, foreign and international documents, selected from government printing office cataloging records on the basis of two criteria: either the title is a depository item selected by five or more of the twenty-five law libraries or is any other document with law-oriented subject headings.

An annual compilation of the monthly lists notes each of the law libraries holding a title.

Bibliography of Law and Related Fields, published weekly by Fred B. Rothman and Company. Most of the "green slips" titles are available from Rothman directly or can be purchased from other book jobbers. Midwest Book Sellers recently began a prepublication identification service of law books published by university presses. Book selectors can also purchase the CDS Alert Service, which is the weekly cataloging information published by the Library of Congress.

Databases

While other legal databases do exist, the preeminent ones are LEXIS and WESTLAW. Both LEXIS and WESTLAW are full text, online, end-user-oriented databases, whose content consists primarily, but not exclusively, of case law. LEXIS was inaugurated in 1973 by Mead Data Central. WEST-LAW, produced by West Publishing Company, started in 1975, and initially consisted of "headnotes" (editorially prepared abstracts of cases) rather than full text. West soon realized that the headnotes-only approach was inadequate, and added full text by 1978.

The coverage of LEXIS and WESTLAW is similar. At this writing LEXIS's United States Supreme Court coverage extends back to 1790, while WESTLAW covers 1880 to the present. WESTLAW has more comprehensive coverage of the Courts of Appeals and District Court cases (from 1880 for both) while LEXIS covers the Courts of Appeals from 1938 and the District Courts from 1948. In the statutory area, both LEXIS and WESTLAW have the *United States Code* online. LEXIS contains the Ohio and New York state codes. WESTLAW has recently put the Illinois code online and promises to expand its state codes coverage. Both databases have specialized files such as tax, securities, admiralty, and federal communications law. Both databases have some unique coverage; for example, WESTLAW has a database for First Amendment law research and LEXIS has one for Delaware corporate law research. Both LEXIS and WESTLAW continue to expand coverage both in new areas and retrospectively.

Despite their similarities, LEXIS and WESTLAW are not exactly alike. Some materials are available on one service but not on the other. For instance, English, Australian, New Zealand, and French materials are available on LEXIS but not on WESTLAW. LEXIS subscribers can also access NEXIS and other news, business, medical, and patents databases. On the other hand, WESTLAW has the capability of searching not only the text of cases, but also West's headnotes and "key-number" classification system.

While neither of these systems is available on DIALOG or BRS, libraries can subscribe directly from LEXIS and WESTLAW at rates that are reasonable in comparison to the high cost of hard-copy purchases. Libraries that have limited need to access the primary legal sources may find that online access, while not inexpensive, may be cheaper than the cost of many hard-copy subscriptions. For example, at this writing, LEXIS is available for a $125 monthly fee, accessible on one's own computer and modem with connect charges of approximately $30 per hour and a per-search charge of between $10 and $20 depending upon which database is accessed.

Publishers and Dealers

Even within a field as narrow as law book publishing, there is substantial specialization among publishers. The major publishers of case reports and statutes are West Publishing Company and Lawyers Co-operative Publishing Company. Other publishers are known for their loose-leaf services. These include the Bureau of National Affairs, Commerce Clearing House, and Prentice-Hall. Some companies specialize in law school casebooks and textbooks, such as Little, Brown and Company, the Michie Company, and Foundation Press. A number of publishers gear their publications towards practitioners, including Shepard's/McGraw-Hill, Clark Boardman and Company, Callaghan and Company, Matthew Bender, and Warren, Gorham and Lamont. Professional organizations in the area of law, such as the American Bar Association and the American Law Institute, have extensive publishing programs. Carswell and Butterworth are well known for their Canadian and British materials. Congressional Information Service (CIS) is the best-known of the microform publishers. Most of their micropublications consist of reprinted congressional hearings and prints used in compiling legislative histories. CIS also publishes extensive indexes to their microfiche. Some publishers specialize in narrow subject areas. For instance, Oceana is known for their international law titles. Fred B. Rothman and Company, William S. Hein and Company, and William W. Gaunt and Sons are primarily known as book jobbers, but also publish legal materials in original, reprint, and micro-formats. Traditionally, only these few dealers have served the law book market. Over the years, as law book budgets have become larger, other book jobbers have become interested. Among these jobbers are Baker and Taylor, Midwest Booksellers, Yankee Book Peddler, and Blackwell North America. Generally these firms do provide higher discounts on trade and university press titles; however, because they are moving into a new market, they are less likely to know the legal publications. Some of them do provide advanced book listings and standing order services.

In 1975, after a number of years of prodding by the American Association of Law Libraries, the Federal Trade Commission published *Guides for the Law Book Industry* (*Code of Federal Regulations*, Title 16, Section 256 et seq.). While these guides have no sanctions attached they do set forth some requirements for publishers who purport to publish law books. The definition of law books under the guides is quite comprehensive, including any sort of materials in any format for use by members of the legal profession. Despite the lack of sanctions accompanying the FTC guides, complaints are filed from time to time with the commission. The American Association of Law Libraries Committee on Relations with Publishers and Dealers actively pursues publications that fall outside the guides, brings these discrepancies to the notice of their publishers, and attempts to get publishers to modify their practices to conform with the regulations. The committee newsletter, the *Publication Clearing House Bulletin*, publishes notices of transgressions and publishers' responses to inquiries from the committee. The *Bulletin* is published four times annually and is available from the committee through the American Association of Law Libraries.

Retrospective Collection Development

A number of factors make retrospective collection development of legal materials more complicated than is true in other areas. Retrospective materials are purchased not merely for their historical significance. Many statutes and case decisions that are quite old are still good law. Similarly, secondary sources such as treatises do not necessarily lose their practical significance merely because they are old. In some areas the law changes extremely slowly. Equity, for instance, is an area of law in which the argument is made that what is just should prevail. One would be hard-pressed to suggest that discussions of justice ever become obsolete. For example, Borchard's treatise, *Declaratory Judgments*, though fifty years old, is still the seminal work in that area. While some complete statutory revisions of an area of the law make previous statutes in the area obsolete, as is true for the new bankruptcy code, this is not always the case. For example, the Uniform Commercial Code (UCC) codified much of commercial law. The UCC was to a degree an attempt to codify the common law in the commercial law area, but for those issues ignored by the UCC, the common law still prevails. Book selectors would have to take such factors into account, not only with regards to selection of new materials, but also in deciding whether or not to weed older materials.

The availability of used, antiquarian, and rare legal materials is a relatively recent phenomenon. It has only been in the past ten or twenty years that the antiquarian law book market has come into being. It is still limited to a very small number of book dealers. The best known of these are Meyer Boswell Books, Bauman Rare Books, and Robert H. Rubin Books. All three regularly issue antiquarian and rare law book catalogs. Other dealers who specialize in the used and antiquarian, but not necessarily rare, law book market, are Thomas J. Joyce and Company, the Austin Book Shop, and Q. M. Dabney and Company.

The used, antiquarian, and rare law book market has traditionally been small because of both few sellers and few buyers. The limited market has insured relatively volatile prices. Buyers should at a minimum check Richard Adamiak's *Law Book Price Guide* to determine whether a particular book has been on the market and at what price. It is, unfortunately, not uncommon to find that no same editions of a given title have been on the market. Buyers must often resort to standard features such as quality of the physical piece, author's reputation, etc., to guess whether a book is worth its price.

Academic law librarians have utilized a variety of sources for retrospective collection development. Among these is the Association of American Law Schools' *Law Books Recommended for Libraries* series, which is unfortunately no longer being updated. Other sources for evaluating retrospective monographic purchases are the Berkeley-Davis Catalog, the Columbia University Law Library's Catalog, and the New York University (NYU) Law Library Catalog. In particular, the NYU Law Library Catalog, though thirty years out of date at this point, is an excellent source because each entry has a brief annotation abstracted from book reviews or other sources.

Comparative, International, and Foreign Law and International Documents

Most law collections select beyond the bounds of United States legal materials. These non-United States materials include: international law (the law governing relations among nation-states); foreign law (the domestic law of foreign states); and international documents (documents published by international organizations such as the United Nations, the Council of Europe, and the Organization of American States). An additional area is comparative law, which is not a body of primary legal materials, but rather consists of the secondary literature comparing the law of foreign states.

Extreme caution should be taken by all but the most experienced selectors in this area as few librarians have much experience with any but the most basic sources of foreign, international, or comparative law. A complete exposition of these important sources is beyond the scope of this chapter. The difficulties inherent in collecting any legal materials are exacerbated for non-American materials. These materials are expensive, due in part to the smaller numbers published. Prices may vary dramatically due to fluctuations in the rate of exchange. The expense of initial purchase may well be multiplied exponentially over time for continuations. Many of the sources are not in English, thus causing one to purchase expensive materials for a small number of users in a language that few may be able to read. Since not many librarians have broad language expertise, processing of new materials in a variety of languages is slow. Few librarians, even those with both Masters in Library Science and law degrees, have any understanding of civil law systems. Yet, most law libraries do collect some international and foreign law materials, as well as international documents.

American law libraries traditionally have collected British legal materials. American common law is a descendant from the English common law. Indeed, in the new American republic the "reception doctrine" required that, in those areas of law for which there was no native American law, American lawyers should look to English law. The reception doctrine, the similarity of language, and the similarity of legal doctrine begin to suggest why American law libraries—even nonacademic American law libraries—have traditionally collected substantial numbers of British materials. Whether this tradition should continue is open to debate.

In selecting non-United States materials, many libraries use as a first criterion the availability of English-language publications. Aside from Great Britain and the former Commonwealth countries, little foreign law is available in English. However, many international law books and international documents are published in English. Indeed, many international organizations have designated English as one of their official languages. While documents published by international organizations are not particularly expensive to purchase, they are generally internal documents with weak bibliographic organization; thus, processing is often difficult and costly. For this reason, book selectors should exercise discretion about what they purchase from international organizations on standing order. One should not burden a cataloging department with extensive original cataloging of nonlegal materials, thus turning an inexpensive purchase into an expensive one.

It should be noted that some international legal materials actually represent part of United States law. For example, treaties to which the United States is a party are published in United States legal sources.

It is imperative that a book selector decide in advance how comprehensively his or her library hopes to collect in this area. As any commitment is quite expensive, some libraries have begun to share resources. On a basic level, for example, some pairs of libraries collect alternate editions of the major British legal treatises. Others have taken more substantial steps. New York Law School, Brooklyn Law School, and City University of New York Law School have started a Joint International Law Program, sharing one librarian who rides circuit among the three libraries. The consortium has committed itself to developing core collections at each institution and deciding on a collection development policy that divides the legal world by subject area.

It is perhaps more important that a library be able to identify these materials bibliographically than that the library actually own them. Major bibliographic tools include: Charles Szladits, *Bibliography on Foreign and Comparative Law: Books and Articles in English*; Harvard Law School Library Catalog of International Law and Relations; *Manual of Law Librarianship, the Use and Organization of Legal Literature*, edited by Elizabeth M. Moys; and John Williams's *Research Tips in International Law*. Interlibrary loan may be the best method of "acquiring" foreign and international law titles.

Selection Sources and Bibliography

Adamiak, Richard, comp. *The Law Book Price Guide: A Market Value Reference for Antiquarian Out-of-Print and Rare Law Books and Documents and Other Law-Related Materials.* Chicago: Richard Adamiak, 1983. (Available from the compiler, 1545 East 60th St., Chicago, IL 60637.)

Advance Bibliography of Law and Related Fields. v.1– . 1968– . Littleton, Colo: Fred B. Rothman. Weekly.

Annual State Documents Bibliography. Chicago: American Assn. of Law Libraries. Government Documents Special Interest Section, 1979. States completed to date include Alaska, Arizona, California, Connecticut, District of Columbia, Indiana, Kansas, Louisiana, Maryland, Massachusetts, Michigan, Missouri, Nevada, New Jersey, New Mexico, New York, Oklahoma, Oregon, Pennsylvania, Texas, Virginia, Washington, and Wyoming. States for which bibliographies are in progress are Delaware, Illinois, Kentucky, Minnesota, North Carolina, North Dakota, Ohio and the Territory of Guam.

Association of American Law Schools. *Law Books Recommended for Libraries.* South Hackensack, N.J.: Fred B. Rothman, 1967.

C.D.S. Alert Service. Washington, D.C.: Library of Congress, Cataloging Distribution Service. Weekly.

Cohen, Morris L. *Legal Research in a Nutshell.* 4th ed. Nutshell Series. St. Paul: West, 1985.

————, and Robert C. Berring. *How to Find the Law.* 8th ed. St. Paul: West, 1983.

Current Law Index. v.1- . 1980- . Belmont, Calif: Information Access Corp. Monthly. (This index, with some additions, appears on computer output microfilm as Legal Resource Index and on optical disk as LegalTrac.)

Dictionary Catalog of the Columbia University Law Library. 28v. Boston: Hall, 1969.

————. *Supplement.* 7v. Boston: Hall. 1973.

Directory of Law Teachers. v.1- . 1922- . St. Paul: West; Mineola, N.Y.: Foundation. Annually.

Hicks, Frederick C. *Materials and Methods of Legal Research.* 3rd ed. Rochester, N.Y.: Lawyers Co-operative, 1942.

Holterhoff, Sarah. "Depository Document Selection in Academic Law Libraries: A Core List of Items Selected." *Government Information Quarterly.* 2:275-89 (1985).

Index to Legal Periodicals. v.1- . 1926- . New York: Wilson. Monthly.

Jacobstein, J. Myron, and Roy M. Mersky. *Fundamentals of Legal Research.* 3rd ed. Mineola, N.Y.: Foundation, 1985.

————, and Meira G. Pimsleur. *Law Books in Print.* 4v. Dobbs Ferry, N.Y.: Glanville, 1976.

Johnson, Nancy P. "Federal Administrative Decisions." *Legal Reference Services Quarterly.* 1:49-65(1981).

Law Books, 1876-1981: Books and Serials on Law and Its Related Subjects. 3v. New York and London: Bowker, 1981.

Marke, Julius J. *A Catalogue of the Law Collection at New York University with Selected Annotations.* New York: Law Ctr. of New York Univ., 1953.

Maru, Olavi. "Measuring the Impact of Legal Periodicals." *American Bar Foundation Research Journal.* 2:227-49 (1976).

"Price Index for Legal Publications." *Law Library Journal.* (Beginning with v.69, 1976, this is an annual article.)

Price, Miles O., and Harry Bitner. *Effective Legal Research; A Practical Manual of Law Books and Their Uses.* New York: Prentice-Hall, 1953.

Publications Clearing House Bulletin. v.1- . 1977- . Chicago: American Assn. of Law Libraries, Committee on Relations with Publishers and Dealers. Quarterly.

Schwartz, Mortimer D., and Dan F. Henke, comps. and eds. *Anglo-American Law Collections: University of California Law Libraries, Berkeley and Davis with Library of Congress Class K Added; Combined Catalog.* 10v. South Hackensack, N.J.: Fred B. Rothman, 1970.

————. *Supplement.* 9v. Littleton, Colo.: Fred B. Rothman, 1979.

Stern, Arlene L., comp. and ed. *Legal Looseleafs in Print*. 1981– . New York: Infosources. Annually.

―――. *Legal Newsletters in Print*. 1985– . New York: Infosources. Annually.

"Survey of Books Relating to the Law." *Michigan Law Review*. (Beginning with v.77, 1978–79, one issue per year, generally Mar., is devoted to book reviews.)

"Survey of Recent Literature in International & Comparative Law." *Maryland Journal of International Law & Trade*. (Beginning with v.9, no. 2, a book review issue will be published periodically.)

Szladits, Charles. *A Bibliography on Foreign and Comparative Law: Books and Articles in English*. Dobbs Ferry, N.Y.: Oceana for Parker School of Foreign and Comparative Law, Columbia Univ., 1955– .

"Title Output and Average Prices." *Publishers Weekly*. Annually since 1932; generally published in Mar. issue.

Triffin, Nicholas, ed. *Law Books Published*. v.1– . 1969– . Dobbs Ferry, N.Y.: Glanville. Quarterly.

A Uniform System of Citation. 14th ed. Cambridge, Mass.: Harvard Law Review Assn., 1986.

Ward, Peter D., ed. *National Legal Bibliography*. v.1– . 1984– . Buffalo: William S. Hein. Monthly.

―――. *National Legal Bibliography Annual*. v.1– . 1984– . Buffalo: William S. Hein. Annual cumulation of the monthly issues.

―――. *National Legal Bibliography, Subject Area Lists*. v.2– . 1985– . Buffalo: William S. Hein. Quarterly. (Beginning with this volume, broad subject compilations are available.)

―――, and Margaret A. Goldblatt, eds. *National Legal Bibliography Part II: Government Documents from Official & Commercial Sources*. v.3, no. 1– . 1986– . Buffalo: William S. Hein. Monthly. (Beginning with this volume, the monthly issue is divided into two parts, separating government documents from other materials.)

Wypyski, Eugene M. *Legal Periodicals in English*. v.1– . 1976– . Dobbs Ferry, N.Y.: Glanville. 3/year.

Yates, Robert D. "Nearly Everything You Want to Know about Data Bases." *American Bar Association Journal*. 71:90–92(Nov. 1985).

Zubrow, Marcia Singal, ed. *Pimsleur's Checklists of Basic American Legal Publications*. AALL Publications Series no.4. 1962– . Littleton, Colo.: Fred B. Rothman. Biennially.

PUBLIC ADMINISTRATION AND POLICY SCIENCES

Gudrun A. Meyer and Jane W. Johnson

Developing collections in public administration and public policy analysis poses challenges to the bibliographer that are common to selection in all interdisciplinary subjects. A brief summary of the field might put the problem into perspective.

Public administration as a separate and distinct field of study began in the late nineteenth century as a specialty within political science. The idea that the public sector is most effectively managed by a cadre of politically disinterested, competent civil servants, selected on the basis of ability and training rather than the prevailing spoils sytem, became the philosophical foundation of the new discipline. Large universities established separate programs of public administration to train the civil servants who were charged with implementing the policies decreed by the legislatures.

In developing the content of public administration programs, theorists and teachers drew extensively upon the existing intellectual resources of political science, business, sociology, psychology, and economics. The growing field of management science proved to be the most rewarding source for new concepts and ideas. From the scientific management movement of the 1920s to current concerns with human resources management, the theories developed in schools of business have exerted a strong influence on public administration thought and practice. Sociology contributed theories of bureaucracy and organizational behavior and psychology contributed theories of motivation. Political science provided insights into legislative processes and the role of administrative law, while economic methodology, based on rationality and maximization of resources, has become the foundation of policy analysis and the evaluation of program effectiveness.

With the increased focus on evaluation, we are now moving into the realm of policy studies. Although frequently taught as part of the public administration curriculum, public policy analysis is a new and complex discipline in its own right. It involves not only the study of program effectiveness mentioned above, i.e., how well a given policy met its intended goal, but also policy design, which posits a goal and then recommends appropriate policies. In doing so, it encompasses all aspects of public life: political, environmental, social, and economic.

Given this broadly diversified background, the public administration bibliographer needs to be aware of current developments as well as relevant selection tools in many areas. This is especially important for policy analysis, where it is often difficult to determine from a book review alone whether or not a particular publication might be relevant to a policy analyst. It has to be assumed that many works pertinent to public policy analysis will be collected as a matter of course by subject librarians in business, social work, sociology, economics, political science, law, urban studies, and the sciences, as well as public administration.

Another important consideration for the bibliographer derives from the principal aim of public administration programs, which is the production of skilled practitioners, rather than scholars. Consequently, bibliographers must be familiar with a number of unconventional materials such as planning studies, city budgets, financial reports, and environmental impact statements, to name but a few. Access to some of these materials can be difficult, but we hope to point to some sources that often list them.

Background Reading

Public Administration has few undisputed classic texts; however, the influence of Chester Barnard's 1939 seminal *Functions of the Executive* on the works of later writers, particularly Herbert Simon, is plain. The latter's *Administrative Behavior*, first published in 1945 is still important to those who study public organizations. Other significant contributors to the field include Dwight Waldo, whose *The Administrative State* has been reissued as a second edition in 1984 with a new preface that assesses its impact on the field since it was first published in 1948. A classic textbook is Felix Nigro's *Modern Public Administration*, first published in 1965, which currently is in its sixth edition. *The Craft of Public Administration*, first published in 1975 by George Berkley, is another text by an important author in the field.

Public policy analysis may be a young field, but nevertheless it has had some outstanding contributors. Carol Weiss's 1972 *Evaluation Research* and Aaron Wildavsky's 1979 *Speaking Truth to Power: The Art and Craft of Policy Analysis* are notable. A broad overview of the subject was presented in 1983 in *The Encyclopedia of Policy Studies*, edited by Stuart S. Nagel; this work does a very good job of conveying the far-flung nature of the field. For the new bibliographer, or one not familiar with the policy sciences, it is an invaluable introduction. The articles are excellent, as are the bibliographies.

Guides to the Literature

Traditionally, Eugene Sheehy's *Guide to Reference Books* has been consulted as a starting point for selecting retrospective general reference sources in the broad disciplines. Public administration is part of the political science section (CJ) in the first edition and in the first and second supplements. Annotations are compact and LC call numbers are given for each entry. The first and second supplements to the ninth edition (1980 and 1982) also list reference works by publication type with succinct annotations. The January and June issues of *College & Research Libraries* has "Selected Reference Books," edited by Eugene Sheehy, which updates the first and second supplements.

The fourth edition of *Walford's Guide to Reference Material* is international in scope and especially valuable for works published in Britain. Walford lists public administration as a discipline and then subdivides the discipline into categories such as police, housing, security, towns, and cities and then further divides these categories by publication type and geographical designation. The annotations are running commentaries on the contents of each volume reviewed. For selectors working in comparative public administration, it is a good starting point. An author, subject, title index is included.

American Reference Books Annual (ARBA) and *Reference Services Review* (RSR) are two additional selection tools for reference materials. ARBA provides reviews of the complete spectrum of reference books published in the United States during a single year plus foreign reference titles that have exclusive distributors in the United States. Government publications are also reviewed on a highly selective basis. Reviews are critical, evaluative, signed, and longer than reviews in *Choice* or *Library Journal*. ARBA lists "Public Policy" as a subdiscipline of political science, which is then further divided into publication types. An author, title, subject index is included.

RSR provides reference librarians and subject bibliographers with information essential to discerning and judicious book selection, as well as guidance in the use of existing reference sources. It emphasizes reviews of recent as well as older reference works, whether monographic or serial, especially as they relate to other works in the same field or with similar purpose. It is a wonderful tool for locating current reviews on the broad disciplines. For example, there was a splendid review of current reference sources in political science in the fall, 1982, issue and another useful review of criminal justice journals in the spring, 1985, issue of *RSR*.

Frederick Holler's *Information Sources in Political Science*, now in its fourth edition, is a valuable source of information in many areas of political science. The 2,400 citations are divided into seven parts; one of those parts is public administration. The public administration section begins by describing the multidisciplinary nature of the discipline; it then lists sources by publication type. Descriptive annotations provide detailed information about each source. The subject index includes a listing by format for each subdivision so you can quickly locate, for example, casebooks for public administration.

Antony Simpson's *Guide to Library Research in Public Administration* identifies published and unpublished sources of information, such as dissertations and reports. Many of the sources listed also are heavily used in other political science fields. Separate chapters annotate literature guides, abstracting and indexing services, published bibliographies, and major periodical publications. An introductory essay emphasizes the interdisciplinary nature of public administration, which necessitates a broad approach to the field. A combined author/title index helps to locate materials listed in the book.

William H. Webb has become the new editor of *Sources of Information in the Social Sciences: A Guide to the Literature*, now in its third edition. The literature of public administration is covered in the political science section and includes a discussion of the historic works written in the field as well as the main bibliographic sources, which are listed and annotated in considerable detail. Webb's book is an outstanding guide to the bibliography of the social sciences. A bibliographer should be familiar with the political science section and with the social sciences in general.

Another publication from the 1970s is Robert Harmon's *Developing the Library Collection in Political Science*. Harmon has written several guides to the literature and focused this handy volume on book selection. The sources listed are for small to medium size libraries. Harmon covers the structure of the discipline and then proceeds with a discussion of general selection sources, noted books in the discipline, selected reference materials by type, and the periodical literature. The annotations are short, usually one or two sentences. LC call numbers are given for each entry. An author-title index completes the volume.

Two other volumes worthy of mention are Mary Rock's *Handbook of Information Sources and Research Strategies in Public Administration* and Howard McCurdy's *Public Administration: A Bibliographic Guide to the Literature*. McCurdy's work is an update of a "standard" retrospective tool first published in 1972. Twelve hundred books have been cited under thirty-three subject categories. A subsection contains anno-

McCurdy, Howard E. *Public Administration: A Bibliographic Guide to the Literature.* New York: Marcel Dekker, 1986.
Lists 1,200 books recognized by scholars as important to the field of public administration. The first section covers 181 of the most frequently cited titles alphabetically by author and includes annotations. Subsequent arrangements are by subject and then alphabetic by author.
The distinguishing feature of this bibliography is a lengthy introductory essay, which provides an excellent overview of the field for the neophyte bibliographer.

tations of 181 major books in public administration selected as most influential by a panel of fifty scholars in public administration. A new selector will find the introduction to this bibliography valuable, as it provides a capsulized survey of the history of the discipline of public administration.

Rock's work is described by the author as a "toolkit" of major information sources and related research strategies in public administration and public affairs. It is a "guidebook" that provides selective, annotated coverage of the major research tools, reference services, and organizations pertinent to the field. The annotations are well written and the work is aimed toward practitioners and public policymakers. This work is regrettably out of print; however, if you can find it, I would highly recommend its use.

Choice describes John Rouse's *Public Administration in America* as the "first annotated bibliography for public administration." It is an annotated bibliography of 1,700 books and periodical articles covering the past fifty years, focusing on the impact of the public bureaucracy of the 1970s. Each annotation usually consists of three to four sentences; content and point of view are summarized and articles as well as books are covered. Separate author, title, and subject indexes are included.

Gerald Caiden's *American Public Administration: A Bibliographical Guide* begins by describing the generic constituents of American public administration and continues the description as a guide in determining the scope of the bibliography. The chapters list reference sources, professional journals, and books, which are then subdivided into subject and types of publications. This volume includes two excellent information resource chapters, one on abstracts, indexes, and bibliographies and the other on professional journals in the field. Unlike Rouse's work, Caiden chose to do without annotations for books, and he excludes articles published in professional, trade, and academic journals. The book includes many current publications and also indicates the availability of three major American online database vendors. Separate author, journal, and abstract indexes are provided in the volume. Taken as a whole, this guide is excellent for retrospective collection development, since it offers a checklist of relevant reference materials a public administration library should own.

Caiden's work is one of three bibliographies recently published by Garland. The other two are Mark Huddleston's *Comparative Public Administration: An Annotated Bibliography* and Nicholas Lovrich's *Public Choice Theory in Public Administration: An Annotated Bibliography*. Each of the three bibliographies follows the same arrangement: an introductory essay, a classified bibliography, various kinds of indexes and, when appropriate, a section on information sources. All three bibliographies primarily emphasize academic and scholarly materials, and identify core journals in the field. The citations are predominantly to materials published since the 1960s. Huddleston's and Lovrich's works are completely annotated. The annotations are excellent, substantial, and informative.

Two other volumes that also should be reviewed are William Murin's *Public Policy: A Guide to Information Sources*, published by Gale, and Douglas Ashford's *Comparative Public Policy: A Cross National Bibliography* published by Sage. John S. Robey's two volumes, *Public Policy Analysis: An Annotated Bibliography* and *Analysis of Public Policy* are also worthwhile. The former is an introductory research guide that covers articles and book reviews for the period 1977–82. The 749 concisely annotated entries are grouped under ten specific policy areas with additional chapters on policy analysis and policy making. Dissertations and conference proceedings are not included. The work is useful in selecting for an undergraduate collection. Robey's other volume is an annotated and alphabetically arranged topical listing of over 1,000 doctoral dissertations at universities in the United States and Canada. The annotations are based on the candidates' abstracts as printed in *Dissertation Abstracts* and their volume and page citations are given. It is a handy tool since it compiles studies of public policy from a wide range of disciplines.

The Subject Catalog of the Institute of Governmental Studies Library from the University of California at Berkeley lists over 300,000 pamphlets, government documents, and periodicals covering a wide range of subjects of public interest, both past and present. The collection dates from 1920 and emphasizes domestic materials; however, the collection does have some English-language material descriptive of problems abroad.

Current Sources

Public administration and the policy sciences are well covered by the general sources of publishing information such as CDS Alert Service, the

Recent Publications on Governmental Problems. v.1– . 1932– . Chicago:
  Merriam Center Library. Monthly.
  Indexing Service.
  Selective listing of books, periodical articles, pamphlets, federal, state and
     local documents, agency publications, and trade association publications.
  Annual cumulated indexes by subject, personal and corporate author, and
     title.
  Although selective, *RPGP* is useful because it lists many relevant publications
  from private and public agencies, as well as trade and professional organizations.

monthly *Book Publishing Record, Publishers Weekly,* and others listed in
any general introduction to collection management. More specific to the
field is *Recent Publications on Governmental Problems,* published by the
Merriam Center Library. It covers journal articles as well as current books
and provides brief annotations, frequently taken from the introduction to
the work. Here can be found some of the more elusive publications of
associations and public policy "think tanks." The acquisitions list from
the Institute of Governmental Studies library at the University of California, Berkeley, is another useful selection tool for nonstandard publications such as pamphlets and research reports.

As good as some of these acquisitions tools may be, to cover organizations, associations, and think tanks adequately, you must get on their
mailing lists for flyers and catalogs. The most important of these are listed
later in the chapter in a separate section. It is important that their publications are acquired in a timely fashion, since they tend to go out-of-
print rather soon. If funds are available and exhaustiveness is desired,
establishing standing orders becomes advisable.

Even though trade publishers generally are well covered by approval
plans and the more comprehensive selection tools, their catalogs are invaluable additional sources for current information on new books and
journals. Several, such as Lexington, Sage, Ballinger, Marcel Dekker, Pergamon, Praeger, and Academic Press are particularly relevant to public
administration. Several of these have established series for which standing
orders should be considered. *Public Administration and Public Policy,
Public Affairs and Administration,* and *Public Administration and Democracy* are notable. The *Pergamon Policy Studies* series in various areas
such as public administration, science and technology, energy and environment and others would be most important to public policy analysis.

Other useful sources for current awareness are the alert services main-
tained by book vendors such as Baker and Taylor's *Directions,* which is
arranged by subject and hence is useful as a selection tool. It covers the
public administration literature very well and includes many association
publications and smaller publishers.

Public Administration Review. v.1- . 1940- . Washington, D.C.: American Society for Public Admin. Bimonthly.
Scholarly Journal.
10–12 lengthy, signed reviews.
Books reviewed are grouped under broad topics. Occasionally, important government or agency publications are also covered.

Administrative Science Quarterly. v.1- . 1956- . Ithaca, N.Y.: Graduate School of Management, Cornell Univ. Quarterly.
Scholarly Journal.
7–10 signed book reviews, extensive "Publications Received" section.
The reviews are excellent and informative, although there may be a time lag between publication and review of up to two years.

Policy Studies Review. v.1- . 1981- . Urbana, Ill.: Policy Studies Organization. Quarterly.
Scholarly Journal
10–12 signed reviews grouped by topics.
"Book Notes" section with brief annotations.
The review essays cover books published one to two years previously. The "Book Notes" section lists more current materials.

Reviews in Journals

The most important general journal carrying book reviews in public administration is *Public Administration Review*, followed by *American Review of Public Administration*. The reviews in *Public Administration*, published by the Royal Institute of Public Administration, provide a more international outlook, although the focus is predominantly British.

Government Publications Review lists newly received books on governmental problems and provides reviews of books, as well as databases and other nonprint materials. More specialized are reviews in journals dealing with subdisciplines such as *Administrative Science Quarterly*, which focuses on organizational behavior and other managerial concerns common to business and public administration. *Public Productivity Review* has few, but lengthy book reviews, while those in *Public Personnel Management* are shorter.

The policy sciences have spawned a great number of new journals, the most useful of which to the bibliographer are *Policy Studies Review* and *Policy Studies Journal*. Both have sections called "Literature Reviews" that provide more or less lengthy reviews and annotations of current works. Many publications from associations and research institutes are included. The "Comments" section in *Policy Studies Review* has lately been highlighting these types of publications and it would be very helpful, were it continued. *The Public Interest* is another journal that carries in-depth reviews, which are very useful to the selector.

Bibliographical Services

Public Affairs Information Service Bulletin, better known as the *PAIS*, is the best periodical indexing system to new literature in public administration. The bibliographer will primarily use it for the identification of the core journal literature in the field. Other sources providing journal lists are *Sage Public Administration Abstracts*, *Sage Urban Studies Abstracts* and *Urban Affairs Abstracts*.

Another source that has to be commented on is *Selected Rand Abstracts*, a quarterly guide to publications of the Rand Corporation. Because a significant number of these studies have application to problems of policy and planning in domestic and foreign affairs, it should not be overlooked by a public administration bibliographer. It abstracts all unclassified books and reports currently published by the corporation. The reviews are well written, descriptive summaries of each report. Each issue has subject and author indexes. Quarterly issues progressively cumulate into an annual volume.

The Council of Planning Librarians' *CPL Bibliographies, Vance Public Administration Series*, and the *Exchange Bibliographies* are topical "running" bibliographies that could serve as selection tools in specific subject areas. The *Exchange Bibliographies*, edited by Mary Vance and published by the Council of Planning Librarians, ceased publication in 1978. The *Exchange Bibliographies*, from 1957 to 1978, was possibly the most comprehensive topical bibliographic service in public administration and urban affairs. Over 1,500 separately bound bibliographies were published, each covering a different aspect of urban management, planning, and public policy. The *Vance* and *CPL* both geared up in 1978 and 1979, to continue a topical bibliographic service for public administration and planning.

The *Vance Public Administration Series* has published over 1,600 bibliographies researching issues in public and urban affairs. Most of these bibliographies have introductory essays or comments on the topic discussed. The bibliography that follows is usually not annotated and quality control may be questioned at times. However, it could be a useful service for identifying information on current topics in public administration and public policy. The *CPL Bibliographies* seem to follow the same format as the *Vance*; however, most of the bibliographies are annotated. These bibliographies are useful for their timeliness and should be included as selection tools for the public administration bibliographer.

Organizations and Associations

As noted previously, much of the public administration literature is published by organizations, associations, and research centers both inside and outside of universities. Outside of the universities, the organizations that should be covered in some depth include the American Enterprise Institute for Public Policy Research, Brookings, Rand, Urban Institute, Hoover Institute, Institute for Policy Studies, Cato Institute, Committee for Economic Development, and the Council of State Governments. Among the professional organizations, the American Planning Association and the International City Management Association are notable. While there are many more listed in the *Encyclopedia of Associations*, these have well defined publication programs and most of them offer standing order plans. Perusing the subject index of *Associations' Publications in Print* will quickly reveal the more prolific publishers.

Research centers at universities are particularly important for policy analysis. The publications of the Center for Urban Policy Research at Rutgers, Yale Institution for Social and Policy Studies, and the National Center for Public Productivity at City University of New York should be considered for acquisition. Addresses for these and many others can be found in the *Research Centers Directory*. All of these publications are not reliably covered by general selection tools, and so reviewing flyers and announcements in current journals is the best way to become aware of them. Again, as with associations, timeliness is very critical because of the short print runs.

Conclusion

It should be clear by now that collection development in public administration and the policy sciences is neither simple nor straightforward. Many additional selection sources are available for different types of materials. We have not addressed ourselves to the selection of local, state, federal, and international documents, which are relevant to public administration, but are the province of the documents librarian. We need to emphasize again that bibliographers in this area are unusually dependent on selectors in almost all subject areas for the broadest coverage. There does exist, however, a core literature and we have attempted to point out the most important access points to it, both for current selection as well as retrospective collection development.

Selection Sources

Administrative Science Quarterly. v.1– . 1956– . Ithaca, N.Y.: Graduate School of Business and Public Admin. Quarterly.

American Book Publishing Record. v.1– . 1960– . New York: Bowker. Montly.

American Reference Books Annual. 1970– . Littleton, Colo.: Libraries Unlimited. Annually.

American Review of Public Administration. v.1– . 1967– . Parkville, Mo.: Midwest Review of Public Admin. Quarterly.

Ashford, Douglas. *Comparative Public Policy: A Cross National Bibliography.* Beverly Hills, Calif.: Sage, 1978.

Associations' Publications in Print. v.1– . 1981– . New York: Bowker. Annually.

Barnard, Chester. *The Function of the Executive.* Cambridge, Mass.: Harvard Univ., 1968.

Berkley, George. *The Craft of Public Administration.* Newton, Mass.: Allyn, 1984.

Caiden, Gerald. *American Public Administration: A Bibliographical Guide.* New York: Garland, 1983.

Choice. v.1– . 1963– . Chicago: Assn. of College and Research Libraries. Monthly.

Coppa and Avery Consultants, ed. *Public Administration and Public Policy.* Monticello, Ill.: Vance Bibliographies, 1980.

CPL Bibliographies. v.1– . 1979– . Monticello, Ill.: Council of Planning Librarians. Monthly.

Directions. v.1– . 1975– . New York: Baker and Taylor. Monthly.

Encyclopedia of Associations. 1975– . Detroit: Gale. Annually.

Exchange Bibliographies. Ed. by Mary Vance. 1957–78. Monticello, Ill.: Council of Planning Librarians. (Ceased publication.)

Government Publications Review. v.1– . 1982– . New York: Pergamon Bimonthly.

Harmon, Robert. *Developing the Library Collection on Political Science.* Metuchen, N.J.: Scarecrow, 1976.

Holler, Frederick. *Information Sources in Political Science.* 4th ed. Santa Barbara, Calif.: ABC Clio, 1985.

Huddleston, Mark. *Comparative Public Administration: An Annotated Bibliography.* Public Affairs and Administration Series v.5. New York: Garland, 1984.

Library Journal. v.1– . 1976– . New York: Bowker. Semimonthly.

Lovrich, Nicholas P., et al. *Public Choice Theory in Public Administration: An Annotated Bibliography.* New York: Garland, 1984.

McCurdy, Howard. *Public Administration: A Bibliographic Guide to the Literature.* New York: Dekker, 1986.

Mosher, Frederick. *Public Administration and Democracy.* New York: Oxford Univ. Pr., 1982.

Murin, William, ed. *Public Policy: A Guide to Information Sources.* American Government and History Information Guide Series v.13. Detroit: Gale, 1981.

Nagel, Stuart, ed. *The Encyclopedia of Policy Studies.* Boston: Little, Brown, 1979.

Nigro, Felix. *Modern Public Administration.* New York: Harper and Row, 1977.

Policy Studies Journal. v.1– . 1972– . Urbana: Univ of Illinois. Quarterly.

Policy Studies Review. v.1– . 1981– . Urbana, Ill.: Policy Studies Organization. Quarterly.

Public Administration Review. v.1– . 1940– . Washington, D.C.: American Society for Public Admin. Bimonthly.

Public Administration Series. v.1- . 1978- . Monticello, Ill.: Vance Bibliographies. Irregularly.

Public Affairs and Administration. 1983- . New York: Garland. Irregularly.

Public Affairs Information Service Bulletin. v.1- . 1915- . New York: Public Affairs Information Service. Monthly.

The Public Interest. v.1- . 1965- . New York: National Affairs, Inc. Quarterly.

Public Personnel Management. v.1- . 1940- . Washington, D.C.: International Personnel Management Assn. Quarterly.

Public Productivity Review. v.1- . 1975- . New York: Ctr. for Productive Public Management. Quarterly.

Publishers Weekly. v.1- . 1976- . Whitensville, Mass.: Bowker. Weekly.

Recent Publications on Governmental Problems. v.1- . 1932- . Chicago: Merriam Center Library. Monthly.

Reference Services Review. v.1- . 1972- . Ann Arbor, Mich.: Pierian. Quarterly.

Research Centers Directory. 1960- . Detroit: Gale. Irregularly.

Robey, John. *Analysis of Public Policy.* Westport, Conn.: Greenwood, 1984.

———. *Public Policy Analysis: An Annotated Bibliography.* New York: Garland, 1984.

Rock, Mary. *Handbook of Information Sources and Research Strategies in Public Administration.* San Diego: Institute of Public and Urban Affairs, 1979.

Rouse, John. *Public Administration in America: A Guide to Information Sources.* Detroit: Gale, 1980.

Sage Public Administration Abstracts. v.1- . 1974- . Beverly Hills: Sage. Quarterly.

Sage Urban Studies Abstracts. v.1- . 1973- . Beverly Hills: Sage. Quarterly.

Selected Rand Abstracts. v.1- . 1963- . Santa Monica: Rand Corp. Quarterly.

Sheehy, Eugene. *Guide to Reference Books.* Chicago: American Library Assn., 1976.

Simon, Herbert. *Administrative Behavior.* New York: Free Pr., 1976.

Simpson, Antony. *Guide to Library Research in Public Administration.* New York: Center for Productive Public Management, 1976.

Subject Catalog of the Institute of Governmental Studies Library. 1978- . Berkeley: University of California.

Urban Affairs Abstracts. v.1- . 1971- . Washington, D.C.: National League of Cities. Weekly.

Waldo, Dwight. *The Administrative State.* New York: Holmes and Meier, 1984.

Walford, Albert John. *Walford's Guide to Reference Material.* 4th ed. London: The Library Assn., 1980.

Webb, William H. *Sources of Information in the Social Sciences: A Guide to the Literature.* Chicago: American Library Assn., 1986.

Weiss, Carol. *Evaluation Research.* Englewood Cliffs, N.J.: Prentice-Hall, 1972.

Wildavsky, Aaron. *Speaking Truth to Power: The Art of Policy Analysis.* Boston: Little, Brown, 1979.

RACE AND ETHNIC STUDIES

Edith Maureen Fisher

All or any combination of the wide spectrum of races and ethnic groups are eligible for inclusion in the development of a race and ethnic studies collection.[1] To develop a strategy for collection development, each developer must weave together the exceptional threads of race and ethnic studies with the common strands of selection and acquisition to create a unique tapestry for the particular library. This essay highlights multiethnic, interdisciplinary resources for identifying and acquiring monographs and series, periodicals and newspapers, proceedings and conference papers, government publications and multimedia materials. It draws on my fourteen years as an ethnic studies collection developer, focusing on specific ethnic groups, and joins an existing body of essays, articles, and reports.[2]

Collections of race and ethnic studies resources are not uniform, and their diversity is significant.[3] The tremendous range, scope, and types of

1. For a discussion of the features to consider in defining an ethnic group, including race, see Stephan Thernstrom, ed., *Harvard Encyclopedia of American Ethnic Groups* (Cambridge, Mass.: Harvard Univ. Pr., 1980), pp. v–vi, 239, 869, 1041–42.

2. Among these are Laura A. Bareno and others, *A Guide for Developing Ethnic Library Services* (Sacramento: California State Library, California Ethnic Services Task Force, 1979); Natalia B. Bezugloff, "Library Services to Non-English-Language Ethnic Minorities in the United States," *Library Trends* 29: 259–73(Fall 1980); Edith Maureen Fisher, "Academic Library Collection Development in Ethnic Studies: Issues for Concern," *Bookmark* 41:32–35(Fall 1982), and *Ethnic and Area Studies Collections: Patterns, Decisions, and Rationales for Establishing, Maintaining, and Providing Access* (Unpublished report, Librarians Assn. of the University of California, 1982); Marilyn W. Greenberg and Patricia Tarin, *Ethnic Services Task Force Collection Evaluation Project* (Sacramento: California State Library, 1982); E. J. Josey and Marva DeLoach, eds., *Ethnic Collections in Libraries* (New York: Neal-Schuman, 1983); Task Force on Library and Information Services to Cultural Minorities, *Report of the Task Force on Library and Information Services to Cultural Minorities* (Washington, D.C.: National Commission on Libraries and Information Science, 1983); Anthea Raddan, "Selecting Non-Fiction Books for a Multi-Ethnic Society," *School Librarian* 32:20–24 (Mar. 1984); American Library Assn. President's Commission on Library Services to Minorities, *Equity at Issue: Library Services to the Nation's Major Minority Groups* (Chicago: American Library Assn., 1985); Patrick Valentine, "Minority Language Selection: Helping Ourselves to Help Others," *Wilson Library Bulletin* 60:26–29 (Jan. 1986).

3. For example, the thirty-three libraries, representing seventy-five diverse ethnic collections serving the needs of black, Chinese, Hispanic, American Indian, and Japanese populations

race and ethnic studies resources contribute to the notion that the major obstacle facing the researcher is simply a matter of the overwhelming amount of available material.[4] The range of a collection might be hemispheric, national, regional, or local. Its scope might be interdisciplinary or be confined to a single discipline. The types of primary, secondary, published and/or unpublished resources collected might be English, bilingual and/or multilingual; retrospective and/or current imprints: print and/or multimedia formats. In the seventies, general ethnic collections enjoyed a kind of priority status as an object of federal support. This status, like federal policy, was implied. It was achieved on the belief that such collection development was a key strategy for libraries in making library and information service available and relevant to minority and ethnic groups. Various budgeting suggestions and recommendations regarding the allocations of funds for ethnic resources collection development are available from many sources.[5]

Selection and Acquisition of Ethnic Resources

The selection and acquisition of ethnic resources is a complex phenomenon. Each specific race and ethnic group, as well as each discipline, is unique. Most collection developers agree that retrospective selection is

in California, are evaluated and profiled in the Marilyn W. Greenberg and Patricia Tarin report on the *Ethnic Services Task Force Collection Evaluation Project* (Sacramento: California State Library, 1982), and the major diverse collections on ethnic minorities—Puerto Rican, Chicano, Spanish Speaking, Afro-American, Native American, Asian American, Caribbeans, Pacific Islanders, and Africans—are profiled in the E. J. Josey and Marva DeLoach book *Ethnic Collections in Libraries* (New York: Neal-Schuman, 1983); additionally, in his issue introduction John J. Grabowski, "Research Centers and Libraries," *Ethnic Forum* 5:3–6 (Fall 1985) discusses diverse ethnic collections including an archives collecting only within one ethnic group (the American Jewish Archives of Hebrew Union College), an archives collecting from a variety of immigrant groups in a broad geographic locale (the Balch Institute of Philadelphia), a public library serving a specific geographic area (the Cleveland Public Library, where the ethnic materials held by the library are only a small part of the institution's total holdings), and he also notes that profiles of several institutions collecting ethnic materials appear in *Ethnic Forum* 1 (Sept. 1981); and also the recent North America Collection Inventory Project (NACIP) *Conspectus* (Washington, D.C.: Office of Management Studies, Assn. of Research Libraries, 1984) includes assessments of participating libraries' diverse literature collections for specific ethnic groups.
    4. Matthew F. Browarek, "Ethnic Research in the Public Library," *Ethnic Forum* 5:30–35 (Fall 1985).
    5. William D. Cunningham, "Federal Policy and Ethnic Collections: What It Is and Other Comments on an Endangered Species," in *Ethnic Collections in Libraries*, ed. by E. J. Josey and Marva DeLoach (New York: Neal-Schuman, 1983), pp. 303–9; also, Laura Bareno and others, *A Guide for Developing Ethnic Library Services* (Santa Barbara, Calif.: California Ethnic Services Task Force, 1979.) p. 33 suggests funding allocations for ethnic collection development, p. 36 recommends needs to consider, and p. 38 discusses cost of materials; Marilyn W. Greenberg and Patricia Tarin, *Ethnic Services Task Force Collection Evaluation Project* (Sacramento: California State Library, 1982), p. 42 recommends use of state monies; Task Force on Library and Information Services to Cultural Minorities, *Report*, pp. 68–78, "Financing Library Programs for Cultural Minorities," includes funding status of public, college and university, and school libraries, financial planning, funding requirements for materials and resources, and other areas, and recommendations; American Library Assn.,

among their most difficult responsibilities. It requires considerable subject expertise along with a good knowledge of the book trade. Out-of-print material, when it can be located, is often very costly to purchase. There are also certain difficulties in the selection of current imprints. Most libraries are automatically saturated with announcements and catalogs from major trade publishers and university presses, yet these are not the only sources for ethnic resources. Making the effort to supplement these announcements and catalogs by soliciting promotional materials from ethnic publishers, and those whose works are not widely reviewed, can be invaluable in the selection of race and ethnic studies resources. Sometimes, however, when these publishers are contacted they have little or no promotional materials or catalogs available, nor are they able to provide review copies of their ethnic resources. Directories for identifying publishers of ethnic resources and other ethnic organizations with information on ethnic groups and resources include Marjorie Joramo's *A Directory of Ethnic Publishers and Resource Organizations*; Rita Torres's *Multicultural/Multilingual Resources: A Vendor Directory*; Len Fulton and Ellen Ferber's *International Directory of Little Magazines and Small Presses*; Katherine Cole's *Minority Organizations: A National Directory*; and Lubomyr Wynar's *Encyclopedic Directory of Ethnic Organizations in the United States.*

It is admittedly difficult to keep abreast of the new ethnic resources, especially those published by small presses and independent publishers. Standard reviewing sources, and to some extent ethnic journals also, are limited in their coverage of ethnic resources. Who gets reviewed and reviews of small press books have been surveyed by Judith Serebnick.[6] The evaluation process for race and ethnic studies resources is difficult without the benefit of reviews and oftentimes the opportunity to examine copies. Those multiethnic newsletters and scholarly journals that review and compile lists of current ethnic resources are:

EMIE Bulletin (v.1– . : 1982–).
Ethnic and Racial Studies (v.1– ; 1978–).
Ethnic Forum; Journal of Ethnic Studies and Ethnic Bibliography (v.1– ; 1980–).
IFLA Round Table on Library Service to Ethnic and Linguistic Minorities Newsletter (v.1– ; 19 –).

President's Commission on Library Services to Minorities, *Equity at Issue* (Chicago: American Library Assn., 1985), p. 14; "Findings" on overall funding for library services, pp. 17–19, various specific recommendations on funding; grants for the development of ethnic collections from Library Services and Construction Act (LSCA) funds have been allocated to eight selected libraries in California, *California State Library Newsletter* 44 (August 1984).

6. Judith Serebnick and John Cullars, "An Analysis of Reviews and Library Holdings of Small Publishers' Books," *Library Resources and Technical Services* 28:4–14 (Jan.–Mar. 1984); and Judith Serebnick, "An Analysis of Publishers of Books Reviewed in Key Library Journals," *Library and Information Science Research* 6:289–304 (July–Sept. 1984).

Sage Race Relations Abstracts. v.1- . 1975- . Beverly Hills, Calif: Sage.
Quarterly.
Abstracts of current monographs and journal articles.
"Bibliographic Essays" provide regular in-depth studies on topical subjects.
Comprehensive abstracts of recent race relations literature providing sufficient
information to accurately evaluate the material, as well as pertinent data to aid
in locating it. Material is abstracted in a wide range of race relations issues
including discrimination, education, employment, health, politics, law, and legislation.

International Migration Review (v.1- ; 1966-).
Interracial Books for Children Bulletin (v.1- ; 1970-).
Journal of American Ethnic History (v.1- ; 1981-).
Journal of Ethnic Studies (v.1- ; 1972-).
*MELUS: Journal of the Society for the Study of the Multiethnic
Literature of the United States* (v.1- ; 1974-).
National Association for Ethnic Studies Newsletter (v.1- ; 1975-).

Of course, in addition to these multiethnic newsletters and journals, there
are specific ethnic group newsletters and journals that should also be
consulted.

MONOGRAPHS AND SERIES

In conjunction with using the varied newsletters and journals already suggested for current imprints, recent race relations books, journal articles,
research papers, and other materials can be identified in *Sage Race Relations Abstracts.* Each quarterly issue includes at least 100 comprehensive
abstracts of recent literature from a variety of publishers, research institutions, universities, and information services. Bibliographies are included,
and the "Bibliographic essays" provide regular in-depth studies on topical
subjects (for example, in 1983 a "Survey of the Literature on Theoretical
Perspectives on Ethnicity and Nationality" was included in volume 8,
numbers 2 and 3).

A major multiethnic publication for identifying retrospective ethnic resources is Wayne Miller's two-volume publication *A Comprehensive Bibliography for the Study of American Minorities.* It contains nearly 30,000
entries representing the most comprehensive bibliographical coverage of
American minorities extant, including references to more specialized bibliographies for every minority group and for every discipline. Sections on
forty-one ethnic groups often include bibliographies; guides to collections;
encyclopedias and handbooks; periodicals; and resources by subject discipline. For those minority groups with extensive coverage, monographs
and other full-length studies are included; for those groups that have

Miller, Wayne Charles. *A Comprehensive Bibliography for the Study of American Minorities.* New York: New York Univ. Pr., 1976.
This bibliography's nearly 30,000 entries represents the most comprehensive bibliographical coverage of American minorities extant, and includes references to more specialized bibliographies for every minority group and for every discipline in which they are available. Historical-bibliographical essays precede each group presenting basic overviews and identifying some of the most useful sources for the study of the group considered.

received less attention, a large number of articles and pamphlets in addition to the fewer number of available books are included. In the interest of making the text as useful as possible, there are exceptions to this general pattern. The section on "Multiethnic Group Studies" includes a list of bibliographies and resources in history and sociology, including regional, immigration, prejudice and discrimination, economics, politics, law, education, and literature. The historical-bibliographical essays preceding each group are designed to present basic overviews and to identify some of the most useful sources for the study of the group considered.

A companion publication, *A Handbook of American Minorities,* also contains essays designed to provide basic historical overviews for many American minorities and bibliographical introductions to some of the most useful sources for their study. This monumental bibliographic work will be continued by the series *Minorities in America: The Annual Bibliography.* The first volume, for 1976, was published in 1985. Each volume in the series will represent a survey of 900 journals and a review of the publications of American university presses, commercial publishers, and the Government Printing Office, as well as a review of abstracts of theses.

Marc Cashman and Barry Klein's *Bibliography of American Ethnology* was published at the same time as Miller's two-volume bibliography, but before publication of his first 1976 annual bibliography. It covers all aspects of ethnicity and race in America. More than seventy ethnic minority groups are included in four main categories—General Ethnology, American Indians, Black Americans, and Other Minorities. Among the subject areas covered are acculturation and assimilation, ethnic literature, ethnicity and education, ethnography, ethnopsychology, genealogy, immigration, race relations, school desegregation, urban ethnicity, folklore, history, language, art, religion, migration, civil rights, etc.

Multiethnic acquisitions lists were useful selection checklists when they were published, such as *A Quarterly Bibliography of Cultural Differences (1964-1982)* from the California State Library. Multiethnic selection checklists exist among the Council of Planning Librarians' *CPL Exchange Bibliographies,* such as "American Ethnic Groups: A Retrospective List

> *Ethnic Studies in North America: A Catalog of Current Doctoral
> Dissertation Research.* Ann Arbor, Mich.: Xerox University Microfilms,
> 1983. Irregularly.
> As the only central source for accessing North American doctoral dissertations,
> University Microfilms International's (UMI) specialized subject catalogs, such as
> this one and other specific ethnic group catalogs, are essential selection tools.
> UMI has the computer search and retrieval system DATRIX (Direct Access to
> Research Information—a Xerox service)—that offers a special "Customized Pro-
> file Search Service" for libraries, institutions, and collection specialists requesting
> information in select subject areas. Custom-selected dissertations matching spe-
> cific research/collection needs can automatically be sent with a "standing order."
> UMI's database can also be accessed by using the online search services of
> Lockheed's DIALOG or Bibliographic Retrieval Service Inc. (BRS).

of Publications," and the bibliographies on specific ethnic groups. Various
specific ethnic group's acquisitions lists are being published.

Ethnic theses and dissertations provide reviews of the literature that
would otherwise be difficult to uncover, and focus on specific aspects of
topics for which there may be few other books to consult. For these
reasons they are vital sources of ethnic information. Guides for identifying
ethnic theses and dissertations include *A Bibliography of Doctoral Research on Minorities: Racial, Religious and Ethnic;* Francesco Cordasco
and David Alloway's *American Ethnic Groups: The European Heritage;
Ethnic Studies in North America: A Catalog of Current Doctoral Dissertation Research;* and Victor Gilbert and Darshan Singh Tatla's *Immigrants, Minorities and Race Relations.*

Approval plans and standing orders can be set up to acquire publications
from trade and commercial publishers and the university presses. The
profile schemes of approval plans most often include ethnic resources in
disciplinary categories or coded subject divisions, such as discrimination,
minority groups, and race relations. Standing orders, serving much the
same purpose as approval plans, eliminate the need to identify and order
each new volume in a series individually. Among the multiethnic series
appropriate for standing orders in an academic collection are:

American Ethnic Groups Series (Arno Press)
Contributions in Ethnic Studies (Greenwood Press)
Ethnic Chronology Series (Oceana)
Ethnic Groups in American Life Series (Prentice-Hall)
Ethnic Groups in Comparative Perspective (Random House)
Ethnic Studies Information Guide Series (Gale Research)
Ethnicity and Public Policy (University of Wisconsin-Milwaukee)
Immigrant Heritage of America Series (Twayne)
Newcomers to a New Land (University of Oklahoma Press)

Relying totally on approval plans and standing orders is, of course, insufficient for race and ethnic studies collection development.

A number of monographs and series for specific ethnic groups are available on microfilm. Among these the *Immigrant in America*, a microfilm collection from Research Publications, reproduces about 6,000 monographs and pamphlets published between 1820 and 1929. It covers two major waves of immigration from Europe—the 1820s and the 1880s—as reflected in materials preserved by the New York Public Library, the Balch Institute of Ethnic Studies in Philadelphia, and the Immigration History Research Center at the University of Minnesota.

PERIODICALS AND NEWSPAPERS

Ethnic periodicals and newspapers constitute a major source of information on the cultural heritage and historical development of individual ethnic groups in the United States, and they may be regarded as unique primary and secondary sources for historical and sociological study of the American people and their culture. Ethnic periodicals are a mainstay in academia, as seen by the nearly 400 pages in the University of California's union list of *Ethnic Serials at Selected University of California Libraries.*[7]

The *Encyclopedic Directory of Ethnic Newspapers and Periodicals in the United States* by Lubomyr and Anna Wynar identifies newspapers and periodicals published by various ethnic groups in the United States and describes their content and bibliographical features. It is limited to sixty-three ethnic groups, arranged in fifty-one sections with a separate chapter devoted to multiethnic publications. The American Indian press and the black American press are excluded.

Patricia Hagood's *Oxbridge Directory of Ethnic Periodicals* contains some 3,500 ethnic newspapers, magazines, journals, newsletters, bulletins, directories, yearbooks, bibliographies, and association publications published in the United States and Canada for over seventy ethnic groups. Multiethnic periodicals and publications on immigration, naturalization, and census data are also listed.

A number of additional lists are available that identify ethnic periodicals and newsletters. Among these are the titles included in Wayne Miller's *A Comprehensive Bibliography for the Study of American Minorities*; Paul Wasserman and Alice Kennington's *Ethnic Information Sources of the United States: A Guide to Organizations*; Ulrich's *International Periodicals Directory*; Bill and Linda Katz's *Magazines for Libraries*; and Margie Domenech's *Oxbridge Directory of Newsletters*.

Individual ethnic group newspapers and periodicals are available on microfilm. The "Ethnic Records Microform Project" (ERMP) established

7. Constance Bullock and others, *Ethnic Serials at Selected University of California Libraries* (Los Angeles: Univ. of California, 1977).

by the Center for Immigration Studies at the University of Minnesota and the Center for Research Libraries (CRL) in Chicago, in conjunction with the Immigration History Group, selectively films ethnic newspapers and other periodicals in order to preserve the historical records of the great immigrations to the United States from Europe. Use of the CRL collection is limited to libraries of institutions that are CRL members or associate members.

The Pennsylvania Ethnic Heritage Studies Center and the University Center for International Studies at the University of Pittsburgh created an index to journal articles, the *Ethnic Studies Bibliography* from the contents of *United States Political Science Documents* (USPSD). There are 150 journals reviewed and listed in the indexes of the latter publication, *USPSD*, by author, subject, geographic area, proper name, and journal. Numerous race and ethnic studies subject headings are included. Print and an online version are available. In addition to this publication, other particular discipline's or general indexes to journal articles, there are journal indexes for certain specific ethnic groups.

PROCEEDINGS AND CONFERENCE PAPERS

Papers presented on ethnic topics at conferences, seminars, symposia, colloquia, conventions, and workshops are often very difficult to identify. Ethnic group studies and ethnic interests can be found among the papers in the *Index to Social Sciences and Humanities Proceedings*. This index includes proceedings from throughout the world, in English and foreign languages, and from a range of disciplines. Each quarterly issue or annual cumulation contains a main section of contents of proceedings; category index; permuterm subject index; sponsor index; author/editor index; meeting location index; and a corporate index including a geographic section and an organization section. Those papers not included in this index remain difficult to identify. Oftentimes they might be identified in the varied ethnic newsletters and journals, in references, or in other citations. Of course a number of the papers are unpublished and thus unavailable, except perhaps from the author.

GOVERNMENT PUBLICATIONS

Materials about ethnic groups are produced by a wide variety and constantly changing group of federal agencies. In Barbara Ford and Laurel Minott's essay "United States Government Publications as Sources for Ethnic Information," examples of useful and interesting ethnic publications are given to illustrate the numerous materials available, and bibliographic control and access through the Federal Depository Library system is discussed. Additional resources can also be identified in the "Ethnic

Groups" section of Judith Robinson's *Subject Guide to U.S. Government Reference Sources.*

Several publications are available for selection of government publications including the microfiche *GPO Sales Publications Reference File*, a books-in-print and for-sale catalog of the Goverment Printing Office publications; *New Books*, a list organized into principal subject areas, such as business and labor, census, education, health, law and law enforcement, etc.; *U.S. Government Books*, a publication available one copy at a time when documents are ordered; and the "Subject Bibliographies," covering 300 topics, which include minorities and civil rights and equal opportunity. Government bookstores, operated all around the country, are available for examining publications and placing special orders.

Regular and irregular columns on new government publications can be found in *Booklist, RQ, School Library Media Quarterly*, and *Wilson Library Bulletin*, oftentimes with an emphasis on ethnic publications.

MULTIMEDIA RESOURCES

The federal law establishing the Ethnic Heritage Studies Program stimulated the growth and development of ethnic curriculum projects in American schools and, at the same time, created a demand for minority ethnic nonprint resources to support the curriculum in elementary, secondary, and postsecondary institutions. College and university libraries have been among the last to adopt nonprint media for educational purposes and many of the selection aids, retrospective lists, directories, and guides are directed toward elementary and secondary schools, making it a challenge for college and university librarians to locate suitable materials.

In the essay "Nonprint Ethnic Resources," Adele Dendy cites a list of criteria by the Council on Interracial Books for Children to assist in the evaluation of nonprint ethnic resources, and notes that the selection of these resources cannot rely solely on reviews, as is typically done with books. Previewing for purchase consideration is seen as central to the evaluation and selection of nonprint resources. "Recorded Ethnic Music: A Guide to Resources," compiled by Norm Cohen and Paul Wells, is available to identify ethnic music.

Lubomyr Wynar and Lois Buttlar, in their *Ethnic Film and Filmstrip Guide for Libraries and Media Centers; A Selective Filmography*, note that although filmographies pertaining to ethnic groups in the United States that are appropriate for use in educational institutions do exist, the majority are related to just a few major groups and in many instances fail to provide adequate filmographic information and description of listed sources. A reference compendium to audiovisual ethnic sources, their publication is a comprehensive annotated guide to films and filmstrips related to the

Wynar, Lubomyr R., and Lois Buttlar. *Ethnic Film and Filmstrip Guide for Libraries and Media Centers: A Selective Filmography.* Littleton, Colo.: Libraries Unlimited, 1980.
This publication is based on a comprehensive filmographic survey of ethnic films and filmstrips available for acquisition or rental. It is an annotated guide to films and filmstrips related to the experience of individual American ethnic groups as well as ethnic topics in general. Because of the existence of the Program for the Study of Ethnic Publications, a good number of the titles listed in this filmography are available for preview and rental through Kent State University.

experience of individual American ethnic groups as well as ethnic topics in general. A separate chapter is devoted to multiethnic audiovisual sources and to general ethnic topics. A list of producers and distributors is provided.

Conclusion

This essay provides only a capsule view of the many resources and tactics necessary for race and ethnic studies collection development. Undoubtedly the selection and acquisition of race and ethnic studies resources is no simple undertaking. The social contribution made by collecting, preserving, and providing access to these resources is unquestionable.

The future of race and ethnic studies collection development is directly related to notions and perceptions of how essential these areas are and how necessary it is for libraries to continue collecting. With technological change there should be new opportunities and challenges for race and ethnic studies collection development.

Both national and international groups of librarians exist that support the selection and acquisition of race and ethnic studies resources. The multiethnic group in the American Library Association is the Ethnic Materials Information Exchange Round Table, and in the International Federation of Library Associations it is the Round Table on Library Service to Ethnic and Linguistic Minorities. There are also individual ethnic group caucuses in state library associations and in the American Library Association.

Selection Sources

A Bibliography of Doctoral Research on Minorities: Racial, Religious and Ethnic. Ann Arbor, Mich.: Xerox University Microfilms, 1972.
Booklist. v.1– . 1905– . Chicago: American Library Assn. 22/year. (Refer to government publications column for ethnic resources.)

Cashman, Marc, and Barry Klein. *Bibliography of American Ethnology*. Rye, N.Y.: Todd, 1976.

Cohen, Norm, and Paul F. Wells. "Recorded Ethnic Music: A Guide to Resources." In *Ethnic Recordings in America: A Neglected Heritage*. Washington, D.C.: American Folklife Center, Library of Congress, 1982, pp. 175–250.

Cole, Katherine W. *Minority Organizations: A National Directory*. Garret Park, Md.: Garrett Park Pr., 1982.

Cordasco, Francesco, and David N. Alloway. *American Ethnic Groups: The European Heritage, A Bibliography of Doctoral Dissertations Completed at American Universities*. Metuchen, N.J.: Scarecrow, 1981.

Council of Planning Librarians. *CPL Exchange Bibliographies*. v.1– . 1958– . Chicago: CPL Bibliographies. Monthly.

Dendy, Adele S. "Nonprint Ethnic Resources." In *Ethnic Collections in Libraries*. Ed. by E. J. Josey and Marva L. DeLoach. New York: Neal-Schuman, 1983, pp. 36–45.

Domenech, Margie, ed. *Oxbridge Directory of Newsletters*. New York: Oxbridge Communications, 1985. (Titles appear in "ethnic" section.)

EMIE Bulletin. v.1– . 1982– . Chicago: Ethnic Materials Information Exchange Round Table. American Library Assn. Quarterly.

Ethnic and Racial Studies. v.1– . 1978– . Boston: Routledge Journals. Quarterly.

Ethnic Forum: Journal of Ethnic Studies and Ethnic Bibliography. v.1– . 1980– . Kent, Ohio: Center for the Study of Ethnic Publications, Kent State Univ. Biannually.

"Ethnic Records Microform Project" (ERMP). Newspaper and Periodical Microfilm. Chicago: Center for Research Libraries. (Available to members only.)

Ethnic Studies Bibliography. v.1–2. 1975–76. Pittsburgh: Pennsylvania Ethnic Heritage Studies Ctr. and Univ. Ctr. for International Studies, Univ. of Pittsburgh. (Refer to *United States Political Science Documents*.)

Ethnic Studies in North America: A Catalog of Current Doctoral Dissertation Research. 1983– . Ann Arbor, Mich.: Xerox University Microfilms. Irregularly.

Ford, Barbara J., and Laurel Minott. "United States Government Publications as Sources for Ethnic Information." In *Ethnic Collections in Libraries*. Ed. by E. J. Josey and Marva L. DeLoach. New York: Neal-Schuman, 1983, pp. 46–62.

Fulton, Len, and Ellen Ferber, eds. *International Directory of Little Magazines and Small Presses*. Paradise, Calif.: Dustbooks, 1984 (Refer to subject index under specific ethnic groups and under "Third World, Minorities.")

Gilbert, Victor F., and Darshan Singh Tatla. *Immigrants, Minorities and Race Relations: A Bibliography of Theses and Dissertations Presented at British and Irish Universities, 1900–1981*. London and New York: Mansell, 1984.

GPO Sales Publications Reference File. v.1– . 1977– . Microfiche. Washington, D.C.: Superintendent of Documents, Government Printing Office. Bimonthly with monthly supplements.

Hagood, Patricia. *Oxbridge Directory of Ethnic Periodicals*. New York: Oxbridge Communications, 1979.

IFLA Round Table on Library Service to Ethnic and Linguistic Minorities Newsletter. v.1– . 19– – . London: Commonwealth Institute. 3/year.

Immigrant in America. Microfilm collection. Woodridge, Conn.: Research Publications, 1983.

Index to Social Sciences and Humanities Proceedings. v.1– . 1979– . Philadelphia: Institute for Scientific Information. Quarterly.

International Migration Review. v.1– . 1966– . Staten Island: Ctr. for Migration Studies of New York. Quarterly.

Interracial Books for Children Bulletin. v.1- . 1970- . New York: Council on Interracial Books for Children. 8/year.

Joramo, Marjorie K. *A Directory of Ethnic Publishers and Resource Organizations.* Chicago: American Library Assn., Chicago: 1979.

Journal of American Ethnic History. v.1- . 1981- . New Brunswick, N.J.: Transaction Periodicals Consortium, Rutgers Univ. Semiannually.

Journal of Ethnic Studies. v.1- . 1972- . Bellingham, Wash.: Western Washington Univ. Quarterly.

Katz, Bill, and Linda Sternberg Katz. *Magazines for Libraries.* New York: Bowker, 1982. (Titles appear in "ethnic groups" section, in sections by specific ethnic group(s), and in sections by subject disciplines.)

MELUS: Journal of the Society for the Study of Multiethnic Literature in the United States. v.1- . 1974- . Cincinnati: Univ. of Cincinnati, Dept. of English. Quarterly.

Miller, Wayne Charles. *A Comprehensive Bibliography for the Study of American Minorities.* 2v. New York: New York Univ. Pr., 1976.

_____. *A Handbook of American Minorities.* New York: New York Univ. Pr., 1976.

_____. *Minorities in America: The Annual Bibliography. 1976.* University Park: Pennsylvania State Univ., 1985.

National Association for Ethnic Studies Newsletter. v.1- . 1975- . Davis, Calif.: National Assn. for Ethnic Studies Publications. Semiannually.

New Books. v.1- . 1982- . Washington, D.C.: Superintendent of Documents. Government Printing Office. Bimonthly.

A Quarterly Bibliography of Cultural Differences (1964-1982). Sacramento: California State Library. Quarterly. (Was a useful selection checklist.)

Robinson, Judith Schiek. *Subject Guide to U.S. Government Reference Sources.* Littleton, Colo.: Libraries Unlimited, 1985.

RQ. v.1- . 1960- . Chicago: American Library Assn. Quarterly. (Refer to government publications column for ethnic resources.)

Sage Race Relations Abstracts. v.1- . 1975- . Beverly Hills, Calif.: Sage. Quarterly.

School Library Media Quarterly. v.1- . 1952- . Chicago: American Library Assn. Quarterly. (Refer to government publications column for ethnic resources.)

Torres, Rita, and others. *Multicultural/Multilingual Resources: A Vendor Directory.* Sacramento: California State Library, California Ethnic Services Task Force, 1979.

Ulrich's International Periodicals Directory. New York: Bowker, 1984. ("Ethnic interest" section lists a variety of titles.)

United States Political Science Documents. v.1- . 1975- . Pittsburgh: Univ. Ctr. for International Studies, Univ. of Pittsburgh. Annually.

U.S. Government Books. v.1- . 1982- . Washington, D.C.: Superintendent of Documents, Government Printing Office. Quarterly.

Wasserman, Paul, and Alice E. Kennington. *Ethnic Information Sources of the United States: A Guide to Organizations.* Detroit: Gale, 1983. (Newspaper and newsletter titles are listed by individual ethnic group.)

Wilson Library Bulletin. v.1- . 1914- . Bronx, N.Y.: Wilson. Monthly. (Refer to government publications column for ethnic resources.)

Wynar, Lubomyr R., *Encyclopedic Directory of Ethnic Organizations in the United States.* Littleton, Colo.: Libraries Unlimited, 1975.

_____, and Lois Buttlar. *Ethnic Film and Filmstrip Guide for Libraries and Media Centers: A Selective Filmography.* Littleton, Colo.: Libraries Unlimited, 1980.

_____, and Anna T. Wynar. *Encyclopedic Directory of Ethnic Newspapers and Periodicals in the United States.* Littleton, Colo.: Libraries Unlimited, 1976.

THE RADICAL LEFT AND RIGHT

Jannette Fiore

In undertaking selection of library materials in the area of the radical Left and Right, two preliminary questions arise. The obvious one is that of definition: what is the "radical" Left and Right? The second and more manageable question is what sort of collection is envisioned, given, on the one hand, the different needs and interests of public, college, and university libraries and, on the other, possibilities that extend from current general information about a few significant groups to a "special" collection of primary materials for either a broad or a more selected range of American radicals.

While "left" and "right" mean different things to different individuals, depending on their political perspectives, there is a sufficiently common understanding of the general meaning of the two terms to permit agreement, in most cases, in placing a given idea or organization either to the left or right of center. "Radical," however, is much more contextual in its meaning, and agreement about the point at which either the Left or the Right becomes radical is not so readily achieved. It is probably enough, for our purposes, to take note of how our own context has shaped our categorizing and collecting habits. A quick review of something so familiar as library practice in assigning subject headings makes clear what most of us know—in the United States, "radical" has generally meant anything to the left, from a democratic socialist movement committed to electoral politics to an advocate of the violent overthrow of the government. By contrast, the radical Right is usually defined so as to include only the extremes: the Ku Klux Klan, various Nazi and neo-Nazi groups, possibly (but not probably) the John Birch Society and, more recently, some elements of the "New Right."

This process is no doubt encouraged by the tendency of the Left to organize itself into political parties and to campaign for a direct role in the governing process, thereby categorizing or labeling itself (i.e., the Communist Labor Party or the Socialist Workers Party). Its counterparts to the right of center have more often, at the extreme, formed secret and semisecret societies devoted to direct and often illegal intervention into community life. Nearer center, they have been represented in a whole complex of policy-shaping bodies—lobbies, advisory groups, and think tanks—which surround, penetrate, and shape the governmental process, usually in the guise of disinterested, nonpartisan experts and concerned citizens, and seldom with explicitly avowed political affiliations.

Similarly, while the periodicals of the Left are likely to identify themselves as such—*In These Times* is "The Independent Socialist Newspaper," *The Guardian* is "an Independent Radical Newsweekly," *Revolutionary Worker* is "the Voice of the Revolutionary Communist Party, U.S.A."—those of the Right generally do not. Thus, publications of the American Enterprise Institute and periodicals such as *Human Events* and *American Spectator* will probably be housed in the general collection, while Left equivalents such as *In These Times* or studies produced by the Coalition for a New Foreign and Military Policy, if they are to be found at all, will more likely be located in a "special" collection, inadvertently or, more often, intentionally stigmatized as "radical."

For purposes of this essay and in my own collecting activity, my working definition of the radical Left and Right is broad rather than narrow, encompassing the parties and groups of the Left, the societies and organizations of the Right, and the think tanks and other policy-influencing bodies of both. I also include a category that is not explicitly left or right, but is perhaps in our time more important than either: the whole range of activist organizations that seek fundamental alterations in American policy or society, either through direct political activity or through shaping public opinion. The Moral Majority, the Pro-choice and Right-to-life organizations, the Freeze or the many Third World "solidarity" groups are among the vital political forces of our era and will doubtless be as much a subject of study for the next generation as the "New Left" of the sixties now is for ours. Most collections, having gone this far, will find it both useful and practical to include other less strictly political viewpoints. The range of material variously designated as "new age," "alternative life style," etc., forms a continuum along which it is difficult to draw any but arbitrary lines.

Defining the Collection

In determining the extent and scope of collecting activity that should be undertaken, the usual criteria apply: What is the user group to be served and what are its needs? What are the broad and ongoing responsibilities of the institution for public service, study, and research? What are its peculiar interests and strengths? Beyond these, if a collection strong in current materials is needed, what are the important issues, especially at the local or regional level, and who are the groups working around those issues? If a more comprehensive historical collection is envisioned, local and regional history and the presence of other significant collections in the area are also important considerations.

Public and small college libraries may conclude that their constituents will be well served by a collection of general information that emphasizes current materials and focuses on major national organizations and/or on locally active groups and locally important issues. A well-chosen collection of current periodicals, backed up with a careful selection of books and pamphlets, may be what is needed. College and university libraries, on the other hand, may want to consider a larger collection that includes both current and retrospective holdings, with back files of a larger number of periodicals, more extensive pamphlet and ephemera collections and, when they can be acquired, manuscript and archival materials.

For the most part, this essay focuses on acquisition of primary materials in the context of a "special" collection (primary, that is, in the sense that, published or not, they are products *of*, rather than works *about*, a given organization, group, or individual). The library that does not wish to go so far as a separately administered collection can treat radical periodicals as it does others and can usefully incorporate pamphlet and ephemeral material into a "current issues" vertical file in an appropriate service unit, especially if long term preservation for a historical collection is not planned. The bibliographer whose responsibilities also include selection of secondary material for a general collection may wish to consult the essays on related disciplines such as political science, history, and sociology in *The Selection of Library Materials in the Humanities, Social Sciences, and Sciences.*[1]

Academic libraries should not assume that a more comprehensive collection will serve exclusively, or even primarily, the needs of graduate students and faculty researchers. Michigan State University's American Radicalism Collection is most heavily used by undergraduates—in a typical spring term research paper "season," we will handle between three and four thousand requests for information from undergraduates. In a sense, such a collection can serve as a laboratory in which students gain their first real experience in critical evaluation of primary materials.

An important corollary to identifying the user constituency is cultivating that constituency. In this respect, a special collection offers an important advantage that to some degree offsets the admitted disadvantages of se-

1. Patricia A. McClung, ed., *Selection of Library Materials in the Humanities, Social Sciences, and Sciences* (Chicago: American Library Assn, 1985).

questering this or any other sort of material. By developing working relationships with faculty, we become familiar with both their individual
research interests and their teaching needs and habits. In turn, we can
educate them in the potential curricular uses of the collection, breaking
through the invisibility that generally surrounds a special collection and
greatly enhancing both its use and its usefulness. There are some disadvantages to this kind of use, the chief being that material receives much
more wear and tear than it otherwise might and we occasionally lose an
item. There are also unanticipated benefits: one of the half-dozen or more
undergraduates doing term paper work on the Ku Klux Klan in a recent
term provided us with a print of a two-hour videotaped interview he
conducted with Michigan Klan leader Robert Miles, who is emerging as
a significant figure in the current interplay of the various groups of the
extreme Right (the Aryan Nation, the Order, et al.). The same term brought
a KKK robe and hood from a different source. Less spectacular but useful
donations of radical publications from grateful users are common occur-
rences, sometimes continuing long after a student has left the area.

Building the Collection

Much has been said in the last decade about the difficulty of acquiring
alternative materials for libraries and most of it applies as much to political
viewpoints as to other alternatives.[2] In the same time period, a great many
very useful tools for librarians have appeared. The bibliographer undertaking to build a collection of radical materials will find that the only
serious constraint on his or her work is time—time to identify what is
needed from the myriad of possibilities and time to pursue it through the
somewhat unconventional means often required. While it is true that
standard reviewing sources and mainstream vendors generally do not serve
our purposes, the absence of these conventional aids is not so great a
handicap as it may seem. Whether your objective is to provide a limited
cross-section of current opinion on important issues or to build an extensive collection documenting the history of a few or many American
radicals, the task is less a matter of identifying and securing any given title
than of acquiring a representative selection of materials—it is not so much
knowing *what*, as deciding *who*, you want.

KNOWING WHO'S WHO

The great practical difficulty in collecting materials of the Left or the Right
lies in identifying and understanding the nature of the multifarious groups

2. James P. Danky, "Acquisition of Alternative Materials," in *Alternative Materials in
Libraries*, ed. by James P. Danky and Elliott Shore (Metuchen, N.J.: Scarecrow, 1982), 12–
30, is a succinct summary of the problems facing librarians in acquiring nonmainstream
materials.

that make up either category. It has always been difficult, on the Left, to sort out the various parties and splinter groups and to ascertain who they are or were, how they interrelate, and what their importance is or was. It has become increasingly so on the Right. At the extreme, sometimes interlinked and sometimes rival KKK, Nazi and neo-Nazi, survivalist and white supremacist groups proliferate, while nearer center, the interlocking relationships of the innumerable "New Right" organizations are practically a study in themselves.

Histories and Studies. Histories of the Left and Right are plentiful and bibliographers familiar with United States political history will have their own preferred sources. Selectors new to the field may find those included here especially helpful. Jonathan M. Kolkey's *The New Right, 1960–1968 with Epilogue, 1969–1980* identifies and categorizes the Right from the Cold War era forward, with extensive use of quotations from right-wing publications and spokespersons and a detailed exposition of the nature and origins of right-wing positions on the issues they address.[3] Alan Crawford's *Thunder on the Right* is one of several works focusing on the New Right, especially as it differs from the mainstream of traditional American conservatism.[4] *The Politics of Unreason; Right-wing Extremism in America, 1790–1970* provides an overview and analysis of the history of the far Right in the United States.[5] Published in the mid-seventies, Ferdinand V. Solara's *Key Influences in the American Right* lists and describes sixty right-of-center organizations and publications, with an interesting scheme of relating them to each other and to the larger political context.[6]

Very useful recent studies include Robert Armstrong's analysis of the components of the Reagan coalition, "Reagan's Uneasy Alliance," in *NACLA Report on the Americas* and several reports by Sasha Gregory-Lewis for *The Advocate*, especially "The New-Right Political Apparatus," and a two-part series, "Danger on the Right."[7] Both Gregory-Lewis studies include detailed charts of the interrelationships of organizations and individuals within the current Right.

Milton Cantor's *The Divided Left, American Radicalism 1900–1975* is a concise account of the twentieth-century American Left; John P. Diggins's *The American Left in the Twentieth Century* is more general but

---

3. Jonathan M. Kolkey, *The New Right, 1960–1968 with Epilogue, 1969–1980* (Washington, D.C.: Univ. Pr. of America, 1983).

4. Alan Crawford, *Thunder on the Right* (New York: Pantheon, 1980).

5. Seymour M. Lipset, *The Politics of Unreason; Right-wing Extremism in America, 1790–1970* (New York: Harper and Row, 1970).

6. Ferdinand V. Solara, *Key Influences in the American Right*, rev. ed. (n.p.: LEA Communications, 1974).

7. Robert Armstrong, "Reagan's Uneasy Alliance," *NACLA Report on the Americas* 15:8–24 (July–Aug., 1981); Sasha Gregory-Lewis, "The New-Right Political Apparatus," *The Advocate* 234:6–9 (Feb. 8, 1978); Gregory-Lewis, "Danger on the Right," *The Advocate* 227:11–16 (Nov. 2 1977), 228:6–10 (Nov. 15, 1977).

Muller, Robert H., Theodore Spahn, and Janet Spahn. *From Radical Left to Extreme Right*. 3v. 2nd ed., rev. and enl. Metuchen, N.J.: Scarecrow, 1972–76. (Vol. 1; Ann Arbor, Mich.: Campus Publishers, 1970.) Bibliography of periodicals; lists approximately 1,500 publications. Ten years old but still extremely useful: organized by categories, e.g., Radical Left, Marxist-Socialist Left, Radical Professional, Labor and Union, Underground, Comics (i.e., underground comics), Libertarian, Utopian, Conservation and Ecology, Liberal, Civil Rights, Prisons, Feminist, Gay Liberation, Racial and Ethnic Pride, Peace, Servicemen's Papers, Conservative, Anti-Communist, Race Supremacist, Metaphysical, UFOs, and Miscellaneous. The work is indexed for (1) editors, publishers and opinions, (2) titles, and (3) place of origin.

also a useful introduction.[8] Walter Goldwater's *Radical Periodicals in America, 1800–1950* includes a very useful genealogical chart and short historical sketches of the parties and groups whose publications he includes.[9] *The American Radical Press, 1880–1960*, edited by Joseph Conlin and produced to accompany the Greenwood reprint series, provides a more thorough study of leftist groups and their publications, organized chronologically and theoretically.[10]

Directories. For both Left and Right, there are a number of useful directories of organizations and publications. The second edition of *From Radical Left to Extreme Right*, by Robert H. Muller et al., is now a decade old but remains the most comprehensive single source for identifying and placing groups, through their periodical publications, across a whole range of possibilities. Laird Wilcox, whose ephemera collections are part of the holdings of the University of Kansas Library, has produced several editions of his directories of the Left and Right. Their usefulness is limited by the fact that each is a simple, unannotated alphabetical listing of organizations, publishers, and publications (with mailing addresses), but for the Right, at least, Wilcox's *Directory* is one of very few tools available. A more useful source for the right wing is Bayliss (Jim) Corbett's *Spectrum*. *Spectrum* lists periodicals, publishers, distributors, and organizations, with the last only organized by the nature of their paramount area of interest. Both the Wilcox and Corbett directories incorporate many of the activist and single-issue organizations of the Right. For not-strictly-political alternatives, if these are to be included, the best single tool is Patricia Case's

8. Milton Cantor, *The Divided Left, American Radicalism 1900–1975* (New York: Hill and Wang, 1978). Histories of the major parties are available; notably David A Shannon, *The Socialist Party of America* (Chicago: Quadrangle Books, 1955) and Irving Howe and Lewis Coser, *The American Communist Party, A Critical History* (Boston: Beacon, 1957); John P. Diggins, *The American Left in the Twentieth Century* (New York: Harcourt Brace, 1973).

9. Walter Goldwater, *Radical Periodicals in America, 1800–1950* (New Haven: Yale Univ. Pr., 1964).

10. Joseph R. Conlin, *The American Radical Press, 1880–1960*, 2v. (Westport, Conn.: Greenwood, 1974).

Case, Patricia J. *Field Guide to Alternative Media: A Directory to Reference and Selection Tools Useful in Accessing Small and Alternative Press Publications and Independently Produced Media.* Chicago: American Library Assn., 1984.
Guide to reference and selection tools.
Published by the Task Force on Alternatives in Print of the ALA's Social Responsibilities Round Table, this is the tool to use to find all the other tools. "The Field Guide attempts to list and describe all available tools that list, index, or review primarily small and alternative press publications and independently-produced media." It includes subject and trade directories, indexes and subject bibliographies, trade and review media, and bookstore and distributor catalogs. Each listing is informatively annotated, with information on price and availability.

Field Guide to Alternative Media, a concise directory of selection tools and sources for a wide range of materials. For older right-wing groups, especially the more obscure ones, the printed guide to *The Right Wing Collection of the University of Iowa Libraries, 1918-1977*, produced to accompany the microform project by that title, is useful, albeit not easy to use. For older organizations and individuals of the Left, the infamous House Un-American Activities Committee reports and Attorneys General's lists do name names.

Other Sources. There are a number of research organizations that publish information, including the Data Center in Oakland, Midwest Research, Inc., in Chicago, and Interchange Resource Center and Group Research, Inc., both based in Washington, D.C.[11] All monitor and report on right-wing activities. For the Left, *American Sentinel* (formerly *The Pink Sheet on the Left*) is useful.[12]

A less conventional approach to placing the elements of the activist population in particular is to look at networking in support of marches, demonstrations, fundraisers, boycotts, and other activities and to examine memberships in umbrella organizations. The Coalition for a New Foreign and Military Policy, for example, lists nearly 50 affiliate organizations with a wide range of political and social interests; the Coalition for Peace through Strength counts over 150.[13] This is a particularly useful strategy

11. Data Center, 464 19th Street, Oakland, CA 94612 ("A project of the Investigative Resource Center, Inc."); Midwest Research, Inc., 343 S. Dearborn, Suite 1505, Chicago, IL 60604; Interchange Resource Center, 1201 16th St., N.W., Washington, DC 20036 (publishers of a bimonthly *Bulletin* and a quarterly *Interchange Report*; Group Research, Inc., 313 Colorado Bldg., 1341 G. St., N.W., Washington, DC 20005 (publishers of *Group Research Report*).
12. *American Sentinental*, Phillips Publishing Co., 7315 Wisconsin Ave., Suite 1200 N, Bethesda, MD 20814.
13. Coalition for a New Foreign and Military Policy, 120 Maryland Ave., N.E., Washington, DC 20002; Coalition for Peace through Strength, 4995 Capitol, S.E., Washington, DC 20003.

for identifying very current groups and for forming at least a preliminary estimate of their general political position. Many of the directories included in Case's *Field Guide to Alternative Media* will assist in identifying networks and coalitions; others will come to your attention through periodicals, mailings and events.

GETTING THE GOODS

Assuming that we have at least a preliminary idea about the nature and scope of the collection we want and have some of the tools in hand, the remaining question is how to get the material. Now that we know what, or at least who, we want, how do we get it?

Current Materials: Periodicals. For current materials, periodicals are the best bargain. A current periodical collection, whether limited or extensive, is relatively easy to establish and a wide range of viewpoints can be covered in ongoing fashion for a relatively small investment of time and money. Radical periodicals tend to be among the cheapest to subscribe to and those of the Left, at least, are relatively well indexed. For a larger collection, a little additional effort can back up the active periodical collection with an extensive file of sample issues. Most publishers will provide a free sample and the rest will sell you an individual issue. Such a sample collection might even be considered by public libraries, whose patrons could thus identify and perhaps subscribe for themselves from a much wider range of material than most libraries can afford to provide regularly for them.

The choice of titles to be included will depend on the intended size and scope of the collection. For left-of-center publications, a logical first step would be to review and select from the titles indexed in the *Alternative Press Index*, although it does not include all of the political party organs. For the Right, Corbett's *Spectrum* has the largest list, though his selections and categorizations are somewhat eccentric and the sheer number of possibilities can be confusing. The novice might more usefully begin by examining the titles from the more selected list of their periodical holdings available from Midwest Research. The *Alternative Press Index*

Alternative Press Index, v.1– . 1969– . Baltimore, Md.: Alternative Press Center. Quarterly.
Periodical index, covering approximately 230 periodicals in each issue. Published quarterly, with a 3–6 month time lag; not cumulated.
Published by the Alternative Press Center, this is the single most comprehensive index of Left and social change periodicals, both scholarly and general, with a few non-U.S. titles included.

Corbett, Bayliss. *Spectrum: A Guide to the Independent Press and Informative Organizations.* 1984– . Winter Haven, Fla.: B. Corbett. Irregularly.
Directory of organizations and publications; earlier editions as *Censored* and *Some Hard to Locate Sources of Information.*
Lists conservative to far-Right and Libertarian publications, booksellers, and organizations, chiefly American but with a relatively large number of foreign entries. Subjects include National Government, Agricultural Movements, Anti-lawyer, Justice and Citizens Rights, Immigration and World Population Problems, etc.; there are more than thirty categories in all. The organization is somewhat eccentric (periodicals by frequency, etc.), as are the descriptive annotations: the Neo-Nazi *National Vanguard*, for example, is an "intellectual pro-White monthly devoted to current trends, White history, survival and renaissance." An earlier edition found the KKK's *Crusader* "literate, temperate and informative."

is an obvious companion purchase; unfortunately, there is no analog for the Right.

Current Materials: Monographs. There are many alternative distributors whose stock includes publications of radical parties and organizations. Where they can be identified, the bibliographer can write directly to the publishing houses of the Left and Right to ask to be placed on mailing lists for catalogs. For the Left, Case's *Field Guide* includes a section for distributors, with annotations describing the range of publications they stock (not all deal in political material). *Spectrum* lists distributors, book stores, and publishing houses of the Right, as does Wilcox's *Directory*, though the latter does not treat them as a separate category. Once catalogs and literature lists are in hand, standard acquisitions methods handle the rest. Many radical groups, especially the new, the locally oriented, and the very topical ones, have no formal publishing and distributing structure, however. With these, an approach we have found effective, albeit costly in time, is to scan incoming periodicals on a regular basis, identifying publications, organizations, and even individuals of interest. Samples of unfamiliar periodicals are requested and orders are placed for books and pamphlets. To organizations, solidarity and support groups, projects and campaigns of many kinds we send a general form request, identifying our collection in terms of its extent, use, and purpose and asking for information about their activities and for a place on their mailing list. (We provide no postage but do supply two prepared mailing labels.) A surprising number of these requests get results, often in the form of substantial packets of material, gift subscriptions for a few issues, and lists of available literature for purchase. The same approach is used with groups and organizations listed in the many directories mentioned earlier and with new ones as they appear.

Looking Backward: Microforms. For a retrospective collection, the bibliographer can accomplish a good deal through simple and conventional means by establishing a base collection in microform. Periodicals of the Left and Right and many of the alternative newspapers of the sixties are now available on film either as single titles or in collections. Major projects include serials, pamphlets, archival and ephemeral materials and are increasingly available. The pamphlet collection of the Tamiment Institute, for example, includes over 8,600 pamphlets originally part of the socialist Rand School Library.[14] *The Right Wing Collection of the University of Iowa Libraries,* mentioned above, incorporates material from 1918–77 for a range of groups that includes even the opponents of fluoridated drinking water. *The Students for a Democratic Society Papers, 1958–1970,* from the collections of the State Historical Society of Wisconsin, covers this popular study topic.[15] Records of major parties, including the Socialist and Socialist Labor Parties, and of organizations such as CORE and the Southern Tenant Farmers' Union, are available—the list goes on.

A relatively new and important microform resource is material released under the Freedom of Information Act (FOIA) from the files of government surveillance agencies; for example, files of the FBI's Cointelpro operations, and projects such as *U.S. Military Intelligence Reports: Surveillance of Radicals in the United States, 1917–1941.*[16] (An unorthodox but sometimes effective approach to acquiring FOIA materials in hard copy is underwriting the cost to researchers for pursuing release of files needed for their research, in exchange for library ownership of the resulting documents.)

Looking Backward: Finding Collections. Beyond resources in microform, retrospective acquisition becomes more difficult. It also becomes more interesting. Older pamphlets and ephemera, as well as periodical runs, are increasingly available in the antiquarian market, but their cost—twelve to twenty-five dollars for a single pamphlet is not uncommon—will probably dictate that such purchases will be limited to areas of very special interest. The bibliographer hoping to build an extensive special collection will want to consider another approach—finding and cultivating local sources with collections of material to sell or—better yet—to donate.

To some extent, as noted earlier, your donor and user constituencies will overlap, but your best sources probably lie outside your immediate user group. Here again, the key is local and regional activity. Was the Communist Party, the Silver Shirts, or the KKK important in your locale?

14. *Radical Pamphlet Literature: A Collection from the Tamiment Library, 1817 (1900–1945)* (Glen Rock, N.J.: Microfilming Corp. of America, 1977).
15. *Students for a Democratic Society Papers, 1958–1970* (Glen Rock, N.J.: Microfilming Corp. of America, 1977).
16. *U.S. Military Intelligence Reports: Surveillance of Radicals in the United States, 1917–1941* (Frederick, Md.: Univ. Pub. of America, 1985).

If so, do participants still survive? There is still time, though it is short, to identify the old-timers who participated in radical activities of the thirties and forties and even the twenties, and not-so-old members of the "New Left" may prove valuable sources. (Faculty can sometimes provide leads and even introductions.) In my experience, many of these individuals still retain large personal collections of pamphlets, books, leaflets, posters, organizational material, etc., which they are prepared to donate or sell at a reasonable price.

Especially when such donors were members of political parties, you may find collections of material otherwise difficult to locate. Over the last several years, the Michigan State University collection has acquired a great deal of Communist Party material, published and internal (drafts of position statements, discussion papers on local and national issues, documents from intraparty conflicts) from the 1950s. From a different source (needless to say) similar materials from the Socialist Workers Party, especially its Johnson-Forest Tendency, have been added. Since our collection had substantial holdings in the Communist Party, U.S.A. and the various Trotskyist groups from the twenties into the mid-forties, these were crucial extensions of areas of strength. In both instances, these materials were only part of collections that extended, in the first case, across the whole range of New Left activity and, in the second, into militant labor activity in the Detroit auto plants.

Another profitable avenue, especially for donations, is through locally based activist organizations. These build extensive working files of information around their areas of interest and often interact with a wide network of like-minded groups with whom they exchange educational materials and reports about their current activities. Because of the topical nature of their work and because they generally have limited office space and small, usually volunteer, staffs, file material that becomes out-of-date (for their purposes, but not for ours) must be disposed of. If you establish working contacts with such groups, your collection may receive cartons of material on subjects ranging from peace, disarmament, and world hunger to Third World revolutions and liberation movements. If a local alternative newspaper still functions in your area, it may well be experiencing a similar problem, as issues exchanged over the years with other publications outgrow the available space and are no longer useful. Call and ask. In all these instances, a willingness to underwrite packing and shipping costs can facilitate donations.

Needless to say, the work of cultivating donors will be easier when the bibliographer shares the outlook of the individual or organization involved, but this is not essential. Political and other activist groups are in the business of persuasion, and the more out of the mainstream they are, the more limited their opportunities to find an audience. Whatever else you can offer, you are providing them an opportunity to be heard, and this can carry you where personal sympathy might not.

By this point, it should be clear that collecting the radical Left and Right really is not all that difficult. Probably, too, it is becoming clear that collecting is only the beginning. If acquiring radical material poses a challenge to traditional library practice, organizing and accessing such material poses a far greater one—but that is another subject and, happily, outside the scope of this essay.

Selection Sources

Alternative Press Center. *Alternative Press Index.* v.1– . 1969– . Baltimore, Md.: Alternative Press Ctr. Quarterly; annual vol. not cumulated.

Case, Patricia J. *Field Guide to Alternative Media: A Directory to Reference and Selection Tools Useful in Accessing Small and Alternative Press Publications and Independently Produced Media.* Chicago: American Library Assn., 1984.

Corbett, Bayliss. *Censored: Hard-to-Locate Sources of Information on Current Affairs.* 13th ed. Winter Haven, Fla.: B. Corbett, 1983.

Muller, Robert H., Theodore Spahn, and Janet Spahn. *From Radical Left to Extreme Right.* 3v. 2nd ed., rev. and enl. Metuchen, N.J.: Scarecrow, 1972–76. (Vol. 1: Ann Arbor, Mich.: Campus Publishers, 1970.)

The Right Wing Collection of the University of Iowa Libraries, 1918–1977. A Guide to the Microfilm Collection. Glen Rock, N.J.: Microfilm Corp. of America, 1978.

Wilcox, Laird M. *Directory of the American Left.* Kansas City, Kans.: Editorial Research Service, 1981.

———. *Supplement.* Kansas City, Kans.: Editorial Research Service, 1983.

———. *Directory of the American Right.* Kansas City, Kans.: Editorial Research Service, 1981.

———. *Supplement.* Kansas City, Kans.: Editorial Research Service, 1983.

SOCIAL WORK

Brenda J. Cox

Collection development in a social work library is a most interesting challenge. The literature of the field is a fusion of information, not just on social work practice per se, but covering numerous related fields, and in many instances there are no clear lines of demarcation. For instance, in the health field emphasis has progressed from strictly treating the physical symptoms to concern for motivational, environmental, and economic factors in health care and the use of human resources in the delivery of services. City planning has expanded to include the conduct of people as they interact with their space. This acknowledgment by other disciplines, that social relationships are significant to their study, has accounted for a cross-fertilization of several fields of study.[1] Developing a collection to accommodate the research needs of the evolving social work field necessitates an understanding of its scope rather than a specific definition of social work. Social work encompases literature on social welfare, the criminal justice system, psychology, mental health, youth, social gerontology, the handicapped, alcohol and drug abuse, health, and industrial social work.[2] Emphases also are placed on women's issues and studies of ethnic minorities. In addition to covering these substantive areas, primary consideration is given to the method or process used in providing services. Therefore, a significant amount of the collection should cover direct services, community organization and development, and social administration as methods of intervention with society.

Grateful appreciation is given to Juanita Portis, Deputy Director, University Libraries, Howard University, and George Martin, Reference Librarian, Howard University, for their helpful comments and suggestions. Many thanks go to Sabrina Thomas and Brenda D. Sims-Grant for their assistance in typing the manuscript.
    1. Robert Morris, "Preface," in *Encyclopedia of Social Work*, 17th ed. (Washington, D.C.: National Assn. of Social Workers, 1977), pp. xii–xiii.
    2. Evelyn Butler, "Social Welfare Libraries and Collections," in *Encyclopedia of Library and Information Science*, v.28. (New York: Dekker, 1980), p. 95.

Clientele

The primary groups served by social work collections are students, researchers, and practitioners who all may have general or very specialized areas of interest. In defining and addressing their various needs, one has to identify the informational requirements and constraints under which these patrons are working. For instance, subject needs of researchers in an academic setting are broader than those of professionals working in a particular issue-oriented organization. Therefore, the collection in the academic setting must have breadth as well as depth in the various fields being covered. Also, researchers may take time to do extensive research, while a practitioner's primary concern may be only to get through his or her case load. A collection geared to current awareness will better serve the needs of this latter group. A few key journal subscriptions and *Social Work Research and Abstracts* may be sufficient.

Collecting Retrospective Materials

Probably the most comprehensive retrospective source available in social work is the *Dictionary Catalog of the Whitney M. Young, Jr. Memorial Library of Social Work*, from Columbia University in New York which was published in 1980. This ten-volume set documents materials in the social welfare field dating back to the 1700s. Volumes nine and ten are agency and projects catalogs, respectively. This is an invaluable resource for identifying materials of historical significance.

The Council on Social Work Education has sponsored the compilation of comprehensive bibliographies of core collections for social work libraries over the last twenty-five years. They can be used to obtain a historical perspective on the field, as well as for identifying some of the classics. *Building a Social Work Library: A Guide to the Selection of Books, Periodicals, and Reference Tools* appeared in 1962. This is a non-annotated bibliography arranged by format. Another major source, *Toward Building the Undergraduate Social Work Library: An Annotated Bibliography*, compiled by Sheldon Gelman, was published in 1971. Although it emphasizes the undergraduate library, the sources identified may also serve as a basis for a graduate library collection. The items are listed alphabetically in the guide, but are coded according to primary subject matter and format.

Gelman's work excludes materials concerning ethnic minorities, since other council publications address this need in a series of bibliographies on five major ethnic minority groups in the United States. These are *The Forgotten American: American Indians Remembered*, by Jere L. Brenna;

Matson, Margaret B., and Sheldon R. Gelman, comps. *Toward Building the Undergraduate Social Work Library: An Annotated Bibliography.* New York: Council on Social Work Education, 1980.
An annotated bibliography.
This work identifies a "core" collection of books and journals for a social work library. In addition to the annotations, each item is coded according to the primary subject(s) covered. Although the title indicates an emphasis on an "undergraduate" collection, the sources identified may also serve as a basis for a graduate library collection.

Poverty, Participation, Protest, Power, and Black Americans, by Charlotte Dunmore; *The Puerto Rican People,* by the Institute of Puerto Rican Studies at Brooklyn College; *Asians in America,* by Harry H. L. Kitano; and *The Chicano Community,* by Eliseo Navarro. Each of these titles is subtitled *A Selected Bibliography for Use in Social Work Education.* With the core collection bibliographies and these supplemental bibliographies, the literature of social work is well documented for this period.

In 1980, Margaret Matson and Sheldon Gelman compiled *Building the Undergraduate Social Work Library: An Annotated Bibliography,* which updated and expanded Gelman's former work. In addition to the annotations, this bibliography also classified the subject matter of the items according to the primary areas of importance. A list of suggested texts for the beginning course in social welfare as well as a list of core periodicals complete the work.

Collecting Current Materials

A most comprehensive and fairly recent bibliography in the field is *Reference Sources in Social Work: An Annotated Bibliography* by James Conrad. This is an invaluable tool for anyone who needs the total picture of reference sources for selection. Conrad identifies pertinent resources in the diverse areas of social work as well as in allied fields. There are

Conrad, James H. *Reference Sources in Social Work: An Annotated Bibliography.* Metuchen, N.J.: Scarecrow, 1982.
An annotated bibliography.
This source identifies a core collection of reference books useful to the field of social work. It categorizes the sources according to format within subjects. The areas covered are general works, allied fields, the fields of service, service methods, and the social work profession. The appendixes include lists of journals, social service organizations, and social work libraries.

Social Work: Journal of the National Association of Social Workers. v.1– .
1956– . Silver Spring, Md.: National Assn. of Social Workers.
Scholarly journal.
About 7–10 reviews per issue.
Approximately 2–3 year lag time in series between publication and reviews.
This major publication of the professional social workers' organization includes
book reviews by scholars in each issue. There is usually at least a two-year lag
time between publication and the appearance of the reviews.

---

also state listings of social work libraries, an inclusive list of social service
organizations, and a list of social work and related journals.

BOOK REVIEWS

Other than *Choice*, current book reviews in this field are not readily available; and even in *Choice*, they are not listed under the field of social work.
Ideally, one would expect to be able to use book reviews from current
journals to assess new publications soon after they are published. However, in this field the reviews in the major journals, *Social Work*, and
Social Casework, etc., appear to be about two years behind the book's
publication. If a librarian waits to read a review before purchasing an item,
the chances are very good that it will not be available in the collection
when it is requested. It is important to remember, especially in academic
settings, that the faculty and other users are receiving announcements at
the same time as the librarian, so one has to make a choice. Either one
makes an educated guess about an item based on prepublication information and orders the book so it is available within a reasonable amount
of time after publication, or opts to wait for it to be reviewed in a scholarly
journal or review publication and risks not having it available when it is
requested and needed. This decision will more than likely be dictated by
the collection development policy.

APPROVAL PLANS

If the selector is affiliated with an institution that uses an approval plan,
some basic concerns need to be addressed. Because of the interdisciplinary
nature of the field, close attention needs to be given to the development
of the social work collection profile. Experience has shown that titles
pertinent to social workers' interests may be classified under another subject, so duplication may be a problem. Another consideration is that the
materials received should relate to the pertinent aspects of the various
areas of interest. Again, the collection development policy may be used
to address the duplication issue. However, the profile will reflect the nu-

ances and relevant areas of the literature as the selector works with and
revises it as necessary.

TRADE PUBLISHER CATALOGS

Another alternative is to develop a strategy guaranteeing exposure to at
least the announcement of current publications of interest. Regularly receiving trade publishers' catalogs is a first step in this process. A selected
list of major publishers for this process contains the following: Haworth
Press, Free Press, Lexington Books, Jossey-Bass, Sage Publications, Springer
Publishing Company, and Addison-Wesley. Several publishers have series
on pertinent issues, such as the Sage Human Services Guides, Springer
Focus on Women Series, Springer Series on Death and Dying, Social Work
and Social Issues Series by the Columbia University Press, and the Social
Science Foundation of Social Welfare Series by Prentice-Hall. By using
Books in Series, other pertinent series can be identified and standing orders
placed for any series in which the selector wants to receive each item.
The alternative would be to order individual volumes as they are published
and take the chance that one would be able to identify everything in a
series.

SUBJECT GUIDE TO FORTHCOMING BOOKS

Using the *Subject Guide to Forthcoming Books* will also facilitate the
identification of prospective publications in specific subject areas. To use
this source effectively one must, again, be cognizant of the subjects to be
covered. Developing a list of subject headings to be covered, similar to a
vertical file listing, is a good idea. As one becomes more knowledgeable
of the field, the list will undoubtedly grow. A selected list of headings
would include:

Abortion	Deinstitutionalization
Adoption	Employee Assistance Programs
Afro-Americans	Families
Aged	Family Therapy
Asian-Americans	Fund-Raising
Birth Control	Groups
Child Abuse	Halfway Houses
Child Welfare	Handicapped
Community Development	Housing
Community Mental Health	Human Sexuality
Corrections	Income Maintenance
Crime	Juvenile Delinquency
Day Care	Mental Health

Mental Illness   Single-Parent Families
Nursing Homes   Social Policy
Parole   Social Welfare
Poverty   Unemployment
Probation   Volunteerism
Rape   Wife Abuse
Recidivism   Women

Society/Agency Publications

Membership in, or being on the mailing lists of, scholarly societies, associations, and institutes whose work is pertinent to social work is essential. Subject-specific research organizations generate studies and statistics that can account for a substantial part of a collection. A selector may determine that the library should acquire all of an organization's publications. In that case a blanket order should be considered. A suggested list of organizations follows.

Alan Guttmacher Institute
360 Park Avenue South, 13th Floor
New York, NY 10010
(212) 685–5858

American Public Welfare Assn.
1125 15th Street N.W.
Washington, DC 20005
(202) 293–7550

Child Welfare League of America
67 Irving Place
New York, NY 10003
(212) 254–7410

Children's Defense Fund
122 C Street N.W.
#400
Washington, DC 20001
(202) 628–8787

Council on Social Work Education
1744 R Street N.W.
Washington, DC 20009
(202) 667–2300

Family Service America
44 East 23rd St.
New York, NY 10010
(202) 674–6100

Institute for Research on Poverty
University of Wisconsin-Madison
Social Science Building, Room 3412
Madison, WI 53706
(608) 262-6358

National Assn. of Social Workers
7981 Eastern Ave.
Silver Spring, MD
(301) 565-0333

National Council on the Aging
600 Maryland Ave. S.W.
West Wing 100
Washington, DC 20024
(202) 497-1200

National Urban League-Washington Operations
1111 14th Street N.W.
Washington, DC 20005
(202) 898-1604

Planned Parenthood Federation of America
810 Seventh Ave.
New York, NY 10019
(212) 541-7800

Project SHARE
P.O. Box 2309
Rockville, MD 20852
(301) 231-9539

Government Documents

GENERAL

In lieu of access to a government documents collection, the selector can use several sources available that identify federal government resources. The best source for identifying government documents is the *Monthly Catalog of United States Government Publications*. It lists items by government document number, but there are also indexes by author, title, subject, series or report number, contract number, stock number, and title key words. The *Government Publications Index* offers a cumulation of the information in the monthly catalog into one alphabet from 1978 to the present on microfilm. The *Index to U.S. Government Periodicals* is another excellent source for identifying relevant information published by government agencies.

Many federal government agencies have publication rooms responsible for the dissemination of information and studies they produce. Hence, rather than dealing with the office responsible for compiling reports or statistics, one can call or write the publication room for the agency. This is also an excellent way to receive free materials. Many government sponsored or generated studies fall under the Freedom of Information Act, which means that a single free copy of each study is available per person. In addition, government reports are frequently sold by the Government Printing Office. For information on state and local programs, contact the appropriate offices within the government structure. Annual reports from the various agencies may also prove useful. Some federal agencies from which pertinent publications may be received are:

Administration on Aging
330 Independence Avenue S.W.
#4146
Washington, DC 20201
(202) 245-0641

Clearinghouse on Drug Abuse Information
P.O. Box 416
Kensington, MD 20795
(301) 443-6500

Data Users Services Division
Customer Service Branch
Bureau of the Census
Washington, DC 20233
(202) 763-4100

Government Printing Office
North Capitol and H Streets N.W.
Washington, DC 20402
(202) 783-3238

National Center Clearinghouse on Child
Abuse and Neglect Information
P.O. Box 1182
Washington, DC 20013
(202) 251-5157

National Institute of Justice/National Criminal
Justice Reference Service
1600 Research Blvd.
Rockville, MD 20850
(301) 251-5500

National Institute of Mental Health
Public Inquiries, Room 15C-05
5600 Fishers Lane
Rockville, MD 20857
(301) 443-4517

National Institute on Alcohol Abuse and Alcoholism
Clearinghouse on Alcohol Information
1776 East Jefferson St.
Rockville, MD 20852
(301) 468–2600

SPECIALIZED

Two categories of information that are important but sometimes hard to acquire are statistical information and information on legislative histories. Population statistics can be retrieved from sources published by the Census Bureau. In addition to *Statistical Abstract of the United States*, the series of *Current Population Reports* (P-20 and P-60) are quite helpful. Publications of the various agencies of the Department of Health and Human Services contain national statistics on social welfare programs. The most comprehensive source of federal government statistics is the *American Statistics Index* (*ASI*) microfiche collection, but its cost precludes purchase in many libraries. *The Statistical Reference Index* is more affordable and an excellent source to use for identifying statistics in government resources other than the federal government. It identifies statistical information found in publications from state and local governments, independent research organizations, trade, professional and nonprofit organizations. Inquiries to local programs or agencies can also produce sources for local statistics.

Information on legislative histories is crucial for policy studies, since all government-sponsored social welfare programs are based in some public law. If a government documents collection is not accessible, there are several sources from which information on government programs may be obtained. The *Catalog of Federal Domestic Assistance* is a good place to start. It provides a basic outline of all government programs, identifies the laws and amendments establishing the programs, and indicates the types of assistance, eligibility requirements, application process, related programs, etc. Having identified the laws authorizing a program, enough information is available to research the history in a law library.

The committees of the United States Senate and House do the background research on all laws, and it is from them that one can receive copies of all public laws, the amendments, and committee reports that went into their making. The *Congressional Staff Directory* may be used to identify the appropriate committee. Also, the Congressional Information Service (CIS) produces a microfiche collection of the same. Printed indexes and abstracts serve as guides to the collection. For information on state and local laws, one should contact appropriate publication offices within state and local governments.

Tests

Sources for identifying instruments (questionnaires) to measure human behavior, and/or social, psychological, political, religious, etc., attitudes are difficult to find. Students and researchers often look for instruments that have already been tested to measure whatever they are studying or to use as guides in developing their own questionnaires. A selected list of proven sources follows.

Beere, Carole A. *Women and Women's Issues: A Handbook of Tests and Measures.*

Brodsky, Stanley L. *Handbook of Scales for Research in Crime and Delinquency.*

Chun, Ki-Taek. *Measures for Social Psychological Assessment: A Guide to 3,000 Original Sources and Their Applications.*

Goldman, Bert A., and John C. Bush. *Directory of Unpublished Experimental Mental Measures.* v.2-4.

———, and John L. Saunders. *Directory of Unpublished Experimental Mental Measures.* v.1.

Goodwin, William L., and Laura A. Driscoll. *A Handbook for Measurement and Evaluation in Early Childhood Education.*

Johnson, Orval G. *Test and Measurements in Child Development: Handbook II.*

Mangen, David J., and Warren Peterson. *Research Instruments in Social Gerontology: Clinical and Social Psychology.*

———. *Research Instruments in Social Gerontology: Health, Program Evaluation and Demography.*

———. *Research Instruments in Social Gerontology: Social Roles and Social Participation.*

Robinson, John P., Robert Athanasiou, and Kendra B. Head. *Measures of Occupational Attitudes and Occupational Characteristics.*

——— and P. R. Stoner. *Measures of Social Psychological Attitudes.*

Shaw, Marvin E. and Jack M. Wright. *Scales for the Measurement of Attitudes.*

Straus, Murray A. and Bruce W. Brown. *Family Measurement Techniques: Abstracts of Published Instruments, 1935-1974.*

Audiovisual Materials

Many social work programs use audiovisual materials and either produce their own videotapes for use in therapeutic or academic settings, or acquire commercially produced tapes. Although many universities have video or media resource centers that provide for the distribution of tapes done in-house, the Human Resource Library in the Department of Social Work of the University of West Florida is a most comprehensive source of tapes in the social work and mental health fields.

The National Audio Visual Center, a division of the National Archives, is the clearinghouse for audiovisual materials produced or supported by the federal government. This facility sells the films but some are available for rental. Since this is a comprehensive collection, it includes many items that may be of interest to those exploring the various areas of social work. A basic catalog with quarterly updates provides lists of media on specific subjects. The center can be contacted at 8700 Edgeworth Drive, Capitol Heights, Maryland 20743-3701; phone (301) 763-1896.

Private vendors offer a wide variety of media formats related to the various issues in the field of social work. An excellent source for identifying those companies that produce films as well as scripts is the "Appendix" in *Video in Mental Health Practice* by Ira Heilveil.[3] It specifies companies and organizations that produce or distribute scripts, educational television, intelligent television, and videotapes.

Indexes and Abstracts

The most important index in the social work field is *Social Work Research and Abstracts*. This publication, issued quarterly by the National Association of Social Workers, abstracts over 150 journals in social work and related fields. Other indexes and abstracts pertinent to the issues in the field of social work that may be used to supplement *Social Work Research and Abstracts* are:

Criminal Justice Abstracts. Hackensack, N.J.: National Council on Crime and
   Delinquency.
Criminology and Penology Abstracts. Leiden: Criminologia Foundation.
Current Literature on Aging. Washington, D.C.: National Council on the Aging.
Human Resources Abstracts. Beverly Hills, Calif.: Sage.
Index to U.S. Government Periodicals. Chicago: Infordata.
Inventory of Marriage and Family Literature. Beverly Hills, Calif.: Sage.
Journal of Human Services Abstracts. Rockville, Md.: Project SHARE.
Sage Family Studies Abstracts. Beverly Hills, Calif.: Sage.

Social Work Research and Abstracts. v.1– . 1965– . Silver Spring, Md.:
   National Assn. of Social Workers.
   Abstracts.
   About 400–800 abstracts per issue. This is primarily an indexing and abstracting
   journal. However, it does have a special section on new doctoral dissertations
   done in the field.

---

3. Ira Heilveil, "Appendix," in *Video in Mental Health Practice: An Activities Handbook.*
(New York: Springer, 1983), pp. 182–86.

Sage Race Relations Abstracts. Beverly Hills, Calif.: Sage.
Sage Urban Studies Abstracts. Beverly Hills, Calif.: Sage.
Social Planning, Policy, Development Abstracts: An International Data Base. San Diego: Sociological Abstracts.
Social Science Citation Index: An International Multidisciplinary Index to the Literature of the Social, Behavioral, and Related Sciences. Philadelphia: Institute for Scientific Information.
Social Service Abstracts. London: Dept. of Health and Social Security.

Journals/Newsletters

The best source for identifying the core journals in the field of social work is the list of titles abstracted in *Social Work Research and Abstracts*. To get a comprehensive view of all titles available, check the most recent edition of *Ulrich's International Periodical Directory*. Although this is not necessarily a selection tool in that it does not contain reviews, it does give an overall picture of what is available and enough pertinent information on individual titles to make an initial determination as to whether a title is worth further exploration.

The following list provides general titles appropriate for most social work collections.

Administration in Social Work. v.1– . 1977– . Haworth. Quarterly.
American Journal of Orthopsychiatry. v.1– . 1930– . American Orthopsychiatry Assn. Quarterly.
Arete. v.1– . 1970– . Univ. of South Carolina, College of Social Work. Semiannually.
Child Welfare. v.1– . 1920– . Child Welfare League of America. Bimonthly.
Community Development Journal. v.1– . 1966– . Oxford Univ. Pr. Quarterly.
Family Planning Perspectives. v.1– . 1969– . Alan Guttmacher Institute. Bimonthly.
Family Process. v.1– . 1962– . Family Process. Quarterly.
Health and Social Work. v.1– . 1976– . National Assn. of Social Workers. Quarterly.
Journal of Continuing Social Work Education. v.1– . 1981– . Continuing Education Programs, School of Social Welfare, State Univ. of New York. Quarterly.
Journal of Gerontological Social Work. v.1– . 1978– . Haworth. Quarterly.
Journal of Marital and Family Therapy. v.1– . 1975– . American Assn. of Marriage and Family Therapy. Quarterly.
Journal of Social Work and Human Sexuality. v.1– . 1981– . Haworth. Semiannually.
Journal of Social Work Education. v.1– . 1965– . Council on Social Work Education. 3/year.
Public Welfare. v.1– . 1943– . American Public Welfare Assn. Quarterly.
Social Casework: The Journal of Contemporary Social Work. v.1– . 1920– . Family Service America. Monthly.
Social Policy. v.1– . 1970– . Social Policy Corp. 4/year.

Social Service Review. v.1- . 1927- . Univ. of Chicago Pr. Quarterly.
Social Work. v.1- . 1956- . National Assn. of Social Workers. 6/year.
Social Work in Education. v.1- . 1978- . National Assn. of Social Workers. Quarterly.
Social Work in Health Care: A Quarterly Journal of Medical and Psychiatric Social Work. v.1- . 1975- . Haworth. Quarterly.
Social Work with Groups: A Journal of Community and Clinical Practice. v.1- . 1978- . Haworth. Quarterly.

Newsletters are useful for obtaining discussions or analyses of topics that are of current interest. They are usually published by special interest organizations that keep abreast of developments in a particular field. And as they are generally published more often than journals, the information in them is more timely. Newsletters are also a good source for identifying nontrade or ephemeral materials available on various topics. The *Oxbridge Directory of Newsletters* is a comprehensive source for identifying newsletters. Listing the newsletters by subject as well as alphabetically, it gives pertinent publication and circulation information.

The following newsletters offer current and prospective information on legislative and administrative actions in their specific areas of study.

CDF Reports. Children's Defense Fund. Monthly.
Children's Voice. Child Welfare League of America. Bimonthly.
Community Development Digest. Community Development Publications. Semimonthly.
Corrections Digest. Washington Crime News Service. Biweekly.
Criminal Justice Newsletter. National Council on Crime and Delinquency. Biweekly.
Day Care U.S.A. Newsletter. Day Care Information Services. Biweekly.
Economic Growth and Revitalization. Community Development Publication. Semimonthly.
Federal Research Report. Federal Research Group. Weekly.
From the State Capitals. Bethune, Jones. Weekly. Series includes:
    Civil Rights
    Family Relations
    Housing and Redevelopment
    Juvenile Delinquency and Family Relations
    Public Assistance and Welfare Trends
    Public Health
    Racial Relations and Civil Rights
    Urban Development
    Women and the Law
Journal of Social Service Research. Haworth. Quarterly.
Marriage and Divorce Today: The Professional Newsletter for Family Therapy Practitioners. Atcom. Weekly.
Planned Parenthood: World Population. Washington Memo. Alan Guttmacher Institute. 20/year.
Sexuality Today: The Professional's Newsletter on Human Sexuality. Atcom. Weekly.

Trends in Housing. National Committee against Discrimination in Housing. Bimonthly.

Washington Social Legislation Bulletin. Child Welfare League of America. Social Legislation Information Service. Semimonthly.

Databases

Databases of possible use to the clientele of a social work library are listed here. Some correspond to indexes available in printed format and are generally available through the vendors BRS or DIALOG. Also provided are area(s) of specialization and producer(s).

Ageline—Aging and the aged. American Assn. of Retired Persons and the National Gerontology Resource Center.

AV-Line—Biomedical and educational audiovisual materials. National Library of Medicine.

Child Abuse and Neglect—Government-sponsored research on child abuse and neglect. U.S. Department of Health and Human Services and the National Center on Child Abuse and Neglect.

CIS (Congressional Information Services)—Federal government legislative histories and committee reports, etc. Congressional Information Service, Inc.

Criminal Justice Periodical Index—Criminal Justice and related topics. University Microfilms International.

DHSS-DATA—Health and Social Services. Department of Health and Social Security, Great Britain.

Dissertation Abstracts Online—Abstracts of doctoral dissertations and masters theses. University Microfilms International.

Drug-Info and Alcohol Use/Abuse—Information on the various impacts of drug and alcohol abuse. University of Minnesota Drug Information Services.

Family Resources—Literature on family life and related topics. National Council of Family Relations.

FARPS (Federal Assistance Programs Retrieval System)—Information on federally funded programs. U.S. Office of Management and Budget.

Handicapped Users Database—Current information pertinent to the needs of handicapped persons. Georgia Griffith.

Marriage and Divorce Today—Family life and social services. Atcom, Inc.

Mental Health Abstracts—Information on biomedicine and psychology. IFI/Plenum Data Company.

NARIC—Rehabilitation information. Rehabilitation Information Center.

National Adoption Network—A referral service and information for family intervention. National Adoption Exchange.

NCJRS (National Criminal Justice Reference Services)—Information on criminal justice research and programs. U.S. Department of Justice and the National Institute of Justice.

Psycho-Info—Psychology. American Psychological Assn.

Social Science Index—Citations from the social sciences and humanities. Wilson.

Social Science Search—A comprehensive listing of information in the social sciences and humanities. Corresponds to the Social Science Citation Index. Institute for Scientific Information.

Social Work Abstracts (SWAB)—Most pertinent information to the field of social work. National Assn. of Social Workers.

Sociological Abstracts—Literature of the field of sociology. Sociological Abstracts, Inc.[4]

Conclusion

For success in developing a social work collection, there is no substitute for being well read in a number of academic disciplines. In many instances, the literature of the field is evolving daily, and the selector has to develop a strategy to keep abreast of new developments. Systematic reviews of the periodical literature, including newspapers as well as some of the previously cited sources, will keep the librarian informed of developing trends. Regular interaction with reference patrons or access to questions can be an invaluable gauge of the research needs of the clientele. The role of faculty advisors or library committees should basically be an advisory one. As the librarian is the one who has access to the broadest scope of the needs of the library clientele, it is reasonable to expect that he or she should be the one to make the final selection decisions, taking into account the advice of the faculty and committee members. Systematically organizing the process to ensure that the various fields of study are covered will produce a collection that will accommodate the needs of the library's patrons.

Selection Sources

American Statistics Index: A Comprehensive Guide to the Statistical Publications of the U.S. Government. v.1- . 1974- . Bethesda, Md.: Congressional Information Service. Monthly.

Beere, Carole A. *Women and Women's Issues: A Handbook of Tests and Measures.* San Francisco: Jossey-Bass, 1979.

Books in Series. 3rd ed. New York: Bowker, 1982.

Books in Series: Original, Reprinted, In-Print, Out-of-Print Books Published or Distributed in the United States in Popular, Scholarly and Professional Series. 6v. 4th ed. New York: Bowker, 1985.

Brenna, Jere L. *The Forgotten American: American Indians Remembered: A Selected Bibliography for Use in Social Work Education.* New York: Council on Social Work Education, 1973.

Brodsky, Stanley L. *Handbook of Scales for Research in Crime and Delinquency.* New York: Plenum, 1983.

4. *Directory of Online Databases.* 7:1 (Jan. 1986).

Brownson, Charles B., and Anna L. Brownson. *Congressional Staff Directory.* Mount Vernon: Congressional Staff Directory, 1985.

Butler, Evelyn. "Social Welfare Libraries and Collections." In *Encyclopedia of Library and Information Sciences.* New York: Dekker, 1980.

Choice. v.1– . 1963– . Middleton: Assn. of College and Research Libraries, American Library Assn. Monthly.

Chun, Ki-Taek. *Measures for Social Psychological Assessment: A Guide to 3,000 Original Sources and Their Applications.* Ann Arbor: Institute for Social Research, 1975.

Congressional Information Service. Index to Publications of the United States Congress. v.1– . 1970– . Bethesda: Congressional Information Service. Monthly.

––––––. *Statistical Reference Index.* Bethesda: Congressional Information Service, 1980. Annually.

Conrad, James H. *Reference Sources in Social Work: An Annotated Bibliography.* Metuchen, N.J.: Scarecrow, 1982.

Council on Social Work Education. *Building a Social Work Library: A Guide to the Selection of Books, Periodicals, and Reference Tools.* New York: Council on Social Work Education, 1962.

Current Population Reports: Population Estimates and Projections. (Series P-20, P-25, P-60) Washington, D.C.: U.S. Bureau of the Census, 1947– .

Dictionary Catalog of the Whitney M. Young, Jr. Memorial Library of Social Work. v.1–10. New York: Columbia Univ.; Boston: Hall, 1980.

Directory of Online Databases. New York: Cuadra/Elsevir, 1986.

Domenech, Margie. *Oxbridge Directory of Newsletters, 1985–86.* New York: Oxbridge Communications, 1985.

Dunmore, Charlotte. *Poverty, Participation, Protest, Power, and Black Americans: A Selected Bibliography for Use in Social Work Education.* New York: Council on Social Work Education, 1976.

Gelman, Sheldon R. *Toward Building the Undergraduate Social Work Library: An Annotated Bibliography.* New York: Council on Social Work Education, 1971.

Goldman, Bert A., and John C. Bush. *Directory of Unpublished Experimental Mental Measures.* v.2–4. New York: Human Science Pr., 1978.

––––––, and John L. Saunders. *Directory of Unpublished Experimental Mental Measures.* v.1. New York: Behavioral Publications, 1974.

Goodwin, William L., and Laura A. Driscoll. *A Handbook for Measurement and Evaluation in Early Childhood Education.* San Francisco: Jossey-Bass, 1980.

Heilveil, Ira. "Appendix." In *Video in Mental Health Practice: An Activities Handbook.* New York: Springer, 1983.

Index to U.S. Government Periodicals. v.1– . 1974– . Chicago: Infordata. Quarterly plus annual cumulation.

Institute of Puerto Rican Studies at Brooklyn College. *The Puerto Rican People: A Selected Bibliography for Use in Social Work Education.* New York: Council on Social Work Education, 1973.

Johnson, Orval G. *Test and Measurements in Child Development: Handbook II.* San Francisco: Jossey-Bass, 1976.

Kianto, Harry H. L. *Asians in America: A Selected Bibliography for Use in Social Work Education.* New York: Council on Social Work Education, 1971.

Mangen, David J., and Warren Peterson. *Research Instruments in Social Gerontology: Clinical and Social Psychology.* v.1. Minneapolis: Univ. of Minnesota Pr. 1982.

_____. *Research Instruments in Social Gerontology: Health, Program Evaluation and Demography.* v.3. Minneapolis: Univ. of Minnesota Pr. 1982.

_____. *Research Instruments in Social Gerontology: Social Roles and Social Participation.* v.2. Minneapolis: Univ. of Minnesota Pr., 1982.

Matson, Margaret B., and Sheldon R. Gelman, comps. *Building the Undergraduate Social Work Library: An Annotated Bibliography.* New York: Council on Social Work Education, 1980.

Monthly Catalog of United States Government Publications. Washington, D.C.: U.S. Government Printing Office. Monthly.

Navarro, Eliseo. *The Chicano Community: A Selected Bibliography for Use in Social Work Education.* New York: Council on Social Work Education, 1971.

Office of Management and Budget. *Catalog of Federal Domestic Assistance.* Washington, D.C.: Office of Management and Budget, 1985.

Robinson, John P., Robert Athanasiou, and Kendra B. Head. *Measures of Occupational Attitudes and Occupational Characteristics.* Ann Arbor, Mich.: Institute for Social Research, 1978.

_____and P. R. Stoner. *Measures of Social Psychological Attitudes.* Ann Arbor, Mich.: Institute for Social Research, 1973.

Shaw, Marvin E., and Jack M. Wright. *Scales for the Measurement of Attitudes.* New York: McGraw-Hill, 1967.

Statistical Abstract of the United States, 1985: National DataBook and Guide to Sources. Washington, D.C.: Government Printing Office, 1985.

Straus, Murray A., and Bruce W. Brown. *Family Measurement Techniques: Abstracts of Published Instruments, 1935-1974.* Rev. ed. Minneapolis: Univ. of Minnesota Pr., 1978.

Subject Guide to Forthcoming Books: A Bimonthly Subject Forecast of Books to Come. v.1- . 1967- . New York: Bowker.

Ulrich's International Periodicals Directory. New York: Bowker, 1985.

Wasserman, Paul, ed. *Statistics Sources.* Detroit: Gale, 1984.

SPORTS AND RECREATION

Patricia McCandless

Although people have always engaged in play, sport, and competitive games, the relative freedom from long working hours brought about by the Industrial Revolution and the concurrent interest in leisure are rather recent phenomena. In simplistic terms, recreation is the voluntary activity humans engage in during their nonworking hours. Sport may therefore be subsumed under recreation as an instance of one such activity. However, both sport and recreation range from spontaneous play to professionalism and a recreation industry.

As disciplines, these fields run the gamut from professional preparation or developing athletic skill to study of human bioscience, especially as people are engaged in various activities, and analysis of those activities in terms of their historic, anthropologic, economic, psychological, or sociological aspects.

Both sport and recreation look at the provision of the activity as well as the mechanics of the activity itself and much endeavor is related to facility design, construction, and management; legal and economic considerations; environmental issues; and usage. Perhaps a remnant of the Puritan attitude toward leisure occasions the examination of the social value or contribution of an activity to an individual's—or humanity's—well-being. Research also focuses on the effect of various activities on particular groups, i.e., various age groups, male versus female, the handicapped, the family unit.

Sport research also examines motor development, biomechanics, locomotion, kinesiology, metabolism, respiration, anthropometry, and disease and injury as they relate to human beings engaged in physical activity. Because of their cross-disciplinary nature, sport and recreation materials cover a wide range and scope. The literature encompasses psychology, medical sciences, biology, education, history, law, sociology, anthropology, commerce, and the arts, so that neither the Library of Congress (GV)

222

nor the Dewey Decimal (790s) classification schemes provide an adequate guide to the literature.

A research collection in sport and recreation consists of both monographs and serials published primarily in English within the last ten years. Significant contributions to the field of sport science have been made by the Germans, whose scholarship should also be reflected in a research collection.

Concerted effort at bibliographic control of sports and recreation literature is a rather recent phenomenon. Indeed, the first subject specific indexes made their appearance in the mid-seventies.[1] These indexes make collection development and reference work in sports and recreation less frustrating, but do not provide comprehensive coverage of this multidisciplinary field. However, recent efforts by the International Association for Sport Information and the World Leisure and Recreation Association to establish international documentation centers may be realized in the near future. UNESCO has just designated the Sports Information Resource Centre (SIRC) in Ottawa, Ontario as the main international sports database. As publisher of the original *Sport Bibliography* and *Sport and Fitness Index* as well as specialized computer bibliographies, SIRC also offers its resources through the SPORT database, accessible through SDC and BRS. This designation as an international database is a welcome step toward more comprehensive bibliographic control.

Both a science and a social science, sports and recreation embrace aspects of many fields: engineering, ergonomics, agriculture, forestry, wildlife management, city planning, gerontology, geography, bioscience, environmental studies, law, public administration, psychology, sociology, tourism, wellness, the arts, nutrition, architecture, education, history, and social work, to name just a few.

Selection and Acquisition of Current Materials

Confronted with this wide spectrum of coverage, the selector must become familiar with the curriculum offered at the particular institution and also with the research interests of the faculty and/or researchers relying on the collection. In a world of exploding resources and a shrinking economy, dialogue and feedback with those people is critical, for most libraries cannot afford to build a comprehensive collection. Within the confines of the defined curriculum and research, nevertheless, it is incumbent upon

1. *Completed Research; Leisure, Recreation and Tourism Abstracts; Physical Education Index; Physical Education/Sports Index* (ceased); *Physical Fitness/Sports Medicine; Sociology of Leisure and Sport Abstracts; Sport and Fitness Index* (ceased); *Sport Search; Sportdokumentation: Literatur der Sportwissenschaft;* and *Sports Documentation Monthly Bulletin.*

the librarian to provide depth and balance and to be cognizant of shifts both within the curriculum and also with the direction of research being conducted locally, nationally, and internationally.

To date, however, little has been written about collection development in sports and recreation. Existing articles generally have focused only on key journals, indexing tools, or reference sources. Of notable exception is Linda Catelli's recent article on sport and physical education collections, although the emphasis is on material for the adolescent and young adult.[2] As of this writing, only minimal investigation of reviewing sources has been conducted, and that research has been confined to sports materials.[3]

MONOGRAPHS

Approval plans, memberships, and standing orders can be utilized to ensure a certain level of coverage of the field, leaving the selector free to pursue more elusive additions to the collection. One useful method of becoming acquainted with new material is to scan incoming journals for advertisements, book reviews, lists of books received for review, blurbs of new publications, and articles of a bibliographic nature. The following journals are particularly useful for identifying new titles:

Adapted Physical Activity Quarterly
American Journal of Sports Medicine
Archives of Physical Medicine and Rehabilitation
Arete
Athletic Journal
Electromyography and Clinical Neurophysiology
Human Movement Science
Journal of Physical Education, Recreation, and Dance
Journal of Sport and Social Issues
Journal of Sport History
Journal of Sport Sciences
Physician and Sportsmedicine
Research Quarterly for Exercise and Sport
Sports Medicine Bulletin

Journals that review recreation sources include:

American Rehabilitation
Annals of Tourism Research
Journal of Leisure Research

2. Linda Catelli, "Physical Education in the 1980s: A Guide for Developing Children and Young Adult Collections," *Collection Building* 5:7–22(Winter 1984).
3. Marshall E. Nunn, "Sports," *Serials Review* 3:37–38(Apr./June 1977); Nancy Dean Cleland, "Comparison of Sports Coverage in *Book Review Digest* and *Book Review Index*," *RQ* 23:451–59(Summer 1984).

Leisure Studies
Parks and Recreation
Special Recreation Digest
Sport and Leisure

To identify reviews of international books in the field, the following journals are most helpful:

British Journal of Physical Education
British Journal of Sports Medicine
Canadian Association for Health, Physical Education and Recreation Journal
EPS: Education Physique et Sport
FIEP Bulletin
International Journal of Rehabilitation Research
International Journal of Sport Psychology
Leistungsport
Loisir & Societe
Olympic Review
Sportwissenschaft

However, one should not be restricted to reading just these or a similar list of most helpful titles. References can crop up everywhere, including the local newspaper or a weekly newsmagazine.

In addition to perusing the standard library selection tools and review sources, the selector of sports and recreation materials also should consult *Resources in Education, Monthly Catalog of United States Government Publications, Government Reports Announcements and Index, Statistical Reference Index, American Statistics Index,* and *CIS Annual* for pertinent report literature conducted or supported by government agencies and statistical data if the collection does not include or have access to a government documents unit. The annual *A London Bibliography of the Social Sciences* is useful for identifying British material, as are *Microlog* and *Canadiana: Canada's National Bibliography* for Canadian materials.

As tedious as it seems, specialized indexes to the literature are worth checking routinely for selection purposes because in addition to journal coverage, books and conference proceedings are indexed as well. The quarterly *Sociology of Leisure and Sport Abstracts* does an excellent job of abstracting individual papers presented at conferences, often before the proceedings have been published. Other unpublished papers cited are frustrating to obtain because the author's affiliation, address, or intention for publication are not given; but the index's document delivery service can supply an urgently needed citation.

Leisure, Recreation and Tourism Abstracts (LRTA) also covers periodic as well as monographic literature and conference proceedings. There is

> *Sociology of Leisure and Sport Abstracts.* v.1- . 1980- . Amsterdam: Elsevier.
>   Quarterly.
> This index is produced by the Information Retrieval System for the Sociology
> of Leisure and Sport (SIRLS), Faculty of Human Kinetics and Leisure Studies,
> University of Waterloo, Ontario. Each issue contains citations to approximately
> 320 current journal articles, conference proceedings, unpublished papers, theses,
> monographs, and government publications covering the field of sport and other
> leisure activities from a social science perspective. It covers material not indexed
> elsewhere in the sport and recreation field and is particularly useful for identifying
> conference proceedings. The availability of theses is noted.

adequate coverage of American materials but, as one might suspect of a publication of the Commonwealth Bureau of Agricultural Economics, the emphasis is upon materials from the British Commonwealth and Europe. The abstracts are of high quality but citations to chapters of books or conferences often vary and contain spelling or typographical errors. *LRTA* recently has begun to cover more leisure, tourism, and hospitality business literature.

Korperkulture und Sport Uberblicksinformation: Sportwissenschaftlich beitrage aus der Deutschen Demokratischen Republik: Informationsbulletin provides coverage of books and dissertations as well as journals. *Sports Documentation Monthly Bulletin* covers papers presented at conferences as well as journal literature and provides complete citations for those conferences at the end of each issue. The new book section at the back of *Sportdokumentation: Literatur der Sportwissenschaft* and the book review section in *Physical Education Index* are good checklists of monographs.

The eight volume set and two volume supplement of *Sport Bibliography* have now become an annual publication. Although the major portion of the citations are to journal literature, conference proceedings and chapters of books are indexed, and its more timely appearance will enhance its

> *Leisure, Recreation and Tourism Abstracts.* v.6- . 1981- . Oxford, England:
>   Commonwealth Bureau of Agricultural Economics. Quarterly.
> Approximately 640 citations to journals, books, conference proceedings, government publications, and dissertations appear in each issue. Materials listed
> cover theory, policy, economic aspects, planning, sociology, psychology, leisure
> of special groups, cultural development, education, natural resources, tourism,
> recreation activities and facilities, culture and entertainment, and home and
> neighborhood activities. Although there is a good coverage of American literature, there is a European and British Commonwealth bias. Because bibliographic
> control of recreation literature is more elusive than sport material, this index is
> indispensable as a selection tool.

Sportdokumentation: Literatur der Sportwissenschaft. v.1– . 1971– .
  Schorndorf: Hofmann. Bimonthly.
Arranged by broad subject categories, this index to sport journal literature and
monographs is often overlooked because of its German origin and difficult-to-
read computer printout format. Each citation is accompanied by an abstract in
either English or German. Of particular interest to selectors is the listing of
approximately 200 monograph titles received for inclusion in future indexes.
This timely coverage is the most comprehensive and international in scope among
all the selection tools, even though German titles are heavily represented. There
is good coverage of nontrade as well as trade publishers.

Physical Education Index. v.1– . 1978– . Cape Girardeau, Mo.: BenOak.
  Quarterly with annual cumulation.
Approximately 1,000 book reviews are indexed each year. Predominantly covering United States trade publishers, the index also includes university presses
and some British publishers. The index becomes a good checklist for selectors
although there is usually a two to three year lag between publication and indexing
of reviews, so many titles may be out-of-print by the time the review is indexed.

---

value as a selection tool for current as well as retrospective acquisitions.
Topically arranged, this index covers the range of sport science and individual sport activities. A good general index is provided.

In addition to these specialized sources, two journals of a more general
nature help the selector to keep abreast of developments in the field. The
International Bulletin of Sports Information has a limited listing of new
monographs and periodicals and enables the selector to keep current with
international developments in bibliographic control of the literature. *Collection Building* is also worth browsing for pertinent articles and bibliographies.

DISSERTATIONS

Research design and review of the literature as well as the findings mandate
the acquisition of dissertations for collections that support a graduate
program. The field is fortunate to have many selective dissertations, master's theses, and selective out-of-print journals available through the University of Oregon microform collection (University of Oregon, College of
Human Development and Performance [Microform Publications], Eugene,
Ore., 1949–). Each year approximately 230 of the most outstanding and
timely dissertations and theses are selected from those reported by the
degree granting institution to the American Alliance for Health, Physical
Education, Recreation and Dance and listed in its annual publication *Completed Research in Health, Physical Education and Recreation.* A subscription to the microform collection provides a printed index and catalog

cards to accompany each shipment. Selective titles may also be ordered on demand. Some universities, however, do not report to *Completed Research*, so *Dissertation Abstracts International (DAI)* also must be consulted. Furthermore, there are pertinent dissertations in *DAI* from other departments such as education, history, biology, and sociology that one might want to add to a comprehensive collection.

Selective dissertations and their availability are also indexed in *Sociology of Leisure and Sport Abstracts* and *Leisure, Recreation and Tourism Abstracts*. The abstracts are useful in helping selectors evaluate whether a dissertation falls within the scope of the collection.

PROCEEDINGS AND CONFERENCE PAPERS

Because many conferences do not commercially publish their papers and because many are not held on a regular basis and so move from location to location (and possibly from publisher to publisher), approval plans seem to fail abysmally in supplying such publications. These sources of empirical, theoretical, and descriptive research are often elusive when not published commercially, as they frequently are not listed in the *Weekly Record*. However, the *Index to Social Sciences and Humanities Proceedings* does cover both commercially and privately published proceedings. This index provides valuable ordering information including prepayment notification. On a broader scale, *Proceedings in Print* and the *Directory of Published Proceedings* also cover privately published conference proceedings as well as those published in journal literature. The *Directory of Published Proceedings* provides better coverage of conferences available for purchase from the National Technical Information Service.

PERIODICALS

A general rule guiding periodical selection is that a journal is only as valuable as the bibliographic access to it.[4] Therefore, first consideration should be the selection of appropriate titles from the journals covered by the indexes in the field. *Physical Education Index, Physical Fitness/Sports Medicine, Sport Search, Sport and Fitness Index, Sportdokumentation,* and *Sports Documentation Monthly Bulletin* list journals surveyed on a regular basis. Until 1981 *Completed Research* also covered journal literature and may be reviewed in giving a sense of relevant titles. *Social Science Citation Index* and *Science Citation Index* may be checked to make evaluative judgments about the scope and relevance of journals under consideration and to identify journals peripheral but applicable to the field. The coverage of *Current Contents/Agriculture, Biology & Envi-*

4. Andrew Delbridge Osborn, *Serial Publications, Their Place and Treatment in Libraries* (Chicago: American Library Assn., 1980), p. 81.

ronmental Sciences; Current Contents/Life Sciences; and *Current Contents/Social & Behavioral Sciences* will also provide insight into building an appropriate journal collection. The advertising and new books sections also alert selectors to new publications.

On a continuing basis, new journals will be announced or reviewed in professional library journals and publisher's flyers. In addition to standard library selection tools, *Serials Review* and *Serials Librarian* are worth browsing for pertinent articles or bibliographies. Most publishers are willing to supply a sample issue for evaluation if a review has not yet appeared or the selector cannot make a decision based solely upon a blurb or announcement. Cleland's research indicates that much of the sports literature is never reviewed, even though since 1970 the publishing output has increased while the percentage of those books reviewed has decreased.[5] In conjunction with *Alternatives in Print,* consulting the *New American Guide to Athletics, Sports, and Recreation; National Recreational Sporting & Hobby Organizations of the United States; Sportsguide Master Reference; Youth-Serving Organizations Directory;* and *Recreation and Outdoor Life Directory* permit a selector to develop lists of organizations and publishers to contact for publications, newsletters, mailing lists, catalogs, etc.

ORGANIZATIONAL PUBLICATIONS

The *New American Guide to Athletics, Sports, and Recreation,* by Craig and Peter Norback, is arranged by activity, and lists national, regional, and local organizations. It is weak on identifying the publishing activity of those groups but it does include a section of sport serials with publisher, address, frequency, and focus provided.

No local, state, or regional organizations are found in the *National Recreational Sporting & Hobby Organizations of the United States,* which lists only organizations with national memberships. Arranged alphabetically by name of the organization, this directory contains a good subject index. Association publications are indicated.

The *Sportsguide Master Reference* is a useful tool for libraries although it appears to be directed toward businesspersons. General sports associations, athletic conferences, and professional leagues and teams associations in North America are listed with publications of each identified. There is also a selective list of sport serials.

A spinoff from the *Encyclopedia of Associations,* the *Youth-Serving Organizations Directory,* can be useful to those who do not have access to the *Encyclopedia;* it is arranged in a similar style.

5. Cleland, "Comparison of Sports Coverage," p.456.

The *Recreation and Outdoor Life Directory* lists national, state, and regional organizations, government organizations in the United States and Canada, and some international organizations if there is significant American participation. Publications are indicated and a section on serials is useful. Also included in this work are sections on research centers and libraries with an indication of those publishing acquisition lists or other titles.

The new *International Directory of Sports Organizations under the Auspices of the International Association for Sports Information* provides information on an international scale, as does the *International Directory of Leisure Information Resource Centres–1980*. International organizations and their activities are also included in *The Recreation Management Handbook,* although it has a heavy emphasis on British organizations. It can be a valuable resource in contacting publishers identified in *Leisure, Recreation and Tourism Abstracts.*

Of wider scope, yet useful because of their subject as well as name indexes, are two Gale publications, *Encyclopedia of Associations* and *Research Centers Directory,* which list any publishing activity of the organizations listed. Another Gale title, *Directory of Directories,* contains sections on "Sports and Outdoor Recreation," "Hobbies, Travel and Leisure," and "Health and Medicine." Both trade and nontrade publishers are included. And finally, but not least, the *Associations' Publications in Print* by Bowker lists newsletters, journals, pamphlets, audiovisual, and free materials as well as trade publications and conference proceedings. Arranged by broad subject categories, the work is enhanced by numerous indexes.

RETROSPECTIVE SELECTION

Desiderata lists may be generated by checking the collection against standard bibliographies. However, because of the relatively recent interest in bibliographic control of the sports and recreation literature, there are no comprehensive checklists of the field. There are, though, a plethora of bibliographies on narrow components of the literature. The Gale Research *Sports, Games, and Pastimes Information Guide Series* and the Chicorel indexes to environment and ecology, the crafts, and urban planning and environmental design are examples of such bibliographies. Robert Higgs's *Sport: A Reference Guide* is a bibliographic essay with useful chapters on research centers, noteworthy collections, and directories. Another retrospective checklist is *Sports and Physical Education: A Guide to the Reference Resources.* Those interested in rare book collecting may wish to check Robert W. Henderson's *Early American Sport: A Checklist of Books by American and Foreign Authors Published in America Prior to 1860 Including Sporting Songs.*

Once lists of desired items are identified—an ongoing process, by the way—traditional means of acquiring those items come into play: out-of-print dealer's catalogs, reprints, and microforms can be utilized as appropriate. Reviewing interlibrary loan requests can also identify gaps in the collection, especially serial titles. However, caution must be exercised to ensure that requests generate from a number of users, not merely a dozen requests from one person.

MISCELLANEOUS SELECTION STRATEGIES

The benefits of making contact with associations and organizations extend as well to contacts with other libraries or documentation centers. Acquisition lists do function as selection tools, so exchanges of lists can be advantageous, especially on an international scale. One such useful list is the monthly Neuerwerbungsliste from the Bundesinstitut fur Sportwissenschaft (Carl-Diem-Weg 4, 5000 Koln 41).

Library of Congress proof slips may also serve as a selection tool, especially since LC is producing a lot of CIP cataloging. However, the selector should be aware that not all items with CIP cataloging will actually be published when the cataloging indicates; some may not be published at all, or published with a variant title. Vendors generally prefer not to hold orders for a delayed publication and title variations may cause some problems for the vendor and acquisition staff.

One final word: make use of personal contacts in the field. Many library users are editors, editorial board members, or contributors to conferences as well as authors themselves, and they have exceptional knowledge of the publishing industry. Their counsel may be sought on questions of delayed publication, changing editorship of journals, sometimes interrupting publication schedules; addresses and activities of professional organizations; and the publication of elusive conference proceedings and papers.

Conclusion

Collection development in any area is an active, not a passive, activity that demands a variety of approaches. The multidisciplinary nature of sports and recreation, combined with the fact that many resources are not trade publications, make collection development in this area a challenge. That which distinguishes one collection from another is the depth and richness of those nontrade materials.

The selector must have a thorough knowledge of the tools of selection, the publishing pattern of the field, and the scope of the collection being developed. Linked to these skills is the ability to recognize and accommodate shifts in the research in the field as well as changes in the curricular and research interests of the clientele served.

Because so few materials are reviewed and those reviews suffer a time lag, the aggressive selector cannot wait for a review to appear before making a decision to acquire a particular title. Probably every selector has been embarrassed by some selection; but small print runs, especially for nontrade materials, mandate timely ordering. Traditional library selection tools, publisher's ads, user's requests, and browsing incoming journals and newsletters and checking appropriate indexes form the backbone of collection strategy in sports and recreation.

Selection Sources

Adapted Physical Activity Quarterly. v.1– . 1984– . Champaign, Ill.: Human Kinetics. Quarterly.

Alternatives in Print. v.1– . 1971– . New York: Neal-Schuman. Biennially.

American Journal of Sports Medicine. v.1– . 1972– . Baltimore: Sports and Medicine Publications. Bimonthly.

American Rehabilitation. v.1– . 1975– . Washington, D.C.: Government Printing Office. Quarterly.

American Statistics Index. v.1– . 1974– . Bethesda, Md.: Congressional Information Service. Monthly with quarterly and annual cumulations.

Annals of Tourism Research. v.1– . 1973– . New York: Pergamon. Quarterly.

Archives of Physical Medicine and Rehabilitation. v.1– . 1920– . Chicago: American Congress of Rehabilitation Medicine. Monthly.

Arete: The Journal of Sport Literature. v.1– . 1983– . San Diego, Calif.: Sport Literature Assn. Biennially.

Associations' Publications in Print. v.1– . 1981– . New York: Bowker. Annually.

Athletic Journal. v.1– . 1921– . Evanston, Ill.: Athletic Journal. Monthly.

British Journal of Physical Education. v.14, no.3– . 1983– . London: Physical Education Assn. of Great Britain and Northern Ireland. Bimonthly. (Continues *Action: British Journal of Physical Education,* v.11–14, no.2, 1980–83; *British Journal of Physical Education,* v.1–10, 1970–80.)

British Journal of Sports Medicine. v.1– . 1968– . Loughborough, Leicestershire: British Assn. of Sport and Medicine. Quarterly.

British Library of Economic and Political Science. *A London Bibliography of the Social Sciences.* v.1– . 1931– . London: Mansell. Annually.

Canadiana: Canada's National Bibliography. v.1– . 1950–1951– . Ottawa: National Library of Canada. Monthly with annual cumulations.

Canadian Association for Health, Physical Education and Recreation Journal. v.1– . 1933– . Vanier, Ont.: Canadian Assn. for Health, Physical Education and Recreation. Bimonthly.

Chicorel, Marietta. *Chicorel Index to Environment and Ecology.* 1st ed. New York: Chicorel Library, 1975.

————. *Chicorel Index to the Crafts.* 1st ed. New York: Chicorel Library, 1974–77.

_____. *Chicorel Index to Urban Planning and Environmental Design*. 1st ed. New York: Chicorel Library, 1975.

CIS Annual: Index to Congressional Publications and Public Laws. v.1– . 1970– . Bethesda, Md.: Congressional Information Service. Annually.

Clotfelter, Cecil F., and Mary L. Clotfelter. *Camping and Backpacking: A Guide to Information Sources*. Sports, Games, and Pastimes Information Guide Series v.2. Detroit: Gale, 1979.

Collection Building. v.1– . 1978– . New York: Neil-Schuman. 3/year.

Completed Research in Health, Physical Education and Recreation. v.1– . 1959– . Reston, Va.: American Alliance for Health, Recreation and Dance. Annually.

Current Contents/Agriculture, Biology & Environmental Sciences. v.1– . 1970– . Philadelphia: Institute for Scientific Information. Weekly.

Current Contents/Life Sciences. v.1– . 1958– . Philadelphia: Institute for Scientific Information. Weekly.

Current Contents/Social & Behavioral Sciences. v.1– . 1969– . Philadelphia: Institute for Scientific Information. Weekly.

Directory of Directories. 3rd ed. Detroit: Gale, 1984.

Directory of Published Proceedings. v.1– . 1965– . Harrison, N.Y.: InterDok. Monthly with annual cumulation.

Ebershoff-Coles, Susan, and Charla Ann Leibenguth. *Motorsports: A Guide to Information Sources*. Sports, Games, and Pastimes Information Guide Series v.5. Detroit: Gale, 1979.

Electromyography and Clinical Neurophysiology. v.1– . 1961– . Louvain, Belgium: Editions Nauwelaerts. 6/year.

Encyclopedia of Associations. 19th ed. Detroit: Gale, 1984.

EPS: Education Physique et Sport. no. 1– . 1950– . Paris: Comite d'Etudes et d'Informations Pedagogiques de l'Education Physique et du Sport. Bimonthly.

FIEP Bulletin. v.43– . 1973– . Cheltenham: Federation Internationale d'Education Physique. Quarterly.

Gardner, Jack. *Gambling: A Guide to Information Sources*. Sports, Games, and Pastimes Information Guide Series v.8. Detroit: Gale, 1980.

Government Reports Announcements and Index. v.1– . 1946– . Springfield, Va.: National Technical Information Service. Biweekly.

Henderson, Robert W., comp. *Early American Sport: A Checklist of Books by American and Foreign Authors Published in America Prior to 1860 Including Sporting Songs*. 3rd ed. Rutherford, N.J.: Fairleigh Dickinson Univ. Pr., 1977.

Higgs, Robert J. *Sport: A Reference Guide*. Westport, Conn.: Greenwood, 1982.

Human Movement Science. v.1– . 1982– . Amsterdam: Elsevier. Quarterly.

Index to Social Sciences and Humanities Proceedings. v.1– . 1979– . Philadelphia: Institute for Scientific Information. Quarterly with annual cumulation.

International Bulletin of Sports Information. v.1– . 1979– . The Hague: International Assn. for Sports Information. Quarterly.

International Directory of Leisure Information Resource Centres-1980. Ed. by James C. Knoop and Gerald S. Kenyon. Waterloo, Ont.: Otium Publications, 1980.

International Directory of Sports Organizations under the Auspices of the International Association for Sports Information. v.1– . 1984– . Haarlem, Netherlands: Uitgeverij de Vrieseborch. Biennially.

International Journal of Rehabilitation Research. v.1– . 1977– . Heidelberg: G. Schnidele Verlag. Quarterly.

International Journal of Sport Psychology. v.1– . 1970– . Rome: Edizioni Luigi Pozzi. Quarterly.

Journal of Leisure Research. v.1- . 1969- . Alexandria, Va.: National Recreation and Park Assn. Quarterly.

Journal of Physical Education, Recreation, and Dance. v.1- . 1930- . Reston, Va.: American Alliance for Health, Physical Education, Recreation and Dance. Monthly.

Journal of Sport and Social Issues. v.1- . 1976- . New York: ARENA: The Institute of Sport and Social Analysis. Semiannually.

Journal of Sport History. v.1- . 1974- . Seattle: North American Society for Sport History. 3/year.

Journal of Sport Sciences. v.1- . 1983- . London: E. & F. N. Spon. 3/year.

Korperkultur und Sport Uberblicksinformation: Sportwissenschaftliche beitrage aus der Deutschen Demokratischen Republik: Informationsbulletin. v.1- . 1976- . Leipzig: Zentrum fur Wissenschaftsinformation Korperkultur und Sport. Quarterly.

Leistungssport. v.1- . 1971- . Frankfurt: Bartels and Wernitz. Bimonthly.

Leisure, Recreation, and Tourism Abstracts. v.6- . 1981- . Oxford, England: Commonwealth Bureau of Agricultural Economics. Quarterly. (Continues *Rural Recreation and Tourism Abstracts.* v.1-5, 1976-80.)

Leisure Studies. v.1- . 1982- . London: E. & F. N. Spon. 3/year.

Loisir & Societe. v.1- . 1976- . Quebec: Dept. of Leisure Studies, Universite du Quebec a Trois-Rivieres. Semiannually.

Microlog. v.1- . 1979- . Toronto: Micromedia Ltd. Monthly with annual cumulation.

Monthly Catalog of United States Government Publications. no.1- . 1895- . Washington, D.C.: Government Printing Office. Monthly.

Murdoch, Joseph S. F., and Janet Seagle Murdoch. *Golf: A Guide to Information Sources.* Sports, Games, and Pastimes Information Guide Series v.7. Detroit: Gale, 1979.

National Recreational Sporting & Hobby Organizations of the United States. v.1- . 1980- . Washington, D.C.: Columbia books. Annually.

Norback, Craig, and Peter Norback. *The New American Guide to Athletics, Sports, and Recreation.* New York: New American Library, 1979.

Olympic Review. no.1- . 1967- . Lausanne: International Olympic Committee. Monthly.

Parks and Recreation. v.1- . 1966- . Alexandria, Va.: National Recreation and Park Assn. Monthly.

Peele, David A. *Racket and Paddle Games: A Guide to Information Sources.* Sports, Games, and Pastimes Information Guide Series v.9. Detroit: Gale, 1980.

Physical Education Index. v.1- . 1978- . Cape Girardeau, Mo.: BenOak. Quarterly with annual cumulation.

Physical Fitness/Sports Medicine. v.1- . 1978- . Washington, D.C.: President's Council on Physical Fitness and Sports. Quarterly.

Physician and Sportsmedicine. v.1- . 1973- . New York.: McGraw-Hill. Monthly.

Proceedings in Print. v.1- . 1964- . Arlington, Mass.: Proceedings in Print. Bimonthly with annual cumulation.

Recreation and Outdoor Life Directory. 2nd ed. Ed. by Steven R. Wasserman. Detroit: Gale, 1983.

The Recreation Management Handbook. 3rd. ed. London: E. & F. N. Spon, 1981.

Reister, Floyd Nester. *Private Aviation: A Guide to Information Sources. Sports, Games, and Pastimes Information Guide Series* v.3. Detroit: Gale, 1979.

Remley, Mary L. *Women in Sport: A Guide to Information Sources.* Sports, Games, and Pastimes Information Guide Series v.10. Detroit: Gale, 1980.

Research Centers Directory. 8th ed. Detroit: Gale, 1983.
Research Quarterly for Exercise and Sport. v.51– . 1980– . Reston, Va.: American Alliance for Health, Physical Education, Recreation, and Dance. Quarterly. (Continues *Research Quarterly,* v.1–50, 1930–79.)
Resources in Education. v.1– . 1966– . Washington, D.C.: Government Printing Office. Monthly.
Schultz, Barbara A., and Mark P. Schultz. *Bicycles and Bicycling: A Guide to Information Sources.* Sports, Games, and Pastimes Information Guide Series v.6. Detroit: Gale, 1979.
Serials Librarian. v.1– . 1976– . New York: Haworth. Quarterly.
Serials Review. v.1– . 1975– . Ann Arbor, Mich.: Pierian. Quarterly.
Social Science Citation Index. v.1– . 1966– . Philadelphia: Institute for Scientific Information. 3/year.
Sociology of Leisure and Sport Abstracts. v.1– . 1980– . Amsterdam: Elsevier. Quarterly.
Special Recreation Digest. v.1– . 1984– . Iowa City: Special Recreation. Quarterly.
Sport and Fitness Index. v.11, no. 4/5–v.12. 1984–85. Ottawa, Ont.: Sport Information Resource Centre. Monthly. (Continues *Sport and Recreation Index.* v.1–11, no. 3. 1974–84.)
Sport and Leisure. v.1– . 1960– . London: Sports Council. Bimonthly. (Continues Sport and Recreation. v.1–21, no. 1. 1960–80.)
Sport Bibliography. v.1– . 1981– . Champaign, Ill.: Human Kinetics. Annually.
Sport Search. v.1– . 1985– . Champaign, Ill.: Human Kinetics. Monthly.
Sportdokumentation: Literatur der Sportwissenschaft. v.1– . 1971– . Schorndorf: Verlag Karl Hofmann. Bimonthly.
Sports and Physical Education: A Guide to the Reference Resources. Comp. by Bonnie Gratch, Betty Chan, and Judith Lingenfelter. Westport, Conn.: Greenwood, 1983.
Sports Documentation Monthly Bulletin. v.1– . 1971– . Birmingham, Eng.: Sports Documentation Centre, Univ. of Birmingham. Monthly.
Sports Medicine Bulletin. v.1– . 1965– . Indianapolis: American College of Sports Medicine. Quarterly.
Sportsguide Master Reference. v.1– . 1981– . Princeton, N.J.: Sportsguide. Annually.
Sportwissenschaft. v.1– . 1971– . Schorndorf: Verlag Karl Hofmann. Quarterly.
Statistical Reference Index. v.1– . 1981– . Bethesda, Md.: Congressional Information Service. Monthly with quarterly and annual cumulations.
University of Oregon. College of Human Development and Performance. [*Microform Publications*] 1949– . Eugene, Ore.: The University. Semiannually.
Weekly Record. v.1– . 1974– . New York: Bowker. Weekly.
Wells, Ellen B. *Horsemanship: A Guide to Information Sources.* Sports, Games, and Pastimes Information Guide Series v.4. Detroit: Gale, 1979.
Youth-Serving Organizations Directory. 2nd ed. Detroit: Gale, 1980.
Ziegler, Ronald M. *Wilderness Waterways: A Guide to Information Sources.* Sports, Games, and Pastimes Information Guide Series v.1. Detroit: Gale, 1979.

URBAN PLANNING

Rona H. Gregory

DEFINITION OF PLANNING

Urban planning is one of the original interdisciplinary academic subjects. Degrees in the subject of city planning were first granted in the 1930s. Since that time, academic planners have engaged in a lively dialogue attempting to define the subject and to agree upon a curriculum to teach it effectively. The first issue of the *Planners' Journal*, published in the spring of 1935, reported on "an effort to establish the place of the so-called 'physical' planner, and to distinguish his field from that of social or economic planning."[1] Forty-five years later, the *Journal of the American Planning Association* was still publishing articles addressing "the planning profession's own long-standing argument about the purpose and method of planning."[2]

Although no consensus exists among planners regarding a single definition of planning, several concepts appear again and again in the professional literature. Planning is often defined as rational decision making:

> Anyone who seeks to arrange events in order to secure desired change in the future is a planner. Planning is simply the application of forethought; the consideration of the most appropriate means of achieving desired ends in the future.[3]

When confronted with the need to define planning, John Friedmann, a noted planner, named "seven modes of thought that ... distinguished planners: scientific objectivity, analysis, synthesis, projection, experiment, utopian concepts, and aesthetic vision. He listed two main elements of planning: forethought and reason."[4]

1. Tracy B. Augur, "What Is Planning?" *Planners' Journal* 1:12(May/June, 1935).
2. George C. Hemmens, "Introduction," *Journal of the American Planning Association* 46:261(July 1980).
3. John M. Hall, *The Geography of Planning Decisions* (New York: Oxford Univ. Pr., 1982), p.3.
4. Robert Conot, "Tracking John Friedmann," *Planning* 12:24(Feb. 1984).

236

The Planning Library

SCOPE

The inability to define planning in a neat and simple fashion is one of the salient characteristics of the field. It is also the primary challenge facing the person responsible for developing and managing library collections. Selectors in the field of planning need to understand the distinctions among the following subjects: urban studies, urban planning, regional planning, community planning, environmental planning, rural planning, and development planning. Although the subjects are often used interchangeably, each represents a different perspective and each is described by a different combination of library materials.

Given the difficulty in defining the subject, it is particularly important to understand both the institutional environment of the library and the nature of the specific program being supported by the library's collections. Is the library an academic library or a government agency library? Does the library maintain a research collection or a working collection? Does the program being supported have a national or international focus? If an academic library, does the program being supported grant doctorates? Does the school perceive itself to be training practicing planners or social scientists? Is the library the only one of its kind within a given region or does it have easy access to supporting collections in the social sciences, policy sciences, engineering, architecture, law, federal and state government documents?

In addition to considering the above questions when establishing the scope of a planning library, the selector also should be aware of staff and budgetary constraints. Selecting materials in the field of planning is labor-intensive; because of the interdisciplinary nature of the field and the lack of consensus concerning its definition, it is difficult to take advantage of approval plans or blanket order plans. A realistic assessment of the present and future availability of staff time and funding to support the collection should be an important factor in determining scope.

TYPES

The majority of planning libraries in the United States can be identified as either academic libraries supporting teaching and research programs in city and regional planning, or government agency libraries supporting the planning activities of governmental units at the city, state, or federal level. Although the two types have much in common, they differ in several important aspects.

Academic planning libraries tend to have a broader collection scope as well as easy access to large research and reference collections in related disciplines. Academic planning libraries tend to be bound by the policies and procedures of the larger library systems of which they are a part; consequently, although often constrained by inflexible classification schemes and cataloging and acquisitions procedures, they reap the benefits of a more consistent, formal budget process and access to relatively greater financial resources. And finally, although nearly all planning libraries are small and thinly staffed, academic planning librarians tend to work in less professional isolation due to the presence of other libraries and librarians on campus.

Bibliographic Structure of Planning Literature

If planning is considered a method, its literature becomes the literature of the social sciences, architecture, engineering, and government. Information is disseminated in several forms: books, serials, reports (including planning reports, government documents, consulting reports, statistical reports, pamphlets), maps and plans, newspapers, newsletters, laws, and regulations.

As well as being able to house different forms of materials, a planning library needs procedures that enable the materials to be kept current and easily accessible. Much material of interest to planners is neither indexed nor published in conventional book format; examples include newspaper clippings, local government documents, newsletters reporting on government activities in housing, community development, economic development, codes and regulations written at all levels of government, and newsletters or annual reports describing the research activities of academic, public, and private research centers.

A selector in the field of planning needs to develop methods for acquiring nonbook material. Often the material is available free of charge; although purchasing cost may not be a factor, it is labor-intensive to collect, process, and provide bibliographic access to such materials. The monitoring and maintenance of clipping files, local government document collections, and materials received via mailing lists require substantial staff time.

Except for the largest academic research libraries, most planning libraries will include more nontraditional than traditional materials. The bulk of the collection will consist of report literature, government documents, socioeconomic statistics including census materials, pamphlets, newspapers and newsletters, maps and plans, and a small number of books. Although historical statistics are needed to confirm or deny the existence of trends, the shelf life of most of the materials is five to ten years.

Journal of the American Planning Association. v.1– . 1925– . Chicago:
American Planning Assn. Quarterly.
Reviews of current monographs.
10–15 critical book reviews an issue.
12–18 month lag between book publication and review.
Features book reviews and occasional review essay. Focuses on professional and
academic viewpoint. List of "Publications Received" is broken down into eighteen categories representing the breadth and scope of planning literature. Lists
contents of current planning periodicals in "Periodical Literature in Urban Studies and Planning."

Specific Selection Strategies

GENERAL PLANNING SOURCES

Once the selector in planning has understood the substantive nature of
the program being supported by the library and has determined an appropriate scope for the collection, specific materials can be selected. There
is no one single comprehensive selection tool in the field of planning.
There are a few major sources that focus on planning in general and many
specialized sources that cover specific disciplines such as sociology and
economics or interdisciplinary subjects such as the environment and urban
studies.

The most important source on planning in general is the *Journal of the
American Planning Association.* The quarterly journal regularly includes
a section of book reviews as well as a list of "Publications Received" and
a list of "Periodical Literature in Urban Studies and Planning." The list
of "Publications Received" is broken down into eighteen categories, representing the breadth and scope of planning literature and including such
topics as the history of planning and cities, planning theory, land use
planning, housing, community development, transportation, environment
and energy, economic development, urban design, and public administration. Such a subject breakdown makes it possible for the selector to focus
on those aspects of planning that are in scope for a particular collection.

A second major source that can be used as a selection tool in the field
of planning is *Recent Publications on Governmental Problems* (RPGP),
published monthly by the Merriam Center Library in Chicago. *RPGP*
covers books, pamphlets, and articles in the fields of planning and public
administration.

In response to . . . numerous requests, *RPGP* has come to serve also as an
acquisitions tool for libraries and agencies, by providing complete order information on each of the publications listed. In recent years book reviews
and annotations were introduced to further facilitate acquisitions decisions.[5]

5. Patricia Coatsworth, "Introductory Note," *Recent Publications on Governmental Problems,* cumulation 53:vi(1984).

Recent Publications on Governmental Problems. v.1– . 1932– . Chicago:
  Merriam Center Library. Monthly.
  Includes brief reviews and annotations.
  Covers books, pamphlets, periodical articles, state and local government
    documents.
  Annual cumulation.
Aware of its growing use as a selection/acquisitions tool, it has added book
reviews and annotations as well as complete order information. Focuses on
public administration/practical planning issues. Many of its sources are not
indexed anywhere else.

The staff of the Merriam Center Library regularly scans approximately
800 periodicals for the purpose of selective indexing; many of the periodicals are not indexed in any other sources. The monthly issues are
cumulated annually. *RPGP* is an essential tool for the selector in planning
because of its coverage of periodical articles, pamphlets, and state and
local government documents.

A third tool of value to the selector in planning is *Urban Affairs Abstracts*, published weekly by the National League of Cities. The staff of
the Municipal Reference Service of the National League of Cities selects
and abstracts articles from the hundreds of materials subscribed to by its
library. Their goal is to provide a current guide to the most relevant urban
literature. In addition to academic, professional, and research journals,
Urban Affairs Abstracts indexes many of the publications of the various
municipal leagues, leagues of cities and/or counties, and state organizations. The weekly lists are cumulated annually.

In addition to the above three general sources, many periodicals include
book reviews and lists of publications received. The book reviews are
mostly of titles published within a three-year period; the lists of publications received tend to be titles published within the past year. It is
important for the selector to scan regularly the periodicals most heavily
used in the library; since those periodicals are the ones being read, the
books being reviewed in them are often sought by users.

The following list of periodicals is representative of those most likely
to be relevant to a planning collection:

American Journal of Sociology   *Environments*
Economic Development and   *Journal of Housing*
  Cultural Change   *Journal of Planning Education*
Ekistics   *and Research*
Environmental Impact   *Journal of Policy Analysis and*
  Assessment Review   *Management*
Environment and Planning   *Journal of Regional Science*

Journal of Social Policy
Journal of the American
  Planning Association
Mass Transit
Neighborhood
Planning
Public Administration Review

Regional Studies
Third World Planning Review
Town Planning Review
Transportation Research
Urban Land
Urban Studies

SPECIALIZED SOURCES

Many of the major reference sources in the social sciences are also useful as specialized selection tools. Titles that fall into that category include *Public Affairs Information Service Bulletin, Sage Urban Studies Abstracts, Index to Current Urban Documents, Environmental Index, Monthly Catalog, Government Reports Announcements and Index*, and the *Monthly Product Announcement*.

Increasingly, sources such as those mentioned above are available in both online and print format (at this writing, only *Sage Urban Studies Abstracts* and *Index to Current Urban Documents* were not available online). Although most online services are marketed and purchased for public use or reference service, their potential value as a collections tool should not be overlooked. Searching for newly issued planning reports by city or region is a simple task online; it can be very difficult to do manually if there is no geographic index. Verifying the title of a government document using the print volumes of the *Monthly Catalog* is an onerous task; a check of the online database is far more efficient. Monthly updates from *NTIS* online are an easy method for tracking all federally funded urban research by specific city or region and/or subject (e.g., urban transportation in Atlanta, housing in Cleveland). A small library may discover that use of the online reference terminal is a relatively inexpensive way to greatly expand the resources available to the collections staff.

The *PAIS Bulletin* indexes "publications on all subjects that bear on contemporary public issues and the making and evaluation of public policy."[6] The materials indexed come primarily from the acquisitions of the New York Public Library, and in particular from the acquisitions of the Economic and Public Affairs Division; books, periodicals, government documents, and reports are indexed. The index is published semimonthly and cumulated annually.

Sage Urban Studies Abstracts is a quarterly publication abstracting books, articles, pamphlets, government publications, significant speeches, and legislative research studies. Although the abstracts are useful in determining

6. "PAIS Selection Policy," *Public Affairs Information Service Bulletin Annual Cumulation 1984*, 70:vii(Oct. 1983–Sept. 1984).

the content and scope of an item, the materials abstracted can be dated due to the quarterly publication schedule. Since there is no annual cumulation, *Urban Studies Abstracts* is awkward to use retrospectively.

The *Index to Current Urban Documents* is a quarterly publication that "makes available complete and detailed bibliographic descriptions of the majority of the local government documents issued annually by the largest cities and counties in the United States and Canada."[7] Although the *Index* is not comprehensive, it is a valuable tool to be used in the identification of major city or county reports. All materials indexed are also available from Greenwood Press on microfiche. As valuable a source as the *Index* is, it should not replace semiannual visits, letters, or phone calls to the local jurisdictions of primary interest to the library. Some important reports never appear in the *Index* due to bureaucratic error.

Environment Index is an annual that reviews the major news and issues affecting the environment as well as indexing recent reports, conference papers, news stories, and journal articles. The index is taken from the monthly issues of *Environment Abstracts*. Some of the indexing categories of interest to planners include energy, environmental design and urban ecology, land use and misuse, population planning and control, solid waste, and transportation. Although the monthly issues of *Environment Abstracts* permit the selector to choose more timely materials, the annual index is a useful means of ensuring that nothing important has been overlooked. Subscribing to the *Environment Index* alone can be a workable solution to the dilemma of providing access to information with limited resources.

The strengths and weakness of the *Monthly Catalog* are common knowledge. Its usefulness as a selection tool in planning is limited by its broad and general scope and by the length of time it takes for a major government report to be indexed. Four other sources published by the federal government are more useful to planning subject specialists. *Recent Research Results* is prepared by HUD USER and published by the U.S. Department of Housing and Urban Development. It contains brief sum-

---

Government Reports Announcements and Index. v.74– . 1974– . Springfield, Va.: U.S. National Technical Information Service. Biweekly.
Annual cumulation.
Available online and in print form.
Index to the research sponsored by the U.S. government. Particularly useful in areas of urban transportation, environmental planning, and economic development. Reports are indexed by subject, keyword, personal author, and corporate author.

---

7. *Index to Current Urban Documents*, cumulated volume 12 (Westport, Conn.: Greenwood, 1983/84), p. 11.

maries of the published reports sponsored by HUD's Office of Policy Development and Research. It is issued monthly and includes an order form and ordering instructions.

Government Reports Announcements and Index (GRA&I) is published by the National Technical Information Service; it is sometimes referred to as the *NTIS Index*.

NTIS, an agency of the U.S. Department of Commerce, is the central source for the public sale of U.S. Government-sponsored research, development, and engineering reports, and for sales of foreign technical reports and other analyses prepared by national and local government agencies and their contractors or grantees.[8]

GRA&I is issued biweekly with annual cumulation. The reports are indexed by subject, keyword, personal author, corporate author, contract number, grant number, report number, and the NTIS order number. *GRA&I* is particularly useful in identifying government reports in the areas of urban transportation, environmental planning, and economic development.

The *Monthly Product Announcement* is published by the U.S. Bureau of the Census and lists the new products available. All formats are covered including paper, fiche, tape, and maps. An order form and ordering instructions are included in each issue. *Data User News* is a monthly newsletter published by the Bureau of the Census. It reports on the programs and activities of the bureau as well as reviewing newly published reports. The newsletter is invaluable in answering the most common questions of the user community, in facilitating networking among data users, and in explaining new programs and products. The *Monthly Product Announcement* and *Data User News* are both essential to building and maintaining a satisfactory census collection.

For planning libraries whose scope includes countries other than the United States, *Urban Abstracts*, *Devindex*, and *UNIPUB Bulletin of New Publications* are important sources. *Urban Abstracts* is published monthly by the Greater London Council. It is published in two separate series; one series covers policy subjects and the second covers technical subjects. The items abstracted are drawn from the acquisitions of the libraries of the

---

Data User News. v.1– . 1965– . Washington, D.C.: U.S. Bureau of the Census. Monthly.
Reviews newly published reports of the Census Bureau.
Newsletter reporting on the programs and activities of the Census Bureau. Essential for networking among data users. Best way to stay informed about changes in the bureau's programs and products.

---

8. *Government Reports Announcements and Index*, 85:13:ii(June 21, 1985).

council. *Urban Abstracts* is also available as an online database called ACCOMPLIS/ACCOMPLINE.

Devindex is an index to selected literature on economic and social development published by the International Development Research Centre in Ottawa, Ontario, Canada. The index is published annually and includes reports and documents from Third World countries as well as from those countries giving aid to the Third World.

UNIPUB Bulletin is issued bimonthly and announces the recent books and reports issued by the United Nations and its agencies, nongovernmental international organizations, and commercial publishers available through UNIPUB. Each citation includes bibliographic information, a brief description of the contents of the report, and review citations. For small libraries that cannot afford standing orders for United Nations publications, the *UNIPUB Bulletin* is an excellent means of identifying planning materials in scope for the collection.

Many other specialized sources for planning literature exist. The decision to purchase and use any specific source for selection or reference purposes should be based upon the scope of the particular library and the resources in staff time and money available to that library.

RETROSPECTIVE SOURCES

Three major types of selection tools for retrospective purchasing exist; they are book catalogs, published bibliographies, and the catalogs produced by the book dealers who specialize in out-of-print materials. Book catalogs are simply photoreproductions of the card catalog of a particular library. Supplements are issued irregularly in an attempt to keep the catalog up to date. Since the supplements are issued so irregularly, book catalogs are used primarily to identify retrospective materials. When used for that purpose, the timeliness of the supplements is less important.

The three most important book catalogs for a planning library are the *Dictionary Catalog of the United States Department of Housing and Urban Development*, the *Catalog of the Avery Memorial Library* at Columbia University, and the *Catalogue of the Library of the Graduate School of Design* at Harvard University. Because those book catalogs describe the holdings of three of the oldest and largest planning libraries in the United States, they are invaluable in documenting the history and development of the field.

Many different published bibliographies exist. Because of the length of time it takes for a bibliography to be compiled and published, they are most useful in identifying retrospective materials. Since 1979, the Council of Planning Librarians has published a series called *CPL Bibliographies*. The bibliographies are reviewed by outside sources and edited by CPL staff in Chicago. Twenty to thirty bibliographies are published each year; the subject matter covers the full range of planning activities. From time to time, CPL publishes an index to the bibliographies in print.

Before the publication of *CPL Bibliographies*, the Council of Planning Librarians published a series of *Exchange Bibliographies*. The *Exchange Bibliographies* originated in 1958 as an informal exchange among a small group of planning librarians. Over the years, the network of authors expanded greatly. The series was finally closed in 1978 when the council had grown large enough to support a more formal publications program. The complete set of *Exchange Bibliographies* (numbers 1–1,565) is available on microfiche from William S. Hein. A comprehensive index to the complete set is available from the Council of Planning Librarians.

Vance Bibliographies has published two continuing series of bibliographies since 1979, Architecture and Public Administration. Although the topics are timely, the bibliographies are not reviewed and edited in a consistent and formal manner. Several hundred bibliographies are published each year. Because of this number, libraries preferring standing orders are required to commit a large sum of money. Since neither series focuses on planning specifically, it is possible for a planning library to stretch limited financial resources by purchasing only those titles requested by staff or users.

Several series published as parts of the Gale Information Guide Library are relevant to planning libraries. Gale intends its Library series to cover the bibliographic sources in major areas in the social sciences, humanities, and current affairs. Some of the series relevant to planning libraries include Urban Studies, Man and the Environment, Economics, and American Government and History.

The third type of source for selectors seeking retrospective materials in the field of planning is catalogs from out-of-print book dealers. Several dealers specializing in art and architecture books also handle planning materials. They include J. B. Muns, H. L. Mendelsohn—Fine European Books, R. Tanner, B. Weinreb Architectural Books Limited, and Blackwell's. Such dealers are invaluable in helping a library to fill in gaps in the collection as well as to replace material that has disappeared or fallen apart due to heavy use.

IMPORTANT TRADE PUBLISHERS

Since few planning libraries collect comprehensively enough in any one subject to make approval plans effective, publishers' catalogs are an important source for current acquisitions. The library should be on the mailing lists to receive the catalogs from as many as possible of the publishers of books in the social sciences, architecture, history, and public policy.

Some of the major publishers include Lexington, Sage, Ballinger, Plenum, Praeger, Wiley, MIT Press, Johns Hopkins University Press, and the University of California Press. The scope of the library will determine which publishers' lists are most used. A selector focusing on urban history, public policy, and environmental concerns will look at a different mix of catalogs than a selector focusing on urban design, environmental psychology, housing, and community development issues.

OTHER PUBLISHERS

Planning literature is most often disseminated through channels other than trade publishers. Many reports are published by academic departments, scholarly societies, research institutes, professional associations, or governmental units. It is essential that the selector identify those groups most likely to publish material in scope for the library's collection and be put on the mailing lists of those groups.

Several reference sources exist to aid the selector in identifying those groups. The *Encyclopedia of Associations*, *Research Centers Directory*, and *Associations Publications in Print* all provide subject access to a variety of groups involved in activities of interest to planners. All three titles indicate the publishing activity of the specific group. *Research Centers Directory* also indicates whether or not a library is affiliated with the group.

The following is a list of some of the major groups involved in research and publishing in the field of planning:

American Planning Association	National Association of Housing
Association of Collegiate Schools	and Redevelopment Officials
of Planning	National League of Cities
Brookings Institution	National Planning Association
Center for Urban Policy Research	Rand Corporation
Conservation Foundation	Regional Plan Association
Environmental Design Research	U.S. Conference of Mayors
Association	U.S. Department of Housing
International City Management	and Urban Development
Association	Urban Affairs Association
Lincoln Institute of Land Policy	Urban Institute

In addition to the major national and regional associations such as those mentioned in the above list, there are local organizations whose activities must be monitored by the selector. Local ordinances, zoning maps, base maps, neighborhood statistics, and planning reports are all examples of material that can only be obtained through contact with city hall or the local issuing agency. Semiannual visits to city hall, a regular reading of local newspapers and newsletters, and personal contact with faculty and/

or researchers using the library are essential as well as effective strategies for identifying and acquiring such material.

Selection Sources

American Journal of Sociology. v.1- . 1895- . Chicago: Univ. of Chicago Pr. Bimonthly.

Associations Publications in Print. 3v. v.1- . 1981- . New York: Bowker. Annually.

Catalog of the Avery Memorial Library of Columbia University. 2nd ed. 19v. Boston: Hall, 1968.

———. Supplements 1-5. Boston: Hall, 1972-82.

Catalogue of the Library of the Graduate School of Design. Harvard Univ. 44v. Boston: Hall, 1968.

———. Supplements 1-2. Boston: Hall, 1970-74.

CPL Bibliographies. no.1- . 1979- . Chicago: Council of Planning Librarians.

Data User News. v.1- . 1965- . Washington, D.C.: U.S. Bureau of the Census. Monthly.

Devindex: Index to Literature on Third World Economic and Social Development. 1976- . Ottawa, Ont.: International Development Research Centre. Annually.

Dictionary Catalog of the United States Department of Housing and Urban Development. 19v. Boston: Hall, 1972.

———. Supplements 1-2. Boston: Hall, 1973-75.

Economic Development and Cultural Change. v.1- . 1952- . Chicago: Univ. of Chicago Pr. Quarterly.

Ekistics. v.1- . 1955- . Athens: Ctr. of Ekistics. Bimonthly.

Encyclopedia of Associations. v.1- . 1975- . Detroit: Gale. Annually.

Environmental Impact Assessment Review. v.1- . 1980- . New York: Plenum. Quarterly.

Environment and Planning. Part A. v.6- . 1974- . Part B. v.1- . 1974- . Part C, *Government and Policy,* v.1- . 1983- . Part D, *Society and Space,* v.1- . 1983- . London: Pion. Monthly.

Environment Index. v.1- . 1971- . New York: Environment Information Ctr. Annually.

Environments. v.1- . 1969- . Waterloo, Ont.: Univ. of Waterloo. Faculty of Environmental Studies. 3/year.

Exchange Bibliographies. nos. 1-1565. 1958-78. Chicago: Council of Planning Librarians.

Government Reports Announcements and Index. v.74- . 1974- . Springfield, Va.: U.S. National Technical Information Service. Biweekly with annual cumulation.

Index to Current Urban Documents. v.1- . 1972- . Westport, Conn.: Greenwood. Quarterly.

Journal of Housing. v.1- . 1944- . Washington, D.C. National Assn. of Housing and Redevelopment Officials. 6/year.

Journal of Planning Education and Research. v.1- . 1981- . Cincinnati: Univ. of Cincinnati. 3/year.

Journal of Policy Analysis and Management. v.1- . 1981- . New York: Wiley. Quarterly.

Journal of Regional Science. v.1- . 1958- . Amherst, Mass.: Regional Science Research Institute. 4/year.

Journal of Social Policy. v.1- . 1972- . Cambridge: Cambridge Univ. Pr. Quarterly.

Journal of the American Planning Association. v.1- . 1925- . Chicago: American Planning Assn. Quarterly.

Mass Transit. v.1- . 1974- . Wasgington, D.C.: Carroll Carter. Monthly.

Monthly Catalog. v.1- . 1895- . Washington, D.C.: U.S. Government Printing Office. Monthly.

Monthly Product Announcement. v.1- . 1980- . Washington, D.C.: U.S. Bureau of the Census. Monthly.

Neighborhood. v.1-7, no. 1. 1977-85. New York: New York Urban Coalition. Quarterly.

Planning. v.1- . 1972- . Chicago: American Planning Assn. Monthly.

Public Administration Review. v.1- . 1940- . Washington, D.C.: American Soc. for Public Admin. Semiannually.

Public Affairs Information Service Bulletin. v.1- . 1915- . New York: Public Affairs Information Service. Semimonthly with annual cumulations.

Recent Publications on Governmental Problems. v.1- . 1932- . Chicago: Merriam Center Library. Monthly.

Recent Research Results. 1979- . Washington, D.C.: U.S. Dept. of Housing and Urban Development. Monthly.

Regional Studies. v.1- . 1966- . Cambridge: Cambridge Univ. Pr. Bimonthly.

Research Centers Directory. v.1- . 1965- . Detroit: Gale. Irregularly.

Sage Urban Studies Abstracts. v.1- . 1973- . Beverly Hills, Calif.: Sage. Quarterly.

Third World Planning Review. v.1- . 1979- . Liverpool: Liverpool Univ. Pr. Quarterly.

Town Planning Review. v.1- . 1910- . Liverpool: Liverpool Univ. Pr. Quarterly.

Transportation Research. Part A-General, Part B-Methodological. v.1- . 1967- . Elmsford, N.Y.: Pergamon. Bimonthly.

UNIPUB Bulletin. 1980- . New York: UNIPUB InfoSource International. Bimonthly.

Urban Affairs Abstracts. v.1- . 1971- . Washington, D.C.: National League of Cities. Weekly.

Urban Land. v.1- . 1941- . Washington, D.C.: Urban Land Institute. Monthly except July/Aug.

Urban Studies. v.1- . 1964- . Essex: Longman. 6/year.

Vance Bibliographies. Architecture Series, no.1- . 1979- . Public Admin. Series no.1- . 1979- . Monticello, Ill.: Vance.

Out-of-Print Dealers

B. Weinreb Architectural Books Ltd.
93 Great Russell St.
London, England WC1B 3QL
Blackwell's
Broad St.
Oxford, England OX1 3BQ

H. L. Mendelsohn
Fine European Books
1640 Massachusetts Ave.
Cambridge, MA 02138.

J. B. Muns
  1162 Shattuck Ave.
  Berkeley, CA 94707

R. Tanner
  47 Theobald Rd.
  Croydon, England CR0 3RN

WOMEN'S STUDIES

Susan E. Searing and Joan Ariel

Feminist scholars have stretched the boundaries of knowledge in the past fifteen years. Growing from a handful of courses in the early 1970s, women's studies is rapidly emerging as a discipline in its own right. Over 450 United States colleges and universities now offer programs or degrees (including several Ph.D.s) in women's studies, and many more courses are taught, ranging from survey lectures to graduate seminars.[1] Community-based noncredit classes and training programs have also multiplied. In 1977, the National Women's Studies Association was chartered; its stimulating conferences attract some fifteen hundred participants each year.

The expanding literature of women's studies reflects this remarkable growth. The field now boasts scores of academic journals, and the monographic output in English alone totals thousands of volumes annually. Periodical indexes, a yearbook of feminist scholarship and activism, and monthly reviewing media represent but a few of the tools now available which, in combination with academic programs, degrees, and publishing, testify to women's studies' maturation.[2]

To date, comparatively little attention has been paid to the bibliographic structure of women's studies, or to collection development strategies and sources in this nascent discipline. Despite advances in the number and quality of materials, and the corresponding progress in bibliographic control, women's studies still poses particular challenges to selectors. We believe the challenges are inherent in the field itself—that feminist knowledge will never be fully codified within the existing academic and publishing institutions, and thus will always require the dedicated use of somewhat eclectic strategies and sources for building library collections.

1. "Women's Studies Programs—1984," *Women's Studies Quarterly* 12: 34–44(Fall 1984).
2. *Women Studies Abstracts*, v.1– , 1972– . (Rush, N.Y.: Rush Publishing), Quarterly; *Studies on Women Abstracts*, v.1– , 1983– (Oxfordshire, England: Carfax), Quarterly; *The Women's Annual: The Year in Review*, v.1– , 1981– (Boston: Hall), Annually; *The Women's Review of Books*, v.1– , 1983– (Wellesley, Mass.: Wellesley College Center for Research on Women), Monthly.

Women's studies emerged from and continues to reflect a revolutionary social movement; for this reason, even core collections must include the materials of both scholarship and feminist activism. In addition, selectors must recognize that feminism and its expression in academia are global movements and require collections international in scope even where, in keeping with the particular campus community and curriculum, non-English-language acquisitions may be limited.[3]

Women's studies has established roots deep within the traditional disciplines. Feminist literary criticism, women's history, and the psychology of women, for example, are all flourishing subjects. From a home base in the humanities and social sciences, feminist scholarship is making significant inroads in the biological sciences. Applied fields—especially business, education, law, and medicine—have also been powerfully transformed.[4]

Yet women's studies remains as strongly interdisciplinary as it is multidisciplinary. Its practitioners encourage the sharing of theories, methods, insights, and applications across intellectual and institutional boundaries. Undergraduate women's studies programs in particular are imbued with an interdisciplinary flavor, and introductory courses are often team-taught. As current projects aimed at integrating the new scholarship on women across the curriculum begin to take hold, women's studies will exert an even greater influence throughout the disciplines at the same time that it becomes more firmly established as a distinct discipline.[5]

The interdisciplinary nature of women's studies hinders the application of simple strategies for identifying relevant materials for library collections. A study of acquisitions and cataloging records at a typical medium-sized campus revealed that less than one-fourth of the titles relevant to women's studies fell into the Library of Congress range of call numbers for "women and feminism," HQ 1101 to HQ2030.[6] Thus a shelflist approach, using

3. For an invaluable compendium of documentation and sources, see Robin Morgan, ed., *Sisterhood Is Global: The International Women's Movement Anthology* (Garden City, N.Y.: Anchor Press/Doubleday), 1984.

4. See, for example, Susan Douglas Franzosa and Karen A. Mazza, *Integrating Women's Studies into the Curriculum* (Westport, Conn.: Greenwood, 1984); Diane L. Fowkes and Charlotte S. McClure, eds., *Feminist Visions: Toward a Transformation of the Liberal Arts Curriculum* (University: Univ. of Alabama Pr., 1984); Dale Spender, *Men's Studies Modified: The Impact of Feminism on the Academic Disciplines* (Oxford: Pergamon, 1981); Betty Schmitz, *Integrating Women's Studies into the Curriculum: A Guide and Bibliography* (Old Westbury, N.Y.: The Feminist Press, 1985).

5. Can women's studies properly be labeled a "discipline?" Leading feminist scholars amiably disagree. Some argue that although women's studies offers brilliant new theories and incisive critiques of traditional methods, it elaborates no methodology of its own. Others point to the organization of the feminist curriculum, the shape of the emerging body of literature, the increasing legitimation of women-focused research, and feminism's undeniable impact on existing scholarly methods, as proof that women's studies must, for all practical purposes, be considered a fledgling discipline. The model of discipline development described by Anne K. Beaubien, Sharon A. Hogan, and Mary W. George in *Learning the Library* sheds some light on this debate (New York: Bowker, 1982, pp. 95–108). In this paper, we use the terms "discipline" and "field" interchangeably.

6. Susan E. Searing, "Report on a Study of Women's Studies Acquisitions at UW-Whi-

the *Weekly Record* or proof slips, can hardly suffice. Furthermore, most of the standard selection tools, even those organized by subject, fail to provide a separate section on women's studies.

Clearly, women's studies' wide angle of vision poses problems for the individual selector. It also raises the fundamental question of who should select and acquire materials. In many libraries, women's studies still is addressed by bibliographers with more traditional subject, language, or area responsibilities, who incorporate the selection of women-related materials in their particular field. While this arrangement may have sufficed a decade ago, such secondary attention no longer proves adequate. In most settings, women's studies collection development is best accomplished by a single selector with a commitment to the integrity of the discipline, someone in a position to monitor holdings across other disciplines, to guarantee balance within the collection, and to acquire the more specific and often elusive materials generated by feminist scholars and activists. Given the growth and establishment of women's studies, we can no longer allow institutional precedents and expediency to dictate selection procedures. The same philosophies of service, principles of quality collection development, and allocation of budgets and personnel that we apply to other disciplines must also be applied to women's studies.

Challenged by the interdisciplinary nature of women's studies, the selector may also face the specter of partisanship. Forthrightly political, women's studies insists that research and writing must benefit women, not merely be about them. Even the most arcane feminist scholarly pursuits envision gender equality as a basic goal. Some librarians may argue that feminist materials are "biased" or "nonobjective," and thus unsuitable for purchase. This same argument, we counter, must then hold true for the scholarly output of generations of male thinkers. To assume that good scholarship and a political viewpoint do not and cannot coexist in a single text—that knowledge is and should be somehow objective and final—is seriously shortsighted. In fact, as mainstream and feminist scholars alike have demonstrated, knowledge is a social, psychological, political, and historical construct, as well as an intellectual or scientific process.[7]

Successful collection development in women's studies requires an openness to the feminist viewpoint. Moreover, selectors must be attuned to the various perspectives within feminism: the contending theoretical schools that derive from (or develop in resistance to) prevailing paradigms such as Marxism, psychoanalysis, or sociobiology; and the compelling voices

tewater," *Feminist Collections* 4: 3–5(Spring 1983). Reprinted in *Alternative Library Literature, 1982/1983*, ed. by Sanford Berman and James P. Danky (Phoenix, Ariz.: Oryx, 1984), pp. 57–58.
7. See, for example, Thomas Kuhn, *The Structure of Scientific Revolutions* (Chicago: Univ. of Chicago Pr., 1970), and Lynne Spender, *Intruders on the Rights of Men: Women's Unpublished Heritage.* (London: Pandora Press, Routledge & Kegan Paul, 1983).

of women with diverse experiences—women of color, lesbians, working-class women, old women, disabled women—in short, all women struggling to make their stories heard and their needs known, in a world where a white male elite, by and large, still controls the creation, dissemination, use, and cost of information.

Let us not fail, however, to credit the publishing establishment for its progress. Trade publishers have responded quickly to the demand for anthologies, textbooks, and popularizations of research, although much still needs to be done. University presses issue an ever-growing number of scholarly studies; and Columbia University, the University of Chicago, and Rutgers University, among others, are notable for their recently established series in women's studies. However, women's studies scholars cannot rely solely on mainstream sources of information. Firm in their belief that the power of the press ultimately belongs only to those who own one, women continue to form collectives and companies to publish their own work. Many feminist presses have blossomed; many have withered; but alternative publishing by and for women remains on the cutting edge of feminist thought. Obviously, a field that relies heavily on non-mainstream materials demands special attention on the part of librarians and faculty designated to develop, maintain, and nurture the library's holdings.

Unfortunately, publishing patterns within women's studies remain virtually unanalyzed. We do not know, except impressionistically, which subfields are experiencing the greatest literature growth. We do not have citation studies or content analyses to tell us how greatly the scholarly and the alternative literatures overlap.[8] We do know that books in the HQs are frequently at the top of circulation statistics, but we don't know how heavily researchers rely on feminist materials from other classifications. Few libraries can pinpoint the rate at which their women's studies holdings are growing, nor even how much money they spend annually on these materials.

For over a decade, librarians responsible for selection in women's studies have been struggling to serve their users and to meet the demands of expanding curricula, usually with budgets far too small to match the rapid growth and diversity of feminist publishing. Independently and through professional networks, selectors began to share strategies, evaluations, exasperations, successes. In 1983, a women's studies discussion group was organized within the Association of College and Research Libraries of the American Library Association. Dedicated to the specific needs of academic

8. An exception to this general dearth of data is Elizabeth Futas's dissertation, "Communication and Information Patterns in the Emerging, Interdisciplinary Area of Women's Studies," Rutgers, 1980. It would be interesting to replicate her research to discover if her major finding—that publishing and citation practices in women's studies most closely resemble practices in the social sciences—holds true in the mid-eighties.

and research librarians in women's studies, the group set an initial high priority to compile a check list of sources for collection development. That document provides the basis for this chapter but goes well beyond what we can present here. It lists, for example, both prominent and little-known publishers of feminist materials, vendors, antiquarian booksellers, and data archives—all with brief descriptions and addresses. We strongly encourage selectors to use the checklist, and to participate in the ongoing networks that the discussion group fosters.[9]

Selection and Acquisition

BACKGROUND

Selectors new to the field of women's studies will find background reading useful to gain an understanding of the scope, principles, and concerns of feminist scholarship. Marilyn Boxer's review essay in *Signs*, supplemented by the chapters on women's studies as an academic discipline in *Theories of Women's Studies* and selections from *Learning Our Way: Essays in Feminist Education*, offer informative introductions.[10] Furthermore, especially since the discipline is still taking shape, any conscientious selector will want to keep abreast of new developments. *The Women's Annual: The Year in Review*, published since 1980 with the dual goal of reviewing the year's scholarship on women and reporting on feminist activity and social action, provides the best single source for current awareness.

AUDIENCE

The readers of *The Women's Annual*—scholars and activists both—reflect the broad audience for women's studies materials. Academic and public libraries alike must develop diversified collections to meet the needs and interest of their communities.

On campuses, the primary audience for women's studies materials are students and teachers directly involved in women's studies classes. Professors may need specialized resources for research on women within their disciplines, in addition to the introductory texts, anthologies, and key monographs that students demand.

9. Joan Ariel, ed., *Building Women's Studies Collections: A Checklist for Libraries, Research and Resource Centers, and Individual Collectors* (forthcoming as no. 8 in the "Bibliographic Essay Series" from *Choice*).

10. Marilyn J. Boxer, "For and about Women: The Theory and Practice of Women's Studies in the United States," *Signs* 7: 661–95(Spring 1982); Gloria Bowles and Renate Duelli Klein, eds., *Theories of Women's Studies* (London: Routledge & Kegan Paul, 1983); Charlotte Bunch and Sandra Pollack, eds., *Learning Our Way: Essays in Feminist Education* (Trumansburg, N.Y.: The Crossing Press, 1983).

The Women's Annual: 1980: The Year in Review, v.1– . 1981– . Boston: Hall. Annually.
Yearbook on feminist scholarship and the women's movement.
10 topical articles, with bibliographies.
Each year, *The Women's Annual* reports on scholarship, activism, and community programs that address issues of concern and interest to women. Barbara Haber, of the Schlesinger Library on the History of Women in America, conceived the series, and each volume to date has been edited by a librarian. Chapters by knowledgeable contributors focus on such topics as education, health, the humanities, international issues, lesbians, mass media and communications, politics and law, psychology, women of color in the United States, and work. Informative overviews provide an important current awareness service. Of particular interest to selectors, however, are the valuable bibliographies at the end of each chapter, which can be used as effective checklists for collection development.

We must remember, however, that like users of public libraries, women in the college community turn to the library for nonacademic needs as well. A women's studies collection should extend beyond the sometimes parochial parameters of the curriculum and encompass materials that address the daily needs and interests of women. In an attempt to "live up to the scholarly ideal of educating and serving the whole person," collections should also contain information on career choices, health matters, sexuality, self-defense, and child care, among other concerns of women's daily lives.[11] In like manner, works of women's studies scholarship are often of interest and use to women not engaged in formal academic pursuits, and public library collections should include the more important of these.

CURRENT MONOGRAPHS

Many academic libraries now rely heavily on approval plans for current monographs. These plans generally provide good coverage of academic and trade publishers, and thereby offer a basic foundation for current selection. While plans may include better-known feminist and other small progressive publishers, e.g., The Feminist Press or Virago, this coverage is usually selective and must be monitored closely.

The standard reviewing media—*Choice, Library Journal, Booklist, Publishers Weekly,* the *New York Times Book Review,* and the rest—have limited usefulness for identifying and evaluating new women's studies monographs. None highlight women's studies titles in a separate section.

11. Neel Parikh and Ellen Broidy, "Women's Issues: The Library Response," *Wilson Library Bulletin* 57: 195–99(Dec. 1982); Esther Stineman, "Issues in Women's Studies Collection Development," *Collection Building* 1: 57–76(1979).

Women's Review of Books. v.1– . 1983– . Wellesley, Mass.: Wellesley College
Center for Research on Women. Monthly.
Scholarly review journal.
About 16 reviews per issue.
3-month to 2-year time lag between book publication and review.
Reminiscent of the *New York Review of Books*, this monthly tabloid features
monographic titles by and about women, evaluated by expert feminist scholars.
Reviews are lengthy, and the editors strive for balanced coverage of mainstream
and small press books. Careful perusal of the *Women's Review* serves as an
enjoyable introduction to the debates that currently engage feminist readers and
writers.

Still, because *Choice* reviews so many titles, it may be the most productive
of the mainstream sources.

Several feminist serials supplement the above sources. The youngest,
The Women's Review of Books, has quickly gained a wide audience among
women's studies faculty. Each monthly issue is likely to generate reader
requests for new titles. Another tabloid, *Motheroot Journal,* is devoted
solely to the products of small presses; however, its irregular publishing
schedule makes it less central to selection than it might be. The Center
for Women's Studies at Ohio State University produces a bimonthly newsletter, *The Women's Studies Review*, with a half dozen reviews by feminist
faculty in each issue. And a new magazine devoted to reviews of literature
by women, *Belles Lettres,* began circulation in September of 1985.

Two quarterly feminist periodicals aimed specifically at librarians carry
reviews in addition to articles, editorials, and general news on the profession. Women Library Workers, a national organization of women working
at all levels in public, academic, school, and special libraries or in related
fields, publishes *WLW Journal.* Its signed reviews of books, serials, films,
records, and vertical file items are succinct and current. *Feminist Collections*, published by the Women's Studies Librarian of the University of
Wisconsin System, carries one to three review articles per issue. Reviewers,
usually faculty, often compare several titles or survey recent publishing
on a topic of interest. *Feminist Bookstore News* is a newsletter and networking tool for bookstore owners and workers, but librarians can profit
from its prepublication notices and the editor's knowledgeable predictions
of best sellers and publishing trends.

All of the abovementioned sources emphasize United States publications
and rarely review materials in languages other than English. *Resources for
Feminist Research/Documentation sur la Recherche Feministe,* a Canadian periodical with many reviews of materials in French and English,
begins to fill this gap. American works are specifically excluded from
coverage. Still, identification of international sources for women's studies

remains frustrating and problematic. Careful review of approval plans (e.g., Touzot for French materials, Harrassowitz for German) or current national bibliographies must be undertaken until a more comprehensive source is available. Fortunately, Virginia Clark, assistant editor at *Choice*, is working on a directory of European women's studies resources, including entries for organizations, archives and libraries, publishers, journals, and bookshops.

Most scholarly journals in women's studies carry reviews, although their coverage may lag one to three years behind publication. *Signs, Feminist Studies, Women's Studies International Forum*, and *Women's Studies Quarterly* all offer a handful of thoughtful assessments in each issue. Feminist magazines and newspapers also highlight books and other media, and are frequently more current in their coverage. In addition to *Ms.*, selectors should consider routinely scanning *New Directions for Women*, which averages ten book reviews per monthly issue, *off our backs*, a long-lived vehicle for radical feminist opinion and news, and *Sojourner*, a Boston-based newspaper with good coverage of recent monographs. Additional reviews may be located by consulting the listing in the back of each quarterly issue of *Women Studies Abstracts* and the book abstracts section in the newer British service, *Studies on Women Abstracts*. In the latter source, one must be alert to British printings of titles previously released in the United States, and vice versa.

Academic librarians will surely want to scan most of these sources; public librarians may wish to be more selective or to rely on *Booklist, Ms.*, and *New Directions for Women* as barometers to indicate women's studies titles of interest to the general reader.

Selectors should not neglect to look for feminist titles among the small press offerings reviewed in such sources as *Small Press Review* and *New Pages*, although the broader objectives of these publications naturally limit the number of women's studies titles they treat. In addition, several major book distributors emphasizing small press titles recognize the importance of feminist materials and include separate listings for women's studies within their catalogs. Most notable among these are Bookpeople and Inland Book. We also recommend the specialized Turtle Grandmother Books for books by women of color.

While they cannot substitute for full reviews, accession lists serve to alert the selector to the latest titles purchased by other libraries. The Marguerite Rawalt Resource Center of the Business and Professional Women's Foundation, the University of Illinois Library, and University of Pittsburgh Hillman Library all issue lists of recent titles added to their shelves. The first emphasizes materials on work and careers, while the others cover the spectrum of women's studies. *New Books on Women and Feminism*, compiled at the University of Wisconsin, is a comprehensive listing of books, nonprint materials, new periodical titles, and children's literature, arranged by subject. Citations are culled from a number of sources, including reviews and publishers' catalogs.

The busy selector will also welcome direct communications from publishers. Indeed, for women's studies, publishers' announcements may provide the most current and complete source for identification of materials. Many of the larger trade and university presses now distribute brochures describing new women's studies titles, and they are only too glad to add interested names to their mailing lists.[12] Small presses, too, invest in mail advertising. For the addresses of the more elusive feminist publishers and progressive publishers that produce a significant number of titles on women, one can consult the checklist compiled by the ACRL Women's Studies Discussion Group of the *Index/Directory of Women's Media*, issued annually by the Women's Institute for Freedom of the Press. Among these numerous publishers, selectors should be certain to contact the following: The Feminist Press, a well-established nonprofit publisher of both classroom texts and books for personal reading; Kitchen Table/Women of Color Press, the first publishing house run by and for Third World women in North America; Naiad Press, the largest publisher of lesbian belles-lettres and nonfiction; Firebrand Books, a new publishing house established by the former editor of the highly regarded Crossing Press Feminist Series; and Virago Press, the foremost British producer of original and reprinted women's fiction.

Librarians can also upgrade their "junk mail" by joining the National Women's Mailing List network. This free computerized system allows its members to identify areas of interest and to receive targeted information from publishers and other organizations.

RETROSPECTIVE SOURCES

New women's studies programs and innovative courses are established every year on American campuses. Thus libraries often find it necessary to survey their holdings and to fill gaps. While the increasing number of specialized bibliographies in women's studies provide fruitful listings, the single best guide to books through 1979 is *Women's Studies: A Recommended Core Bibliography*, by Esther Stineman. *New Books on Women and Feminism* can serve to update Stineman until the planned supplement is published.

An increasing number of out-of-print book dealers specialize in works by and about women. The ACRL/WSDG checklist identifies over thirty such firms, all of which have prepared catalogs devoted to women's materials.

12. Cathy Loeb, "Breaking into Print II: Feminist Publishing in the Mainstream," *Feminist Collections* 5: 3–8(Summer 1984).

Stineman, Esther. *Women's Studies: A Recommended Core Bibliography.*
Littleton, Colo.: Libraries Unlimited, 1979.
Selected annotated bibliography.
Coverage through mid-1979.
Representing a core collection for a library supporting an undergraduate women's studies curriculum, this pioneering volume cites 1,763 books and periodicals. The annotations (which are often pointedly evaluative) are grouped in twenty-six chapters by subject or type of publication—anthropology, history, poetry, reference, etc. A forthcoming supplement will highlight core materials published between mid-1979 and 1985. Author, title, and subject indexes enhance both volumes.

Important retrospective materials for the study of women are also available in microform. The *History of Women* collection from Research Publications, Inc., includes printed books, periodicals, pamphlets, manuscript items, and photographs; over 10,000 pieces in all. The *Gerritsen Collection of Women's History 1543–1945,* from Microfilming Corporation of America, is an international assemblage of nineteenth and early twentieth-century books, pamphlets, and periodicals. The *Herstory* set and its supplements, available from the Women's History Research Center, reproduces periodicals and other ephemeral sources from the 1960s and early 1970s, many of them already quite rare. These are but a few of the important archival collections now readily accessible through microform sets from Harvester Press, Microfilming Corporation of America, Research Publications, and University Microfilms International, among others.[13]

REFERENCE BOOKS

Reference books claim a central place in a developing field such as women's studies. They lead researchers to older materials previously undiscovered, and they supply conceptual organization and bibliographic control for a wealth of new information. Many of the sources already noted review reference books; they are given special attention in *Feminist Collections.* The *American Reference Books Annual* has featured a chapter on women's studies for several years, with thoughtful evaluations of recent tit
les. The monthly *Reference Report* provides a welcome awareness service for new reference titles and reviews, if one is willing to scan the list for women's studies sources.

For retrospective selection of reference materials (as well as research guidance), Susan Searing's *Introduction to Library Research in Women's Studies* comes in handy. Patricia Ballou's *Women: A Bibliography of Bib-*

13. Sarah Pritchard, "Microform Resources in Women's Studies at the Library of Congress" (Washington, D.C.: Library of Congress, General Reading Rooms Div., 1985).

Feminist Collections. v.1– . 1980– . Madison: Univ. of Wisconsin System
Women's Studies Librarian. Quarterly.
Newsletter.
2–4 review essays per issue.
3-month to 2-year lag between book publication and review.
This newsletter runs to thirty-plus pages and is aimed at a diverse audience of
librarians, faculty, independent researchers, and members of the loosely knit
"women-in-print" network. Each issue has regular columns on periodicals, reference works, nonprint media, and miscellanea ("Items of Note"), plus book
reviews by expert faculty, librarians, or community activists. Recent feature
articles have surveyed feminist small press and mainstream publishing, inter-
viewed authors and editors, reported on women's scholarship outside the United
States, and highlighted special library collections.

---

liographies and Jane Williamson's *New Feminist Scholarship*, although
both dated, remain useful for identifying bibliographies. Public and academic libraries alike should compare their holdings to Beth Stafford's 1982
basic checklist in *Reference Services Review*.

PERIODICALS

Periodical literature plays a vital role in a dynamic discipline such as wom-
en's studies. Here, periodicals fall into two categories—academic and activist—although the dual commitment of feminist publishing often blurs
this distinction. *Signs: A Journal of Women in Culture and Society*, widely
recognized as the most prestigious of the scholarly journals, belongs in
every academic library, whether or not a formal women's studies program
exists on the campus. Other key interdisciplinary journals include *Women's
Studies Quarterly*, *Women's Studies International Forum*, *Feminist Studies*, and *Sex Roles: A Journal of Research*. *Frontiers*, notable for its commitment to "bridge the gap between university and community women
[and] to find a balance between academic and popular views on issues
common to women," is an excellent choice for both academic and public
library collections.

Many specialized journals reflect the influx of feminist scholarship in
the traditional disciplines. Too numerous to list here, their ranks include
the *Psychology of Women Quarterly*, *Harvard Women's Law Journal*,
Tulsa Studies in Women's Literature, *Women and Health*, and *Women's
Art Journal*.

Feminists also publish a wide range of literary journals and "journals
of ideas," each with its own personality and ideological flavor. Among
the best, in our opinion, are *Sinister Wisdom*, *Ikon*, *Calyx*, *Helicon Nine*,
Conditions, and *13th Moon*. These are but a handful of the bountiful

crop; selectors should request sample copies and choose those most suited to the needs of their collections and the interests of their communities.

Women's studies is inescapably pluralistic, and the many voices of feminism and women's studies scholarship have given rise to periodical titles reflecting the diversity of perspectives. *Common Lives/Lesbian Lives, Lilith: The Jewish Women's Magazine, Sage: A Scholarly Journal on Black Women*, and *Third Woman*, to name a few, provide important examples that should be included in serial collections.

Since this chapter can only hint at the variety of periodicals currently available about women, selectors should regularly consult other more comprehensive listings. *Feminist Periodicals*, which reprints the tables of contents from over seventy English-language periodicals, can be skimmed to get a sense of each publication's content and style, although the coverage of literary and nonacademic titles is selective. The *Annotated Guide to Women's Periodicals in the U.S. and Canada*, issued twice a year, organizes its extensive listings by subject and provides comparative, albeit brief, descriptions. The *Annotated Guide*, the *Index/Directory of Women's Media*, and *Feminist Periodicals* serve as up-to-date sources for addresses and subscription rates for periodicals. Bibliographic data on older periodical titles can be found in *Women's Periodicals and Newspapers from the 18th Century to 1981*, edited by James P. Danky.

As every selector knows, subscriptions must be entered with care, for they represent an ongoing commitment of funds. One typical criterion for adding new periodical titles is the availability of indexing. If a periodical is covered by an index or abstract heavily used by library patrons, one can predict a corresponding demand for the periodical. *Feminist Periodicals* notes index coverage for the seventy-plus titles it includes. Unfortunately, there is no current published list of periodical titles covered in *Women Studies Abstracts*, the major indexing tool in women's studies. *Studies on Women Abstracts* carries a list of the titles it covers, but the list does not appear to be accurate. Regrettably, standard indexes continue to ignore many serials essential to women's studies, but the selector may find some guidance in the recent library literature.[14]

Although a conservative and perhaps narrowly pragmatic approach to periodicals selection will weight heavily the criterion of index availability, treating this desirable factor as a requirement will only diminish the quality of women's studies holdings and eliminate articles and perspectives critical to the discipline. Two cases illustrate this important point. *Conditions*

14. Helen Rippier Wheeler, "A Feminist Researcher's Guide to Periodical Indexes, Abstracting Services, Citation Indexes, and Online Databases," *Collection Building* 5:3–24(Fall 1983); Mary Alice Sanguinetti, "Indexing of Feminist Periodicals," *The Serials Librarian* 8: 21–33(Summer 1984); Jane Williamson, "Feminist Periodicals: A Beginner's Guide," *The Serials Librarian* 8: 13–20(Summer 1984); Charlotta Hensley, "Sinister Wisdom and Other Issues of Lesbian Imagination," *Serials Review* 9: 7–19(Fall 1983); Ellen Gay Detlefsen, "Issues of Access to Information about Women," *Special Collections* 3(forthcoming).

and *Sinister Wisdom* are excluded from mainstream indexes and receive sporadic indexing in alternative sources. At the same time, they are often deemed "not scholarly enough" to include in research library collections. Yet *Conditions Five*, issued in 1979, was the first widely disseminated articulation of feminism from the viewpoint, voice, and experience of black women; in many ways, it served as a springboard for subsequent pathbreaking and influential publications such as *All the Women Are White, All the Blacks Are Men, But Some of Us Are Brave: Black Women's Studies* and *This Bridge Called My Back*.[15] For close to a decade, *Sinister Wisdom* has pioneered the publication of theoretical, critical, personal, and political writing by lesbian feminists, writing that has often been neglected, even silenced, by more established journals. In 1983, *Sinister Wisdom*'s double issue, "A Gathering of Spirit," offered a rare collection of North American Indian women's writing and art.[16]

Libraries neglect such periodicals to the short- and long-term detriment of their collections. If budgets are limited, cooperative collection development within systems or among libraries should be employed to insure this vital coverage.

OTHER PRINT SOURCES

In addition to monographs and periodicals, selectors must be alert to a variety of other printed resources appropriate, and sometimes essential, to collections in women's studies.

As in any academic field, conferences serve as a key means of communicating new theories and methodologies. The major professional gathering—the annual conference of the National Women's Studies Association—as yet produces no regular proceedings series, but many specialized conferences and colloquia result in pathbreaking monographic volumes.

Dissertations, of course, offer an excellent source of data and analysis. They are difficult to identify, however, because doctoral degrees in womens studies per se are rarely granted. University Microfilms International issues occasional catalogs of theses that may be classified as women's studies; identification of useful dissertations can also be achieved through online access to *Dissertation Abstracts International* using key words related to women or feminism.

The National Council for Research on Women links the growing number of centers and organizations "which provide institutional resources

15. Gloria T. Hull, Patricia Bell Scott, and Barbara Smith, eds., *All the Women Are White, All the Blacks Are Men, But Some of Use Are Brave: Black Women's Studies* (Old Westbury, N.Y.: The Feminist Press, 1982); Cherrie Moraga and Gloria Anzaldua, eds., *This Bridge Called My Back: Writings by Radical Women of Color* (Watertown, Mass.: Persephone Press, 1981).
16. This special issue has been expanded and reissued as a monograph: Beth Brant (Degonwadonti), ed., *A Gathering of Spirit* (Rockland, Me.: Sinister Wisdom Books, 1984).

for feminist research, policy analysis, and educational programs."[17] Most issue occasional working papers and informational packets. Bibliographic control of materials from research centers is poor; within the coming decade, the National Council hopes to correct this situation through the development of a national online database for women's studies. Meanwhile, librarians are advised to correspond directly with the various centers to ascertain their offerings. An annotated directory of National Council member centers is published annually in the *Women's Studies Quarterly*.

There are many sources for pamphlet materials and other items suitable for vertical files. *WLW Journal*, mentioned above, features a regular column on ephemeral materials of interest to women. *On Campus with Women*, the newsletter of the Project on the Status and Education of Women of the Association of American Colleges, highlights research reports, statistical compilations, and position papers that might otherwise escape the attention of educators and librarians. The National Women's History Project also has a large catalog of curriculum materials suitable for public, school, and academic libraries. Program manuals and reports that result from federally sponsored projects are distributed through the Women's Educational Equity Act Publishing Center.

Since there is no current national directory of women's organizations, the *Encyclopedia of Associations* remains the best guide for locating potential sources of association or agency publications. Although unfortunately dated, the *Women's Action Almanac* offers another productive resource for this task. Librarians will also want to consult local, state, and regional directories wherever they are available.

Women's studies collections are significantly strengthened through the inclusion of government publications. Both the United States federal government and the United Nations print reams of information on and for women, from statistical surveys to self-help booklets. Intergovernmental agencies and international organizations also gather and disseminate data highly relevant to women's studies and increasingly reflective of the expansion of global feminism. Feminist organizations that collect and disseminate information in this arena include:

> ISIS International Women's Information and Communication Service, which since 1974 has developed an "extensive pool of documentation and information comprising a network of 10,000 contacts in 130 countries (and) 50,000 items—periodicals, newsletters, pamphlets, books, manuscripts, information about films, projects, groups—by and about women from all over the world."[18] Its 1983 publication, *Women*

---

17. *Women's Studies Quarterly*, 12:17 (Spring 1984).
18. "About ISIS," in *Women in Development: A Resource Guide for Organization and Action* (Philadelphia: New Society Publishers, 1984), p. 221.

ISIS International Women's Information and Communication Service. *Women in Development: A Resource Guide for Organization and Action.*
Philadelphia: New Society Publishers, 1984.
Sourcebook and bibliography.
International scope.
Coverage primarily 1970s to early 1980s.
ISIS is "an international women's information and communication service . . . established in 1974 in response to demands from women in many countries for an organization to facilitate global communications among women" (p. 221). *Women in Development* focuses on five key areas related to women in developing countries: multinational corporations, rural development and food production, health, education and communication, and migration and tourism. For each of these topics, overview articles providing substantive information and analysis are followed by annotated resources for reserch and organizing. These lists include resource centers, books and pamphlets, recommended periodical articles, and audiovisual materials from governmental, intergovernmental, and development agencies, as well as feminist and other action-oriented groups.

in Development: A Resource Guide for Organization and Action, provides a wealth of information useful for developing the international scope of collections in women's studies.

Women's International Resource Exchange (WIRE), a clearinghouse and distribution center for the evaluation and dissemination of materials about women in the Third World and Third World women in the United States.

Change, a London-based organization "founded to research and publish reports of the condition and status of women all over the world."

AUDIOVISUAL SOURCES

Feminist education often incorporates affective, experiential learning. Audiovisual materials are popular classroom tools in women's studies; thus libraries and media centers should assure their accessibility. The standard nonprint reviewing media should be scanned routinely. Unfortunately, the single newsletter devoted to reviewing audiovisual resources about women, the *Catalyst Media Review,* ceased publication in 1985. Brief notes on new films and recordings continue to appear in the *Media Report to Women* and *On Campus with Women. New Books on Women and Feminism,* despite its print-oriented title, also highlights audiovisual materials.

Michigan Media has produced an annotated list, "Films and Videocassettes for Women's Studies," and the National Film Board of Canada offers a United States edition of their catalog entitled "Beyond the Image: A Guide to Films about Women and Change." These lists, used in conjunction with Kaye Sullivan's two-volume *Films for, by and about Women* and Joan Nordquist's *Audiovisuals for Women*, will assist in the selection of nonprint sources. In addition, some two hundred films and videotapes about women from the early eighties are described in a filmography compiled by Margaret Hohenstein and available from the University of Wisconsin Women's Studies Librarian.

Sound recordings and music selections can be identified through several sources. Ladyslipper's annual *Catalog and Resource Guide of Records and Tapes by Women* is an invaluable compendium for ordering recording by an extensive variety of women musicians, writers, and composers. *The Music of Women: A Selection Guide*, compiled by Nancy Vedder-Shults, is a useful annotated core discography in four sections: concert; jazz, blues, and gospel; folk; and women's music. For spoken recordings—literary, autobiographical, and political—convenient sources include the Poet's Audio Center, the Pacifica Radio Archive, and the American Audio Prose Library; all issue catalogs.

As with microform and periodical selection, cooperative acquisitions of films and other audiovisual materials will help stretch budgets while assuring access to important, if sometimes expensive, sources.

Conclusion

Both challenging and frustrating, collection development in women's studies requires a degree of commitment and creativity matched in few other academic disciplines. The expanding parameters and fluid boundaries of the literature itself may cause difficulties.

We must stay abreast of the new specializations emerging within women's studies and spawning ever more esoteric books and journals, yet recognize meanwhile that cross-disciplinary anthologies and survey works continue to break new conceptual paths. We must be aware of feminist scholarship's impact on more traditional disciplines, as well as of the rapid growth and changes within women's studies itself. As we reach the end of the United Nation's Decade for Women, global feminism and the international women's movement demand increasing attention, but we face inadequate bibliographic control of non-English-language publications and official documents, and a glaring need for translations of both literary and nonfiction works.

In the face of this predicament, there is no room for parochialism in women's studies collection development. If we are to be truly comprehensive (and true to the goal of bibliographic control), every avenue to information must be taken. Selectors cannot depend on a single source, nor even a single group of sources. Scholarly and "popular" frequently intersect and long-standing distinctions between academic and public library collections converge. Feminist challenges to the conventional categories of knowledge may confound us, as reserachers turn to source materials previously scorned by scholars and academic librarians alike—household journals, mass market romances, cookbooks, beauty manuals—to document, investigate, and illuminate the lives of women. If women's studies is both academic and activist, experiential as well as experimental, collection development programs must reflect that diversity, and selectors must search out materials without regard to artificial boundaries of subject or discipline.

As women's studies gains academic recognition and legitimation, and thus increased publication through mainstream channels, libraries are, almost automatically, integrating this material into our collections. Yet a great many works crucial to the study of women's lives, and to the development of feminist theory, scholarship, and action are not caught by the conventional nets of acquisitions and bibliographic control. Selectors in women's studies cannot rely upon (and should, in fact, seriously question) the inherently biased standards of "the academic gatekeepers," those people in the academic and mainstream publishing communities, still predominantly male or male-identified, who set the criteria for scholarly excellence, define knowledge, and administer its distribution, including its distribution to libraries.[19] Unlike other disciplines, women's studies is informed and continually revitalized by a radical social movement; to retain that vitality and the essential promise of the fundamental transformation of race-, class-, and gender-biased structures, women's studies selectors must insure comprehensive coverage and ready access to the materials of the small, radical, and feminist publishers worldwide who are the voices of this movement.

Selection Sources

American Audio Prose Library. 915 East Broadway, Columbia, MO 65201; 314–874-1139.
American Reference Books Annual. v.1– . 1970– . Littleton, Colo.: Libraries Unlimited. Annually.
Ariel, Joan, ed. *Building Women's Studies Collections: A Checklist for Libraries, Research and Resource Centers, and Individual Collectors.* Forthcoming as no. 8 in the "Bibliographic Essay Series" from *Choice.*
Ballou, Patricia K. *Women: A Bibliography of Bibliographies.* Boston: Hall, 1980.
Belles Lettres. v.1– . 1985– . 6/year. P.O. Box 987, Arlington, VA 22216; 301–294-0278.
Bookpeople. 2929 Fifth St., Berkeley, CA 94710; 415-549-3030.

19. Lynne Spender, *Intruders on the Rights of Men.*

Business & Professional Women's Foundation. Marguerite Rawalt Resource Center. *Selected Acquisitions.* 6/year. 2012 Massachusetts Ave., N.W., Washington, DC 20036; 202–293–1200.

Catalyst Media Review. v.1–4. 1981–85. New York: Catalyst. Quarterly.

Change International Reports. Parnell House, 25 Wilton Rd., London SW1V 1JS, England.

Danky, James P., ed. *Women's Periodicals and Newspapers from the 18th Century to 1981.* Boston: Hall, 1982.

Feminist Bookstore News. v.1– . 1976– . 6/year. P.O. Box 882554, San Francisco, CA 94188.

Feminist Collections: A Quarterly of Women's Studies Resources. v.1– . 1980– . Univ. of Wisconsin System Women's Studies Librarian. Quarterly. 112A Memorial Library, 728 State St., Madison, WI 53706; 608–263–5754.

Feminist Periodicals: A Current Listing of Contents. v.1– . 1981– . Madison: Univ. of Wisconsin System Women's Studies Librarian. Quarterly.

The Feminist Press. 311 East 94th St., New York, NY 10128.

Feminist Studies. v.1– . 1972– . College Park, Md.: Women's Studies Program. Univ. of Maryland. 3/year.

Firebrand Books. 141 The Commons, Ithaca, NY 14850; 607–272–0000.

Hohenstein, Margaret, comp. "Films and Videotapes about Women." Madison: Univ. of Wisconsin System Women's Studies Librarian, 1984.

Index/Directory of Women's Media. v.1– . 1972– . Washington, D.C.: Women's Institute for Freedom of the Press. Annually. 3306 Ross Place, N.W., Washington, DC 20008; 202–966–7783.

Inland Book. Box 261, 22 Hemingway Ave., East Haven, CT 06512; 201–467–4257.

Kitchen Table/Women of Color Press. P.O. Box 2753, New York, NY 10185.

Ladyslipper Catalog and Resource Guide of Records and Tapes by Women. Annually. Ladyslipper, Inc., P.O. Box 3130, Durham, N.C. 27705.

Media Report to Women. v.1– . 1972– . Washington, D.C.: Women's Institute for Freedom of the Press. 6/year.

Mehlman, Terry. *Annotated Guide to Women's Periodicals in the United States and Canada.* v.1– . 1982– . Richmond, Ind.: Women's Program Office. Earlham College. Semiannually.

Michigan Media. "Films and Videocassettes for Women's Studies." 400 Fourth St., Ann Arbor, MI 48103; 313–764–5360.

Morgan, Robin, ed. *Sisterhood Is Global: The International Women's Movement Anthology.* Garden City, N.Y.: Anchor Press/Doubleday, 1984.

Motheroot Journal: A Women's Review of Small Presses. v.1– . 1979– . Pittsburgh: Motheroot Publications. Quarterly.

Ms. v.1– . 1972– . New York. Monthly.

Naiad Press. P.O. Box 10543, Tallahassee, FL 32302.

National Film Board of Canada. "Beyond the Image: A Guide to Films about Women and Change." National Film Board of Canada, 1251 Avenue of the Americas, 16th floor, New York, NY 10021–1173; 212–586–5131.

National Women's History Project. P.O. Box 3716, Santa Rosa, CA 95402.

National Women's Mailing List. P.O. Box 68, Jenner, CA 95450.

New Books on Women and Feminism. no.1– . 1979– . Madison: Univ. of Wisconsin System Women's Studies Librarian. Irregularly.

New Directions for Women. v.1– . 1972– . Englewood, N.J. 6/year.

"New Materials from Hillman Library." In *Women's Studies Program Newsletter.* Women's Studies Program, Univ. of Pittsburgh, 2632 Cathedral of Learning, Pittsburgh, PA 15260.

New Pages: News and Reviews of the Progressive Book Trade. v.1– . 1980– . Grand Blanc, Mich. 3/year.

Nordquist, Joan. *Audiovisuals for Women.* Jefferson, N.C.: McFarland, 1980.

off our backs. v.1– . 1970– . Washington, D.C. Monthly.

On Campus with Women. v.1– . 1971– . Washington, D.C." Project on the Status and Education of Women. Assn. of American Colleges. Quarterly. 1818 R St., N.W., Washington, DC 20009; 202–387–1300.

Pacifica Radio Archive. (Microfiche catalog and titles cassette catalog.) 5316 Venice Blvd., Los Angeles, CA 90019.

Poet's Audio Corner. *Collector's Catalog.* Watershed Foundation, P.O. Box 50145, Washington, DC 20004.

Reference Report. v.1– . 1982– . Detroit: Grenoble Books. Monthly.

Resources for Feminist Research/Documentation sur la Recherche Feministe. v.1– . 1979– . Toronto: Ontario Institute for Studies in Education. Quarterly. (Formerly *Canadian Newsletter of Research on Women,* 1972–1978.)

Searing, Susan E. *Introduction to Library Research in Women's Studies.* Boulder, Colo.: Westview, 1985.

Small Press Review. v.1– . 1967– . Paradise, Calif.: Dustbooks. Monthly.

Sojourner. v.1– . 1975– . Cambridge, Mass.. Monthly.

Stafford, Beth. "Women's Studies: A Reference Collection for Public Libraries." *Reference Services Review* 10: 11–15(Winter 1982).

Stineman, Esther. *Women's Studies: A Recommended Core Bibliography.* Littleton, Colo.: Libraries Unlimited, 1979.

Studies on Women Abstracts. v.1– . 1983– . Oxfordshire, Eng.: Carfax. 6/year.

Sullivan, Kaye. *Films for, by, and about Women.* Metuchen, N.J.: Scarecrow, 1980.

———. *Films for, by and about Women, Series II.* Metuchen, N.J.: Scarecrow, 1985.

Turtle Grandmother Books. P.O. Box 33964, Detroit, MI 48232.

Vedder-Shults, Nancy. *The Music of Women: A Selection Guide.* Wisconsin Women Library Workers, 1984. P.O. Box 1425, Madison, WI 53701.

Virago Press. 41 William IV St., London WC2N 7HE, England. Dist. in the United States by Merrimack Publishers Circle, 250 Commercial St., Manchester, NH 03101.

Williamson, Jane. *New Feminist Scholarship: A Guide to Bibliographies.* Old Westbury, N.Y.: Feminist Pr., 1979.

WIRE, Women's International Resource Exchange. 2700 Broadway, Rm. 7, New York, NY 10025; 212–666–4622.

WLW Journal. v.1– . 1976– . Berkeley, Calif.: Women Library Workers. Quarterly.

Women in Development: A Resource Guide for Organization and Action. Geneva: ISIS International Women's Information and Communication Service, 1983. ISIS, P.O. Box 50 (Cornavin), 1211 Geneva 2, Switzerland. United States ed. available from New Society Publishers.

Women Studies Abstracts. v.1– . 1972– . Rush, N.Y.: Rush Publishing. Quarterly.

Women's Action Alliance. *Women's Action Almanac: A Complete Resource Guide.* Ed. by Jane Williamson, Diane Winston, and Wanda Wooten. New York: Morrow, 1979.

Women's Educational Equity Act Publishing Center. Educational Development Center, Inc., 55 Chapel St., Newton, MA 02160; 800–225–3088.

Women's History Research Center. 2325 Oak St., Berkeley, CA 94708; 415–548–1770.

The Women's Review of Books. v.1– . 1983– . Monthly. Wellesley College Center for Research on Women, Wellesley, MA 02181–8255.

Women's Studies: Selected Acquisitions. Women's Studies/WID Unit, 415 Library,
  Univ. of Illinois, Urbana, IL 61801; 217-333-7998.
Women's Studies International Forum. v.1- . 1978- . Elmsford, N.Y.: Pergamon.
  6/year.
Women's Studies Review. v.1- . 1972- . Center for Women's Studies, Ohio State
  Univ. 6/year. 207 Dulles Hall, 230 West 17 St., Columbus, OH 43210. Biweekly.
Women's Studies Quarterly. v.1- . 1972- . New York: Feminist Pr. Quarterly. 311
  East 94th St., New York, NY 10128.

Editors and Contributors

NANCY ALLEN was the Communications Librarian at the University of Illinois, Urbana, from 1978 to 1984. During that time she published *Film Study Collections; A Guide to Their Development and Use*, and, with Robert Carringer, *Unpublished Film and Television Scripts at the University of Illinois at Urbana Library*, along with several other articles and papers. In 1984, she became Assistant Director for Services at Wayne State University. Maintaining her interests in media-related information, she is active in the ACRL Arts Section, and is presently working on a annotated bibliography of research literature on children and mass media.

JOAN ARIEL, Women's Studies Librarian at the University of California, Irvine, since 1981, previously worked as a public librarian in the Alameda County (California) Library System. She is the founding chair of the Women's Studies Discussion Group of ALA's Association of College and Research Libraries. Her publications include *Building Women's Studies Collections: A Checklist for Libraries, Research and Resource Centers, and Individual Collectors* (*Choice*, 1986), and *Women's Legal Rights in the United States: A Selective Bibliography* (American Library Assn., 1985), in addition to women's studies reviews and articles in *Feminist Collections, Serials Review*, and *RQ*.

ROBERT BELLANTI is Head of the Graduate School of Management Library at the University of California at Los Angeles (UCLA). Before that he was the Associate Director for the Pacific Southwest Regional Medical Library Service at the UCLA Biomedical Library and Head of that Library's Interlibrary Loan Division. He also worked for four years as Serials Librarian at the University of Nevada at Las Vegas.

BRENDA J. COX has been the Social Work Librarian at Howard University since 1978. Before that she worked as the Adult Institutions Librarian and as a branch librarian in the D.C. Public Library System, Washington, D.C. She started her career as a catalog librarian at the West Virginia State College, Institute, West Virginia.

271

JANNETTE FIORE has been the Head of Rare Books and Special Collections at the Michigan State University Libraries since 1974. She is a reviewer for *Choice* and is the author of "Popular Culture and the Academic Library: The Nye Collection" (*Drexel Library Quarterly*, v.16, no.3, July 1980).

EDITH MAUREEN FISHER has been the Ethnic Studies Collection Developer at the University of California, San Diego, since 1972. She has a Certificate in Ethnicity and Librarianship from the Department of Library Science at Queens College of the City of New York. Among her publications are "Minority Librarianship Research: A State-of-the-Art Review" (Library and Information Science Research; An International Journal 5: 5–65, [Spring 1983]) and "Academic Library Collection Development in Ethnic Studies: Issues for Concern" (Bookmark 41: 32–35, [Fall 1982]). She presented a paper on "Whitewash: The Concealing of Information on Women of Color" for the Librarians Task Force of the National Women Studies Assn., at the 1985 Annual Conference.

RONA H. GREGORY served as Subject Specialist for City and Regional Planning and Collection Manager for the Rotch Library of Architecture and Planning at the Massachusetts Institute of Technology for six years. Before working at M.I.T., she received graduate degrees in both regional planning and library science.

JANE W. JOHNSON, Social Sciences Collection Management Librarian, Virginia Commonwealth University, previously served as Reference Librarian at VCU and at the University of Georgia and as the Head of Online Bibliographic Searching Service at VCU from 1978 to 1983. She has published book reviews in *Southeastern Librarian* and an online searching column in *Education Libraries*.

ARLENE E. LUCHSINGER is Assistant Director for Branches at the University of Georgia Libraries and was formerly a cataloger at Georgia State University and the University of the South. She has degrees in botany and is coauthor of *Smith's Guide to the Literature of the Life Sciences* (1980) and *Plant Systematics* (1979 and 1986).

PATRICIA McCANDLESS is the Applied Life Studies Librarian and Assistant Director of the Life Science Council Libraries at the University of Illinois at Urbana-Champaign. As project director of an Office of Management Studies, Association of Research Libraries public services grant entitled "The Invisible User," she is coauthor of *The Invisible User: User Needs Assessment for Library Public Services*, published by ARL. Among her other publications is a bibliography of "sports medicine" materials for public library collections that appeared in *Illinois Libraries*.

NEOSHA A. MACKEY is Head of Reference at Southwest Missouri State University. She was Head of the Home Economics Library at the Ohio State University from 1980 to 1985. As a member of the American Home Economics Association, she began identifying and organizing librarians with responsibilities in home economics. She has also served as a consultant to assess home economics library collections.

GUDRUN A. MEYER is the Collection Management Librarian for Public Administration and Business at Virginia Commonwealth University.

TRACEY MILLER served as Collection Development/Reference Librarian for four years at the Graduate School of Management Library at the University of California at Los Angeles. Before that she worked as Head Librarian and Assistant Business Librarian at the University of Colorado's William M. White Library and as Business Librarian at Denver Public Library.

BETH M. PASKOFF, Science Bibliographer at Louisiana State University since 1978, formerly served as medical librarian at the Veterans Administration Hospital in Baltimore, and at the Washington, D.C. Hospital Center. She is also an adjunct member of the faculty of the L.S.U. School of Library and Information Science, where she regularly offers a course in Resources in Science and Technology. She has reviewed books for *ARBA* and *JASIS* and has published in *RQ*.

EDWIN D. POSEY is Engineering Librarian and Associate Professor at the Siegesmund Engineering Library of Purdue University. Before this he was engineering librarian at Princeton University. He is author of several journal articles, and coauthor of *Approval Plans and Academic Libraries* (Oryx Press, 1977).

JUDITH L. RIEKE is currently Serials Librarian at the Medical Center Library at Vanderbilt University, Nashville, Tennessee. She was Head of the Map Department at the Sterling C. Evans Library, Texas A&M University. She has written articles on different facets of maps and map libraries and has been active in the Map and Geography Round Table of the American Library Association.

BILL ROBNETT is the Director of the Division of Reader Services in the Fondren Library of Rice University. He was an instructor in Biology at the University of Agriculture of Malaysia, Technical Editor for an environmental engineering corporation, and Science Librarian at Oberlin College. Robnett has written several biological sciences papers in scholarly journals, and authored the Biology essay for ALA's *Selection of Library Materials in the Humanities, Social Sciences, and Sciences*.

EILEEN ROWLAND has been with the library of the John Jay College of Criminal Justice since 1971, initially as Acquisitions Librarian, subsequently as Head of Technical Services, and since 1975 as Chief Librarian. She is an advocate of librarian participation in disciplinary associations and helped establish a Library Committee in the Academy of Criminal Justice Sciences (ACJS). Her published columns and articles generally relate to library and archival resources for criminal justice study and research. She has edited and contributed to a "Library Resources" Column in *ACJS Today* since 1983.

SUSAN E. SEARING, Women's Studies Librarian for the University of Wisconsin System since 1982, previously worked as a reference librarian at Yale. She is the author of *Introduction to Library Research in Women's Studies* (Westview Press,

1985); of *Women's Studies: A Recommended Core Bibliography, 1980–1985* with Catherine Loeb and Esther Stineman (Libraries Unlimited, forthcoming); of *Women's Legal Rights in the United States: A Selective Bibliography* with Joan Ariel and Ellen Broidy (American Library Assn., 1985); and of numerous articles, bibliographies, and book reviews in the fields of women's studies and library science.

BETH J. SHAPIRO, Deputy Director at the Michigan State University Libraries, served as social science collections coordinator and urban affairs bibliographer before assuming her present duties. In addition to editing the Social Sciences Section of *The Selection of Library Materials in the Humanities, Social Sciences, and Sciences*, she has written about both librarianship and the sociology of sport in journals such as the *Journal of Academic Librarianship, Insurgent Sociologist, Journal of Sport History*, and the *Sociology of Sport Journal*.

CHARLES THURSTON is Education/Reference Librarian at the University of Texas at San Antonio Library. He held a similar position at Sterling C. Evans Library, Texas A&M University. He holds a B.A. in Elementary Education from Luther College and M.A. degrees in Library Science and Social and Philosophic Foundations of Education from the University of Minnesota.

JOHN H. WHALEY, JR. is at Virginia Commonwealth University. He is a frequent speaker on various issues in collection management and development and has published a number of articles in the field. He is one of the editors of the book *Selection of Library Materials in the Humanities, Social Sciences, and Sciences* and edits the series The Last Quarter Century published by the American Library Association.

CARL A. YIRKA is Associate Librarian and Adjunct Assistant Professor of Law at New York Law School. He previously worked at Indiana University Law Library (Bloomington); Northwestern University Law School Library; Chase Law School Library, Northern Kentucky University; and Cincinnati Law Library Association. He has been active in the American Association of Law Libraries, serving as chair of the committee on Relations with Publishers and Dealers in 1981–82. He currently teaches Advanced Legal Research at New York Law School.

Index

Pamela Hori

Numbers in boldface indicate pages on which full descriptions appear.

275